T0320082

HOW TO GET PUBLISHED IN THE BEST MARKETING JOURNALS

How to Get Published in the Best Marketing Journals

Edited by

David W. Stewart

Loyola Marymount University | Los Angeles, USA

and

Daniel M. Ladik

Seton Hall University, South Orange, NJ, USA

EE Edward **Elgar**
PUBLISHING

Cheltenham, UK • Northampton, MA, USA

Published by
Edward Elgar Publishing Limited
The Lypiatts
15 Lansdown Road
Cheltenham
Glos GL50 2JA
UK

Edward Elgar Publishing, Inc.
William Pratt House
9 Dewey Court
Northampton
Massachusetts 01060
USA

A catalogue record for this book
is available from the British Library

Library of Congress Control Number: 2019951040

This book is available electronically in the **Elgar**online
Business subject collection
DOI 10.4337/9781788113700

ISBN 978 1 78811 369 4 (cased)
ISBN 978 1 78811 370 0 (eBook)

Printed and bound by CPI Group (UK) Ltd, Croydon, CR0 4YY

Contents

Figures and tables

Chapter 15

Biographies of editors and contributors

Editors

Daniel M. Ladik (Ph.D., University of South Florida. MBA, Saint Joseph's University, M.A., Saint Joseph's University, B.A., Saint Joseph's University) is an Associate Professor of Marketing in the Stillman School of Business at Seton Hall University. His main teaching and research interests include personal selling and sales management, servant leadership, digital marketing, and buyer behavior with articles appearing in the *Journal of the Academy of Marketing Science*, *Journal of Public Policy & Marketing*, *Marketing Letters*, *Industrial Marketing Management*, *Journal of Marketing Theory and Practice* and other leading journals. Prior to Seton Hall University, Professor Ladik taught in the Sawyer Business School at Suffolk University in Boston.

David W. Stewart (Ph.D., Baylor University, M.A., Baylor University, B.A., Northeast Louisiana University) is President's Professor of Marketing and Business Law in the College of Business Administration at Loyola Marymount University in Los Angeles. He has previously served as a tenured member of the faculty and in various administrative roles at Vanderbilt University, the University of Southern California, and the University of California, Riverside. He was the 1988 MSI Visiting Scholar at General Motors Corporation and served as a manager of research for Needham, Harper, and Steers Advertising (now DDB) early in his career. David has authored/co-authored over 250 publications and 12 books, including *A Primer on Consumer Behavior: A Guide for Managers* and *Accountable Marketing: Linking Marketing Actions to Financial Performance*, among others. He is past Editor of *Journal of Marketing*, the *Journal of the Academy of Marketing Science* and the *Journal of Public Policy & Marketing*. He is the current Vice President for Publications of the American Marketing Association and founding chair of the Marketing Accountability Standards Board. Dr. Stewart's research has examined a wide range of issues including marketing strategy, the analysis of markets, consumer information search and decision making, effectiveness of marketing communications, public policy issues related to marketing and methodological approaches to the analysis of marketing data. Dr. Stewart has been awarded the American Marketing Association's Award for Lifetime Contributions to Marketing and Public Policy, the Elsevier Distinguished Marketing Scholar Award by the Society for Marketing Advances and the Cutco/Vector Distinguished Marketing Education Award by the Academy of Marketing Science. He has also received the American Academy of Advertising Award for Outstanding Contributions to Advertising Research for his long-term contributions to research in advertising. Dr. Stewart has been an officer in numerous professional organizations including the American Marketing Association, the American Statistical Association, the Society for Consumer Psychology, and the

American Psychological Association. He has consulted with numerous organizations and has offered executive education programs in more than 25 countries on five continents.

Contributors

James R. Bettman is the Burlington Industries Professor of Marketing at the Fuqua School of Business and Professor of Psychology and Neuroscience at Duke University. He received his B.A. (mathematics-economics) and Ph.D. (administrative sciences) from Yale. His research focuses on consumer information processing, constructive preferences, how decision makers adapt, effects of emotion and stress on decision making, and how people use consumption in forming their identities. Professor Bettman's publications include two books, *An Information Processing Theory of Consumer Choice* and *The Adaptive Decision Maker*, and a monograph, *Emotional Decisions: Tradeoff Difficulty and Coping in Consumer Choice*. His 127 research papers appear in books, journals, and proceedings in marketing, consumer research, psychology, management, and neuroscience. He is a member of the editorial boards for the *Journal of Consumer Research* and *Journal of Consumer Psychology*, is an associate editor for the *Journal of Marketing Research*, and has served as co-editor for the *Journal of Consumer Research* and editor of Monographs of the Journal of Consumer Research. Professor Bettman received the Duke University Dean's Award for Excellence in Mentoring in 2006, has chaired or co-chaired 45 Ph.D. committees at Fuqua and at UCLA, and received the Circle of Champions Award from the Ph.D. Project Marketing Doctoral Students Association for his efforts to recruit and mentor Ph.D. students of color. Professor Bettman is a Fellow of the American Marketing Association, the American Psychological Association, the American Psychological Society, and the Association for Consumer Research and has received numerous career contribution awards.

Ruth N. Bolton is Professor of Marketing at the W.P. Carey School of Business, Arizona State University. She is the recipient of the 2016 American Marketing Association/Irwin/McGraw-Hill Distinguished Marketing Educator Award and the 2007 recipient of the Christopher Lovelock Career Contributions to Services Award. Both awards are given to only a select few marketing academics; they recognize distinguished service and sustained outstanding contributions to the field of marketing. She previously served as 2009–2011 Executive Director of the Marketing Science Institute. Dr. Bolton studies how organizations can improve business performance over time by creating, maintaining and enhancing relationships with customers. Her recent research has focused on the customer experience, multi-channel management and high technology, interactive services sold in global business-to-business markets. She previously held academic positions at Vanderbilt University, the University of Oklahoma, Harvard University, University of Maryland, and the University of Alberta. She also spent eight years with Verizon, working on projects in the telecommunications and information services industries. Dr. Bolton's earlier published articles investigate how organizations' service and pricing strategies influence customer satisfaction, loyalty and revenues. She has extensive experience with survey research design, as well as the econometric analysis of large-scale, integrative data bases. Her research is typically conducted in partnership with businesses, such as the Marriott Corporation, Hewlett-Packard and Schneider National Inc. She has also participated in executive education programs around the world. Dr. Bolton has published articles in the *Journal of Consumer Research*, *Journal of Marketing*, *Journal of Marketing Research*, *Journal of Service Research*, *Management Science*, *Marketing Science*, and other leading journals. She previously served as editor of the *Journal of Marketing* (2002–2005) and Area Editor of the *Journal of Marketing Research* (2005–2007), as well as serving on the Editorial Review Boards of other leading marketing journals. She has also served on the Board of Trustees of the Marketing Science Institute and the Board of Directors of the American Marketing Association. She currently serves on the Board of Directors of the Sheth Foundation as Vice-President. She received her B.Comm., with honors, from Queen's University (Canada), and her M.Sc. and Ph.D. from Carnegie-Mellon University.

Linda Ferrell is Professor and Chair of the Marketing Department at the Harbert College of Business at Auburn University. She served on the faculty at Belmont University, University of New Mexico, University of Wyoming, University of Northern Colorado, Colorado State University, and University of Tampa. She co-managed a $2.5 million grant for business ethics education through the Daniels Fund Ethics Initiative at the University of New Mexico. Dr. Ferrell earned a Ph.D. from the University of Memphis. She has published in *Journal of the Academy of Marketing Science*, *AMS Review*, *Journal of Business Ethics*, *Journal of Public Policy & Marketing*, *Journal of Business Research*, as well as others. She has co-authored numerous books including *Business Ethics: Ethical Decision Making and Cases*, 12th edition, *Business and Society*, 6th edition, *Management*, 3rd edition, *Business: A Changing World*, 10th edition, and *M: Business*, 6th edition. Dr. Ferrell is on the Board of Directors of Mannatech, Inc. a NASDAQ listed, health and wellness company. She serves on the Executive Committee and Board of the Direct Selling Education Foundation. She is on the Cutco/Vector College Advisory Board. She is Immediate Past President of the Academy of Marketing Science and Past President of the Marketing Management Association. She is a recipient of the Marketing Education Innovation Award from the Marketing Management Association. Dr. Ferrell also serves as an expert witness in ethics and legal disputes.

O.C. Ferrell is the James T. Pursell, Sr. Eminent Scholar in Ethics and Director of the Center for Ethical Organizational Cultures at Auburn University. He has served on the faculty at Belmont University, the University of New Mexico, University of Wyoming, Colorado State University, University of Memphis, Texas A&M University, University of Michigan, Illinois State University, Southern Illinois University, and the University of Tampa. Dr. Ferrell is President of the Academy of Marketing Science. He served as Vice President of Publications for the Academy of Marketing Science for ten years. He led an initiative with AACSB International on publishing ethics. He is Past President of the Academic Council of the American Marketing Association. He received the AMS Cutco/Vector Distinguished Educator

Award for contributions to the marketing discipline. Additional recognition includes being the first recipient of the Marketing Education Innovation Award for the Marketing Management Association, Lifetime Achievement Award from the Macromarketing Society and special award for service to doctoral students from the Southeast Doctoral Consortium. He has published in the *Journal of Marketing*, *Journal of Marketing Research*, *Journal of the Academy of Marketing Science*, *Journal of Business Ethics*, *Journal of Public Policy & Marketing*, *AMS Review*, *Journal of Business Research*, as well as others. He writes weekly business ethics summaries and reviews for the *Wall Street Journal* with a subscriber list of over 6,000. Dr. Ferrell has served as an expert witness in high profile marketing cases.

Gary L. Frazier (D.B.A., MBA, Indiana University; B.A., B.S., Bemidji State University) is the Richard and Jarda Jurd Chair in Distribution Management and Professor of Marketing in the Marshall School of Business and the University of Southern California. He is an expert on structuring and managing channels of distribution and has published extensively in leading marketing journals. He is a past editor of *Journal of Marketing*. He has won several awards for his teaching including Marshall's Golden Apple Award in 2008. Professor Frazier has consulted and taught for a number of major corporations including Coca-Cola, General Electric, Honeywell, IBM, Intel, Microsoft, and Weyerhaeuser and is active in expert witnessing. He served as an advisor to the Justice Department in its examination of Microsoft. Before joining USC in 1984, Professor Frazier served on the faculty at the University of Illinois.

Ronald Paul Hill, Ph.D. in Business Administration from the University of Maryland, is a Visiting Professor of Marketing and holds a Dean's Excellence Faculty Fellowship at the American University, Kogod School of Business. He has authored over 200 journal articles, books, chapters, and conference papers on topics that include impoverished consumer behavior, marketing ethics, corporate social responsibility, human development, and public policy. Outlets for this research are *Journal of Marketing Research*, *Journal of Consumer Research*, *Business and Society*, *International Journal of Research in Marketing*, *Human Rights Quarterly*, *Journal of the Academy of Marketing Science*, and *Harvard Business Review*. His term as Editor of the *Journal of Public Policy & Marketing* extended from July 2006 until June 2012, and he began editing *Journal of Consumer Affairs* in 2018. His recent awards include: 2012 Williams-Qualls-Spratlen Multicultural Mentoring Award of Excellence, 2012 Villanova University Outstanding Faculty Research Award, 2010 Pollay Prize for Excellence in the Study of Marketing in the Public Interest, 2013 AMA Marketing and Society Special Interest Group Lifetime Achievement Award, 2013 Alan N. Nash Distinguished Doctoral Graduate Award, and VSB 2014 McDonough Family Faculty Award for Research Excellence. His 2014 article won the *Journal of Public Policy & Marketing* Thomas Kinnear Award in 2016, his 2015 *Journal of Consumer Affairs* article won the best paper award in 2016, and his 2015 *Journal of Macromarketing* article won the Slater Award in 2016, and he received the 2017 Marketing Management Association Master Scholar Award.

Joel D. Huber is the Allan D. Schwartz Professor of Marketing at the Fuqua School of Business, Duke University. He received an A.B. *cum laude* in Philosophy from Princeton University (1967) and an MBA (1970) and a Ph.D. (1975) from the Wharton School of the University of Pennsylvania. He has taught at the Krannert School of Business, Columbia University and the Wharton School, but spent most of his teaching at the Fuqua School of Business. At Fuqua he was Associate Dean for Programs and was the Director of the inaugural Weekend MBA Program. He was among the first Associate Editors for *Journal of Consumer Research* (1997–2003) and instituted the first A/E system as editor for *Journal of Marketing Research*. He has been Associate Editor for *Marketing Science* and *Journal of Consumer Psychology* and is currently an Associate Editor for *International Journal for Research in Marketing*. Joel Huber is the first Editor-in-Chief for the *Journal of the Association for Consumer Research*. His research focuses on how people make decisions and how to assess the values underlying those decisions. In particular, he has explored ways to measure consumer values with efficient choice-based conjoint designs and has clarified how people make decisions when confronted with different contextual relationships among alternatives.

Constantine S. Katsikeas is the Arnold Ziff Research Chair and Professor of Marketing and International Management, and the Founding Director of the Global and Strategic Marketing Research Center at Leeds University Business School, University of Leeds. He is the Editor-in-Chief of *Journal of International Marketing*, published by the American Marketing Association, Marketing Editor of *Journal of International Business Studies*, and an Area Editor of *Journal of the Academy of Marketing Science*. He has published in *Journal of Marketing*, *Strategic Management Journal*, *Organization Science*, *Journal of International Business Studies*, *Journal of International Marketing*, *Journal of the Academy of Marketing Science*, *Journal of World Business*, and other journals. He has led executive education programs and taught managers from various firms including Toyota, Aramco, Coca-Cola, Siemens, Philip Morris, Mitsui Chemicals, A1 Telekom Austria, Mercedes-Benz, GlaxoSmithKline, and Johnson & Johnson.

Ujwal Kayande is the Associate Dean (Academic) and Professor of Marketing at Melbourne Business School. He is also Founding Director of the Centre for Business Analytics. He teaches marketing strategy and analytics on the MBA, Master of Business Analytics and Executive Education programs. Ujwal is co-director of the Digital Marketing and Analytics Executive Education Program jointly delivered by the University of Oxford and Melbourne Business School. After completing his Ph.D. at the University of Alberta, Ujwal held faculty positions at Penn State University, Australian National University, UNSW, University of Pennsylvania and others. He has received numerous accolades for teaching-excellence and his research has been awarded by the American Marketing Association (Lehmann Award), European Marketing Academy (*IJRM* Best Paper) and the Australia–NZ Marketing Academy (Distinguished Researcher). Ujwal currently serves on the Editorial Boards of the *Journal of Marketing Research* and the *Journal of Service Research*, and was on the Editorial Board of the *Journal of Marketing* from 2012 to 2018. From October

2018, he is an Area Editor for the *International Journal of Research in Marketing*. He also sits on the advisory boards of two start-ups. A frequent media commentator in *The Australian*, *Australian Financial Review*, *Daily Telegraph* and other publications, Ujwal consults globally on marketing strategy and analytics.

V. Kumar (VK) is the Regents' Professor, Chang Jiang Scholar (HUST), Richard and Susan Lenny Distinguished Chair and Professor of Marketing, Executive Director, Center for Excellence in Brand and Customer Management, and the Director of the Ph.D. Program in Marketing at the J. Mack Robinson College of Business, Georgia State University. VK was previously the ING Chair Professor, and Executive Director, ING Center for Financial Services at the University of Connecticut, Storrs, Connecticut. Dr. Kumar teaches a variety of courses including Database Marketing, E-Marketing, Customer Relationship Management, New Product Management, Marketing Models, International Marketing Strategy, International Marketing Research and Multivariate Methods in Business. Dr. Kumar has taught in the MBA Programs in Australia, France, India, Spain, Holland, and Hong Kong. Dr. Kumar has lectured on marketing-related topics at various universities in the U.S., Europe (including the University of Cambridge and London Business School in the United Kingdom; INSEAD in France; IESE-Barcelona and University of Zaragoza in Spain; University of Kiel and University of Munster in Germany; Tilburg University and Nijenrode University in the Netherlands; Hanken Business School, Finnish School of Business and Turku School of Business in Finland; Catholic University at Leuven in Belgium; Lancaster University, University of Leeds, and Brunel University in the United Kingdom; and Stockholm School of Economics in Sweden), China (Fudan University, Huazhong University of Science and Technology, Tsinghua), India (Indian School of Business, Indian Institute of Management, Management Development Institute, Indian Institute of Technology, Institute of Management Technology), Russia (Moscow School of Management), Australia (University of Sydney, Queensland University of Technology, Griffith University, University of Queensland, Curtin University), Brazil (FGV University, PUCPR – Curitiba), Turkey (Boğaziçi University and Koc̨ University), Mexico (Monterrey Institute of Technology, ITESM), South Africa (Nelson Mandela Metropolitan University Business School), Israel (IDC University, Ben-Gurion University of the Negev, Hebrew University of Jerusalem), Dubai (Institute of Management Technology), and Singapore (Singapore Management University and Nanyang Technological University). He has also conducted numerous executive development seminars in North America, South America, Europe, Asia, Africa, and Australia. He has also been invited to be a keynote speaker in many conferences worldwide. Dr. Kumar received in 2017–2018 Best Teacher and in 2012 Outstanding Teacher Award at Georgia State University, 2007 Teaching Excellence Award, and 2007 MBA Teacher of the Year Award at the University of Connecticut, 1996 Melcher Award for Faculty Excellence in Teaching, 1994 NationsBank Master Teaching Award and the Melcher Faculty Teaching Excellence Award for five years between 1990–1994 and 1995–1996 at the University of Houston. For the academic year 1991–1992, Dr. Kumar also has been recognized as the recipient of the University of Houston Teaching Excellence Award.

Donald R. Lehmann's research focuses on individual and group choice and decision making, the adoption of innovation and new product development, and the management and valuation of marketing assets (brands, customers). He is also interested in knowledge accumulation, empirical generalizations and information use. Lehmann has published more than 100 articles and books, serves on the editorial boards of several academic journals and is the founding editor of *Marketing Letters*. He is a past president of the Association for Consumer Research, former executive director (1993–1995, 2001–2003) of the Marketing Science Institute, and former co-editor of the *International Journal of Research in Marketing*.

Mary Frances Luce is the Robert A. Ingram Professor of Marketing at the Fuqua School of Business at Duke University. Professor Luce's research interests include the role of emotion in consumer decision making with applications to medical decision making. She received her Ph.D. in Business Administration (Marketing) from Duke University in 1994. She was on the faculty of the Wharton School of Business, University of Pennsylvania from 1994 until 2004 and she then re-joined Duke's Fuqua School of Business. Professor Luce's research has appeared in such publications as *Health Psychology*, *Journal of Consumer Research*, *Management Science*, *Journal of Marketing Research*, and *Marketing Science*. She was a co-editor of the *Journal of Consumer Research* (with Ann McGill and Laura Peracchio) for a three-year term and was president of the Association for Consumer Research (2017). She has also served as the faculty dean for the Fuqua School of Business.

Deborah J. MacInnis (Ph.D., University of Pittsburgh; B.A., Smith College) is the Charles L. and Ramona I. Hilliard Professor of Business Administration and Professor of Marketing at USC's Marshall School of Business. Her work focuses on the role of emotions in consumer behavior and branding. She has received the *Journal of Marketing*'s Alpha Kappa Psi and Maynard Awards for the papers that make the greatest contribution to marketing thought and the Long-Term Contribution Award from the *Review of Marketing Research*. She has served as Co-Editor and Associate Editor of the *Journal of Consumer Research* and Associate Editor for the *Journal of Marketing* and the *Journal of Consumer Psychology*. Debbie is co-author of a leading textbook on consumer behavior, several edited volumes on branding, and an upcoming book on developing, enhancing and leveraging brand admiration. She is former Treasurer, and President of the Association for Consumer Research and former Vice President of Conferences and Research for the American Marketing Association's academic council. She is the winner of local and national teaching awards. She has also served the Marshall School of Business as Vice Dean of Research and Strategy and Vice Dean of the Undergraduate Program. She has also received the USC Mellon mentoring award for her mentoring work with faculty. Her consulting includes work with major consumer packaged goods companies, business-to-business marketers and advertising agencies.

Vikas Mittal is the J. Hugh Liedtke Professor of Marketing at the Jones Graduate School of Business. Prior to joining Jones, he was the Thomas Marshall Professor of Marketing at the Katz Graduate School of Management. Dr. Mittal holds a Bachelor's in Business Administration from the University of Michigan and a Ph.D. in Management from Temple University. Before joining Katz, he was on the faculty at Kellogg Graduate School at Northwestern University. In addition to publications in leading marketing journals, Dr. Mittal has published extensively on decision making in journals such as *Organization Studies*, *Organization Science*, *Journal of Applied Psychology*, *Journal of Psychiatry*, *Organization Behavior and Human Decision Processes*, and *Personality and Social Psychology Bulletin*. He currently serves on the editorial boards of numerous journals. In 2014 his article was included in the top-50 articles for highest impact on marketing academics and practice. In 2013 his paper was one of the top three papers in the special issue on consumer identities for the *International Journal of Research in Marketing*. In 2006, Professor Mittal was awarded the William F. O'Dell Award for making the most significant, long-term contribution to the theory, methodology, and practice of marketing. In 2009 he was ranked as the 5th most prolific author published in the top marketing journals. He also received the 2001 FedEx Excellence in Service Research award, as well as numerous other awards. His courses are highly sought after in the MBA as well as the executive education program. He won the excellence in teaching award at the Katz Graduate School three years running, and was voted the best professor by the executives in the 2003 IEMBA program in Brazil. At the Jones School he won the teaching excellence award in 2013 for his teaching in the professional MBA program.

Christine Moorman is the T. Austin Finch, Sr. Professor of Business Administration at the Fuqua School of Business, Duke University. Her research examines the nature and effects of learning and knowledge utilization by consumers, managers, organizations, and financial markets. She studies these topics in the context of innovation, alliances, and public policy. Her research has been published in the *Journal of Marketing Research*, *Journal of Marketing*, *Journal of Consumer Research*, *Marketing Science*, *Journal of Public Policy & Marketing*, *International Journal of Research in Marketing*, *Academy of Management Review*, *Administrative Science Quarterly*, and *Harvard Business Review*, and is supported by grants from the National Science Foundation and the Marketing Science Institute. Christine is founder of The CMO Survey (www.cmosurvey.org) which is dedicated to improving the value of marketing in firms and in society. She wrote *Strategy from the Outside In: Profiting from Customer Value* (winner of the 2011 Berry Book Prize with George Day), authored *Strategic Market Management* (with Dave Aaker), and edited *Assessing Marketing Strategy Performance* (with Don Lehmann). She has served on the Board of Directors and chair of the Marketing Strategy SIG for the AMA, as Director of Public Policy for ACR, and as an Academic Trustee for MSI. Professor Moorman is the Editor-in-Chief of the *Journal of Marketing* and previously served as an Associate Editor for the *Journal of Marketing* and the *Journal of Marketing Research*. She was named the American Marketing Association/Irwin/McGraw-Hill Distinguished Marketing Educator in 2018 and an AMA Fellow in 2017, received the 2012 Paul D. Converse award for significant contributions to the field of marketing, and the 2008 Mahajan Award for Career Contributions to Marketing Strategy.

Cornelia 'Connie' Pechmann is Professor of Marketing at The Paul Merage School of Business, University of California Irvine. She conducts lab and field experiments to study controversial marketing messages including tobacco and drug messages and social media messages. She has received numerous grants to study adolescents' response to tobacco-related advertising and product placements. Her recent work examines the use of social media for online self-help groups and she has received a $2.5M NIH grant to develop Tweet2Quit for smoking cessation. Professor Pechmann has published numerous articles in leading marketing journals (*Journal of Consumer Research*, *Journal of Consumer Psychology*, *Journal of Marketing Research*, *Journal of Marketing* and *Journal of Public Policy & Marketing*) and public health journals (*American Journal of Public Health*, *Tobacco Control*) and her work has received extensive press coverage. She is past Editor of the *Journal of Consumer Psychology* (2012–2015), an Area Editor at *Journal of Marketing*, a Top 50 Marketing Scholar, and a Who's Who in Economics. She received the 2009 Pollay Prize for Research in the Public Interest and the 2005 *Journal of Consumer Research* best article award. Her research has been presented to the U.S. Congress, the California State Legislature and the National Association of Attorneys' General. Professor Pechmann has an M.S., MBA, and Ph.D. from Vanderbilt University.

John H. Roberts is a Professor of Marketing in the UNSW Business School and a Fellow of the London Business School and Fudan University. He has extensive senior executive experience and the company that he founded, Marketing Insights, an Asian leader in strategic marketing consulting, is now a part of the world's largest marketing information company, AC Nielsen. John is winner of the American Marketing Association's John A. Howard Award, its William O'Dell Award, and its Advanced Research Techniques Best Paper Award. He has also been a Finalist in the John Little Award for the best paper in marketing science three times and the Gary Lilien Marketing Science Practice Prize three times. John sits on the Editorial Boards of the *Journal of Marketing Research*, *Journal of Forecasting*, *Marketing Science*, *International Journal of Research in Marketing*, and *Australian Journal of Management*. He has won the AGSM @ UNSW Business School Distinguished Teacher Award, the Australian and New Zealand Academy of Marketing Distinguished Educator Award, and has been Runner Up in the London Business School EMBA Distinguished Teacher Award. John is a Fellow of the Australian Academy of Social Sciences, the Australian Institute of Management, the Australian Marketing Institute, the Australian Market and Social Research Society, and the Australian and New Zealand Academy of Marketing, as well as being a U.S. Harkness Fellow and a Fellow of the U.K. Twenty First Century Trust. John has recently been elected Vice President of Practice, Informs Marketing Science Society (ISMS) for a period of two years. He has been a visiting professor at Stanford, M.I.T., the University of Hamburg, and the Hong Kong University of Science and Technology. John has served on the Academic Advisory Boards of the Marketing Science Institute (based in Cambridge, MA), the Chief Marketing Officers' Council (Menlo Park, CA), the Centre for Brand Management and Marketing (Hamburg), and AiMark (Tilburg), the Applied Economics Bulletin and Quantitative Abstracts in Marketing. He sits on the Australian Research Council's College of Experts.

Richard Staelin is the Gregory Mario and Jeremy Mario Professor of Business Administration at the Fuqua School of Business, Duke University. He graduated from the University of Michigan and taught at Carnegie-Mellon University (13 years), the University of Chicago (one semester) and the Australian Graduate School of Management (one year) prior to his arrival at Duke in 1982. Since then he has been Deputy Dean (twice), Associate Dean of Executive Education, Executive Director for the Teradata Center for CRM and the initial Managing Director of GEMBA at Duke. He has served on over 40 Ph.D. committees and published over 100 papers in academic journals. His work spans a wide range of topics and methodologies, including channel management, information search, quality of health care, service marketing and public policy. Staelin has received best paper awards at the *Journal of Marketing Research*, *Journal of Marketing*, and *Marketing Science*, and the Outstanding Educator award and the Converse award from the AMA. He was elected an inaugural Fellow in ISMS and a Fellow in INFORMS. He was the President of ISMS, the INFORMS Society of Marketing Science. He was the editor of *Marketing Science* for three years and the Guest Editor for *Journal of Marketing*'s special issue on Customer Relationship Management. He was Chairman of the Board of Directors for a small biotech firm (BioElectronics) and served on the Board for a new start-up named Bivarus.

Stefan Stremersch holds the Desiderius Erasmus Distinguished Chair of Economics and the Chair in Marketing at the Erasmus School of Economics (ESE). Professor Stremersch's research is in the areas of innovation, marketing of technology and science, healthcare and pharmaceutical marketing, and international marketing. His research is largely situated in high technology markets (ICT, Telecom, consumer electronics, and video games) and pharmaceuticals, and led to published articles in the major scholarly journals including, among others, the *International Journal of Research in Marketing*, the *Journal of Marketing*, the *Journal of Marketing Research*, *Marketing Science and Management Science*. Professor Stremersch has won several prestigious awards including the Harold H. Maynard Best Paper Award from the *Journal of Marketing*, the J.C. Ruigrok Prize for the most productive young researcher in the social sciences in the Netherlands, awarded every four years to an economist, and the Rajan Varadarajan Early Career Award from the American Marketing Association in 2008. He also has an affiliation with IESE Business School, Barcelona, and is editorial or policy board member of several journals including the *Journal of Marketing*, *Journal of Marketing Research*, *Marketing Science* and *International Journal of Research in Marketing*. He served together with Don Lehmann as editor of the *International Journal of Research in Marketing* from 2006 to 2009. Professor Stremersch is also scientific director of the Erasmus Center for Marketing and Innovation and of the Erasmus Healthcare Business Center.

John O. Summers is the Professor Emeritus of Marketing at Kelley School of Business at Indiana University. He earned his bachelors, masters, and doctorate degrees from Purdue University. His work has appeared in the *Journal of Marketing Research*, *Journal of Marketing*, *Journal of Consumer Research*, *Journal of the Academy of Marketing Science*, *Journal of Business Research*, *Journal of Business*

Administration, and the *Journal of Advertising Research*. He served on the Editorial Review Board of the *Journal of Marketing Research* from 1972 through 1998.

Stephen L. Vargo is a Shidler Distinguished Professor and Professor of Marketing at the University of Hawai'i at Manoa. He also is an Ander Foundation Visiting Professor at the CTF Service Research Center at Karlstad University, Sweden and has held visiting positions at the Judge Business School at the University of Cambridge, the University of Warwick, the University of Maryland, College Park, and other major universities. He has articles published in the *Journal of Marketing*, the *Journal of the Academy of Marketing Science*, the *Journal of Service Research*, *Management Information Systems Quarterly*, and other top-ranked journals. Professor Vargo has been awarded the Harold H. Maynard Award and the AMA/ Sheth Foundation Award for his contributions to marketing theory. Clarivate Analytics (formally Thomson-Reuters) recently named him on its Web of Science "*Highly Cited Researchers*" list (top 1 percent) and has identified him as one of the *World's Most Influential Scientific Minds* in economics and business for a fifth consecutive year.

Russell S. Winer (Ph.D.) is the William Joyce Professor of Marketing at the Stern School of Business, New York University. He currently serves as the Deputy Chair of the Marketing Department. He received a B.A. in Economics from Union College and an M.S. and Ph.D. in Industrial Administration from Carnegie Mellon University. He has been on the faculties of Columbia and Vanderbilt universities and the University of California at Berkeley. He has written three books, *Marketing Management*, *Analysis for Marketing Planning* and *Product Management*, a research monograph, *Pricing*, and has co-edited *The History of Marketing Science*. He has authored over 80 papers in marketing on a variety of topics including consumer choice, marketing research methodology, marketing planning, advertising, and pricing. Professor Winer has served two terms as the editor of the *Journal of Marketing Research*, is Editor Emeritus of the *Journal of Interactive Marketing*, has been a Senior Editor for *Marketing Science* and the *International Journal of Research in Marketing*, and is currently an Associate Editor of the *Journal of Consumer Research*. He is a past Executive Director of the Marketing Science Institute in Cambridge, MA. Professor Winer is a founding Fellow of both the INFORMS Society for Marketing Science and the American Marketing Association and is the 2011 recipient of the American Marketing Association/Irwin/McGraw-Hill Distinguished Marketing Educator award.

Preface

Marketing is a remarkably diverse discipline. At its core is one of the most fundamental and complex of human activities – how a society provides for itself. At an individual level these activities include identification of needs, gathering information, allocation of resources, decision-making, consumption, and disposal, among others. At an organizational level these activities require specialization of labor and resources, role definitions, power relationships, and administrative structures, and so on. At a societal level, marketing entails the influence of culture, social norms, and legal and regulatory dimensions. The complexity of such multi-level activities lends itself to research anchored in quite different disciplines, psychology, economics, sociology, anthropology and political science, among others and that uses an extraordinary array of research methods, ranging from qualitative to quantitative and naturalistic field observations to laboratory experiments. One result of the complexity and diversity of marketing is the creation of a challenge for publication of scholarship. There is no simple formula for publication. There are, however, some general guidelines for publication in marketing in general and in specific areas within marketing. The purpose of this book is to collect these guidelines in one place for developing scholars.

It is important to appreciate that publication in journals is an inherently creative process. When viewed through the lens of creativity it is easier to understand why frustration and failure occur. For every blockbuster motion picture there are another nine that are only so-so, if not outright flops. Some of the greatest works of art are painted over other less impressive or failed projects. Although never pleasant, failure is a part of the creative process. Building on failure, with the help of colleagues, mentors, editors and reviewers is a part of being successful in the long run. The contributors to this volume echo the need for persistence and the importance of learning from failure.

The contributors to this book are current and former editors, reviewers and accomplished scholars who have published in marketing's leading journals. The journals with which the contributors have been involved include the *Journal of Marketing*, the *Journal of Marketing Research*, the *Journal of International Marketing*, the *Journal of Public Policy and Marketing*, the *Journal of Consumer Research*, the *Journal of the Association for Consumer Research*, *Marketing Science*, the *Journal of Consumer Psychology*, the *Journal of the Academy of Marketing Science*, the *Journal of Interactive Marketing*, the *International Journal of Research in Marketing*, and *Marketing Letters*. The contents of the book are a distillation of the wisdom and experience of these contributors. The chapters are original contributions or reprints from other publications that specifically focus on the publication process – how to select a topic with a high probability of publication, how to craft an informative and readable paper that clearly articulates its unique contribution(s) and its place within the broader literature, and how to navigate the review process and address comments of reviewers and editors.

The book is divided into four sections. The first section focuses on the general process of publication in the marketing literature. The second section focuses on writing for specific types of marketing journals or about specific types of research, ranging from behavioral research to quantitative research and from basic research to more applied work on strategy and policy. The third section offers a discussion of the role of reviews and reviewers in the publication process. This section also includes a discussion of the process through which an award-winning paper was ultimately accepted for publication from the perspective of the editor who accepted the paper and the author who wrote the paper. Finally, the last section of the book provides a chapter with a general summary of best and worst practices in the publication process and a chapter offering the collective advice of five current and past editors.

It is our hope that the content of this book will help jump-start the scholarship and successful publication outcomes of developing scholars. We hope the book also finds its way onto reading lists and course syllabi in doctoral programs in marketing where it might serve as the catalyst for further discussions and a deeper understanding of the publication process.

David W. Stewart
Daniel M. Ladik

Acknowledgements

The editors and publishers wish to thank the authors and the following publishers who have kindly given permission for the use of copyright material.

American Marketing Association via the Copyright Clearance Center's RightsLink service for: Deborah J. MacInnis (2011), 'A Framework for Conceptual Contributions in Marketing', *Journal of Marketing*, **75** (4), July, 136–54.

Elsevier via the Copyright Clearance Center's RightsLink service for: John H. Roberts, Ujwal Kayande and Stefan Stremersch (2014), 'From Academic Research to Marketing Practice: Exploring the Marketing Science Value Chain', *International Journal of Research in Marketing*, **31** (2), June, 127–40.

Emerald Group Publishing for: David W. Stewart (2008), 'Academic Publishing in Marketing: Best and Worst Practices', *European Business Review, Special Issue: Academic Journals and Academic Publishing*, **20** (5), 421–33.

Springer via the Copyright Clearance Center's RightsLink service for: John O. Summers (2001), 'Guidelines for Conducting Research and Publishing in Marketing: From Conceptualization Through the Review Process', *Journal of the Academy of Marketing Science*, **29** (4), Fall, 405–15; Donald R. Lehmann and Russell S. Winer (2017), 'The Role and Impact of Reviewers on the Marketing Discipline', *Journal of the Academy of Marketing Science*, **45** (5), September, 587–92.

SECTION I

THE PUBLICATION PROCESS

Introduction to section I

Publication of a paper in a journal is the culmination of a process. The publication process begins with an idea that is developed and refined until it lends itself to empirical research or conceptual elaboration. The idea must be place in the context of extant research and theory, and something 'new' must be identified. Idea development is followed by empirical research, conceptual elaboration, and/or theory development. The idea, its elaboration, and the results of any empirical research or theory development then need to be documented in a fashion that is accessible and meaningful to readers in some well-defined audience. That audience is the readership of the journal for which the paper is intended. Throughout the development process it is helpful to obtain feedback by having others read and comment on the evolving paper and by making formal and informal presentations where ideas can be discussed, sharpened and polished. At some place in the cycle, the feedback and refinement process reach the point of diminishing returns, which suggests it is time to submit the paper. Submission starts a process of review and revision, which results in publication or rejection by the target journal. Rejection may result in revision of the paper for another journal based on feedback, and the process begins again.

The joys of receiving an acceptance letter and seeing a paper published online or in print are part of the rewards for work that goes into the process of crafting a publication. However, if a publication is really successful, publication is not even the end of the process. Successful and influential publications are read, are cited and impact theory, future research and/or practice. It is useful to remember that the real objective of scholarship is the creation and communication of new knowledge. Publication is just a vehicle for achieving this objective.

The three papers in this section of the book provide insights into the publication process. The first chapter is an update of an earlier paper (published in 2008) by the editors of this book (Ladik and Stewart). It provides the results of a survey of reviewers regarding what they look for when reviewing papers and what they view as the criteria for publication of a paper. Editors and reviewers serve as gatekeepers in the publication process, so it is fitting that the first chapter of the book provides the perspectives of these gatekeepers as an introduction. The second chapter is a reprint of a paper by John Summers that originally appeared in the *Journal of the Academy of Marketing Science*. This paper provides a useful and comprehensive summary of the publication process.

The third chapter, by O.C. Ferrell and Linda Ferrell, focuses on the important topic of ethics. While there have always been important ethical dimensions of the publication process, the proliferation of retractions of papers in leading journals in multiple disciplines has served to highlight the need for attention to ethical issues. Some ethical issues, such as blatant plagiarism of the work of others, are easily discoverable and generally recognized as inappropriate. Other ethical issues are not so easily detected and are more nuanced. Chapter 3 provides a helpful introduction to these issues.

The three chapters in this first section of the book will likely raise as many questions as they answer. This is the motivation for the remainder of the remaining chapters of the book.

[1]

The contribution continuum revisited

Daniel M. Ladik and David W. Stewart

The (most) *common mistake is not to "tell a story," but only assemble different related parts. "Telling a good story" means to critically analyze what has been done before and demonstrate convincingly why something is changing. A significant contribution to knowledge does not happen in isolation and needs to be contextualized to the current situation.*

Publishing in academic journals is challenging, especially for doctoral students and young assistant professors. Despite being understood that one needs to make a contribution in order to reach final publication, making the contribution is easier conceptualized then operationalized. Specifically, for this reason, we created "The Contribution Continuum" (Ladik and Stewart 2008), asking editors their thoughts on how to make a contribution. Briefly, we defined "a contribution is made when a manuscript clearly adds, embellishes, or creates something beyond what is already known" (Ladik and Stewart 2008, p. 157).

Given the focus of this volume is on helping young scholars to develop their research, we wanted to revisit the spirit of "The Contribution Continuum" and this conversation. This time, however, we did not ask editors their thoughts on what is a contribution. By contrast, the research presented here asked reviewers:

In 150 words or less, what is the most common mistake you see when author(s) attempt to make a contribution to knowledge?

The results presented here are not from a random set of reviewers. Instead, we asked the strongest, most experienced reviewers their thoughts on common pitfalls in the manuscript creation process. With this objective, we first approached editors from the 39 SSCI marketing and related journals describing this project and then asked for a list of their strongest reviewers such as those who had won awards for their efforts, as well as reviewers who earned their way to associate or area editor positions. In total, we received 249 nominations from the editors, and we are thankful to the 104 reviewers who responded to our request for this study.

The direct question listed above produced just over 10,000 words detailing the common challenges they experience in the review process. After close analysis, we felt the four most common categories of mistakes were, authors (1) who submit grammatically unapproachable manuscripts reducing the contribution's clarity, (2) who argue that "*a gap*" justifies contribution, (3) who fail to position their research into an ongoing conversation in the literature, and (4) who overlook *to whom* (that is, which constituents) are the intended audience of their research. For each of these pitfalls, we outline the hazards using direct quotes from the reviewers. With each theme, we also provide recommendations on how to avoid the particular publication mistake highlighted. This research concludes with a rubric highlighting two or three pitfalls for each stage of the manuscript creation and submission process.

Grammatically unapproachable manuscripts

The most common mistake is submitting a paper that is poorly written. If it is not well written it doesn't make any difference what the content is because you cannot get to the content.

The old adage "you never get a second chance to make a first impression" rings true in the manuscript creation and contribution making process. The last thing an author wishes to do is imbue an unfavorable reaction at the outset of their contribution argument leading to reviewer comments like "*a premature and sloppy initial*" *submission* or (if) "*the paper is not well-written, it makes it hard to understand the contribution.*" The Introduction is where scholars make the case that their research does have a contribution and is worthy of being part of the ongoing conversation in the literature. From the Introduction, the manuscript should logically flow as per the contribution statement and the outline set by the authors. Yet, authors could easily handicap themselves by confusing the reader with grammatically unapproachable text leading to reviewer comments such as, "*I see a lot of papers being rejected partly because of exposition. Such papers might have had a chance otherwise, but they are so poorly written that reviewers do not see enough contribution to warrant a revision.*"

Similarly to grammatically unapproachable text, research is often submitted for review to which "*ideas are not communicated in the most effective manner.*" Meaning, the presentation, logic and flow of a manuscript could just as easily obscure a contribution as poorly structured syntax. On this point, one reviewer stated, "*a major problem is lacking a consistently rigorous presentation of the research and by implication, its relevance.*" In an analogous comment, another reviewer opined that, "*many manuscripts lack a precise writing style that guide the reader through the manuscript's logic and appropriateness.*"

Submissions that lack clarity create an unfortunate effect in the minds of the reviewer, meaning an unfavorable view of the strength of the overall contribution:

I think clarity is the key, and lack of clarity is the most common mistake. Authors need to be: (1) clear about the contribution (be specific about how the paper builds upon prior work), (2) clear about theory (precisely lay out the mechanisms and effects), and (3) clear about methods and analyses (others should be able to replicate method, and findings should be as plainly laid out as possible). If the authors aren't clear on any of these points, then the reviewers (and readers) won't know what to make of the work.

Keep in mind that it is not the reviewer's job to logically organize the author's intentions and to uncover a manuscript's true potential. Of course, the reviewers will be helpful and offer suggestions, but they also ultimately decide if the manuscript goes forward or is rejected. On this thought, one reviewer stated, "*manuscripts are too long and generally not polished enough ('let's see what reviewers want'). Overall, the research is not mature enough to be sent out for review; consequently, the reviewer doesn't see how the authors can turn the manuscript within one round into a publishable paper.*" Another reviewer lamented, "*problems appear when research rigor is compromised by a 'good enough' attitude. Often this appears in terms of a not-ready-for-primetime 'draft' of a manuscript that nonetheless is submitted, with the associated poor writing.*" Authors must understand that if they adopt a mindset with the expectation that the review process is to help them fix an undeveloped manuscript, they should expect that very few of their papers will be asked for a revise and resubmit recommendation from a reviewer.

To conclude this pitfall, this reviewer stated it well:

> *The number one bit of feedback I find myself giving in the review process involves the manuscript's lack of focus. So many papers I read fail to make the research contribution clear and unambiguous to the reader. The overall scope of the research often tries to accomplish too much, without probing the important question(s) with any meaningful depth. Related to this is imprecise use of terminology and lack of definitional structure. However, I see all of these as being related to the research program's lack of focus. A clearly defined focus and articulation of contribution are key to communicating the value of your work.*

Recommendations

Fortunately, this pitfall has a few direct and straightforward practices which could alleviate reviewer comments like those highlighted above. First, use a professional proofreading service. As simple as this sounds, it is a valuable first step in the publication creation process, radically reducing any grammatically unapproachable text. Second, have a minimum of two or three friendly reviews to verify that the presentation, logic, and flow of your intended contribution argument is as sound as you believe it should be. Often, we are too close to our research and cannot see any other perspective than our own. Ask former doctoral program associates or new department colleagues for a friendly review. This is a great way to stay in touch with your doctoral program and also develop new relationships within your current department. Third, go back to the proofreading service after incorporating the friendly reviewer comments into the revised manuscript. One reviewer specifically suggested presenting your research at conferences:

> *Don't leave it to the review process to "discover" where you lack clarity. Find out beforehand by sharing your paper with colleagues, presenting at conferences, and so on, to broaden your perspective and to overcome your own subjectivity and biases. The research itself will benefit, as well as your ability to communicate that research to others.*

Our final reviewer comment summarizes this theme well:

> *In my reviews I always recommend the submitters read chapters 1, 2, and 3 of William Zinsser's* On Writing Well. *One of my favorite quotes:* "I write in order to understand my own ideas." *When something is as poorly written as most of what I read on first submission it is evidence that the writer does not understand his or her own ideas.*

Arguing for "a gap" in the literature

> *An identified research gap does not equal a contribution to knowledge. Oftentimes authors*

fail to move beyond gap identification and flesh out why the area is worthy of academic study. For example, how does the research gap add to theory and practice?

Simply put, "*a gap*" in and of itself, is not a contribution and many reviewers listed this pitfall as one of the most common mistakes in the manuscript creation process. Specifically:

Believing any "gap in knowledge" needs to be filled.

Often, authors think of their contribution in terms of "filling a gap" in the literature, and they are motivated to make this gap seem as large as possible.

To justify a research topic simply because there is no research to date yet.

Often authors confuse contribution with mere newness ("nobody yet studied this").

They argue "there is a lack" without convincingly discussing why filling it is relevant.

They focus on "gaps" in the literature versus why those gaps are important and to whom.

Focusing on novelty but forgetting about relevance. Yes, it has not been tested previously, but there might be a reason for this?

Compared to other disciplines, such as economics or psychology, the marketing literature is quite young. In other words, it is just as easy to argue that the marketing literature is nothing but gaps as it is to argue that any one gap could be a significant contribution. Metaphorically speaking, when we look out into the night sky, we can see nothing but stars. In reality, there is significantly more dark space between those stars than we can easily comprehend. By focusing just on one gap between stars, we might lose the bigger picture and miss an entire constellation. One reviewer touched on this point well, stating:

[A]uthors are defining their contribution in a narrow and specific way that suits their data or approach. The review of the existing literature is often not comprehensive enough, and the bigger picture is missed. Authors also see an area that has not been researched as a white space where the contribution is obvious ("first to study this"), but the relevance of the research question is ignored (maybe that is why others have not looked at it).

Reviewers identified two specific author pitfalls when arguing that "a gap" is a contribution. First, authors assume that "a gap" also equates to "being interesting." One reviewer delineated this point perfectly, "*many authors still think that researching something that has not been researched before, is in itself a contribution. However, if a certain relationship has not been researched before, it might simply be because there's nothing interesting to research there.*" The second "gap" mistake is when authors confuse a theoretical gap with a contextual or constituents' gap. For instance, "*too often authors confuse a different context for a contribution. The author says 'it hasn't been done in country X or discipline Y' when that is, without justification, insufficient for a contribution to knowledge. Why would we expect it to be different in the different context?"* Another reviewer lamented that authors, *"focus too much on the theoretical 'gap' without seeing if that gap is there for a reason (that is, no point in exploring) or if filling the gap is actually consequential for some stakeholders."*

Recommendations
Our strongest recommendation is for authors to not only remove "gap" verbiage from their manuscripts, but also to remove "gap" thinking from their mindset. When trying to make a contribution in a literature that is nothing but gaps, authors could be handicapping their contribution argument from the outset, therefore thinking myopically. The concern here is that even a well-written and methodologically rigorous manuscript, but which lacks an interesting question, still has the potential to be rejected, especially from the top publications, as this reviewer suggested well:

> *A junior researcher may often err on the side of conservatism and in wanting to secure a safe and possibly quick publication will limits his or her research imagination to the confirm or disconfirm empirical findings. Work produced may be technically sound but the value of contribution points to our discipline, modest. They may take comfort in trialed and tested gap-spotting techniques to justify their work, and in doing this end up producing work that while rigorous, is not always interesting.*

In closing, if an author focuses more on the "gap" and not on the literature around their contribution, it's too easy for a reviewer to dismiss the research as "minor" or "incremental." Foreshadowing towards the next theme, authors should focus less on the theoretical "gap" and more on how to position this contribution within the ongoing conversation in the literature.

To conclude this theme, this reviewer summarized this theme well:

> *Authors say – in so many words – that they shed light on something "new" or not well understood but don't tell us what they then "see" or what we're supposed to learn; or they identify a gap but don't tell us why it is important to learn something new about the "gap" or don't bother to tell us how they fill the gap and why we should be interested. But most often the problem is that authors do not identify a clear and coherent context of theoretical contribution at all – they point out all kinds of gaps, problems, aims, and objectives but don't explain what their study actually shows and how their findings complement, correct and extend some existing stream of literature/body of theoretical knowledge.*

Where is the conversation?

> *They do not explicitly articulate what has been done in the literature, what the article adds and why that is relevant. Hence very often the main issue is that the contribution (which may be present) is not sufficiently well spelled out. Most research would benefit from making a stronger case for how the article changes/deepens our insights into a generalizable, theoretically sound phenomenon.*

While arguing for "a gap" in the literature may be the most common pitfall itemized by the reviewers, failing to position their contribution within an ongoing conversation in the literature is the most devastating mistake authors make in the manuscript creation process. Not clearly articulating what your research has added beyond what is already known is setting oneself up for failure in the review process. Not surprisingly, many reviewers strongly noted this theme stating, "*a frequent mistake is that authors do not make the CONSEQUENCES of their study explicit. What exactly follows from it, and which value does this piece of knowledge add for what reasons?*"

Related to not articulating the contribution well, reviewers commented that authors also do not position their contribution well vis-à-vis what has preceded their submitted research and how it will change the conversation going forward, explicitly, "*they don't position their work clearly. Without a clear positioning (that is, what work does this build on? – what do we already know?), it is hard for the review team to assess the magnitude of the contribution.*" Another reviewer recommended the importance of accomplishing this goal in the Introduction, detailing, "*not being clear and straightforward about the (intended) contribution over the existing research in the Introduction (first 1–3 pages). (Realistic) Positioning is critical at the beginning so as to steer how a reviewer reads and evaluates the study.*"

Recommendations

Our definition of what is a contribution (Ladik and Stewart 2008) is very specific. We view the literature as an ongoing conversation and a contribution occurs when an author adds something beyond what is already known to that conversation. The implication of this is that the ongoing conversation in the literature will change as a result of your research. If another researcher attempts to join this conversation after your research is published in the literature, your research should be referenced as part of their contribution argument.

When talking to young scholars about making a contribution to the literature, perhaps an apt analogy is that of a house party. We have all experienced this phenomenon; when attending a house party, for some reason or another, everyone ends up in the kitchen. Let's pretend that you were a little late to the party, but you wanted to join this lively conversation in the kitchen which happens to presently focus on the English Premier League. After listening to the ongoing conversation for a while that focused on arguments pertaining to which teams will finish in the Top 4 and in what order, a short lull in the conversation occurs. Recognizing this opportunity to join the conversation, you interject, "Did you see what happened in the Formula 1 race this weekend in Monaco? What a crash!"

While the Monaco comment was stated with much enthusiasm, it did not add anything to the ongoing conversation about the Top 4 teams in the English Premier League. The comment was not positioned well versus the comments on the teams who are in contention for those Top 4 slots. The comment did not add anything beyond what was already known, and the conversation in the kitchen did not change as a result of your thoughts. Maybe there is an active Formula 1 conversation in the garage or out on the lanai one could join. In the kitchen, however, the Monaco comment did not change the conversation, and therefore, you did not make a meaningful contribution.

To avoid this particular pitfall, we recommend that authors clearly outline how the research adds something beyond what is already known and what could change in the literature. Many authors treat the Introduction and the Literature Review sections as *"history lessons."* The reviewer does not need a historical account in summary form of previously published literature. In the top journals, many of the reviewers selected by the editor will most probably be the references the author summarizes in their history lesson. Furthermore, when authors present a history lesson, they invariably struggle with developing strong hypotheses because they are not specific to what could change in the ongoing conversation in the literature as a result of their analysis.

As opposed to a "history lesson", authors should focus on how their research *"fits"* into the conversation that preceded it. Illustratively speaking, the following shows an example of how an author could position their research:

- Some author publishes Paper A which creates the construct of Subject X and found an effect.
- Another author publishes Paper B on Subject X found this effect again and added another theory to extend its robustness.
- A third author publishes Paper C on Subject X found this effect again but outlined explicit boundary conditions for the effect.
- You then submit your research, Paper D on Subject X for review to a journal. You clearly position Paper D versus the ongoing conversation in the literature (Papers A, B, C) and show via classic theory testing, which theories in the literature hold and which do not agree with the theory that supports Subject X. As a result, the conversation in the literature (Papers A, B, and C) changed as a consequence of Paper D. All further papers on Subject X should appropriately reference Paper D.

To conclude this pitfall, the comment below hits many of the pain points outlined by the reviewers: (1) not explicitly stating their contribution, (2) arguing for some sort of *"gap"* as opposed to positioning a contribution within an ongoing conversation, (3) failing to state their contribution clearly in the Introduction, and (4) not exploring friendly reviews and outside opinions before journal submission to verify that the presentation, logic, and flow of a manuscript is sound:

> *The most common mistake I see is that authors do not explicitly state their contribution to knowledge. They suggest a topic has not been studied before, or that two concepts have not been studied together, but they never say why their research question should be answered, why it is important to theory, and what contribution it makes to the field. If they would take the time to explicitly write out their contribution – in the introduction of the paper – they would often find out that the contribution is not clear in their own minds, or that it is smaller than they thought it was. Or non-existent.*

Who is the intended audience?

> *Casting their contribution in terms of "it's never been done before" rather than in terms of "here's how the behavior of an important constituency will change as a result of our paper."*

Once the authors have established the contribution (that is, adding something beyond what is already known) and how it is positioned within the ongoing conversation in the literature, authors must be mindful of who will be impacted by this new information. The opening reviewer comment uses the word "constituency," and we cannot think of stronger terminology to describe this pitfall. Every published paper has an intended audience and some authors, "*overlook to whom (that is, which constituents) are the intended audience of their research.*"

Many papers have an academic audience and authors should be clear on how the conversation will change among this community. Please note, some academics are looking for a theoretical contribution, but it may also be the case that an academic audience could be looking for a change in teaching practice or novel ideas on running a business school. Some reviewers complained about overlooking non-academic audiences with overly complex methodology, stating "*by design, many projects have no chance of making a compelling contribution to non-academic stakeholders.*" Another reviewer pointed directly to a managerial audience, stating, "*not adequately explaining 'why' addressing the gap is important for knowledge development and/or managerial practice.*" Lawmakers, both on the local level or in Washington D.C., could be another vitally important constituency impacted by your research. Society at large is also another significant constituency which could be impacted by academic research.

Recommendations

Not only should the contribution be stated clearly in the Introduction of the manuscript, but the authors should also be explicit on who will be impacted by the results. We suggest this is an issue authors discuss meticulously with their friendly reviewers. Some of our top journals are general, like the *Journal of Marketing*, meaning the onus is on the authors to be specific on audience impact. Other journals have certain constituencies preordained as per the mission of the publication such as the *Journal of Retailing*, the *Journal of Public Policy & Marketing* or *Journal of Advertising*. We recommend not only to review the target outlet's mission statement, but also review three or four of the most recent letters from the editor which outline the current editor's mindset. Invariably, the editors will detail contribution areas and constituencies for the publication.

To conclude the four pitfalls, the following reviewer said it well:

> *Contributions to knowledge are relatively subjective and do entail the question of "contribution to whom." As a researcher interested in the intersection of consumer well-being and public policy, with a focus on the broad potential for substantive impact for society at large, I have become concerned with papers that seem to be so focused on finding a unique "surprise" that the specific research procedures, methods, and analyses are designed to only deliver the extremely novel finding. This sometimes seems to lead to extremely unusual procedures, methods, and contexts associated with the desire for the "surprise" finding. If this contribution to knowledge is solely focused on the theoretical domain, this may be very reasonable. However, if the implications for the substantive domain are positioned as of interest, the contribution seems limited, and, in a worst-case scenario, potentially misleading. If there are reported implications to applied marketers or society at large, generalizability and replicability of findings become important. Clarifying the contribution to what type of knowledge and for whom the knowledge is intended is critical.*

Conclusion: What is the story?

> *The most common mistake here is the absence of an overarching theoretically anchored conceptual story in the study. This absence of such a story limits the potential of the study to make a substantive contribution to existing knowledge in terms of theory development and the advancement of management practice in the field.*

The goal of this chapter, as well as the other chapters in this volume, is to help young scholars develop their research and make a strong contribution. With this objective, we asked some of the strongest reviewers in our discipline what are the most common manuscript mistakes, and they expressed, authors (1) who submit grammatically unapproachable manuscripts reducing the contribution's clarity, (2) who argue that "*a gap*" justifies contribution, (3) who fail to position their research into an ongoing conversation in the literature, and (4) who overlook *to whom* (that is, which constituents) are the intended audience of their research.

The opening quote of this chapter and the one that initiates the Conclusion section highlights the final pitfall we would like to stress to developing scholars; "*The most common mistake I see is when authors do not know how to turn significant research findings into a forceful, compelling narrative, thereby making it <u>unclear</u> what the contribution is*" (emphasis added). Although each manuscript has a set of distinct sections that are in a common order, it does not follow that a collection of disjointed sections that do not mesh well together creates a contribution. This is especially apparent when the manuscript has multiple authors who are each responsible for their respective section and do not review for article cohesiveness. Moreover, the lack of "*a forceful compelling narrative*" leads to exploring smaller or minor research questions as opposed to something more substantial:

> *When I review, I am having to use too many times a concluding sentence of the kind "In sum, I suggest taking a step back and reconsider the research question." As Eitan Muller told the IJRM ERB few years ago, we focus on providing perfect answers to small questions instead of providing good answers to big questions.*

What is missing from many manuscripts is a what one reviewer called a "*strong narrative arch*", detailing:

> *Another, shortcoming I often encounter is the lack of a strong narrative arch. What I mean by that is that often authors conduct a series of studies and then superficially combine them into the manuscript without really focusing on what is the story here and thereby what is the contribution. Just because the results are significant does not mean that the contribution is worthwhile.*

Each section of the manuscript should logically lead to the next and the storyline should be consistent throughout. The Abstract should match the Introduction and Discussion sections. The Introduction states the contribution and sets the outline for the manuscript. The Literature Review succinctly positions the conversation towards the research Hypotheses. The Method is appropriate for the research questions argued for in the Introduction. The Results are not overstated and the Discussion not only matches the Introduction but also does not make conclusions which are not supported by the data. Research is, *"about using evidence, theory, and logic to weave a 'true' story; when that story is less than compelling, the ultimate result is research that lacks impact and fails to advance domain knowledge (and thus often fails to publish well)."* The most common word a reviewer will use when *"the story"* or *"narrative arch"* is lacking, is *"disconnect"* as the presentation, logic, and flow of a manuscript is disjointed therefore clouding the contribution argument.

In closing, we are indebted to the 104 expert reviewers who took the time to provide the treasure trove of excellent comments for the manuscript construction-and contribution-making process. We hope these words of wisdom will echo in your thoughts when working on your research projects. That said, not all of their comments fit neatly within the four dominant themes outlined in this chapter. At the same time, we did not want these valuable comments to fall by the wayside and instead, used them to create **The Master Mistake Rubric** which is included in the Appendix. The rubric highlights, section by section, common pitfalls in the manuscript creation process and we hope you keep this document handy, therefore avoiding these sure-fire mistakes. Best of luck with your research!

Reference
Ladik, Daniel M. and David W. Stewart (2008), "The Contribution Continuum," *Journal of the Academy of Marketing Science*, 36, 157–65.

Appendix: The Master Mistake Rubric: sure-fire strategies to guarantee article rejection

The most common mistake I see is that authors often fail to remember that editors and associate editors are tasked with publishing papers that are Accurate, Impactful, and Rigorous (AIR). It's not enough to have one of these things without the others. For example, many authors work very hard to produce air-tight, rigorous research, and then they may be surprised that it gets rejected because it doesn't do enough to move the discipline forward. Others may have a "big idea" that has the potential to drive future research but falls short because the paper lacks rigor. Underneath both of these issues is the pitfall where authors often look to prior research published in a journal and assume that the contribution level and rigor required to publish an article in the past is sufficient today. We must move forward as a discipline and, if we're successful, requirements on all three elements of AIR must increase over time.

Before submission

- *"Misalignment with the journal, not speaking to the audience of the journal."*
- *"Another mistake is that the contribution does not fit the audience of the journal. For instance, authors provide a substantial contribution, but the journal is looking for theoretical contributions."*
- *"Poor writing. Problems with the organization of the paper, problems with clarity, grammar issues."*
- *"They choose something that is too narrow. That is, the contribution is too narrow to be meaningful for any stakeholder (researchers, marketing managers, public-policy makers, and so on.)"*
- *"The most common mistake I see is that authors don't really position papers for the journals they are targeting, so that I am left wondering whether they had even read a single paper in the journal the paper has been submitted to."*

Title and abstract

- *"Other mistakes that lead to a rather negative impression straight from the start are an unbalanced abstract (often emphasizing the study's background rather than findings or value of them) or an abstract appearing different from the actual paper, and when the introduction is sloppily written or feels too broad or beside what the title or abstract presented."*
- *"Overpromising in the title or the abstract. This leaves the reader feeling underwhelmed at best and misled at worst."*
- *"The abstract often summarizes the paper but doesn't necessarily highlight what is new for different audiences and sets of literature. This is assuming there is a contribution in the first place, of course."*

Introduction

- *"The first is not clearly communicating, early in the paper (e.g., the introduction) exactly what the contribution of the paper is and how it moves us beyond what is currently known. I tell my doctoral students that they 'must' be able to do this clearly and early as this is what will ultimately catch the reader's attention and cause them to read the paper with interest."*

- *"Typically, the introduction does not effectively establish the study's importance or its contribution to the extant literature."*
- *"Young scholars frequently do not adequately show how their work augments or extends previous work (by using, for example, a literature table listing existing and intended new contributions)."*
- *"Taking four pages to state the objectives of the paper. These should be clear after a paragraph or two. If it is hard to explain the contribution, odds are there is little."*

Literature review

- *"A key mistake is not anchoring the research in a strong theory. This is evident in the literature review where the discussion does not identify the key issues that need closer examination."*
- *"Presenting the literature review as a set of facts instead of offering implications. The point of the review is to indicate why and how the paper differs (or to set up the design of the study)."*
- *"Oftentimes, the conceptual framework is underdeveloped, overly brief, and based on implied or unsubstantiated opinion. Other problems with the conceptual framework include blending several theoretical foundations together without establishing their compatibility; and, introducing theories from different disciplines without establishing their importance, relative to related theories in marketing, or adequately explaining them."*
- *"Most researchers don't ever identify a good set of research questions to guide their project. They ask relatively mundane questions based on past papers they have read, that are not very interesting or novel."*
- *"The paper is not well positioned in the literature (how does it add to the conversation?)."*
- *"The article ignores past research (claiming a contribution when there is not)."*
- *"Not fully accounting for the existing literature. In order to contribute to literature, the author needs to start from a foundation of what is already known."*
- *"Not offering meaningful insight in conceptual development (citing facts, not offering analysis/synthesis)."*
- *"Not knowing previous literature so arguing something is a significant contribution even if it's minor or has already been shown."*

Hypotheses

- *"Common difficulties with the research design concern the measurement scales. Oftentimes, scales are created or adapted without adequately establishing their appropriateness for examining the research hypotheses/ questions."*
- *"Every hypothesis should have a rigorous rationale behind it, but in my*

personal opinion the most interesting questions are: (1) those where the hypothesis can go multiple ways (e.g., the DV goes up or down) and there are theoretically different explanations for it or (2) those where authors aim to explore an interesting phenomenon that we see happening in the managerial world."

- *"A related problem is that oftentimes, it seems as if the author is developing hypotheses post hoc after the data analysis reveals some significant results, that were not expected or part of the original theoretical investigation."*
- *"By this I mean that authors often describe their hypothesis but fail to connect the hypothesis to prior literature and/or fail to explain how the differences between prior literature and the current work are meaningful/important."*

Method

- *"Not considering if their research method best answers the research question posed. Specifically, given the research question, what makes their methodology, data, institutional context the best-in-class in terms of answering the question?"*
- *"The article includes moderators or mediators without any theoretical basis."*
- *"Authors find relationships between variables in data sets and attempt to position the paper as if the hypotheses were a priori."*
- *"The paper mixes 'theories' to propose paths in a theoretical model."*
- *"The constructs and variables are not (well) defined."*
- *"Flawed methods. Incomplete reporting, confounded study designs, inadequate methods, procedural issues in the study."*
- *"Not connecting the conceptual argument to the methodology/analysis that is chosen."*

Discussion

- *"An additional clear mistake is a section with unclear theoretical and managerial implications."*
- *"The discussion section oftentimes does not identify new insights gained from the study findings or explain how they add meaningfully to the literature."*
- *"Not considering implications beyond theory (that is, public policy, managerial implications)."*
- *"Papers often lack implications. If there are no policy relevant variables, it is often unclear what any decision maker should do with the findings. Conjecture is not sufficient."*
- *"Related to this is an inability to interpret what the research has found and impart meaning to it. Often the managerial implications are forced or nonexistent."*
- *"Authors fail to return to develop the theoretical postulates offered in the literature review in their discussion."*
- *"Authors fail to distinguish sampling boundaries from theoretical 'limitations' of the research."*

[2]

Guidelines for Conducting Research and Publishing in Marketing: From Conceptualization Through the Review Process

John O. Summers
Indiana University

A primary mission of institutions of higher learning is the generation and dissemination of knowledge. The low acceptance rates at the leading research journals in marketing, typically in the single digits to low teens, suggests the need to increase the quality of the research manuscripts produced. This article presents a set of guidelines for researchers aspiring to do scholarly research in marketing. Discussed are issues such as developing the necessary research skills, conceptualizing the study, constructing the research design, writing the manuscript, and responding to reviewers. Also presented are the author's personal observations concerning the current state of research in marketing.

This article is intended for doctoral students and those researchers who are beginning or are early in their careers and would like to increase their journal acceptance rates. The experienced author with several major publications and years of reviewing experience will find little, if anything, "new" to them. What follows are the author's reflections on more than a quarter century of guiding doctoral students and reviewing for, and publishing in, some of the leading journals in marketing. The author's remarks primarily relate to research that involves the collection and analysis of primary data (e.g., case studies, surveys, and experiments). Not addressed are such things as review papers, theory development not based on empirical research, and quantitative marketing models.

Journal of the Academy of Marketing Science.
Volume 29, No. 4, pages 405-415.
Copyright © 2001 by Academy of Marketing Science.

Manuscript Acceptance Rates at Leading Marketing Journals: From Single Digit to Low Teens

The acceptance rate at the leading research journals is currently averaging around 10 percent. Because editors are limited in the number of pages they can have in each issue, a journal's acceptance rate is constrained by the number of manuscripts submitted and the average length of the manuscripts accepted. Hence, as the overall quality of the manuscripts received by a journal increases over time, its standards for acceptance also rise.

For most top journals, there isn't a dramatic drop in quality between the top 10 percent of manuscripts received and the next best 10 percent, and most of the manuscripts submitted to the leading journals are reasonably well-done. About 80 percent of the manuscripts submitted are rejected on the initial round of reviews. There are several basic reasons for rejecting manuscripts reporting on empirical studies. These include the following:

1. The research questions being investigated are not very interesting (e.g., studies that are mainly descriptive and lack theoretical implications).
2. The research, although well executed, does not appear to make a sufficiently large contribution to the literature (e.g., the study largely replicates past research with minor modifications).
3. The conceptual framework is not well developed (e.g., lacks precise conceptual definitions of the constructs and/or compelling theoretical rationale for the hypotheses).
4. The methodology is seriously flawed (e.g., the sample is inappropriate for the research question, the validity of one or more key measures is

406   JOURNAL OF THE ACADEMY OF MARKETING SCIENCE   FALL 2001

suspect, and/or the experiment lacks experimental realism).

5. The writing is so confused that an invitation to revise and resubmit is considered unlikely to result in an acceptable manuscript.

For a detailed discussion of the weaknesses in manuscripts cited by the reviewers of one leading journal along with some guideposts for authors, see Varadarajan (1996).

To be published in a respected peer-reviewed journal, a study must be judged as meeting the currently accepted standards for scholarly research. Moreover, the study must be judged as more worthy than others competing for the same journal space. What should researchers do to increase the chances that their studies will make a significant contribution to marketing knowledge and be among those that are eventually published by one of the leading research journals? Answering this question is the major focus of this article.

SCHOLARLY RESEARCH ON SUBSTANTIVE ISSUES IN MARKETING

This section presents a set of 12 guidelines for researchers aspiring to do scholarly research in marketing. These guidelines deal with developing the necessary set of research skills and the research process.

Develop a Broad Set of Methodological Skills

Developing a broad set of methodological skills (e.g., qualitative research methods, survey research methodology, and experimental design) is critical to becoming a productive researcher. Those with a limited set of methodological tools are restricted in what they can study and what they can learn from their research. For example, someone with weak or no training in qualitative research methods is very limited with regard to developing grounded theory in his or her research area of interest, and researchers without a background in experimental design are likely to use surveys to test causal hypotheses. Developing a broad set of methodological skills early in one's career provides long-term benefits because one can rely on this same set of skills for many years. Many of the research techniques used today were developed several decades ago. For example, much of the most important work on reliability and validity was published during the 1950s and 1960s.

Learn to Be a Critical Reader of the Literature

It is important to become practiced in reading the literature in a critical manner. When researchers take an "accepting point of view" in reading the literature and focus on the conclusions of these studies, it will seem to them as if everything has been done, and they will feel disappointed that they had not thought to do these studies first. It is only when researchers look for flaws and/or limitations in the research they read that they begin to develop ideas for building on this research. For example, with regard to the conceptual framework, readers should concern themselves with whether the conceptual definitions are sufficiently unambiguous and whether the theoretical rationale provided for each of the hypotheses is convincing. With regard to survey research methodology, they might consider whether there is a serious problem with shared method variance and/or whether the measures used validly capture the constructs of interest. The limitations identified in existing research alert the researcher to opportunities for making contributions to the research area of interest.

Focus on Developing Hypotheses to Be Tested

As researchers start reading the literature, it is important that they begin thinking about identifying the hypotheses they might want to test. This will help them develop some structure for their conceptual frameworks and construct boundaries for their empirical studies. This, in turn, will allow them to determine which articles in their general area of interest are most central to the empirical study they plan to design. In deciding what hypotheses to investigate in the empirical study, thought should be given to the potential contribution to the literature and the feasibility of developing a rigorous research design for testing them. Researchers who fail to focus on developing hypotheses as they review the literature often end up spending many months or even a year reading the literature without having identified a single hypothesis they want to test.

Use the Literature to Stimulate Your Thinking

It is critical that the existing literature be used to stimulate one's thinking beyond that of merely understanding what is covered in each of the individual articles reviewed. In this regard, researchers need to consider such things as why different studies may have produced what seem to be conflicting results and what overall inferences one can draw from the studies as a group. They also should concern themselves with how existing conceptual frameworks might be improved. For example, have previous researchers overlooked important antecedents or consequences? Have past studies failed to consider potential mediators or moderators? Researchers must avoid allowing the literature to constrain their thinking. One aid for doing this is for researchers to constantly ask themselves what they personally believe about the phenomenon of interest. These are issues that researchers should concern themselves with *as they are reviewing the literature* rather than only after all of the literature has been read.

Put It on Paper

Researchers should write down their ideas as they occur to them and maintain a file. Failure to immediately commit one's ideas to paper means that time will be wasted trying to rediscover old ideas, and some ideas may be lost forever. The mere act of writing down their ideas often makes researchers more aware of ambiguities in their thinking. Frequently, arguments that seem so clear in their heads become unraveled when they write these down. This permits researchers to identify the problems in their current thinking and work to resolve them. Finally, committing one's thoughts to writing makes it much easier to get constructive feedback from others.

Don't Work in Isolation

It is difficult for most researchers to conceptualize a tight research study without interacting with others, if for no other reason than that it is difficult for people to evaluate their own work. This is particularly true for less-experienced researchers. Doctoral students who have infrequent interaction with their dissertation committees almost always take a long time to complete their dissertations. It is often the case that researchers clarify their own thoughts, identify problems with their conceptual framework, and discover new ideas solely as a result of communicating their current thinking to others. The mere process of orally explaining their thoughts to others forces researchers to examine their ideas more deeply. Hence, it is almost always a mistake for researchers to wait until they feel their conceptual frameworks are very well developed before exposing them to others. Although almost anyone willing to listen and read what has been written can be helpful, particularly valuable are those who constantly ask for clarification and question the researcher's assumptions, conceptual definitions, and theoretical rationale. These interactions are especially beneficial when researchers have previously committed their ideas to writing.

Develop Precise Conceptual Definitions for the Constructs

The conceptual definitions of the constructs of interest warrant special attention. Constructs are the building blocks of theory. Without well-developed conceptual definitions for the constructs, it is impossible to develop a coherent theory. For example, we cannot develop a

meaningful theoretical rationale for why Construct A should be related to Construct B if the exact meaning of each of these two constructs has not been established. Moreover, it is impossible to develop a valid measure of a construct that is not precisely defined.

Avoid developing pseudodefinitions. Some authors will talk about some Construct A being a result of or the cause of some other Construct B. However, one cannot define a construct in terms of its antecedents or its consequences. Moreover, trying to do so means that the proposed theoretical linkage between A and B would not be empirically testable (i.e., it could not be falsified); rather, it would be true by definition. Another type of pseudodefinition one finds in the literature involves merely giving examples of what is included in a construct (e.g., Construct A includes such things as . . .). These pseudodefinitions invariably provide an incomplete listing of the construct's content and fail to indicate what is not included in the construct. The central role of constructs requires that researchers make reasonably certain that their constructs are well defined before moving on to other aspects of their conceptual framework or to their research designs.

Evaluate the Hypotheses

The hypotheses to be tested also need to be evaluated before designing the empirical study.

- Are the hypotheses clearly written?
- Is each of the hypotheses falsifiable?
- Do any of the hypotheses involve truism or tautologies?
- Are any of the hypotheses trivial in the sense that others would be likely to question the methodology of any study that reported negative results?
- Is the theoretical rationale provided for each hypothesis compelling?
- Are there any additional theoretical arguments that would strengthen the conceptual support for the hypotheses?
- Do the hypotheses to be tested represent a cohesive set?

It is important for researchers to aggressively solicit criticism of all aspects of their conceptual framework. It is only when continued exposure of the conceptual framework to criticism ceases to uncover serious flaws and all necessary revisions have been made that researchers should move to the design phase. The time to revise the conceptual framework is before the data are collected. After the data are collected, researchers are severely restricted by the available measures as to what changes they can make in their conceptual frameworks.

408 JOURNAL OF THE ACADEMY OF MARKETING SCIENCE FALL 2001

Identify the Intended Contributions

At this point, it is important to make explicit the intended contributions of the study and to evaluate them. The contributions of a study can be conceptual, empirical, or methodological in nature. *Conceptual contributions* could involve such things as:

1. improved conceptual definitions of the original constructs;
2. the identification and conceptual definition of additional constructs to be added to the conceptual framework (e.g., additional dependent, independent, mediating, and/or moderator variables);
3. the development of additional theoretical linkages (i.e., research hypotheses) with their accompanying rationale; and
4. the development of improved theoretical rationale for existing linkages.

Empirical contributions would include such things as:

1. testing a theoretical linkage between two constructs that has not previously been tested,
2. examining the effects of a potential moderator variable on the nature of the relationship between two constructs,
3. determining the degree to which a variable mediates the relationship between two constructs, and
4. investigating the psychometric properties of an important scale.

When *field studies* are being used, *methodological contributions* might involve changes in the design of past studies that:

1. reduce the potential problems with shared method variance through the insightful use of multiple methods of measurement,
2. increase the generalizability of the research through more appropriate sampling procedures,
3. allow the investigation of the plausibility of "third-variable explanations" for the results of past studies, and/or
4. enhance the construct validity of key measures through the use of refined multiple-item measures and/or the use of measurement approaches that do not rely on self-reports.

With respect to *laboratory experiments, methodological contributions* might involve such things as modifications in the experimental procedures that serve to:

1. increase the internal, ecological, and/or external validity of the experiment;

2. improve the construct validity of the putative causes and effects (e.g., through the development of improved manipulations of the independent variables and/or the improvement of multiple-item scales for the dependent variables);
3. enhance statistical conclusion validity;
4. increase the experimental realism of the experiment; and/or
5. decrease the plausibility of demand artifacts.

Not infrequently, less-experienced researchers try to design their studies to contain many such contributions in an attempt to make certain that the overall contribution of their research will be sufficiently high. Pursuit of this approach is often associated with the risk of the researcher's time and effort getting so spread out among many tasks that every aspect of the study is poorly done. The important issue is not how many contributions a study will make but rather the *significance* of each contribution. One should be concerned with such things as the degree to which a proposed contribution fills some important gap in the literature. For example, a study could make a very substantial contribution by demonstrating that a previously unidentified moderator variable could explain what previously appeared to be conflicting results in past research. Feedback from successful researchers with a reputation for being candid is very helpful in pruning the list of intended contributions to those likely to have the greatest impact on the research area of interest.

Designing the Empirical Study

When the conceptual framework has been set and the intended contributions of the study determined, it is time to consider the details of the research design. Although past research in an area can serve as a valuable guide, it is important to recognize that no study is without methodological shortcomings. One should always be cognizant of the methodological weaknesses and/or limitations of published research and attempt to overcome these limitations in one's own work. For example, to the degree that previous measures appear to lack content validity, consideration should be given to revising some of the items used in these scales and developing new items to add.

The time for researchers to get critical feedback on their research designs is before they collect their data. Although researchers can make some modifications to their conceptual frameworks (e.g., clarify conceptual definitions, provide additional theoretical rationale for some of the hypotheses) even while their manuscripts are under review at a research journal, nothing can be done to improve the research methodology once the data have been collected. Moreover, if the data are seriously flawed, no amount of rewriting of the manuscript can overcome this fact.

Experts on the particular research methods being used should be solicited to critique the research design *before* the data are collected. Moreover, they should be encouraged to be as critical and detailed as they are when reviewing manuscripts for a journal.

Pretesting Questionnaires

A rigorous pretest of the questionnaire can almost always provide valuable information on how it might be improved. Unfortunately, many pretests are not very rigorous and only give the researcher a false sense of security. For example, when conducting a pretest of a questionnaire, many researchers will ask a small sample from the population of interest to complete the questionnaire and when they are finished ask them if they noticed any problems. If those in the pretest sample complete all items on the questionnaire and do not report any problems with any of the items, these researchers conclude that the questionnaire is without serious flaws. However, this conclusion is seldom justified. Participants often mark responses to the most confusing questionnaire items and never question what these items were intended to measure. When asked after completing a questionnaire whether any part of it was confusing, participants typically say little, if anything, even when many of the questions are confusingly worded. There are several plausible reasons for this situation. First, pretest participants may be constrained in the time and thought they are willing and able to devote to filling out questionnaires. Second, they may not be sufficiently skilled and/or experienced at detecting and articulating problems with questionnaire items. Finally, they may be reluctant to be critical, even when asked to.

Pretesting of the questionnaire is especially critical if new scales are being constructed or previous scales have been significantly revised. To determine what pretest participants really think about their questionnaires, researchers must be very aggressive in extracting this information. For example, as the pretest participants complete the questionnaire, the researcher might ask these participants whether they can think of more than one way to interpret what each item is asking and to report these interpretations. This should be done separately with each participant one question at a time. The researcher might also ask these participants to explain why they responded the way they did on each item. However, this approach will work only if the participants are perceptive and willing to devote a significant amount of time thinking about each item. One insightful and articulate pretest participant who is committed to providing constructive criticism is worth more than 20 reluctant pretest participants.

Whenever feasible, it is a good idea to use multiple-item scales because these scales are usually more reliable than single-item scales and their reliability can be easily measured when the scales are reflective. When building multiple-item, reflective scales, it is useful to administer the questionnaire to a small sample (e.g., approximately 30 participants) after the initial pretest has been conducted and revisions made. This allows researchers to determine if their items are producing the anticipated pattern of correlations. When this pattern is not achieved, the sample correlation matrix can be used to identify problem items. These items can then be revised or discarded based on a careful analysis of the content of each item.

Pretesting Experiments

Experiments involving human subjects are even more difficult to design and pretest than are surveys. When developing a new experimental design, it is critical that an extensive evaluation of the design be undertaken. In addition to pretesting the measures, researchers need to be concerned with whether (1) the experiment has a sufficient amount of experimental realism, (2) the experiment contains demand artifacts, (3) the manipulations provide the intended variance in the independent variables, and (4) the manipulations might be causing unintended variance in other variables that might have an impact on the dependent variables of interest. After evaluating their own initial experimental designs and making the necessary revisions, researchers should ask one or two individuals with special expertise in experimental design (e.g., those who routinely review manuscripts reporting experimental studies for the leading research journals) to examine their experimental designs and materials and to comment on what they feel the weaknesses of the designs might be. After revising their designs, researchers should recruit three or four insightful and articulate individuals to serve as initial pretest participants. These participants should be asked to provide a verbal protocol as they proceed through the experiment in a thoughtful manner. After all necessary revisions have been made, a pretest using participants from the population of interest should be conducted. The primary purpose of this pretest is to collect manipulation and confounding check measures. This will tell researchers whether their manipulations are working as planned. If the dependent variables are assessed during this pretest, they should be measured *after* the manipulation and confounding checks. Given a sufficient sample size for the pretest, it will not be necessary to include manipulation and confounding checks in the main experiment.

Unless a behavioral experiment largely replicates a past research design, failure to identify several significant problems in the initial design is reason for concern. It is rarely, if ever, the case that a newly developed research design does not contain several serious methodological problems. Hence, when the initial pretest does not reveal serious defects in the research design, the researcher

410   JOURNAL OF THE ACADEMY OF MARKETING SCIENCE   FALL 2001

should strongly consider conducting a second, more rigorous pretest.

CRAFTING MANUSCRIPTS FOR SCHOLARLY JOURNALS IN MARKETING

When researchers do an excellent job of conceptualizing their studies, developing and executing their research designs, and analyzing their data, the most difficult part of their work is behind them. Researchers need not be talented or creative writers to report the results of well-conceptualized and executed studies. They only need to be organized, accurate, and concise in their writing. All well-written manuscripts have three characteristics in common: (1) an introduction that "sells" the study; (2) tight logic, clarity, and conciseness throughout all sections; and (3) a creative and insightful Discussion and Conclusions section.

Introduction—Selling the Study

To convince readers of the importance of their studies, authors need to accomplish the following four goals in the indicated order:

1. Establish the importance of the general area of interest.
2. Indicate in general terms what has been done in this broad area.
3. Identify important gaps, inconsistencies, and/or controversies in the relevant literature.
4. Provide a concise statement of the manuscript's purpose(s), the contributions the manuscript makes to the literature.

The contributions noted should relate back to the gaps, inconsistencies, and controversies identified earlier.

In establishing the importance of the general area of interest, one need not develop long and complicated arguments or discuss the detailed results of several articles. Establishing the importance of the topic area can often be accomplished rather quickly and easily as the following sample text suggests:

_____ researchers have devoted considerable attention to developing and testing models of _____ (e.g., cite several prominent articles in the area).[1]

Next, the author should indicate in general terms what has been done in the broad area. A lot of journal space need not be devoted to achieving this goal. It is not expected or desirable that authors report the detailed findings of individual studies. For example, consider the following sample text:

Previous research has addressed several aspects of _____ : (1) _____ (cite two to three relevant articles), (2) _____ (cite two to three relevant articles), and (3) _____ (cite two to three relevant articles).

The results of the studies cited need not be reviewed when the current article focuses on different issues than those covered in the studies cited.

Then, researchers need to identify important gaps, inconsistencies, and/or controversies in the literature. This serves to establish the need for additional research in the topic area of interest. This task, like those that precede it, can be achieved in a concise manner. For example, consider the following sample text:

However, in addition, _____ encompasses several unexplored dimensions that lately have attracted research attention in other disciplines (cite two to three relevant articles).
Some of these unexplored _____ appear to be important and worthy of investigation in the context of _____.
An investigation of these issues is important because _____.
Furthermore, previous empirical research has focused primarily on _____ . Very little research has been done on _____ .

Finally, and most important, the researcher must provide a concise statement of the manuscript's purposes, the contributions the manuscript makes to the literature. This statement should follow logically from the text that identifies gaps, inconsistencies, and/or controversies in the literature. For example, consider the following sample text:

In this study we seek to extend _____ by addressing the gaps in _____ . The study investigates the impact of four _____ : (1) _____ , (2) _____ , (3) _____ , and (4) _____ . In addition, interrelationships among _____ are examined.

Researchers should avoid trying to develop a long list of contributions (conceptual, empirical, and methodological). Inevitably, several of these "contributions" will be of low importance and will divert the reader's attention from the major focus of the study. Researchers must make clear what *major* contributions their studies make and explain why these contributions are important. It is a mistake to assume that readers will decipher the importance of the study from a description of what was done. The failure to clearly specify the importance of the study in the introduction is often the result of not having given enough thought to this issue *before* the study was conducted.

Writing Quality

Writing quality is often a reflection of the clarity of the author's thoughts. Overly vague ideas invariably lead to confused writing or the lack of any writing. It is generally the case that when authors have trouble writing, the problem lies primarily with the clarity of their thoughts as opposed to their ability to phrase their ideas properly. As such, authors should first question their understanding of what they want to communicate when they are having difficulty writing.

The manuscript must be clearly written, concise, and characterized by tight logic. When evaluating their own writing, authors will often ask themselves whether the text is consistent with their ideas. This is far too low a standard to use because it does little, if anything, to ensure that the reader will understand the author's message. Instead, one should adopt Stevenson's standard: "Don't write merely to be understood. Write so that you cannot possibly be misunderstood."

Authors need to ask themselves whether it is possible to derive either unintended meaning or no meaning at all from what they have written. The aggressive search for alternative interpretations of one's text is a key to identifying ambiguous and confusing passages.

Jargon, the specialized vocabulary of a discipline, can be useful by adding precision and conciseness to researchers' writings. However, it is frequently misused (overused) in an attempt to make a manuscript appear more sophisticated. Unfortunately, it typically achieves the opposite effect. All such terms should be defined where they first appear unless their meaning is (1) invariant and (2) well-known to most readers.

Conciseness in writing is a virtue, particularly when publishing in research journals. Since journal space is scarce and costly, the contribution-to-length ratio is an important consideration in a journal's decision as to whether or not to accept a manuscript for publication. While writing in a succinct manner can be a daunting task for first-time authors, examining particularly well-written articles in the target journal can be very helpful. For example, consider the following passages that deal with conceptual definitions, theoretical rationale for hypotheses, and research methodology:

> *Conceptual definitions:* "_____ is defined as _____
> ." (If borrowed, cite the source.)
> *Rationale for hypotheses:* "Considerable evidence from previous research suggests that _____
> _____ ." (Cite two to three key articles.)
> "Furthermore, _____ (cite "leading experts") argue that _____ , they hypothesize _____ ."

> *Research methodology:* "Data were obtained through self-administered questionnaires from _____ in three _____ ."
> "A total of _____ usable responses were obtained for an overall response rate of _____ ."
> " _____ was measured by an ___ item instrument based on the research of _____ (cite key article)."

Each of the above passages contains a lot of information while using very few words.

Another way to keep the length of a research manuscript reasonable is to be parsimonious in the use of references. Often, two or at most three well-chosen references will provide sufficient support for a position. Moreover, too many references may make the manuscript difficult to read.

Sections involving reviews of the literature deserve special attention. It is unsatisfactory to provide a series of summaries of individual studies when reviewing past research. These consume journal space without adding anything to our understanding of the literature. As Churchill and Perreault (1982) observe, a review should "advance the field by virtue of its insightful, integrative, and critical evaluation of the state of work in a subject area." A good review section will provide a *synthesis* of the literature and make clear what is "known" with a fair amount of certainty and where the gaps are.

A Creative and Insightful Discussion and Conclusions Section

The Discussion and Conclusions section is the last thing readers see, and it can have a large impact on their impressions of the research being reported. This section should build on the Introduction section. In this regard, it needs to reaffirm the importance of the study by showing how the study reported fits into the literature (e.g., what gaps in the literature it fills). The study's contributions and their importance should be made clear by communicating the study's implications for theory and practice. To merely summarize the empirical results is an inappropriate strategy.

It is important to clearly distinguish between conclusions and speculation when writing the Discussion and Conclusions section. Conclusions must be clearly supported by the data. However, authors may have valuable, informed speculation to share. As Churchill and Perreault (1982) observe, "Good science and good 'speculation' are not incompatible, but each should be clearly labeled so that the two are not confused" (p. 286). A few interesting ideas can go a long way here. While the Discussion and Conclusions section should not be dominated by speculation, authors should identify new issues raised by the study's findings and/or provide insightful (nonobvious) directions for future research.

Self-Edit the Manuscript

The initial draft of even the most carefully prepared manuscript can always be significantly improved. As such, the initial draft should be revised prior to submitting the manuscript to others for their evaluation. It is difficult for authors to edit their own writing. In addition to the problem of being critical of one's own work, authors know what they wanted to communicate. This makes it difficult for them to notice ambiguities and omissions in their manuscripts. However, there are things writers can do to reduce these problems. Laying their manuscripts aside for a few weeks reduces writers' familiarity with their papers. This can help them develop a fresh perspective and be more open to changes. Another strategy involves analyzing the manuscript from the point of view of someone who knows little or nothing about the topic area. This would include such things as checking to see whether the specialized terms have been clearly defined and whether the logic underlying each of the arguments made and the positions taken are readily apparent. Finally, authors should ask themselves whether their students would be likely to understand most of what they have written. If not, the manuscript needs to be reworked.

Solicit Critical Feedback Before Submission

"A colleague who will read what is written, then question its assumptions, ask what's new, and quibble about its language is a person to be cultivated" (Markland 1983:142).

Getting feedback from colleagues before a manuscript is submitted to a journal can significantly increase the chances of the manuscript being ultimately accepted for publication, but only if the feedback solicited is highly critical and authors respond to this feedback in a positive fashion. Authors should select critics with extensive reviewing experience and ask them to treat their manuscripts like they would if they had received these manuscripts from a journal editor for review. It is not essential that these critics be experts in the topic area of interest. A strong reviewer can usually provide excellent feedback on manuscripts dealing with a wide range of topics. The feedback writers receive from their colleagues on various aspects of the manuscript (e.g., conceptual definitions, theoretical rationale, measurement of the constructs, and writing) can provide valuable guidance as to how authors might improve their manuscripts.

Should the "reviews" received from an initial set of colleagues contain few substantive criticisms and/or suggestions for major changes, authors should consider soliciting critiques from a second set of colleagues because it is unlikely that the first set of colleagues were being sufficiently critical. Almost all of the approximately 10 percent of the manuscripts that are eventually accepted for publication at leading research journals are the subject of substantial reviewer criticism and go through at least one major revision. Anyone who spends the time to give highly critical, constructive feedback to an author is doing the author an enormous favor.

Responding to the Reviewers

Authors are seldom pleased by the reviewers' reactions to their manuscripts. After their initial reading of the reviewers' comments, authors are frequently angered and/ or depressed because they feel the reviewers have not fairly judged their work, some reviewers more so than others. There is a natural tendency for authors to want to prove the most critical reviewers wrong, an approach that is dysfunctional to the goal of getting their manuscripts published. Authors need to pause to recover from their initial emotional reaction and develop a pragmatic approach to dealing with the reviews. They need to keep in mind that even the most critical reviewers are not vindictive and most of what they say is valid criticism. Reviewers for the leading research journals tend to be very successful researchers, and they typically spend from 1 to 2 days preparing their reviews for a single manuscript. The manuscript revision process must be guided by a careful consideration of the suggestions and critical comments of the reviewers and the editor.

When, even after careful consideration, the *specific content* of a reviewer's comment *appears* to be unjustified, authors should examine whether the comment is the product of some other problem with the manuscript. For example, authors may sometimes feel the reviewers are asking about issues already covered in their manuscripts or that the reviewers do not understand what the authors are doing. When this happens, it is best for authors to consider how they organized and explained things in their manuscript. It may be that the authors need to better communicate what was done. Reviewers spend considerable time and effort reading each manuscript. If they are confused, it is likely that the journal's readers will also be confused.

In addition to carefully studying the reviewers' individual comments, authors should look for trends in each reviewer's comments. It may be that several of a reviewer's comments are all related to a single basic problem. Reacting to the comments individually may not fix this problem and could even create additional problems by producing a disjointed manuscript. Authors should also look for recurring themes across reviewers. Studying the related comments as a group may give authors a better understanding of the underlying problem and lead to a stronger paper than would a piecemeal approach. Moreover, any shortcomings that are noted by more than one reviewer deserve special attention.

Authors should try to respond to *all* of the reviewers' comments in a positive fashion. It is always in the author's best interest to set a tone for courtesy when responding to reviewers. The accepted norm is professionalism and courteousness even when communicating disagreements with the reviewers and the editor.

After making the necessary revisions to their manuscripts and formulating their responses to the reviewers, authors should prepare a thorough set of revision notes that address both the major themes included in each review and the reviewers' individual comments. A separate set of responses should be prepared for each reviewer. The revision notes are easiest for reviewers to follow when each of their individual comments is followed by the authors' detailed responses.

THE STATE OF RESEARCH IN MARKETING: SOME PERSONAL OBSERVATIONS

While it is easy for an experienced reviewer to be critical of any study, research in marketing has greatly improved during the past two decades. Researchers are giving increased attention to providing a solid theoretical base for their studies. Theories developed in other disciplines have been widely used for this purpose. Purely descriptive studies have all but disappeared. More thought is also being given to how a given study fits into the existing literature and what contribution it makes. Because today's research studies are more theory based and tightly linked to the literature, the results of these individual studies are more easily generalized to other contexts.

Today's quantitative studies are more rigorously designed than past research. More attention is being given to the development and/or use of multiple-item measures of the central constructs and to providing evidence regarding the psychometric properties of the measures used in the study, primarily internal-consistency measures of reliability (e.g., coefficient α). Greater attention is being paid to selecting subjects that are appropriate for the research question of interest. There is less reliance on college undergraduate student samples. Finally, the results of today's studies are less open to alternative interpretations than past studies.

However, there are areas that are in need of improvement. These include (1) theory building research; (2) claims regarding convergent and discriminant validity; (3) use of single-source, self-report data; and (4) experimental realism.

Lack of Theory-Building Research

Marketing researchers have devoted little attention to theory-building research. It is difficult to think of many empirical articles in marketing whose primary purpose is to develop theory as opposed to merely introducing marketers to theories developed in other disciplines (e.g., psychology and sociology) and/or testing existing theories. As a discipline, marketing has become content with borrowing theory from other disciplines. Several factors may contribute to this situation. First, most of our doctoral programs do not do a good job of teaching the qualitative research methods (e.g., conducting field interviews and case studies) that are essential to developing grounded theory.[2] Many doctoral programs devote very little time to these methods even though one could argue that rigorous qualitative research is more difficult to conduct, analyze, and report than are surveys or experiments. As a result, most graduates are not skilled at theory-building research. Second, many in our discipline appear to believe that qualitative research is inherently not as rigorous or prestigious as quantitative research (e.g., surveys and experiments) and, therefore, the results are difficult to publish. This belief seems to be reinforced by the fact that few doctoral dissertations are based on qualitative research, and one seldom sees a rigorous qualitative research study published in any of the leading research journals in marketing. It may also be due, in part, to the negative reactions of some researchers to those qualitative researchers who seem to feel that their research findings do not need to be objectively verifiable. For too many of the qualitative studies published in the past two decades, it is difficult, if not impossible, for other researchers to determine whether the authors' conclusions are adequately supported by the data collected and/or to replicate the authors' findings.

Psychometric Properties of Measures

The vast majority of authors' claims regarding the convergent validity of their measures are unwarranted (i.e., maximally different methods of measurement are rarely used), tests for discriminant validity are typically very weak, and test-retest reliability is rarely examined.[3] Although authors often claim to have provided evidence regarding the convergent validity of their measures, it is usually the case that they use the same interitem correlations as evidence of both reliability and convergent validity. Furthermore, in many studies, it appears that the researchers have sacrificed the content validity of some of their measures by deleting items in their initial scales to develop unidimensional scales.[4] Often, the remaining items reflect a much narrower construct than that originally contemplated. Researchers need to give more consideration to using *formative scales* (i.e., scales for which

414   JOURNAL OF THE ACADEMY OF MARKETING SCIENCE

FALL 2001

the observed measures are considered to form the abstract unobserved construct) in those situations where attempts to develop unidimensional *reflective scales* (i.e., scales whose item scores are considered to be caused by, or reflective of, the construct of interest) fail to result in measures with acceptable content validity. When this occurs, it is often the case that the construct is composed of several different aspects or dimensions that are not highly correlated.

Single-Source Self-Report Data

A long-standing issue regarding studies employing surveys is that many involve self-reports and/or key-informant reports from a single source.[5] Data are never collected from any other source, and the survey respondents provide measures for both the independent and the dependent variables. The single-source issue is less of a concern when several of the variables are objective and/or factual in nature (e.g., the respondent's age and corporate profits as a percentage of sales) and, therefore, more likely to be independently verifiable from other sources. However, when most or all of the measures involve summary judgments of an attitudinal or perceptual nature, common method variance becomes a serious concern in interpreting the correlations between these measures. Another related problem with single-source data involving self-reports and/or key informants relates to the consistency motif. A great deal of past research on cognition and attitudes has shown that respondents have an urge to provide answers that they feel are logically consistent. This creates problems because respondents will often have lay theories of how the variables of interest should be related.

Experimental Realism

Perhaps the most frequent and serious problem with experiments in marketing is the lack of experimental realism (i.e., the degree to which the experiment involves the participants, forces them to take it seriously, and has an impact on them).[6] Experiments that ask the participants to role-play without previously having had similar task-related experiences and/or for which there are no meaningful consequences for the participant tend to lack experimental realism. In these situations, the respondents are most likely to tell the experimenter what they feel is a reasonable response. Unfortunately, participants are not always able to predict how they would behave in a given situation.

REVIEWING FOR SCHOLARLY JOURNALS IN MARKETING

Although they are frequently the targets of authors' anger, reviewers provide an indispensable service to the discipline. Without them, no top research journal could operate. Most reviewers are among the most prolific authors in the field. They serve as reviewers because they want to help the discipline advance, because they feel they owe it to their discipline, because of the prestige of being a member of an editorial board, and/or because they enjoy the reviewing process. How reviewers perform their jobs has a huge impact on how manageable editors' positions and authors' tasks are likely to be. Below are some guidelines for reviewers that help editors and/or authors fulfill their responsibilities.

1. Clearly identify all of the major problems with the manuscript that are within the reviewer's areas of expertise. Reviewers should avoid taking strong positions on issues that are not within their areas of expertise.
2. When making global evaluations (e.g., the writing is unclear, the theoretical rationale for the hypotheses are weak, etc.), provide specific examples supporting these evaluations.
3. Indicate which problems are major and which are minor.
4. Indicate which flaws appear to be correctable and which are not.
5. For correctable flaws, indicate what might be done to fix them.
6. For uncorrectable flaws, indicate which should be discussed in the Limitations section.
7. If the manuscript is considered to be potentially publishable with revisions, clearly indicate what must be done to make the article acceptable.
8. When recommending rejection of an article, specify the specific reasons (e.g., uncorrectable flaws). Provide a convincing argument as to why these flaws justify rejecting the manuscript.
9. Be tactful in writing the Comments to the Authors. Start these comments with some positive statements about the manuscript. Avoid making personal comments and using words with negative connotations (e.g., *naive* and *hopelessly confused*).
10. When not too time-consuming, direct the authors to articles or books that may be useful to them in revising their manuscripts and/or designing their next study. For example, if the theoretical rationale provided for a hypothesis is weak, cite previous research that might help the authors develop stronger rationale.
11. Avoid suggesting that the authors cite literature that is only loosely related to the research issues of interest.
12. Avoid asking the authors to cite the reviewer's articles unless they are central to the research.
13. Be open to alternative paradigms for studying the research questions of interest.
14. Allow the authors some flexibility to write the article they want to write.
15. Provide timely reviews (i.e., within 30 days).

SUMMARY

A major key to getting one's research accepted for publication and dissemination in a leading journal is paying careful attention to doing the best job possible at every step of the research and publication process, starting with developing the research idea through preparing the final revision of the manuscript. The success of each step is dependent on the steps that preceded it (e.g., it is impossible to develop valid measures of constructs without having developed precise conceptual definitions of these constructs). Hence, it is important for researchers to check the adequacy of each completed aspect of their studies before proceeding to the next stage. Too frequently, researchers do not seek feedback from their colleagues until they have written the first draft of their manuscript. Moreover, feedback is only helpful when it is solicited from those with high levels of expertise, those providing the feedback are motivated to be highly critical, and those receiving the feedback are receptive to constructive criticism. Being responsive to criticism is especially critical when going through the review process at a major journal. Not infrequently, a publishable study never gets in print because the author chooses to argue with the reviewers, ignores the reviewers' comments, and/or otherwise fails to adequately address the reviewers' and editor's concerns and incorporate their suggestions in the revised manuscript.

Research in marketing has improved greatly both conceptually and methodologically during the past quarter century. However, much remains to be done. Theory-building research is lacking in marketing. Survey researchers should reduce their reliance on single-source, self-report data and use maximally different methods when trying to assess convergent validity. Finally, experimenters need to be more concerned with the experimental realism of their studies.

ACKNOWLEDGMENTS

The author thanks A. Parasuraman, Thomas Hustad, Scott MacKenzie, Cheryl Jarvis, and the editor for their constructive comments on previous drafts of this article.

NOTES

1. This sample text is based on material found in Kohli (1985), as are most all sample texts presented in this section. Basically, the verbiage specific to Kohli's study was stripped from Kohli's article to provide a sample text appropriate for a wide range of studies. This basic approach can and should be used with other particularly well-written articles.

2. For an excellent discussion of building theories from case study research, see Eisenhardt (1989).

3. For the most authoritative treatments of convergent and discriminant validity, see Campbell and Fisk (1959) and Campbell (1960).

4. For an authoritative discussion of content validity, see Cronbach (1971).

5. For an excellent discussion of the problems associated with single-source, self-report data, see Podsakoff and Organ (1986).

6. For an authoritative discussion of experimental realism, see Aronson and Carlsmith (1968).

REFERENCES

Aronson, Elliot and J. Merrill Carlsmith. 1968. "Experimentation in Social Psychology." In *The Handbook of Social Psychology*. 2nd ed. Vol. 2. Eds. Gardner Lindzey and Elliot Aronson. Reading, MA: Addison-Wesley, 1-79.

Campbell, Donald. 1960. "Recommendations for APA Test Standards Regarding Construct, Trait, or Discriminant Validity." *American Psychologist* 15 (August): 546-553.

———— and Donald W. Fisk. 1959. "Convergent and Discriminant Validation by the Multitrait-Multimethod Matrix." *Psychological Bulletin* 56 (March): 81-105.

Churchill, Gilbert A., Jr. and William D. Perreault, Jr. 1982. "*JMR* Editorial Policies and Philosophy." *Journal of Marketing Research* 19 (August): 283-287.

Cronbach, L. J. 1971. "Test Validation." In *Educational Measurement*. 2d ed. Ed. R. L. Thorndike. Washington, DC: American Council on Education, 443-507.

Eisenhardt, Kathleen M. 1989. "Building Theories From Case Study Research." *Academy of Management Review* 14 (4): 532-550.

Kohli, Ajay K. 1985. "Some Unexplored Supervisory Behaviors and Their Influence on Salespeople's Role Clarity, Specific Self-Esteem, Job Satisfaction, and Motivation." *Journal of Marketing Research* 22 (November): 424-433.

Markland, Murry F. 1983. "Taking Criticism—And Using It." *Scholarly Publishing: A Journal for Authors and Publishers* 14 (February): 139-147.

Podsakoff, Philip M. and Dennis W. Organ. 1986. "Self-Reports in Organizational Research: Problems and Prospects." *Journal of Management* 12 (4): 531-544.

Varadarajan, P. Rajan. 1996. "From the Editor: Reflections on Research and Publishing." *Journal of Marketing* 60 (October): 3-6.

ABOUT THE AUTHOR

John O. Summers (Ph.D., Purdue University, 1968) is a professor of marketing in the Kelley School of Business at Indiana University. His work has appeared in the *Journal of Marketing Research*, the *Journal of Marketing*, the *Journal of Consumer Research*, the *Journal of the Academy of Marketing Science*, the *Journal of Business Research*, the *Journal of Business Administration*, and the *Journal of Advertising Research*. He served on the Editorial Review Board of the *Journal of Marketing Research* from 1972 through 1998.

Publishing ethics: managing for success

O.C. Ferrell and Linda Ferrell

Overview

The academic community has expectations that research and publications will be based on ethical conduct; but, implementing publishing ethics is complicated. The assumption that both new and experienced scholars are competent to fulfill their responsibilities can be challenged. All dimensions including conducting research, authorship, reviewing, and working with journal editors and publishers involve ethical decisions that can include gray areas. There are specific issues such as plagiarism, conflicts of interest, human subjects, and manipulation of data to obtain desired results. The Committee on Publishing Ethics (COPE) provides cases on all of these issues where advice is rendered based on concerns or conflicts. For most publishers and editors, COPE is the gold standard on publishing ethics.

Doctoral students receive little or no ethics training on publications. When ethics training is required in order to receive federal funding, often universities offer ineffective compliance or do not comply at all (National Science Foundation 2017). The best doctoral students and young scholars obtain mentors who may not engage in ethical publishing. Students also learn standards and requirements from senior scholars (Eden, Dean, and Vaaler 2018). On the other hand, many students receive little mentoring because the focus is on doing research and getting published. Most academic associations provide very few sessions or training programs on publishing ethics.

As pressure for elite publications increases globally, there is much more diversity in attitudes toward publishing ethics. Chinese scholars can be paid thousands of dollars for articles with a high impact factor. Leading Chinese universities publish their cash-per-publications policies. This trend is advancing globally, with other countries and the United States paying for publications. The cash bonus for publications may create more pressure to use questionable approaches to publishing. For example, a Chinese scholar could offer to share the bonus with a seasoned scholar. This could create ethical issues related to ghost or guest authorship where one scholar may not contribute enough to merit authorship but both authors share in financial rewards. This is just an example of how the publishing environment is changing, creating new ethical issues.

There are many opportunities to engage in unethical behavior in academic publishing. This chapter will examine major issues that have been identified by publishers, editors, universities, and various academic associations as well as the most recognized source for publishing ethics, the Committee on Publishing Ethics (COPE). Specific issues addressed will include conducting research, authorship, plagiarism, conflicts of interest, human subjects, and reviewing. In addition, we provide an overview of the publishing environment. We explain that the failure to have ethical leadership in the publishing process provides the opportunity to use unethical practices to maximize one's publishing success. A code of publishing ethics is provided to address issues corrected in this chapter.

COPE provides guidance

This review on publishing ethics is guided by COPE, a nonprofit organization that strives to help authors, publishers, and editors to achieve best practice in ethics of scholarly publishing. COPE's main goal is for ethical practices to become the norm within the publishing culture. In an effort to develop this review we have used the Code of Conduct and Best Practice Guidelines for Editors and Code of Conduct for Journal Publishers that has been combined into one "Core Practices" document. The core practices which the COPE document emphasizes are as follows: (1) Allegations of Misconduct, (2) Authorship and Contributorship, (3) Complaints and Appeals, (4) Conflicts of Interest/Competing Interests, (5) Data and Reproducibility, (6) Ethical Oversight, (7) Intellectual Property, (8) Journal Management, (9) Peer Review Processes, and (10) Post-Publication Discussions and Corrections. In addition to these ten core practices, COPE provides its members and followers with helpful flowcharts that provide guidance to implement advice when faced with alleged misconduct, a searchable database with over 500 cases of misconduct dating back to 1997, international standards, eLearning and discussion documents, and auditing tools for editors, among many other services (COPE Governance 2018).

COPE provides publishers with over 500 cases that address past examples of plagiarism, illegitimate publishing, conflicts of interest, human subject disputes between authors, and allegations of misconduct, among many other topics and categories, with some cases containing additional resolution and follow-up information. The COPE case database serves as a resource for editors and researchers for publication ethics. Members of COPE bring their cases to the Forum or the Council, where the cases are reviewed and discussed between the members of the Forum/Council. After review, the members provide thoughts, feedback, and advice to the original member who brought them the case. The member who brings the case for review has final discretion on how to handle the case and what decision they make moving forward. It should be noted that COPE advice is not given for the purposes of citing or relying upon for court cases or proceedings (About COPE 2018).

COPE codes, cases, and review papers provide the background and were used to validate most of the content in this chapter. A review of cases and advice from COPE covers almost all types of publishing ethics, misconduct, and acceptable practices. In addition, some emerging issues were included based on 10 years of experience as a vice president of publications for a top tier journal.

Background

Trust in publications is the glue that holds the integrity of the academic community together. Establishing a high integrity publishing culture requires both ethics and compliance. Publishing ethics should be based on principles and standards of conduct to ensure high quality scientific findings. To maintain high standards there is an important role for the author, editor, reviewer, and publisher. Together a culture of integrity should exist that includes compliance as well as values to guide publishing decisions. Unlike ethics in firms, there is less defined leadership to guide high integrity and publishing culture in academic publishing. There is no central oversight or reporting system. There is almost no training or education on publication ethics.

The first step in promoting publishing ethics is identifying the issues and risks of all stakeholders in academic publishing. Next is understanding how authors, editors, reviewers, and publishers make decisions. It is difficult to determine acceptable publishing ethics unless the stakeholders in this process have principles and standards that are understood. Publishers, professional associations, universities, and nonprofit organizations such as COPE provide guidance with codes, rules, and best practices.

While there are many publishing ethics codes, they are not uniform and often address different issues. Codes should drive training, monitoring, and compliance to ensure uniform publishing behavior in the academic community. These are necessary components that are weak or absent in publishing ethics. To make things more complicated, professional associations sometimes have conflicting standards. The Academy of Management (AOM) allows proceedings for AOM journal review to be published in AOM journals (AOM Code of Ethics 2018). The Academy of Marketing Science (AMS) copyrights proceedings would consider the same or embellished manuscript unacceptable for AMS journals. The use of any content from the proceeding would need to be documented. When authors have little mentoring or training and conflicting ethical publishing requirements, mistakes can be made. Many of the codes and guidelines such as COPE are intended to be advisory rather than prescriptive. There is no governing body that provides oversight over publishing ethics. Issues are addressed on a case-by-case basis by publishers, professional associations, universities, and other organizations associated with the author of the publication. For example, universities have strong rules and control through approval of research involving human subjects (Institutional Review Board (IRB)). But in other publishing ethics areas, such as manipulation of findings or authorship, there is almost no oversight. The appropriate committee deals with cases as they occur. Sometimes decisions are rendered by faculty who are not experts on publishing ethics. Some accusations of publishing misconduct in universities are based on personal conflicts and political agendas, not facts.

Therefore, a key problem in improving publishing ethics relates to little proactive involvement in making ethics a key concern in academic publishing. Involvement by all stakeholders is more to investigate and take action when misconduct occurs. In many cases involvement is reactive based on conflicts involving authorship, disputes, reviewers, discovering plagiarism, conflicts of interest, manipulation of data as well as fraud in some aspect of the publication process. Ethical misconduct may occur by authors, editors and reviewers, and publishers. In fact, in many disciplines there are more for-profit or predatory journals than legitimate journals. All of this occurs because of the absence of high integrity publishing environments with established programs, risk management, communication systems, training, monitoring, and enforcement of misconduct policies. In reality, there is no one major stakeholder responsible for publishing ethics. Misconduct often occurs because publishing ethics is only a minor concern of all stakeholders.

While universities and professional associations and publishers have codes of ethics, this is not adequate for establishing a culture of publishing integrity. These codes and policies are not effectively communicated to authors. At many universities there are no courses, workshops, or even discussions of codes of ethics for publishing. The focus is on how to get published. Pressure to get published, combined with the opportunity to manipulate or deceive, creates a situation where pressure is so great that researchers can rationalize misconduct to achieve their goals of publication. This situation is often referred to as the fraud triangle. In many cases researchers cheat to obtain a degree, tenure, or other academic rewards. Therefore, the stakes are high and the rewards are great for engaging in publishing misconduct. It is likely that most misconduct is never discovered. This is because most investigations are the result of accidental discovery, complaints or conflicts by individuals that are directly involved in the publication process. This publishing ethics environment is not effective because of limited leadership or proactive involvement in developing values, norms, and visible artifacts to promote ethics. If government and corporations only relied on whistle blowers to deal with ethical issues, we would have the same environment that we have in publishing ethics today – in our opinion a system that provides tremendous opportunity for misconduct.

Organizations not only have values, norms, and codes of ethics, but also provide training and compliance standards that are enforced. Many in the academic community start their publishing journey without ever reviewing codes of ethics on publishing or even having discussions with peers and mentors about the acceptability of certain practices. It is typical in empirical work to try to make data fit a model then to toss out hypotheses that are not significant and report only acceptable hypotheses using the methods and tests that are found to support the framework. Researchers are driven to manipulate data to make a perfect fit because many reviewers also have a poor understanding of publishing ethics. They may reject research with results that are mixed in significance tests because of a failure to understand that nonsignificant results are also important in scientific research.

With the goal of improving publishing ethics, this chapter will review some of the major issues facing scholars in making ethical decisions. Various guides for understanding these issues as well as concerning inappropriate behavior are addressed. We provide a code of publishing ethics that could be the basis for discussions about some of the issues we address. We want this code to be open access for others to discuss, modify, or use in improving publishing ethics.

Conducting research

Research projects should be designed to use the most appropriate methodology to address the topic under investigation. Results should be reported accurately. This only occurs if researchers use methods and software they understand. Possibly one of the greatest problems in publishing integrity relates to statistical manipulation: lack of full disclosure. Studies or hypotheses that do not show statistically significant results may be highly useful in discovery. Many new scholars have not been taught the value of insightful results in explaining their findings.

A major area of concern is related to survey research that is often used in business research. Does the sample reflect the population? Journal articles should report truth, objectivity in an accurate manner in which it was conducted (Babin, Griffin, and Hair 2016). If the desired outcomes are not reached, objectivity and the elimination of bias require full disclosure of the results. When scientific research is conducted it requires skill in interpreting and explaining what the outcome can add to existing knowledge. This process should avoid making the data fit a desired outcome by eliminating part of the study that does not fit the anticipated or desired outcome. Scientists can possibly advance knowledge more by explaining unexpected regularities rather than pre-existing expectations (Alba 2012).

All aspects of the research should provide a high integrity approach, and in empirical studies the sample of respondents should be appropriate. Some studies are not appropriate for student samples, and that decision is important in planning the research design. In business, research platforms like Mechanical Turk (MTurk) provide inexpensive and convenient online crowdsourcing. For example, 27 percent of all surveys in the *Journal of Consumer Research* used MTurk samples over a four-year period of time. MTurk grew from 9 percent in the first year to 43 percent in the fourth year, indicating researchers were finding an easy, inexpensive way to do experiments (Chandler and Paolacci 2017). Some journals such as the *Journal of Advertising Research* will not accept MTurk samples because MTurk workers often misrepresent their identity, ownership, or behavior in order to get paid (Wessling, Huber, and Netzer 2017). Researchers should examine the strengths and weaknesses of alternative sample sources and find the most representative sample for the population under investigation (Hulland and Miller 2018).

Secondary or archived data needs to be identified and described in sufficient detail. Data that is many decades old may not be representative of the population today. The quality of archived data should be accessed. Because the data exists does not make it sufficient to use it in a scientific analysis. Researchers need to understand why the data was collected and if it is rigorous, reliable, and adequate. If the purpose of gathering the data does not match the purpose of the research project, there needs to be a defense of why it is acceptable to use the data. Finally, the methodology used to gather the data is important to defend in using it in a research project.

It is important to avoid the manipulation of data or to fabricate data to achieve desired research results. This includes avoiding the deleting of data that does not support the desired research outcome. Observations that 95 percent of the hypotheses in recent articles are supported creates the question about only reporting desired results (Babin, Griffin, and Hair 2016). Many editors and reviewers expect hypotheses to be supported. In fact, Armstrong (2003) found that reviewers in top journals expect hypotheses to be supported 80 percent of the time. Therefore, researchers may be driven to eliminate unsupported hypotheses to gain an acceptance. The desired results can be obtained by running many different statistical tests or eliminating part of the data set. The result is the scientific community does not have the opportunity to analyse relationships that are not statistically significant. Nonsignificant results can be more interesting and informative in some studies than significant results. Explanation for why results are nonsignificant provide many insights that could be useful in future research.

Internal validity relates to whether the evidence or data supports the results and rules out alternative explanations. In empirical studies it ensures that the experiment or research design determines the correct cause and effect. For example, the selection of a sample has a direct impact on internal validity. Smith et al. (2015) cast doubt on MTurk respondents. They found they were more likely to be Asian, reside outside the United States, and tend to be "speeders" relative to panel respondents working for a small amount of compensation at a fast rate. This creates questions about the internal validity of these respondents for some types of research.

Internal validity may also relate to archival qualitative or other types of research. In the case of archival or secondary data, in order to have internal validity there needs to be an understanding of the respondents or observations, how the data were collected, and an assessment of measures. There is often a bias in developing association of predictors related to cause and effects. All of these concerns relate to the integrity of the research.

Plagiarism

Understanding what plagiarism is can be challenging. Plagiarism stems from failing to reference the published or unpublished work of others in the submission of a paper under new authorship, often in a different language and country. The Academy of Management Journal's definition of plagiarize "is to present as new and original an idea or product derived from an existing source" (Academy of Management Journal 2012, p. 749). Plagiarism is an act of fraud if the intention is to deceive others. If there is not intent then there needs to be an explanation of why it occurred. Plagiarism can also be viewed as a form of theft. It is an attempt to steal the work of others and pass it off as one's own content. Plagiarism can involve serious legal consequences because it can be a violation of copyright laws. It can involve direct copying with only minor changes with no reference of the original source. It can be self-plagiarism also known as ideoplagiarism when one uses work previously published. In some cases the work may be co-authored with other professors. Copying phrases, sentences, or parts of a paragraph without credit to the source is also a form of plagiarism.

While plagiarism includes both words and ideas, all academic work rests on the foundation of others. Academic integrity requires the use of citations to acknowledge the ideas of others. Intentional copying or the use of ideas that are known to be the work of others is the defining aspect of plagiarism. On the other hand, everyone has acquired knowledge based on everything we have experienced or learned in our life. There will always be concepts in our acquired knowledge that are based on the work of others. Therefore, there may be sentences, terms, or concepts that are widely used in articles.

Turnitin as well as other plagiarism software is used by publishers, the academic community, and others to detect plagiarism. But plagiarism checkers have to be interpreted. The computer software can only match text with existing text. Some sentences or strings of text could be common expressions. For example, George Washington was the first president of the United States. There is debate about what percentage of matched text constitutes plagiarism and it also depends on the nature of the subject matter. In general, anything over 25 percent should raise concerns. But in conceptual articles where many concepts are quoted, 30–40 percent matching may be acceptable. The text-matching software may not detect paraphrasing so it takes experienced scholars to catch this type of plagiarism. Only editors can make final decisions of text-matching analysis.

A survey of 400 researchers, authors, and editors revealed that 95 percent of the editors and 84 percent of the researchers report they occasionally or regularly see plagiarism (Wireless News Jacksonville 2012). There is no doubt that many scholars and students engage in plagiarism on a regular basis. Many may think that it is acceptable because it is so widespread.

Plagiarism and duplicate publication are different based on the culture in various countries. An examination of retracted papers that are withdrawn due to academic misconduct in the publication process indicates retraction for plagiarism. In one study, China retracted the most papers for plagiarism with a plagiarism retraction rate of 16.8 percent. This rate was much lower than Italy and Turkey with over 60 percent of the retractions for plagiarism. The United States had a plagiarism rate of 8.5 percent in retracted papers (Amos 2014). Duplicate publication involves publishing the same content more than once. This form of redundant publication is especially high in China with 29.4 percent of the retractions involving duplicate publication while it is 13.1 percent in the United States (Amos 2014).

The variation in plagiarism across different cultures and countries indicates different publication environments. This could relate to different values and norms related to publishing as well as pressure and the impact of mentors and peers involved in the publication process. Journal editors should be mindful of these different views of plagiarism and duplicate publication.

Authorship
Authorship is one of the major concerns in publishing ethics. All authors are required to take public responsibility for their articles. An author needs to be involved in developing the objective of the article, and if data is used there should be some involvement in acquisition, analysis, and reporting of the results. Involvement means awareness and understanding about the methods used and the accuracy and potential limitations. All co-authors should be involved in drafting and reviewing the content. This means all co-authors read, understand, and contribute in some way to intellectual development. Co-authors should approve and be responsible for the final manuscript. Finally, all authors must be accountable for all aspects of the article. If challenged about the integrity of the article, they should be able to understand what was done and defend their role in developing the article.

Those who do not qualify for authorship include those that edit, acquire funding, or supervise a research group. Those that advised, only collected data, or participated in technical editing or suggesting research methods should be acknowledged for their contribution. These requirements for authorship are standard requirements in the scientific community.

Honorary, guest or also called ghost authorship occurs when an author is listed that did not participate or meet the requirements of authorship (Enago Academy 2018). Guest authorship is one of the biggest concerns in publishing integrity. Guest authorship is often provided to add a co-author that might make the article more prestigious. There are ethical issues in not providing adequate credit for those that wrote the article. There is also an ethical issue when a researcher that provided assistance or helped write the paper is omitted and not acknowledged. Cash-per-publication policies throughout the world are providing rewards for guest authorship. Authorship is the most frequent issue associated with publishing ethics. Some of the most typical authorship disputes relate to who deserves authorship, author order on the manuscript, and the use of ideas or proceeding from work without acknowledgement (COPE 2013a). A COPE forum found that the most common issue is an author who is left off the paper, or the paper is published without the co-author's name on it. A host of issues in disputes over authorship relate to the role of graduate students assisting in the research and debating or defending they should be an author. The following case has been abstracted from COPE case files:

> After undergoing first round revisions pertaining to a paper's format, it was found that the main author excluded a few co-authors from the revised version and failed to notify the journal of the change. The manuscript underwent complete evaluation and was accepted for publication. The excluded authors did not contact the journal until 7 months after publication. The main author assured the journal that he informed the excluded authors. The excluded co-authors in the published version claimed they were involved in the manuscript but withdrew the case because they wanted to keep their personal relationships intact. (COPE Case 15-06, 2015)

This case illustrates the complexity of authorship disputes. This type of case is extremely typical. Often a research team starts working on a project and some team members fail to complete their assignments or fail to complete work used in the final manuscript. Usually when co-authors are excluded, they had limited involvement in the final development of the article or communication about the article did not exist for an extended period of time. There are many reasons for names being removed from the final manuscript. In this case, a personal relationship caused the case to be withdrawn. In other cases, there can be charges of unethical conduct at the university level or even court actions when the offended party can show evidence of damage. Publishers and owners of the copyright make the final decision in most cases.

The key to managing authorship is transparency and complete disclosure of the contributions of others. Authorship should be discussed at the start of the project. All aspects of the authorship plan should be discussed. It does not happen often, but a co-authorship agreement would be an excellent way to avoid disputes. This would include the role and expectation of each participant and even the order of authorship. In other words, the subject of authorship should be a part of the work relationship at the very start of the project. Keeping a record of discussions and continuing to discuss authorship as the project evolves is important (Albert and Wagner 2003). If there is a written authorship agreement, the probability of a dispute is remote.

Conflicts of interest
A conflict of interest related to an author is a situation to take advantage of their position for personal benefit. This could result from relationship between researchers, editors, journal staff, and publishers. Authors are sometimes asked to declare conflicts of interest that may exist due to their relationships or funding for sponsored research. Conflicts of interest exist when an author, reviewer, or editor has financial or personal

relationships that bias or influence behavior (Johnson 2010). Personal relationships including family, friends, competitors, and peers that can relate to biasing a publishing outcome are conflict of interest concerns. Even institutional affiliations could cause an editor or publisher to advance the interest of individuals in that institution.

Other forms of conflict of interest include knowing or recognizing the author of a manuscript they are reviewing. Suggesting reviewers that know the author's work and will probably recognize the author should be avoided. Another issue is an editor-in-chief publishing in their own journal. This is acceptable if handled with rigor or clearly labeled as an editorial or commentary. If an editor-in-chief publishes a few articles, especially to establish a special issue or topic, it is acceptable in most cases. But frequent publishing could be questioned. Therefore, it is okay for an editor to publish in his or her journal, but this opportunity should not be exploited.

An area that should be addressed in codes of publishing ethics involves editors following a course of action consistent with the editor of another journal in accepting each other's articles. This can be expanded to an editor of journal A not only accepting journal editor B articles but also accepting the articles of journal B doctoral students or close associates. Then journal B follows a course of action consistent with A to advance their publications. This has been observed based on the frequency that editors of competing journals publish each other's articles.

Giving authors an opportunity to nominate reviewers can have benefits but also creates an opportunity to create a conflict of interest. This occurs when there is a reviewer that may recognize the author and possibly has a relationship with the author. Therefore, authors should only nominate reviewers that are considered knowledgeable and independent. An issue of concern is fake reviewers. One publisher identified authors who set up email accounts to create aliases as reviewers and then reviewed their own work. Recently Springer Nature retracted 64 articles after finding the peer review process had been manipulated.

Predatory journals also create a conflict of interest. Predatory journals operate as a vanity press and usually charge substantial fees for submission. Thousands of these journals are open-access website publishers that unprofessionally exploit authors and the academic community for their own profit (McLeod, Savage, and Simkin 2018). They are based on a fraudulent business model and lack of transparency. Publishers misrepresent everything from their location to their academic credibility. There is a website (https://predatoryjournals.com/) devoted to helping educate academicians on predatory journals which follows the diligent efforts of Jeffrey Beall (Gupta 2018).

Some consistent characteristics of predatory journals include: a journal that has a very similar name to an existing and respected journal, taking a country name in the title and replacing it with a different country, low or middle income country publisher, spelling and grammatical errors, distorted graphics or images on the website, no journal impact factor, indicating being indexed by Google Scholar, email submission of manuscripts (not through a publisher platform), some do not disclose an editor, not mentioning COPE somewhere on the website, and no policies dealing with integrity issues (such as retractions, corrections/errata or plagiarism) (Shamseer et al. 2017). Other factors include high page fees for publication (and notifying authors of the fees after acceptance), soliciting submissions through email contact, quick turnaround and acceptance, creating bogus scholars on editorial review boards, no peer reviews, improper use of ISSNs, and falsified publication location (predatoryjournals.com 2018).

Charging an article processing fee is often done with understanding that the user only has to pay if the article is accepted. Often these journals attempt to create legitimacy by selecting journal names that are very similar to legitimate names. Some of these so-called journals do not even copyright the manuscript. This is a form of self-publishing or pay to publish which in no way provides academic integrity in scholarship. These publication outlets create a conflict of interest that has the potential to damage legitimate publishers, authors, universities, and professional disciplines (McLeod, Savage, and Simkin 2018). A problem with predatory journals is lack of knowledge by young scholars as well as some administrators about how they operate. These journals could not be so successful unless many scholars used them as an opportunity to get published. Many deans and department chairs are approached for funds to pay the fees for publication. Unfortunately, many in the academic community are not aware of this self-publishing scheme. This is because publishing ethics is not a part of most academic programs. The focus is on getting published, not integrity and legitimacy in publishing. Fortunately, most universities use objective factors such as impact factors as well as ranking by scholarly organizations and avoid counting these publications as acceptable.

Human subjects
Human subjects should provide informed consent that results in voluntary participation. The informed consent should not be coerced or improperly pressured to participate in the research process. This includes student respondents. Students who are given credit for participating should be given an alternative assignment if they want to withdraw from the research at any time. Confidentiality should be maintained, and the privacy of respondents or involvement should be protected.

Human subjects are the only major area of publishing ethics that results in oversight by a university compliance system. This resulted from experiments where respondents were placed in situations where there could be stressful pressure to perform or even situations where there could be damage to the respondent.

U.S. federal oversight and compliance with regulations to protect human subjects create the IRB. The IRB has a mandated staff and all human subject research has to be approved. The U.S. Department of Health and Human Services supervises the compliance system to oversee the development, testing and evaluation of human subjects to develop or contribute to knowledge. Still some professors avoid going through IRB because of the time it takes to comply.

The IRB boards require researchers to complete ethical training, submit proposals, and there can be required changes in how human subjects are involved to satisfy IRB requirements. There have been many critics of IRB as a system to protect human subjects. Major concerns are inequalities between weak and powerful actors. Even with IRB, oversight professors have much power over students and may be able to require participation against their will. As mentioned earlier, the National Science Foundation (2017) finds universities offer ineffective compliance or no compliance.

Many researchers are critical of IRB. In the social sciences, especially business, respondents are often panel members or other paid respondents. The IRB process is designed to include health and medical research so the process can be complex and take much time. Much research in the social sciences does not need that level of scrutiny. Most importantly, researchers should comply with the process, and it is unique to each university and institution.

Reviewers

All legitimate journals must have a peer review system. COPE provides guidelines and cases to provide guidance for peer reviewers. The scientific community depends on peer reviewers to maintain the integrity of research and the development of knowledge.

The double-blind review means that the reviewer should refuse to review if they can identify the author. In return, the reviewers should not self-identify or provide any comment that could provide their identity. The review should be objective without any personal biases about the subject matter or research design. For example, if the subject matter is business ethics and the reviewer does not believe that research in this area is important, then this bias should disqualify the reviewer.

A reviewer should not accept a review if they do not have the expertise to review the article. In addition, the reviewer needs to contact the editor if he or she wants to use someone to consult with regarding some aspect of the manuscript. The most important thing is to respect the confidentiality of the review process. In addition, the reviewer should report any concern about publishing ethics misconduct. This requires the reviewer to understand what constitutes issues such as plagiarism and conflicts of interest. These types of misconduct are often reported by reviewers.

To maintain the integrity of the review, suggestions and comments should be based on solid academic research and knowledge. Opinions should be supported by facts or evidence or provide a defense for recommendations. Reviewers should be careful not to suggest that their work be cited unless it is absolutely necessary to defend a suggestion. Suggesting one's own cites just to increase the reviewer's citations is not acceptable.

A problem in the review process is bias that the researcher has to use a specific theory or methodology. Reviewers may insist on the latest fad in statistical analysis when it is not required. Therefore, the current peer-review process can be a subjective, social construction of knowledge more than objective new discoveries (Bedeian 2004). A new or unique discovery could be rejected if not consistent with the reviewer's view of the world. Reviewers often have biases and their own lens when conducting a review (Bedeian 2004). Many journal editors are finding it difficult to find enough reviewers for the number of manuscripts received. This has resulted in most journals desk-rejecting almost half of all manuscripts received. Most journals are placing increased pressure to return reviews in a very short period of time, such as 30 days. This results in reviewers not spending enough time on the review and a failure to focus on issues that could improve the manuscript. Sometimes the focus is negative, with an attempt to only find out what is wrong without constructive statements to develop and improve the manuscript. Accepting the review should carry the responsibility to do a balanced constructive review.

Reviewers must recognize that authors should respond to their criticisms and try to improve the contribution to knowledge. On the other hand, the editor could discourage the author from addressing some criticisms (Ortinau 2011). The notes to reviewers from the author should address concerns. If the author uses a direct quote or suggestion in the revision, it is best practice to acknowledge the reviewer as the source of the contribution. Reviewers should expect the author to use some of their ideas and should refrain from providing information they do not want the authors to use. The relationship between the reviewer and researcher should be collaborative. For the peer review system to function, all participants recognize the importance of contributing their insights and knowledge. Editors have a responsibility to make decisions based on the insights and facts from the review process.

Conclusion

Publication ethics is important to maintain the integrity of scholarly research. There are many issues beyond those discussed in this chapter that need to be addressed in maintaining integrity. There are many practices that become accepted that are potentially questionable. In general, it is believed there is more opportunity for misconduct today than in the past. This is possible because of advances in technology and the ability to manipulate data using many diverse statistical analysis packages.

The most significant issues relate to the lack of education and training of doctoral students and faculty to understand the required standards of high integrity publishing. There are issues related to the pressure on doctoral students to publish almost by the time they enter their doctoral programs. Dissertations often become the extension of the chair's research program and the student's work is routinely co-authored with the dissertation chair. This is acceptable if the student is not exploited and the relationship works for the mutual benefit of both persons. The danger is the student not being able to develop their own independent publishing career.

Many universities resolve conflicts and misconduct without proactive involvement in improving the quality of research. Some issues are so complex that university committees and ethics officers are not prepared to resolve issues. There is a need for more leadership at the university level to address publishing ethics. Education and training in publication ethics is left to mentors, and there is limited discussion unless there is an obvious issue to be resolved. To address this issue there needs to be more support from accreditation organizations as well as universities and institutions. Teaching material on publishing ethics, such as online certifications or certificates, could be helpful.

The pressure for both scholars and universities to publish in top tier journals has created rewards for researchers to engage in questionable behavior. Some of the rewards involve course releases, chairs or professorships, salary adjustments, and cash-per-publication programs. These rewards have increased incentives for gift authorship. The number of co-authors of articles seems to be increasing because it is a way to increase the number of articles published to receive rewards.

Academic associations have not taken a leadership role in promoting publishing ethics. While codes of ethics exist, there is no information about if and how they are used by scholars. Publishers rely on COPE to provide ethical guidelines when there are conflicts or disputes, and some publishers provide publishing ethics guidelines and other assistance (COPE 2013b). Most editors are selected not because they have expertise on publishing ethics but because they excelled in publishing articles.

Editors have many opportunities to manipulate publishing by the selection of reviewers and through subjective decisions about who gets published. The entire system can be influenced by political action of authors, reviewers, and editors.

The purpose of this chapter is to provide information and address issues that relate to publishing ethics. To be proactive and assist in improving publishing ethics, we have developed a code of ethics for publishing that addresses most of the issues we have discussed. This code of ethics (see Appendix) is based on the best practices that we have reviewed. A code of ethics consists of general statements that should be inspirational that include rules of conduct (Ferrell, Fraedrich, and Ferrell 2019). Basic principles of acceptable and unacceptable types of behavior are included in a code of conduct. Regardless of the subject matter, the code should provide assistance to support an ethical culture. We have developed a code of ethics that should provide an opportunity for discussion, modification, and even debate. The code should provide and highlight the key issues. However, the code should not be so comprehensive that it is used as a 'stand-alone' reference when misconduct occurs. We want the code to be open access to encourage others to contribute to making it more effective and useful.

References

"About COPE" (2018), *Unethical Research / Committee on Publication Ethics: COPE*, publicationethics. org/about (accessed 2018).

Alba, J.W. (2012), "In defense of bumbling," *Journal of Consumer Research*, 38, 981–87.

Albert, T. and E. Wagner (2003), "How to handle authorship disputes: a guide for new researchers," *The COPE Report*, 32–34.

Amos, K.A. (2014), "The ethics of scholarly publishing: exploring differences in plagiarism and duplicate publication across nations," *Journal of Medical Library Association*, 102, 87–91.

"AOM Code of Ethics" (2018), *Academy of Management*, http://aom.org/About-AOM/AOM-Code-of-Ethics.aspx (accessed 2018).

Armstrong, J.S. (2003), "Discovery and communication of important marketing findings: evidence and proposals," *Journal of Business Research*, 56, 69–84.

Babin, B.J., M. Griffin and J.F. Hair (2016), "Heresies and sacred cows in scholarly marketing publications," *Journal of Business Research*, 69, 3133–8.

Bedeian, A.G. (2004), "Peer review and the social construction of knowledge in the management discipline," *Academy of Management Learning and Education*, 3, 198–216.

Chandler, J.J. and G. Paolacci (2017), "Lie for a dime: when most prescreening responses are honest but most study participants are imposters," *Social Psychological and Personality Science*, 8, 500–508.

COPE (2013a), "Authorship, contributorship, who's doing what, and what do we need?" *COPE*, June 3, 2013.

COPE (2013b), COPE ethical guidelines for peer reviewers, https://publicationethics.org/files/Ethical-guidelines-for-peer-reviewers-0.pdf (accessed 2019).

COPE Case 15-16 (2015), Authorship dispute, 2015, *Committee on Publishing Ethics*.

"COPE Governance" (2018), *Unethical Research / Committee on Publication Ethics: COPE*, publication ethics.org/about/governance (accessed 2018).

Eden, L., K.L. Dean and P.M. Vaaler (2018), *The Ethical Professor a Practical Guide to Research, Teaching and Professional Life*, London: Routledge.

Enago Academy (2018), "Ghost authorship vs. honorary authorship in scientific research," *Enago Academy*, May 25, 2018, www.enago.com/academy/difference-between-honorary-and-ghost-authorship-in-scientific-research/ (accessed 2019).

Ferrell, O.C., J. Fraedrich and L. Ferrell (2019), *Business Ethics: Ethical Decision Making and Cases*, London: Cengage Learning.

Gupta, K. (2018), "Opinion: pay-to-play publishing," *The Scientist Magazine*, www.the-scientist.com/opinion/opinion-pay-to-play-publishing-34875 (accessed 2018).

Heimer, C.A. and J. Petty (2018), "Bureaucratic ethics: IRBs and the legal regulation of human subjects research," *AnnualReviews*, www.annualreviews.org/doi/abs/10.1146/annurev.lawsocsci.093008.131454 (accessed 2018).

Hulland, J. and J. Miller (2018), "Keep on Turkin'?" *Journal of the Academy of Marketing Science*, 46, 789–94. https://doi.org/10.1007/s11747-018-0587-4.

Johnson, C. (2010), "Conflict of interest in scientific publications: a historical review and update," *Journal of Manipulative and Physiological Therapeutics*, 33, 81–6.

McLeod, A., A. Savage and M.G. Simkin (2018), "The ethics of predatory journals," *Journal of Business Ethics*, 153, 121–31.

National Science Foundation (2017), OIG review of institutions' implementation of NSF's responsible conduct of research requirements, Office of Inspector General. OIG Tracking No. RP120300006, July 25.

Ortinau, D.J. (2011), "Writing and publishing important scientific articles: a reviewer's perspective," *Journal of Business Research*, 64, 150–156.

Predatoryjournals.com, accessed December 19, 2018.

Shamseer, L., D. Moher, O. Maduekwe, L. Turner, V. Barbour, R. Burch, J. Clark, J. Galipeau, J. Roberts, and B.J. Shea (2017), "Potential predatory and legitimate biomedical journals: can you tell the difference? A cross-sectional comparison," *BMC Medicine*, 15, 1–14.

Smith, S., C.A. Roster, L.L. Golden and G.S. Albaum (2015), "Respondent data quality in managed consumer panels and MTurk samples," *Journal of Business Research*, 69 (8), 3139–48.

Wessling, K.S., J. Huber and O. Netzer (2017), "MTurk character misrepresentation: assessment and solutions," *Journal of Consumer Research*, 44, 211–30.

Wireless News Jacksonville (2012), "Survey shows plagiarism a regular problem," *IThenticate*, www.ithenticate.com/press/plagiarism-survey-2012 (accessed 2019).

Appendix: Publishing code of ethics

This code of ethics should be considered as guidelines that are advisory, based on existing best practices. The guidelines were developed to assist in informing and promoting integrity in academic publishing. There will always be judgments about best practices, and the code is designed to provide guidance on the most appropriate way to address publishing integrity. The purpose of the code is for providing information, not creating new standards. The scientific community has developed principles, standards, and guidelines that this code represents. The Committee on Publishing Ethics (COPE) is an excellent source for additional guidelines and cases on specific breaches of publication ethics and the resolution of conflicts.

1   Conducting Research
   1.1   Research projects should be designed to use the most appropriate methodology to address the topic under investigation.
   1.2   All data sources and methods should be accurately disclosed.
   1.3   Sources of potential bias should be identified and any errors discovered should be reported.
   1.4   When reporting findings, there should be no manipulation of findings, omission of data, or deletion of hypotheses that were found not significant.
   1.5   The discovery of errors requiring corrections or clarifications should be made available at any stage of the research and publishing process.
   1.6   Internal validity should be ensured by appropriate research design and sample selection in empirical research.

2   Authorship
   2.1   Only those that contribute to the conception, design, and writing of the article should be considered co-authors. This means they contribute substantially to writing and revising the manuscript.
   2.2   In planning the research, it is important to determine those who will qualify for authorship, contributors but not authors, and the order of authorship should be established.
   2.3   The practices of placing co-authors on the article for reasons other than their active participation is not acceptable, in that it creates gift authorship.
   2.4   Before submitting a manuscript, all co-authors involved should agree to take responsibility for the final manuscript.
   2.5   Any form of contribution of others including the development of ideas, gathering data, technical assistance, or providing comments should be in the acknowledgements.
   2.6   Those that edit, suggest research methods, or only collect data should be acknowledged but should not be listed as authors.

3   Plagiarism
   3.1   The use of published or unpublished ideas or content should be referenced.
   3.2   When two or more papers share the same conceptual framework, hypothesis, and/or data, all previous articles should be identified. Redundant publication should be avoided when papers are published without proper cross references.

3.3 All references should be based on the original publication, not taken from the reference of other publications.

3.4 Since plagiarism among junior authors may result from poor mentorship or supervision, senior or experienced co-authors should provide appropriate oversight to prevent plagiarism.

3.5 Copying or adopting sentences from a wide range of sources without documentation should be avoided.

3.6 Self-plagiarism, or ideoplagiarism, should be avoided by citing previous work. This is especially important when co-authors are associated with the previous work.

4 Conflicts of Interest

4.1 Any interest or involvement that could influence the editor or reviewers should be disclosed.

4.2 Self-publishing in a predatory journal and claiming a legitimate peer reviewed article is a conflict of interest.

4.3 Suggesting reviewers that know the author's work or are close associates should be avoided.

4.4 Financial support of the research should be acknowledged if material.

4.5 Editors have a responsibility not to develop reciprocation agreements or behavior that results in mutual exchange of publishing each other's work.

4.6 Attempting to influence editors by providing special rewards or benefits with the expectations of special publishing favor is not acceptable.

5 Human Subjects and Respondents

5.1 Subjects or respondents should provide informed consent allowing for voluntary participation.

5.2 Informed consent should not be coerced or improperly pressured on any participant in the research process.

5.3 Subjects or respondents should be allowed to withdraw from the research at any time.

5.4 The privacy and the confidentiality of subjects and respondents should be protected.

5.5 Organizational compliance and training for human subjects and respondents must be implemented as required.

5.6 Since IRB can vary between organizations, researchers should inquire about requirements any time they obtain data for analysis that is based on human subjects.

6 Reviewing

6.1 Respect the confidentiality of the peer review and do not involve others to assist without permission.

6.2 Do not conduct a review unless you have expertise in the subject matter.

6.3 Report any ethical violations or irregularities such as plagiarism or conflicts of interest by reporting observations to the editor.

6.4 Reviewers should withdraw from reviewing a manuscript if they recognize the authors.

6.5   Provide appropriate feedback of the strengths and weaknesses of the manuscript. If possible, support should be provided for opinions.

6.6   Provide suggestions based on academically valid reasons, avoiding unjustified criticisms.

SECTION II

TAILORING YOUR WORK TO YOUR AUDIENCE

Introduction to section II

Marketing is a diverse discipline. Its journals differ on many factors: the focus of their content, the methods they prefer, the length of papers they publish, the balance between theoretical and empirical emphasis, the importance of pure knowledge versus application, and a host of other dimensions. Coursework in marketing doctoral programs generally focuses on theories and methods. Such courses usually assure that students are well-versed in relevant theoretical perspectives and understand the appropriate use of specific research methods. It is less common to find coursework or even books that address the norms for research and publication within the various sub-fields of marketing. Section II of this book provides insights into these normative differences.

The section begins with a general discussion of the positioning of a manuscript by Gary L. Frazier in Chapter 4. Positioning is a simple and direct statement of what a paper is about and what it contributes. Many papers, regardless of their specific focus and orientation, do not fare well in the review process because they are not well positioned, or even positioned at all. There are, of course, issues that are specific to particular types of research. Thus, Chapter 5, by Connie Pechmann, focuses on papers with a behavioral orientation. Chapter 6, a reprint of a paper by Roberts, Kayande and Stremersch, addresses papers with a more quantitative focus.

Conceptual and theoretical papers are especially difficult to publish in marketing, though those that are published tend to have an unusually large influence on the field. Chapter 7 is a widely cited reprint of a paper by Deborah J. MacInnis that provides insights into what works and does not work when crafting a conceptual paper. Like conceptual and theoretical papers, papers with more of a managerial focus also face unique issues in the publication process. This is because such papers are expected to straddle the divide between more academic research and applied implications. Thus, in Chapter 8, V. Kumar addresses writing papers that focus on strategy. In Chapter 9, Ronald Paul Hill examines the crafting of papers with a policy orientation. In Chapter 10, Constantine S. Katsikeas considers the writing and publication of papers with international dimensions.

Finally, different areas within marketing often have different requirements related to sampling and samples. In Chapter 11, Vikas Mittal discusses the general area of sample selection and the unique issues that may arise depending on the focus and orientation of the research reported in a particular paper.

[4]

On the positioning of research papers in the marketing discipline

Gary L. Frazier

Introduction

This chapter focuses on the positioning of research papers in the marketing discipline. Positioning is indicating where a paper stands in comparison to other papers focusing on the same issue, topic or construct. Positioning is mainly implemented by clearly stating the issue, topic, or construct being addressed and stressing its importance, while expounding upon the primary incremental contribution or contributions of the research.

More specifically, successful positioning is accomplished by (1) selecting an issue, topic or construct to focus upon, (2) explaining why the issue, topic or construct is important to the discipline, (3) reporting what is currently known about the issue, topic or construct based on extant empirical research, (4) expounding upon the intended primary incremental contributions of the research in the Introduction of the paper, and (5) clarifying the achieved incremental contributions of the research in the Discussion section of the paper. Of course, arriving at an effective title for the paper that incorporates the issue, topic or construct in some fashion and discussing the positioning briefly in the abstract of the paper are extremely important as well. Effective positioning is therefore multi-faceted.

The proper positioning of a paper is vital to its eventual acceptance and publication. That is, effective positioning enhances the chances of a paper gaining acceptance and publication in a major journal. Weak positioning frequently leads to rejection.

Issue, topic or construct selection

The marketing discipline centers on how end-customers are catered to and served by business firms. An understanding of how customers in business to customer and business to business markets make buying decisions is, therefore, critical within the discipline. Moreover, an understanding of how firms attempt to establish brand equity, segment and target customer segments, and manage the product, price, promotion, and place strategic variables (among other factors) in attracting and maintain customer relationships is critical as well.

Consumer behavior researchers can select from among a broad variety of issues, topics or constructs to focus their papers on what influences customers in making their buying decisions for products and services. Modeling researchers can examine any issue, topic, or construct relating to consumer behavior or firm strategy, including product and innovation management, often utilizing mathematical models grounded in game theory. Strategy researchers frequently focus on problems faced by marketing managers and/or sales managers in performing their jobs relating to building brand equity, targeting of customers, product development, product introduction, portfolio management, pricing, advertising, social media, sales promotions, sales force management, and channel management. Research methods are also the focus of many research papers.

Whatever the issue, topic or construct, it must be defined clearly and precisely. Cloudy descriptions and construct definitions lead to major problems. For example, within channel management, the study of the interfirm power construct is central. However, to this day, many conceptual definitions of the construct are unclear and lack precision, confusing power with its application and associated outcomes. Progress on understanding the interfirm power construct has been impeded as a result, in part, because shoddy definitions lead to weak research and rejections of papers.

In addition, why it is so important to examine the issue, topic or construct within the marketing discipline must be elaborated upon in detail. If the importance of the issue, topic or construct is underdeveloped and superficial, the chances of acceptance will be low. For example, within sales force management, salesperson compensation is a highly important issue for research, as it impacts salesperson motivation, satisfaction, and retention, as well as customer reactions to sales overtures. The anticipated impact of sales compensation on salesperson and customer behaviors must be thoroughly explained in such papers. If the importance of salesperson compensation is not firmly established, even though it may appear obvious, the paper will be on weak ground.

The purpose of a paper follows from the issue, topic or construct being focused upon. Normally, the purpose of a paper is simply to illuminate the issue, topic or construct, further enhancing the knowledge base for the welfare of the marketing discipline.

Review of prior research

What is currently known about the issue, topic or construct based on extant empirical research must be carefully and meticulously summarized. Such a summary is often included in the Introduction of the paper rather than in a separate section thereafter. A table is frequently included, highlighting the research papers and their findings on the issue, topic or construct of interest.

Literature reviews are frequently limited to major papers on the issue, topic or construct appearing in top journals in the field and related disciplines (for example, economics, strategy, organizational behavior, psychology, sociology). However, if publications in lesser journals and other outlets have helped to shape the research area, they need to be reviewed and summarized as well. Reviews should not be limited to papers published only in the journal where the research paper is submitted. The summary within the paper should provide a clear picture of the existing knowledge base on the issue, topic or construct. The review process flags papers that do a poor job of summarizing what is currently known. In essence, the authors must show they are experts on what is understood about the issue, topic or construct. This is critical in the paper gaining credibility in the review process. A paper must be published before it can have any impact.

Importantly, a literature review in a research paper is different than in a dissertation. In research papers, positioning is not a history lesson. That is, chronological order of publications or a comprehensive history of publications is normally unimportant in a research paper, whereas it is often stressed in a dissertation in order for the individual to exhibit to his or her committee that they have mastered the literature. A full-blown history of publications in a research paper takes too long and can even be distracting. A journal article's audience and purpose differ from the audience and purpose of a dissertation.

Intended incremental contributions

Within the Introduction, the primary intended incremental contributions of the paper must be outlined. Intended incremental contributions follow from the review of extant research. That is, what represents a contribution cannot be ascertained until what is currently known about the issue, topic or construct is clarified.

Journal space is limited. Only the very best research papers making the most contribution can be accepted and published. Therefore, the intended incremental contributions of the paper are critical in shaping value judgments within the review process made by reviewers, area editors, and editors-in-chief.

Careful attention must be paid to what are the primary intended incremental contributions of the paper. If they seem pedestrian, the chances of the paper gaining acceptance are dim. For example, if the sole intended incremental contribution of a paper on channel communication between supplier salespeople and distributor top management is that a paucity of research exists on the construct, it is unlikely this will be persuasive. More depth and thought is needed in highlighting what incremental contributions the paper is intended to offer to the marketing discipline.

Sometimes a single intended incremental contribution is sufficient. For example, McCarthy and Fader (2018) examine customer-based corporate valuation and contribute by offering a new model that can accurately value non-contractual firms. This single intended incremental contribution is valuable enough for the marketing discipline to warrant acceptance and publication of the paper. Other papers may need to state more than one intended incremental contribution. Obviously, it is a matter of judgment. Three intended incremental contributions are often warranted, with one or two being too few and four or more diffusing what the paper actually intends to accomplish.

Achieved incremental contributions

Sometimes intended incremental contributions stated in the Introduction are the same as achieved incremental contributions of the research. This often occurs because intended incremental contributions are prepared only after the entire paper is written and are the same as achieved contributions. In such cases, incremental contributions of the research still must be elaborated upon in the Discussion section, in greater depth than their initial mention in the Introduction.

At other times, intended incremental contributions are prepared prior to complete theory development, data collection, and data analysis, and may not all be achieved. In such cases, which incremental contributions actually were delivered upon must receive attention in the Discussion section.

My preference is to compose intended incremental contributions of the research early in the research process. They will serve to guide details of how theory development, data collection, and data analysis are actually conducted, thereby enhancing the overall quality of the research effort. As a result, what is intended to be achieved often is not due to natural difficulties in carrying out a research project. In my judgment, admitting such occurrences and realities enhances credibility in the review process.

Title

The title of the paper should reflect the paper's positioning in some manner. At the very least, the issue, topic or construct being focused upon in the research must be mentioned within the title. The title is meant to suggest to readers what the paper focuses upon.

Abstract

The basic positioning of the paper should be mentioned in the Abstract. The discussion must provide a brief perspective on what the paper is all about and what it intends to accomplish. It is like the first few seconds of a commercial. Failing to get attention will lead to less impact.

Discussion

This chapter centers on the positioning of research papers in the marketing discipline. Positioning is directly indicating where a paper stands in comparison to other papers focusing on the same issue, topic or construct. Positioning is mainly implemented by clearly stating the issue, topic, or construct being addressed and its importance, expounding upon the primary incremental contributions of the research in the process. How successful positioning can be accomplished in a manuscript was thoroughly examined in this chapter.

The success rate for papers submitted to the top marketing journals is low, usually under 10 percent. Part of the explanation is simply competition. There are many able researchers submitting their papers to the top journals with a limited number of spaces available for publication. However, a more important explanation is simply the quality of the research, which can involve positioning of the paper, preciseness of the conceptual definitions of constructs, soundness of the conceptual framework, adequacy of the sample frame, the reliability and validity of the measures, use of appropriate analytical techniques, interpretation of the findings, and writing ability of the authors, among other factors.

Thus, positioning is not the only factor that will determine whether a paper is accepted or rejected. However, positioning of a paper is too important to be ignored. Positioning is frequently not formally covered in either Ph.D. classes or in the mentoring of Ph.D. students and junior faculty by more senior faculty, at least in any depth. Some notion of positioning is sometimes picked up based on the school of hard knocks, learned by having papers rejected at the major journals and receiving associated feedback. It is hoped that this chapter will aide researchers in understanding what the positioning of a paper entails, avoiding huge mistakes as a result.

Planning of a research project can be challenging. The starting point is selecting an issue, topic or construct to focus on, which is often mind numbing, especially for young researchers, and is accompanied with high risk. This is because the selection of an issue, topic or construct should normally lead to a long-term research program of ten or more years in duration. The brand equity of a researcher is impacted by the focus and specialty of their research program. Each researcher must become known for something they have accomplished. Being a generalist is normally the wrong way to go.

However, passion must be part of the equation as well. That is, one must truly love the research thrust of their research program. Excellent research takes too much time and effort for lack of passion to exist.

Aside from the passion or perhaps part of passion, the importance of the issue, topic or construct to the marketing discipline must be considered in selecting a research focus. A safe approach is to examine an issue, topic or construct that is of vital concern to marketing practitioners. Relevant research will impact how marketing practitioners actually make decisions and conduct their work. The associated research program will not only help the researcher gain promotion, but also help marketing managers make better decisions.

Sometimes it may be advisable to select an issue, topic or construct that is not receiving widespread attention by other researchers. In this way, the uniqueness of a paper and related research project is unlikely to be impacted by what other researchers are doing. Many fear that if someone beats them to the punch, their paper and its uniqueness will be adversely affected. This should be a real fear.

Knowledge of the literature on the issue, topic or construct is critical. This simply is a matter of motivation and hard work. The quest for understanding what is known about an issue, topic or construct must be unrelenting and ongoing, as new research papers regularly appear. Grasping what is known about an issue, topic or construct is a lifelong endeavor.

For individual research papers, nothing is more important than shaping the intended incremental contributions. These contributions must be substantial. Some notion of the targeted journal and the likely reviewers of the paper must be sought. For example, the *Journal of Marketing* desires articles that contribute to both the academic discipline of marketing and to marketing practitioners, while the *Journal of Consumer Research* does not directly seek articles with critical implications for marketing practitioners. A grasp of which reviewers and area editor may be assigned to a paper and their associated value systems provides insight into which incremental contributions may sell. Within the Discussion section, an elaboration of the paper's achieved incremental contributions should cement its quality in the mind of the review team.

Conclusion

The effective positioning of a paper is critical to its success, including gaining publication in a major journal and amassing a large number of citations. The purpose of this chapter was to illuminate positioning, that is, what it is and how it can be achieved. It is hoped the chapter will prove useful to researchers as they shape their research programs and associated papers. Positioning cannot be an afterthought. It must receive attention throughout the development of any research project, from early stages to late stages. Appropriate positioning will guide all aspects of the research program and, therefore, tremendously impact its quality.

Reference

McCarthy, Daniel and Peter Fader (2018), "Customer-Based Corporate Valuation for Publicly Traded Non-contractual Firms," *Journal of Marketing Research*, LV (October), 617–35.

[5]

How to publish consumer research based on experiments in the top marketing journals

Cornelia 'Connie' Pechmann

This chapter is intended to provide guidance to junior academics in marketing and other fields about how to publish consumer research based on experiments in the top marketing journals. By the top marketing journals, I mean *Journal of Consumer Research, Journal of Marketing Research, Journal of Marketing, Journal of Consumer Psychology* and *Journal of the Academy of Marketing Science.* All of these are on the *Financial Times* list of leading business journals. Some of the information in this chapter is also relevant to publishing experiment-based consumer research in other marketing journals like the *Journal of Business Research, Journal of Retailing, Journal of Public Policy and Marketing, Journal of Interactive Marketing, Journal of Advertising,* and *Marketing Letters,* because these journals are increasingly adopting the standards of the top journals. My goal is to provide guidance to consumer researchers who primarily use the experimental method. I will not be discussing research that adopts the CCT (consumer culture theory) paradigm or the modeling paradigm.

Researchers who use the experimental method and want to publish in a top marketing journal should strive to make a contribution to knowledge that is solidly grounded in empirical data, but also provides a big picture insight that is generalizable across different substantive contexts. In other words, what the top marketing journals seek is a big picture idea, that is empirically supported, but that makes a fundamental theoretical advance that contributes not only to marketing but to academia in general. It should be possible to summarize this insight in a single sentence, for example, "savoring an upcoming experience heightens on-going as well as remembered consumption enjoyment" (Chun, Diehl, and MacInnis 2017, p. 101). The big picture insight often derives from testing theory-based hypotheses that were identified at the onset using a deductive approach. Alternatively, the insight may bubble up inductively from studying consumers in action, but nonetheless the paper should highlight the theoretical insight, not the specific consumer context, and should stress that the context studied is just one example of a larger empirical phenomenon. Purely empirical papers as well as purely theoretical papers are difficult to publish in the top marketing journals. By purely empirical papers, I mean papers that report findings about a specific marketing, business, policy or consumer context, but provide little in the way of fundamental theoretical insights that allow for understanding and generalizability to other contexts. These papers are viewed as offering more limited contributions. Papers that develop a theoretical framework but do not provide empirical data to support the framework are also viewed as making more limited contributions; but meta-analyses are fine.

One main aim of this chapter is to highlight three distinct pathways to developing papers that make experiment-based big picture theoretical contributions to knowledge. The three pathways involve providing: (1) fundamental insights about humans that are demonstrated in a consumer context; (2) fundamental insights about consumers; or (3) fundamental insights about how marketers or policy makers may affect or be affected by consumers. The third type of paper may arguably seem the most suitable for the top marketing journals, but these papers have declined in prevalence, to such an extent that the *Journal of Marketing* now explicitly encourages them (Moorman et al. 2018). Based on my experience, consumer researchers that employ experiments and that want to publish in the top marketing journals should choose one of these pathways, at the time they write up their research, and ideally from the onset.

In this chapter I first discuss the essential elements of any consumer research paper that targets a top marketing journal. These essential elements include a compelling storyline, empirically-based theoretical contributions to knowledge, multiple complementary experiments, and full transparent reporting of methods and results. Next, I discuss the main sections of a paper: the introduction, the theory section, the methods, and the results. I differentiate between papers that are based on the three distinct research pathways, and I discuss both similarities and differences in how a paper should be written based on the chosen pathway. I illustrate my points about the three research pathways using three papers that were recently published in *Journal of Consumer Research*, which are summarized in a table (Table 5.1). In addition, I provide a checklist for researchers to facilitate manuscript preparation (Table 5.2). A main point I want to convey is that experiment-based consumer research papers in the top marketing journals should use the introduction and theory sections to build their storylines for making a fundamental contribution, based on their chosen pathway. However, all papers should include the essential elements, and all should convey their methods and results fully.

A realistic perspective about publishing in a top marketing journal
Authors should start with a realistic perspective about publishing in a top marketing journal. Most U.S. marketing journals report acceptance rates of 8 percent or less, meaning that 92 percent or more of the submissions are rejected, sometimes even after revisions. If a submission fits within the type of work the journal publishes and hence makes it past the desk rejection stage, acceptance rates are higher, but still surprisingly low. Solid research is routinely rejected at the top marketing journals due to a perceived lack of a big picture insight. Top marketing journals are highly selective because they receive a very large numbers of submissions from the U.S., Europe, Asia, and elsewhere; and also from other business or basic disciplines. In addition, U.S. marketing journals do not solely publish consumer research based on experiments, but also other types of research, and so a large pool of well-trained researchers have to compete for very scarce journal space. Consequently, consumer researchers should expect to receive at least some and perhaps many rejection decisions. Even in the best case scenario, researchers should be prepared to undertake

Table 5.1   Examples of three pathways to making experiment-based big-picture theoretical contributions

Pathway and Example	Introduction	Theory	Methods	Results
Human Insights Pathway: Coleman, Williams, Morales, and White (2017), Attention, attitudes, and action: When and why incidental fear increases consumer choice	**State big picture insight:** Negative feelings have been found to increase choice deferral, but we propose that fear will reduce choice deferral	**Build supportive theory:** The functional approach to discrete emotions indicates fear elicits attention, positive evaluations and a desire to act	**Use standard methods and report them fully:** 6 studies with MTurk or student samples, ave. 250/study, fear manipulated as the IV except once measured, time horizon manipulated as a moderator, choice deferral as the DV, attention as a mediator, 1 study of actual product choice	**Use standard analyses and report results fully:** ANOVA, t-tests, bar graphs; Hayes mediation, tables; logistic regression, chi-square, bar graphs; spotlight, line graphs
Consumer Insights Pathway: Bellezza, Paharia, and Keinan (2017), Conspicuous consumption of time: When busyness and lack of leisure time become a status symbol	**State big picture Insight:** Conspicuous consumption has focused on the scarcity of goods, but we focus on the scarcity of individuals' time	**Build supportive theory:** Non-busyness used to signal status but, in today's consumer culture, busyness signals more human capital, scarcity, and greater status	**Use standard methods and report them fully:** 6 studies with MTurk, Qualtrics or student samples, ave. 300/study, busyness manipulated as the IV, social mobility both manipulated and measured as a moderator, perceived status as the DV, perceived scarcity as a mediator, 1 study of actual social media posts	**Use standard analyses and report results fully:** ANOVA, t-tests, bar graphs; Hayes mediation, line graphs; logistic regression, regression, chi-square, bar graphs; spotlight, line graphs
Marketer or Policy Insights Pathway: Argo and Dahl (2018), Standards of beauty: The impact of mannequins in the retail context	**State big picture Insight:** Social comparisons to similar others have been studied, but we focus on comparisons to global social norms	**Build supportive theory:** Mannequins convey a global social norm about beauty standards, threatening those with low self-esteem	**Use standard methods and report them fully:** 6 studies with student samples, ave. 125/study, mannequin presence manipulated as the IV, self-esteem measured as a moderator, product evaluation as the DV, conveyance of beauty standards as a mediator, 1 study of actual retail purchases	**Use standard analyses and report results fully:** Linear regression, spotlight analyses, bar graphs, Hayes mediation

Note: All examples are from *Journal of Consumer Research*.

Table 5.2   Checklist for a consumer research paper based on experiments aimed at a top marketing journal

Essential Elements	Clear and compelling storyline; apparent in headings, paragraph starts, and graphs	
	Empirically-based theoretical contribution is delineated, that is, a big picture insight	
	Multiple complementary studies, typically 4–7, sometimes more, rarely less	
	Primarily experiments, with at least one study measuring actual behavior	
	Appendices used to facilitate transparency and reproducibility	
	Jargon terms defined at the onset, minimal jargon used, and no acronyms	
	Compliant with journal style guide, and relevant articles from the journal cited	
Introduction	Focal consumer or marketing context identified and its importance delineated	
	Specific relevant literatures identified, along with gaps that are filled	
	Clear and convincing statements made about fundamental contributions	
	The research context, findings and implications are comprehensively summarized	
	The assertions clearly and accurately reflect the actual empirical work and results	
Theory	Subsections discuss each relevant topic and its connections to the current work	
	Pertinent work is included, that accurately conveys the story about contributions	
	Hypotheses stated informally in the text, or formally with numbering and indenting	
	Small number of interesting and important hypotheses, for example, 2–5 hypotheses	
	Overview of studies linked to the fundamental contributions	
Methods	Design and sample sizes disclosed, typically 50+ per cell for online MTurk samples	
	Participants described including number recruited, and number dropped by reason	
	Participant screening methods disclosed, and demographics described, if applicable	
	Manipulations and measures from the literature used, and repeated across studies	
	Manipulation checks and measurement reliabilities provided	
Results	Details of all analyses and results disclosed, including all variables in all models	
	Spotlight or floodlight analyses used for interval predictor variables, if applicable	
	Logistic regression analyses used for dichotomous outcome variables	
	Tests of mediation mirror the hypotheses, for example, using Hayes bootstrap analyses	
	P-values reported to 2–3 decimal places, and marginal p-values disclosed	
	Covariates identified ideally a priori, justified, and consistent across similar studies	

major revisions that may involve new data collection and/or new theorizing. However, researchers who are responsive and persistent, and who try different journals if initially rejected, should be able to publish their work in respected marketing or business journals.

Consumer researchers should also be prepared to pursue a project possibly for many years before successfully publishing a paper in a top marketing journal. It often takes years to understand all relevant literatures, generate viable research ideas that are sufficiently path breaking, run pilot studies followed by numerous full-fledged studies, analyse the data, write up the results, submit to a journal, complete multiple revisions, and possibly submit to alternative journals with revisions there too. The process from beginning to end is typically very lengthy, despite the fact that a marketing journal will generally provide reviews within about two to three months of submission. To handle the extensive workload, and to ensure that the research team has the requisite skills and knowledge, it is common for consumer research papers to include three or more authors. Single authored papers, while they exist, are becoming rarer. Hence, many business schools no longer require faculty who are going up for tenure to produce single authored papers. However, they do expect these faculty to be the lead authors on some papers and to produce papers with junior colleagues.

Many junior academics assume that if they obtain interesting and consistent empirical results across numerous studies, including a behavioral study or a field study, they are virtually guaranteed publication in a top marketing journal. In reality, though, how well the paper is written is at least as important as the results that are reported. Therefore, it is important to understand what is expected in the write-up, as I explain below. It is also important to ask knowledgeable colleagues to provide honest comments on a paper before sending it out for formal review, make revisions based on their comments, and make additional revisions based on the reviewer and editor comments, even if the paper is rejected at that specific journal.

Essential elements of a consumer research paper for a top marketing journal
An important element of a consumer research paper is that it should tell a clear, compelling and consistent story about the research contributions, one that even a casual reader can readily grasp. To tell the story well, the paper should include a plot overview in the abstract and introduction, a plot development in the theory section, and a plot resolution in the results section. As a journal editor, I found that a submission was ready for publication when I could skim through it and immediately appreciate the storyline, by reviewing the section headings, paragraph starts, and graphs. Skimming is common among reviewers, editors and readers. Hence, researchers should skim through their own papers before submission, as if they were busy reviewers or readers, to see if a clear and compelling storyline is conveyed, within these salient elements of the paper.

In addition, a consumer research paper that targets a top marketing journal should seek to delineate fundamental theoretical insights that can be appreciated by other disciplines, and by educated adults generally. By theoretical contribution, I do not mean that a specific theory must be tested and extended, for example, Assimilation-Contrast Theory (Cunha and Shulman 2011) or the Question-Behavior Effect

(Spangenberg et al. 2016). Most papers start with a focal theory or a defined research area, and this is important, but it is only a starting point. To be publishable in a top marketing journal, a paper should make a fundamental contribution to our body of knowledge broadly construed, that is, provide a big picture insight, which I label and is often labeled a theoretical contribution. Identifying at least one major contribution is essential; and creating a laundry list of weaker contributions will not do it. The contribution should be understandable to any educated reader. The contribution should not be of the form that "past research studied X not Y, so we studied Y." Top marketing journals are not looking for incremental work; they are looking for fundamental contributions to knowledge. These fundamental contributions should be emphasized throughout the paper, starting in the abstract, and in the contribution statement if one is required. Marketing journals do not expect researchers to be modest; instead, researchers should repeatedly highlight their contributions.

Typically, a consumer research paper that is targeted at a top marketing journal should include multiple empirical studies that are highly complementary. These studies will often have the same independent variables and outcome measures, but they will explore different mediators (process variables) and/or moderators (used to study boundary conditions and/or test mediating processes). Typically, three to six studies are included in a single paper, and a few papers report ten or more studies. A paper will rarely include just one or two studies, because this will not be sufficient to rule out rival explanations or to fully support one theory to the exclusion of others.

Consumer researchers most typically conduct carefully controlled lab experiments that factorially manipulate all predictor variables and randomly assign participants to condition. They also increasingly include at least one study that has greater realism, which perhaps measures a key construct, analyzes a real-world dataset, and/or studies consumers in the field, to demonstrate that the effects are generalizable outside the lab. Researchers at the top business schools are often given large research budgets, for example, in the thousands or even tens of thousands of dollars annually, to pay for participants, equipment (for example, eye tracking), field studies, and so forth. Therefore, consumer researchers from other schools should obtain whatever resources are needed to ensure high-quantity and high-quality empirical research.

Consumer researchers should ensure that their methods and results are fully reported and transparent, consistent with current top journal reporting standards, which are becoming increasingly rigorous (Pechmann 2014). Researchers should therefore ensure that they are up-to-date with the current transparency reporting requirements at the top journals, which most importantly seek to facilitate reproducibility. In order to provide full information and yet comply with a journal's page length limitations, researchers should generally use appendices to provide supplemental materials, for example, the study manipulations and measures and non-critical analyses. In most top marketing journals, footnotes are discouraged; the information should be included in an appendix instead. Acronyms should be avoided, meaning that words should be spelled out throughout the paper. Jargon should be minimized, with key jargon terms clearly defined at the onset. Renaming well-known constructs should be avoided. Before submitting a manuscript to any journal, researchers should ensure that it is in compliance with the journal's style guide, and that it cites relevant literature from that journal. Furthermore, researchers should ensure there is no identifying information in any part of the submission including the methods. The specific data collection locations (for example, university x) should not be identified.

Front end of the paper: delineating fundamental contributions

Writing the introduction
A very important part of the write-up is the introduction, including but not limited to the title and abstract, because these set the stage for the entire paper. A consumer research paper should typically start by highlighting the consumer or marketing issue that it will address. This should be done in a way that accurately reflects the empirical methods and results that are to follow. In addition, researchers should highlight the importance of what they are studying, for example, by talking about its prevalence, market value and/or impact on individual and/or societal wellbeing. Researchers should include citations that verify the importance of their topic, and sometimes real-world examples can help as well.

Furthermore, the introduction should clearly and convincingly state the various ways in which the research makes fundamental theoretical contributions to the literature, contributions that span multiple disciplines. Researchers should identify the specific literature or literatures to which they are making fundamental contributions, and then clearly and accurately delineate their contributions. It is not sufficient to say that the research addresses gaps in the literature; instead, fundamental new insights should be identified that are meaningful and worthy of attention at a top journal. The authors should also make it clear why their research is important: What did we learn that we did not know before, and why does it matter? Big picture ideas should be conveyed, that academics in other disciplines can appreciate, and even non-academics can appreciate. Some marketing papers also try to speak to marketing practitioners or policy makers, but it is becoming rarer for them to be the primary audience.

Typically, at the end of the introduction to the paper, the research context, findings and implications are summarized in an easy-to-understand and yet technically accurate manner. If readers can quickly and accurately understand the main points of the paper, they will often have a more positive reaction to it. A common mistake that researchers make is that they inadvertently set up the wrong expectations, so their studies do not meet expectations; and reviewers typically react harshly to this. For instance, researchers may describe their studies as addressing an important and prevalent phenomenon, but they actually study a lesser phenomenon. Or researchers may say they found certain results, but in reality they found different or weaker results. It is better to be honest and up-front from the onset. Examples of how strong introductions are written are provided below, using three papers that were published in top marketing journals, representing the three pathways to making fundamental contributions that I identified earlier: human insights, consumer insights, and marketer or policy insights.

Human insights: introductory section   The human insights pathway to publishing in a top marketing journal involves providing fundamental insights about human behavior, and by demonstrating these insights in a consumer context. This type of paper could be published in a psychology journal, but consumer researchers are increasingly writing such papers for top marketing journals. I will illustrate this pathway using Coleman, Williams, Morales, and White (2017), "Attention, attitudes, and action". This paper uses the human insights pathway because it focuses on how incidental fear may affect choice deferral, and then studies this behavior in a consumer context, by looking at product choice deferral. The use of a consumer or marketing context provides a differentiator relative to a pure psychology paper.

The introduction to Coleman et al. (2017) highlights the consumer context that is studied and its importance, noting that "closing the sale is the final and one of the most critical components of any consumer transaction," but that situational factors can affect choice deferral, and "we propose that one such situational factor is the incidental emotion of fear" (p. 283). The introduction also makes clear and convincing statements about the paper's fundamental contributions, stating that:

> According to previous research, general feelings of negativity increase the likelihood that consumers will defer the decision (Luce 1998). Taking a functional approach, however, we suggest that under some circumstances, the negative emotion of fear may actually *reduce deferral* because of its specific set of associated psychological and behavioral responses. (Coleman et al. 2017, p. 284)

Moreover, this paper's introduction discusses the relevant literature and research gaps to be filled: "no research to date has examined the consumer implications of the coordinated set of responses to fear on choice. Previous research has tended to consider how one isolated response associated with a given emotion might carry over and impact a subsequent decision" (p. 284). At the end of the introduction, the findings and implications are summarized: "we examine the effects of the responses associated with incidental fear, demonstrating how they collectively impact consumers' willingness to choose now ... by increasing attention to and liking of the current choice set, while concurrently compelling consumers to take action" (p. 284).

Consumer insights: introductory section   The consumer insights pathway to publishing in a top marketing journal involves contributing fundamental insights about consumers' thoughts, feelings, perceptions, or behaviors, and when and why consumers might have these various reactions. These papers essentially help consumers learn about themselves. This is an increasingly common pathway to publishing in the top marketing journals. I will demonstrate this pathway using Bellezza, Paharia, and Keinan (2017), "Conspicuous consumption of time: When busyness and lack of leisure time become a status symbol". This paper employs the consumer insights pathway because it focuses on consumers who assert to be busy, and how this affects how others perceive their status in today's consumer culture. I use it as an example of the consumer insights pathway because, when consumers assert to be busy, they either purposefully or unintentionally "sell themselves" to others to enhance their status. As the authors argue, this moves the research into the realm of consumer culture and conspicuous consumption. However, the boundaries between a human insight and a consumer insight can be diffuse and are often determined by the write-up rather than the research per se.

In the introduction to Bellezza, Paharia, and Keinan (2017), the consumer context is identified explicitly and its importance is delineated: "In contemporary American culture, complaining about being busy and working all the time has become an increasingly widespread phenomenon. On Twitter, celebrities complain about 'having no life'" (p. 119). The introduction also makes clear and convincing statements about fundamental contributions: "we uncover an alternative kind of conspicuous consumption that operates by shifting the focus from the preciousness and scarcity of goods to the preciousness and scarcity of individuals" (p. 119). The introduction identifies relevant literatures, along with gaps it fills: "Research in economics, sociology, and consumer behavior on the consumption of time has focused on the antecedents of time allocation decisions (Becker 1965), examining how individuals divide their time ... we examine how these time allocation decisions are perceived by others" (p. 119). The specific studies, findings and implications are summarized at the end of the introduction, for example: "We find that Americans, who perceive their society as particularly mobile and believe their work may lead to social affirmation, are very likely to interpret busyness as a positive signal of status" (p. 119).

Marketer or policy insights: introductory section   The marketer or policy insights pathway to publishing in a top marketing journal involves offering fundamental insights about how marketers, social marketers, or marketing-related policy makers may affect consumers, or how consumers may affect them. These insights are generally demonstrated in a marketing or policy context and are directly applicable to the focal stakeholder groups: marketers, social marketers and/or marketing-related policy makers. By social marketers I mean marketers who work in the nonprofit world or in non-governmental organizations (NGOs). I will discuss the marketer or policy insights pathway using Argo and Dahl (2018), "Standards of beauty: The impact of mannequins in the retail context". This research focuses explicitly on a marketing phenomenon: marketers use of mannequins in retail apparel stores, to display and promote apparel products. The research also directly studies the effects of the mannequins on consumers, by investigating whether, when and why the mannequins may inadvertently decrease consumers' evaluations of the promoted products.

The introduction to this paper states its importance: this is "the first academic investigation into the impact of female mannequins in the retail context" and that "the global apparel industry is valued at $3 trillion" (p. 974). Fundamental contributions to knowledge are delineated, by noting that it is shown that consumers are "impacted by a novel type of source – an inanimate object" and that such objects "are dissimilar from consumers because they are not real" and yet "they are capable of creating a global social threat through normative information they make salient and this can have a profound impact on individuals who are sensitive to appearance-related cues (that is, those low in appearance self-esteem)" (p. 975). The relevant literature and novel contributions are highlighted: "Our finding that the social comparison is occurring at a global level departs from previous research, which has focused on social comparisons occurring at the individual level" (p. 975). At the end, the findings and implications are summarized: "we find that the use of female mannequins as a retail promotional tool is less effective for consumers low in appearance self-esteem" … "when the mannequin displays an appearance-related product" and this has "a detrimental impact on their product evaluations" (p. 975).

Writing about the theory
The theory or conceptual framework section of a consumer research paper is generally divided into subsections that provide different literature reviews. Each subsection identifies one or more bodies of literature, and summarizes highly pertinent findings, to illustrate how past work is connected to the current work. Researchers should discuss all the work that is directly related to their storyline about fundamental contributions, regardless of the discipline in which it was published, rather than focusing solely on work on marketing or consumers. While researchers should read broadly, they should nonetheless be selective about what references they cite in a paper and avoid the temptation to share all they know. Researchers should focus on work that is directly on point and tells a simple and coherent story about how they make fundamental contributions. The literature reviews should not be organized by article, nor should they be ordered chronologically; instead, they should be organized by topic. That is, the reviews should not discuss article 1, then article 2, and so forth. Instead, topic 1 should be presented, then topic 2, and so forth.

The theory section of the paper should lead into the study hypotheses, which may be stated informally within the text, or stated formally with consecutive numbering. The hypotheses should be derived from past literature, and yet make novel contributions. Hence, it is important to focus both on similarities with and differences from past work. Typically, a small number of hypotheses are tested in a single paper, for example, from two to five hypotheses. A consumer research paper in a top marketing journal will rarely test a long list of hypotheses. In other words, the focus should be on identifying and testing a small number of highly interesting and important hypotheses, rather than a large number of less interesting ones. The theory section typically ends with an overview of the studies to follow, that illustrates how the studies build on one another to yield fundamental contributions.

Human insights: theory section   Coleman et al.'s 2017 paper shows how a theory section can be written if the human insights pathway is used. The first subsection discusses the literature on incidental fear and decision making, decision making (choice) deferral and its causes, and general negative emotions and choice deferral. The second subsection discusses the literature that suggests that the discrete negative emotion of incidental fear elicits attention, positive evaluations, and the desire to act. Hypotheses are stated: "we predict that incidental fear will narrow attention to the current choice set … result in higher memory for focal product information and lower memory for (peripheral) information … [and] more favorable evaluations … [and] a heightened desire to act … [and] prompt consumers to make a choice, rather than defer" (p. 286). Next, the six studies in the paper are outlined along with the hypotheses they will test. Then, the novelty of the research is re-stated, including its focus on one discrete negative emotion (fear), an entire suite of responses to this emotion, and a predicted reduction in choice deferral rather than an increase in deferral.

Consumer insights: theory section   Bellezza, Paharia, and Keinan's 2017 paper illustrates how a theory section can be written if the consumer insights pathway is used. The first subsection defines busyness as time at work versus leisure, a definition that is confirmed in a pilot study. The next subsections discuss the literature on how leisure implies status, and the researcher's rival hypothesis that busyness may instead imply status due to perceptions of greater human capital (for example, competence) and scarcity, similar to perceptions of luxury goods. The final subsection discusses the literature on social mobility and hypothesizes that busyness only signals higher status when a busy person is perceived as socially mobile.

Marketer or policy insights: theory section   Argo and Dahl's (2018) paper demonstrates how a theory section can be written if the marketer or policy insights pathway is used. It addresses how marketers may influence consumers, while still making fundamental contributions to knowledge. The conceptual background section starts with the literature on social norms and discusses how mannequins in retail apparel stores may convey a global social norm about beauty standards. The next subsection discusses the literature related to why consumers with low appearance self-esteem may be negatively influenced by retail mannequins. Three hypotheses are developed: That consumers with low appearance self-esteem will rate a product more negatively when it is displayed on a mannequin (versus not), but only if the product is appearance-related; and this will be because the mannequin will make salient a threatening normative beauty standard. The researchers stress that their prediction that the mannequin effects are caused by the conveyance of normative beauty standards is contrary to prior literature which would implicate comparisons to similar others instead.

Back end of the paper: full reporting of methods and results

Writing about the methods

The method section of a consumer research paper should be written to ensure full disclosure and reproducibility of the studies, and it should use appendices as needed to provide supplemental information, appendices which are increasingly online. Recently, researchers have been attempting to reproduce social science experiments, often with very disappointing results (Open Science Collaboration 2015), and so it is important to provide enough information to allow for reproducibility. The methods that should be fully disclosed include the experimental design (that is, factors, levels, and if between-subjects or within-subjects), participants, manipulations, measures, analyses, and covariates, for each study that is reported.

While full disclosure of stimulus materials and measures is not required at all marketing journals, it benefits the researchers to provide such materials, because a large number of papers are rejected due to a lack of information about the methods. In addition, providing a detailed description of all methods facilitates the review process and minimizes the number of review rounds. Some marketing journals go further and require that datasets and/or statistical models be provided, so it is important to check the journal's current disclosure requirements.

Consumer researchers typically recruit participants from Amazon's Mechanical Turk (MTurk), undergraduate student subject pools or classes, or Qualtrics. In general, reviewers and editors expect larger sample sizes with MTurk studies than with studies involving undergraduate subjects, who are in shorter supply. For easy-to-recruit online samples like MTurk, it is typically recommended that at least 50 participants be included in each cell of the design. The number of participants in each study should be fully disclosed including the total number recruited, the number dropped by specific reason, and the final sample size. The final number of participants in each cell of the design should also be reported. Sample sizes should ideally be determined a priori, for example, using power analyses.

Any methods for screening participants should be fully reported, and the demographics of the final sample of participants should be described. Studies conducted online, for example, on MTurk, typically use a standard attention check to identify participants that did not pay attention to the survey questions, and these participants are dropped from the statistical analyses. If the prevalence of inattentive participants is very high, the study is typically redone with higher compensation and/or better screening (for further guidance on this, see Oppenheimer, Meyvis, and Davidenko 2009). Participants are also dropped from the statistical analyses if they did not complete a dependent measure. This type of information should also be fully disclosed. Many reviewers require that the same criteria be used to drop participants across all studies. If participants are dropped after the data collection because it is decided post hoc that they did not qualify, for example, were not interested in the focal product, it is often beneficial to provide analyses that include these participants in an appendix. In addition, the researchers should report whether the results change due to the inclusion or exclusion of these participants.

Consumer research papers typically use highly consistent methods across studies, for example, the same manipulations and measures tend to be used repeatedly. Most commonly the independent variable is manipulated to enhance experimental control, but it may be measured in at least one study to examine generalizability. For instance, a consumer orientation or predisposition may be manipulated in most studies through an essay-writing task, but then measured in one study to ensure the results hold.

All stimulus materials (for example, manipulations, instructions, and study setups) should be briefly described in the text, and then preferably provided in the appendix, for example, using screen shots. Similarly, all measures should be briefly described in the text, with reliability statistics if applicable (for example, coefficient alpha), and preferably provided verbatim in the appendix. If content coding is conducted, inter-rater reliability statistics should be reported in the text, and the coding scheme should preferably be included in the appendix. If the same manipulation, measure or coding scheme is used across multiple studies, the researchers should provide the details in the first study in which it was used. Manipulation checks should generally be reported for each manipulation that is used, in each study. Manipulations and measures should be drawn from previous published research, and multi-item measures should be used, whenever possible. If no directly suitable manipulations or measures are available, researchers should try to modify related ones. It is important that researchers provide their stimuli, manipulations and measures in their papers, to allow future researchers to use or modify their materials.

Human insights: methods section Coleman et al.'s 2017 paper illustrates how a methods section can be written for the human insights pathway. Six studies are reported, using either MTurk or student samples. The sample size is about 250 participants per study, except in a behavioral study of snack choice which includes 111 students. Cell sizes are reported, and dropped participants are disclosed. In virtually all studies, the independent variable is manipulated as the type of emotion induced (for example, fear, sadness, or control). Manipulations from the literature are used, and manipulation checks are provided along with measurement reliabilities. In one study, emotion is measured as trait fear. Some studies include a manipulated moderator (for example, time horizon: present versus future) to help understand the underlying processes. The dependent variable is a standard choice deferral task from the literature, except in the behavioral study where actual choice of snacks is assessed. Some studies measure a mediator, for example, attention (via recall). Online appendices provide the stimulus materials.

Consumer insights: methods section Bellezza, Paharia, and Keinan's 2017 paper demonstrates how a methods section can be written for the consumer insights pathway. Six studies are reported that use either MTurk, Qualtrics or student samples. The sample size averages about 300 per study, but ranges from 112 for an initial two-condition study to 474 for a study of real brands. In virtually all studies, the independent variable is manipulated as a target person's level of business, and manipulation checks are reported. The dependent variable is the target person's perceived status, and virtually all studies also measure mediators (for example, perceived competence and scarcity), with the measures derived from the literature. Two studies measure moderators: perceived social mobility and culture (Italian versus U.S. participants). A pilot study serves as a field study; actual social media posts are content coded. An online appendix is used to provide the stimulus materials, and the results of the pilot study and several supplemental studies.

Marketer or policy insights: methods section Argo and Dahl's 2018 paper shows how a methods section can be written for the marketer or policy insights pathway. Six studies are reported, all with undergraduate students, who see real retail mannequins. In the behavioral field study, students go to an actual retail store and try on clothing the mannequin is wearing. The sample size ranges from 75 to 193 participants per study, and dropped participants are disclosed. The studies generally manipulate the mannequin (present or absent), and either the type of product on the mannequin (appearance-related or not, with a manipulation check), or mannequin completeness (for example, with or without a head). The main moderator, appearance self-esteem, is measured across all studies. The dependent variable is product evaluation and/or willingness to pay for the product, and a mediator is sometimes measured as well (conveyance of beauty standards). The measures are provided, and are consistent across studies, and measurement reliabilities are reported. The mannequins are depicted in an appendix.

Writing about the results
Consumer research papers should fully disclose the details of their statistical analyses,

including all variables used in all models, and all empirical results. It is recommended that all p-values be reported out to two or three decimal places (see journal style sheets for more specific guidance) and marginal p-values should always be disclosed. Marketing journals have generally stopped mandating p-values of .05 or less, and will generally publish papers that include some studies with marginal p-values, as long as most of the hypothesized effects are statistically significant across studies. Consumer researchers most commonly report the results of ANOVA models, because their predictor variables are manipulated. Then, relevant means are reported along with 1 degree-of-freedom (1df) t-tests or F-tests for pairwise comparisons of the means. Also, tables, bar graphs and/or line graphs provide the cell means.

If a predictor variable is measured on an interval scale, it is generally inappropriate to artificially dichotomize that variable, for example, use a median split (Pham 2015). Researchers should instead make full use of the continuous nature of the data, through appropriate regression analyses. Instead of pairwise comparisons of means, typically spotlight analyses are reported that examine effects at +/– 1 standard deviation from the mean of the interval variable, or floodlight analyses are reported that examine effects at smaller intervals and show the turning point from non-significance to significance (Fitzsimons 2008, Spiller et al. 2013). Spotlight results are typically illustrated in a bar graph, while floodlight results are typically illustrated in a line graph. If an outcome is dichotomous, for example, choice, logistic regression analyses are reported. In addition, relevant proportions are reported, along with pairwise comparisons using 1df chi-square tests or z-tests of proportions, and tables or bar graphs illustrate the proportions.

Consumer researchers generally hypothesize that an independent variable affects a process mediator and subsequently the dependent measure; and that these effects may be magnified or attenuated by a moderator or contingent factor. In such cases, researchers should report full-factor ANOVA models (or logistic regression models) that test the effects of the independent variable, along with the moderator if applicable, on (a) the mediator and (b) the dependent variable, along with means or proportions and follow-up pairwise comparisons. Then, researchers should report tests of mediation, typically using the appropriate Hayes (2013) model identified by number, and Hayes bootstrap analyses. Or researchers can use other bootstrap approaches for special cases like repeated-measures (within-subject) designs. Researchers could instead use structural equation modeling (SEM), but this approach has become less common in the top marketing journals. Mediation analyses and results are generally reported in the main text, often with a line graph (see Hayes 2013). Mediation may also be tested through moderators that manipulate the underlying processes, for example, by manipulating an emotion that moderates an effect, rather than measuring the emotion.

Consumer researchers sometimes include covariates in their studies to control for extraneous variables, increase power and/or reduce sample sizes (see tutorial by Meyvis and Van Osselaer 2017). For instance, hunger may be used as a covariate in food consumption studies. A highly appropriate use of covariates is when a measured predictor variable (for example, gender) is correlated with another variable (for example, workplace tenure or product interest) which is included as a covariate because it poses a rival hypothesis for the results. Nevertheless, the use of covariates has become quite controversial in the consumer research field, due to concerns about the selective inclusion or exclusion of covariates in different studies to yield p-values at or below .05. In addition, in the past, some researchers did not report their covariates, arguing that this was an inconsequential and extraneous detail.

To avoid any problems regarding covariates, researchers should fully report any covariates that are used in their models, justify the use of these covariates, and use the covariates consistently across similar studies (even if the covariates are sometimes non-significant). In addition, researchers should try to choose their covariates at the onset of their research project, and they should state whether their covariates were chosen a priori or included post hoc. If there is a weak justification for the covariates and/or the covariates were included post hoc, researchers may want to reconsider using these covariates. If these covariates are retained, the researchers should report their results both with and without the covariates, for example, with one set of results in the appendix, and state in the main text if the inclusion or exclusion of covariates changes their results. Note that covariates should generally be unnecessary if an experiment is conducted with manipulated variables, random assignment of individual participants to conditions, a large sample size, and adequate power overall, considering additional factors like manipulation strength. If covariates never attain statistical significance, and therefore do not affect the results, it is generally appropriate to state this and then drop them for parsimony.

Human insights: results section   As an example of a results section for a paper using the human insights pathway, we return to Coleman et al. (2017). This paper reports ANOVA results, followed by planned pairwise comparisons of means (t-tests), with p-values reported out to three decimal places. Tables provide cell means and standard deviations, and/or bar graphs illustrate the cell means. Mediation is tested using Hayes models (identified by model number) and bootstrapping analyses, and tables provide detailed mediation results. When the dependent variable is measured as dichotomous choice, logistic regression is used, followed by planned pairwise chi-square tests, and a bar graph depicts the cell proportions. When the independent variable is measured on an interval scale (trait fear), a spotlight analysis is conducted (+/– 1 SD), and a graph depicts the results. In the trait fear study, because anger is a rival explanation for the results, it is appropriately included as a covariate.

Consumer insights: results section   As an example of a results section for a paper using the consumer insights pathway, we return to Bellezza et al. (2017). This paper reports ANOVA results, followed by planned pairwise comparisons of means (t-tests), with p-values reported out to three decimal places. Bar graphs typically illustrate the cell means and standard errors. Mediation is tested using Hayes models (identified by model number) and bootstrapping analyses, and line graphs provide detailed mediation results. Some mediation results are provided in the online appendix. When the moderator is measured on an interval scale (perceived social mobility), a floodlight analysis is carried out and a line graph used to depict the results. One study includes covariates but reports that the same results obtain even without the covariates. Because mediators are extensively used, a correlation matrix of dependent measures and mediators is provided to demonstrate discriminant validity.

Marketer or policy insights: results section   As an example of a results section for a paper using the marketer or policy insights pathway, we return to Argo and Dahl (2018). Every study in this paper uses the measured predictor variable of appearance self-esteem, and so linear regression analyses are conducted that mean-center the variables. This is generally followed by spotlight analyses (+/– 1 SD) with bar graphs illustrating the results. Eight bar graphs are included to clearly convey the results. Mediation is tested using Hayes models (identified by model number) and bootstrapping analyses, and the results are reported in the text. No covariates are included in any analyses.

Summary and conclusions

As this book chapter has discussed, to be publishable in a top marketing journal, consumer research based on experiments must generally make fundamental big picture theoretical contributions which have a solid empirical basis. However, there are three possible pathways to making such fundamental contributions; researchers can either: (1) provide fundamental insights about humans which are demonstrated in a consumer context; (2) provide fundamental insights about consumers themselves; or (3) provide fundamental insights about how marketers or policy makers influence consumers or vice versa. Two of these pathways do not directly address marketing stakeholders, which may be surprising to outside observers, but this has been the trend in the top marketing journals for a while.

It is sometimes possible to focus on practical marketing questions in an initial study, and then do additional studies to make more fundamental contributions. For instance, Kettle et al. (2016) analyzed a large dataset provided by the financial firm HelloWallet, and found that consumers who concentrated their debt repayments, that is, paid off a few accounts first, ultimately reduced their debt faster. To publish their work in a top marketing journal, the researchers then conducted several additional experiments, testing three different process explanations for this effect. One process explanation was supported: Participants inferred progress from a proportional balance reduction. While the initial finding was not novel, the test of three process explanations was novel. As this example shows, there are several routes to making fundamental contributions.

In this chapter, I also provide a checklist to help consumer researchers who conduct experiments to prepare their manuscripts for submission to top marketing journals. This checklist is applicable regardless of the specific pathway that is chosen for making fundamental contributions to the literature. While some researchers might view the current rather specific standards for top journal articles as constraining, these standards make the research production and evaluation processes more predictable and controllable, which benefits both younger and more senior scholars. While consumer researchers should be guided by their own knowledge and intuition, they should also take into account the standards and norms that influence top marketing journal reviewers and editors, and I hope this book chapter will help them do this.

References

Argo, Jennifer J. and Darren W. Dahl (2018), "Standards of beauty: The impact of mannequins in the retail context," *Journal of Consumer Research*, 44 (5), 974–90.

Bellezza, Silvia, Neeru Paharia, and Anat Keinan (2017), "Conspicuous consumption of time: When busyness and lack of leisure time become a status symbol," *Journal of Consumer Research*, 44 (1), 118–38.

Chun, Hae Eun, Kristin Diehl, and Deborah J. MacInnis (2017), "Savoring an upcoming experience affects ongoing and remembered consumption enjoyment," *Journal of Marketing*, 81 (3), 96–110.

Coleman, Nicole Verrochi, Patti Williams, Andrea C. Morales, and Andrew Edward White (2017), "Attention, attitudes, and action: When and why incidental fear increases consumer choice," *Journal of Consumer Research*, 44 (2), 283–312.

Cunha, Marcus and Jeffrey D. Shulman (2011), "Assimilation and contrast in price evaluations," *Journal of Consumer Research*, 37 (5), 822–35.

Fitzsimons, Gavan J. (2008), "Death to dichotomizing," *Journal of Consumer Research*, 35 (1), 9.

Hayes, Andrew, F. (2013), *Introduction to Mediation, Moderation, and Conditional Process Analysis: A Regression-Based Approach*. New York: Guilford Press.

Kettle, Keri L., Remi Trudel, Simon J. Blanchard, and Gerald Häubl (2016), "Repayment concentration and consumer motivation to get out of debt," *Journal of Consumer Research*, 43 (3), 460–77.

Meyvis, Tom and Stijn M.J. Van Osselaer (2017), "Increasing the power of your study by increasing the effect size," *Journal of Consumer Research*, 44, 1157–73.

Moorman, Christine, Harald van Heerde, C. Page Moreau, and Robert W. Palmatier (2018), Guiding editorial principles for the *Journal of Marketing*, accessed May 22, 2019 at https://www.ama.org/academics/Pages/What-are-the-Guiding-Editorial-Principles-for-Journal-of-Marketing.aspx.

Open Science Collaboration (2015), "Estimating the reproducibility of psychological science," *Science*, 349 (6251), aac4716.

Oppenheimer, Daniel M., Tom Meyvis and Nicolas Davidenko (2009), "Instructional manipulation checks: Detecting satisficing to increase statistical power," *Journal of Experimental Social Psychology*, 45 (4), 867–72.

Pechmann, Cornelia (2014), "Editorial regarding the new submission guidelines at the Journal of Consumer Psychology," *Journal of Consumer Psychology*, 24 (1), 1–3.

Pham, Michel Tuan (2015), "Is it OK to dichotomize? A research dialogue," *Journal of Consumer Psychology*, 25 (4), 650–51.

Spangenberg, Eric R., Ioannis Kareklas, Berna Devezer, and David E. Sprott (2016), "A meta-analytic synthesis of the question–behavior effect," *Journal of Consumer Psychology*, 26 (3), 441–58.

Spiller, Stephen A., Gavan J. Fitzsimons, John G. Lynch, and Gary H. McClelland (2013), "Spotlights, floodlights, and the magic number zero: Simple effects tests in moderated regression," *Journal of Marketing Research*, 50 (2), 277–88.

[6]

Intern. J. of Research in Marketing 31 (2014) 127–140

Contents lists available at ScienceDirect

Intern. J. of Research in Marketing

journal homepage: www.elsevier.com/locate/ijresmar

ELSEVIER

From academic research to marketing practice: Exploring the marketing science value chain

John H. Roberts [a,*], Ujwal Kayande [b], Stefan Stremersch [c,d]

[a] London Business School and Australian National University, Canberra, Australia
[b] Melbourne Business School, Melbourne, Australia
[c] Erasmus School of Economics, Erasmus University Rotterdam, The Netherlands
[d] IESE Business School, University of Navarra, Barcelona, Spain

ARTICLE INFO

Article history:
First received in 28 September 2012 and was
under review for 4 months
Available online 1 October 2013

Area Editor: Dominique M. Hanssens
Guest Editor: Marnik G. Dekimpe

ABSTRACT

We aim to investigate the impact of marketing science articles and tools on the practice of marketing. This impact may be direct (e.g., an academic article may be adapted to solve a practical problem) or indirect (e.g., its contents may be incorporated into practitioners' tools, which then influence marketing decision making). We use the term "marketing science value chain" to describe these diffusion steps, and survey marketing managers, marketing science intermediaries (practicing marketing analysts), and marketing academics to calibrate the value chain. In our sample, we find that (1) the impact of marketing science is perceived to be largest on decisions such as the management of brands, pricing, new products, product portfolios, and customer/market selection, and (2) tools such as segmentation, survey-based choice models, marketing mix models, and pre-test market models have the largest impact on marketing decisions. Exemplary papers from 1982 to 2003 that achieved dual – academic and practice – impact are Guadagni and Little (1983) and Green and Srinivasan (1990). Overall, our results are encouraging. First, we find that the impact of marketing science has been largest on marketing decision areas that are important to practice. Second, we find moderate alignment between academic impact and practice impact. Third, we identify antecedents of practice impact among dual impact marketing science papers. Fourth, we discover more recent trends and initiatives in the period 2004–2012, such as the increased importance of big data and the rise of digital and mobile communication, using the marketing science value chain as an organizing framework.

© 2013 The Authors. Published by Elsevier B.V. Open access under CC BY-NC-ND license.

1. Introduction

Does marketing science research affect marketing practice? Which decisions have marketing science articles supported? To which tools has marketing science contributed? Which marketing science articles have had dual impact on both science and practice? These are key questions that we address in this paper. We define *marketing science* as the development and use of quantifiable concepts and quantitative tools to understand marketplace behavior and the effect of marketing activity upon it. From this definition, one would consider it reasonable for marketing scientists to seek impact on marketing practice, i.e., seek relevance.

However, marketing scientists have recently rekindled the age-old debate on rigor versus relevance. On the one hand, marketing science has been very successful in attracting scholars from other fields such

as economics, statistics, econometrics and psychology. This inflow of talented scientists from other fields has clearly added to the rigor of marketing science and has allowed the development of new techniques. On the other hand, a number of academic scholars have recently called for more emphasis to be placed on the application of marketing science to industry problems, rather than rigor per se (e.g., Lehmann, McAlister, & Staelin, 2011; Lilien, 2011; Reibstein, Day, & Wind, 2009). Such application may also show positive returns to firms. Germann, Lilien, and Rangaswamy (2013) find that increasing analytics deployment by firms leads to an improvement in their return on assets.

Despite the importance of this debate for our field and the strong interest in the drivers of academic impact (e.g., see Stremersch & Verhoef, 2005; Stremersch, Verniers, & Verhoef, 2007), empirical examination of the impact of marketing science on practice is rare. Valuable exceptions are Bucklin and Gupta (1999), Cattin and Wittink (1982), Wittink and Cattin (1989), and Wittink, Vriens, and Burhenne (1994). However, their application areas were narrow. Wittink and his colleagues studied the commercial use of conjoint analysis in North America and Europe, while Bucklin and Gupta studied the usage of scanner data and the models that scholars have developed to analyze them. Other scholars

* Corresponding author.
  E-mail addresses: jhroberts@london.edu (J.H. Roberts), U.Kayande@mbs.edu (U. Kayande), stremersch@ese.eur.nl (S. Stremersch).

http://dx.doi.org/10.1016/j.ijresmar.2013.07.006
0167-8116 © 2013 The Authors. Published by Elsevier B.V. Open access under CC BY-NC-ND license.

128   *J.H. Roberts et al. / Intern. J. of Research in Marketing 31 (2014) 127–140*

have conceptually reviewed the impact of marketing science and prescribed areas in which marketing science might have an impact in the future. In a special issue of the *International Journal of Research in Marketing*, Leeflang and Wittink (2000) summarized the areas in which marketing science has been used to inform management decisions. Roberts (2000) acknowledged the breadth of marketing science applications, but lamented the depth of penetration of marketing science (i.e., the proportion of management decisions informed by marketing science models). Lilien, Roberts, and Shankar (2013) take an applications-based approach to best practice. However, there has been no broad systematic investigation of which marketing science articles and tools have been applied, the decisions that these concepts and tools have informed, and the perceptions of different stakeholders of the usefulness of marketing science in informing decisions. We aim to address this void.

We develop the concept of the *marketing science value chain*, which captures the diffusion of insights from academic articles in a direct (e.g., from article to practice) or indirect (e.g., from article to marketing science tool to practice) manner. We survey the primary agents in this value chain – marketing managers, marketing science intermediaries (marketing analysts), and marketing academics – to calibrate the practice impact of marketing science in all its facets.

2. Methodology

2.1. The framework: The marketing science value chain

An important step in our methodology is a conceptualization of the marketing science value chain. Our representation of this chain, illustrated in Fig. 1, depicts activities (full arrows) by which marketing science is translated from academic knowledge to practical tools, and

thence to marketing action, as well as the participants involved in the chain.

First, new knowledge (marketing science *articles*) is developed, often but not always, by marketing academics.[1] Second, knowledge conversion occurs when new knowledge in articles is adapted and integrated into practical *tools and approaches*, often but again not always, by marketing intermediaries, such as market research agencies (e.g. ACNielsen or GfK), marketing and strategy consultancies (e.g., McKinsey or Bain), specialist niche marketing consulting firms (e.g. Advanis or Simon-Kucher Partners), or the marketing science division of a marketing organization (e.g. Novartis or General Mills). Third, knowledge application occurs when marketing managers implement marketing science knowledge via practical tools to make *marketing decisions*.

While we contend in Fig. 1 that marketing intermediaries play a critical role in the diffusion process, we allow for a direct path as well (disintermediation). For example, marketing academics may work directly with marketing managers to have their tools adopted (marketing science push) or a firm's internal analysts may actively seek out solutions to address the firm's specific problems (marketing science pull). Alternatively, the locus of conceptual innovation may fall further down the value chain (user innovation). Moreover, diffusion may occur through routes other than through intermediaries (for example, via specialist books such as Lilien, Kotler, & Moorthy, 1992; Wierenga & van Bruggen, 2000, and Lilien, Rangaswamy, & De Bruyn, 2007 or general texts such as Kotler & Keller, 2012). In other words, the "direct" influence in Fig. 1 may include a number of further sub-stages that we do not explicitly identify or calibrate.

2.2. The elements: Decisions, tools and articles

In Fig. 1, we identify three core elements in the marketing science value chain: decisions, tools, and articles. Selection of stimuli in each of these elements is a critical part of our methodology, especially considering the scope of our study. Not only have thousands of marketing articles been published across many journals, but marketing managers make decisions to solve marketing problems in a wide variety of areas (pricing, promotions, sales force management, etc.), using a considerable range of marketing science tools (segmentation tools, choice models, etc.) to assist in that decision making. To make our calibration practically feasible, we decided to limit the three sets of stimuli to 12 decision areas, 12 marketing science tools, and 20 marketing science articles. We decided on these limits iteratively, by trading off the need for a comprehensive classification of the decisions, tools, and articles against the time required for respondents to react to the stimuli. In Section 3.5 we discuss the dynamics of these three elements.

2.2.1. Decisions

Marketing decisions refer to the choice of management actions regarding any part of the firm's marketing activity. To categorize marketing decisions, we followed a four-step procedure. First, we examined subject areas used at the major marketing journals and in leading marketing management textbooks. Second, we integrated and synthesized these lists to create an exhaustive inventory. Third, we aggregated the different decision areas into higher order categories, to create a manageable number. Finally, we tested our list with practicing managers and the Executive Committee of the Marketing Science Institute, and refined it based on their feedback. Our final list of marketing decision areas is:

1. *Brand management*: Developing, positioning and managing existing brands.

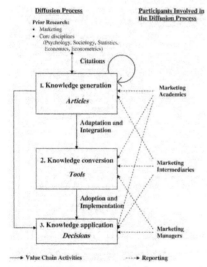

Diffusion Process

Prior Research:
* Marketing
* Core disciplines
  (Psychology, Sociology, Statistics, Economics, Econometrics)

Citations

1. Knowledge generation

Articles

Adaptation and Integration

2. Knowledge conversion

Tools

Adoption and Implementation

3. Knowledge application

Decisions

Participants Involved in the Diffusion Process

Marketing Academics

Marketing Intermediaries

Marketing Managers

⟶ Value Chain Activities   ⤍ Reporting

Fig. 1. The marketing science value chain.

---

[1] For example, a study of *Marketing Science* over the period 1982–2003 shows that of 1072 article authors, 1001 of them were academics (93.4%) Authors with multiple articles are counted as many times as they have (co-)authored an article.

J.H. Roberts et al. / Intern. J. of Research in Marketing 31 (2014) 127–140   129

2. *New product/service management*: New product development, management and diffusion.

3. *Marketing strategy*: Product line, multi-product and portfolio strategies.

4. *Advertising management*: Advertising spending, planning and design.

5. *Promotion management*: Promotion decisions.

6. *Pricing management*: Pricing decisions.

7. *Sales force management*: Sales force size, allocation, and compensation decisions.

8. *Channel management*: Channel strategy, design, and monitoring.

9. *Customer/market selection*: Targeting decisions.

10. *Relationship management*: Customer value assessment and maximization, acquisition, retention, and relationship management.

11. *Managing marketing investments*: Organizing for higher returns and internal marketing.

12. *Service/product quality management*: Any aspect of quality management.

2.2.2. Tools

Tools are approaches and methodologies that can be used to support marketing decisions. To categorize marketing science tools, we followed a procedure similar to the one used for marketing decisions (using marketing research and marketing analysis texts). Our list of tools is:

1. *Segmentation tools*: latent class segmentation, cluster analysis, etc.

2. *Perceptual mapping*: multidimensional scaling, factor analysis, etc.

3. *Survey-based choice models*: conjoint analysis, discrete choice, etc.

4. *Panel-based choice models*: choice models, stochastic models, etc.

5. *Pre-test market models*: ASSESSOR, durable pre-testing, etc.

6. *New product models*: diffusion models, dynamic models, etc.

7. *Aggregate marketing response models*: marketing mix models, etc.

8. *Sales force allocation models*: Call planning models, etc.

9. *Customer satisfaction models*: Models of service quality, satisfaction, etc.

10. *Game theory models*: Models of competition, channel structure, etc.

11. *Customer lifetime value models*: Loyalty and direct marketing models, etc.

12. *Marketing metrics*: Accounting models, internal rate of return, etc.

2.2.3. Articles

We selected candidate articles for the twenty marketing science articles by applying four filters. First, we filter the journals and time period from which to sample. Second, we select 200 articles in the sampled journals and time period, which have made the highest academic impact, measured by age-adjusted citations. Third, we reduce the list of 200 to 100, by weighing impact with the likelihood to which an article represents marketing science. Fourth, we reduce the list of 100 high-impact marketing articles to the 20 articles that marketing intermediaries rated as most impactful on marketing practice. Next, we explain this procedure in greater detail.

For the first filter, our aim was to achieve a good representation of major marketing journals, which we based on prior scientometric work in marketing (Stremersch et al., 2007). We excluded the *Journal of Consumer Research (JCR)* as it is not an outlet that typically publishes marketing science articles. We added *Management Science*, because it consistently features in the *Financial Times* Top 45, for example, and has a marketing section. This step thus led us to the following selection of journals: *International Journal of Research in Marketing (IJRM)*, *Journal of Marketing (JM)*, *Journal of Marketing Research (JMR)*, *Management Science (MGS)* and *Marketing Science (MKS)*.

Next, we assessed how long the journals were covered in the Social Science Citation Index. Young journals need time to mature and become academically and practically impactful, which may make them less suited for our goals, even if they are a top journal. *IJRM* is the youngest top journal in the set and was not included in the Social Science Citation

index until 1997. Therefore, in 2006, it was very unlikely for *IJRM* articles from the period 1997–2003 to have amassed enough citations to be among the top 200 age-adjusted cited articles and be included in our further analytical steps. Later analyses on an expanded sample that included *IJRM* showed this assessment to be accurate. The most highly ranked *IJRM* article was Geyskens, Steenkamp, and Kumar (1998) at rank 255. We selected the period 1982–2003 as observation window. We chose the start year of our data to coincide with the launch of *Marketing Science* in 1982. We chose the end year of 2003 to allow articles at least 2 full years for their impact to materialize (this is common in citation studies, see Stremersch et al., 2007).

Second, we rank-ordered the resultant 5556 articles on their academic importance, as measured by age-adjusted citations (see Stremersch et al., 2007 for a similar procedure). As citations show a time trend, we first de-trended our measure by regressing the number of citations of an article i ($CITE_i$) on the number of quarters (Q_i) that have passed between publication and the quarter in which we gathered the citations and its square (Q_i^2), including a constant (across all articles). We conducted this study in the 3rd quarter of 2006 and, thus, we obtained the stock of citations that were in ISI databases, in that quarter.

As $CITE_i$ shows over-dispersion, we specified a negative binomial count model and optimized with quadratic hill climbing. As expected, our results indicated an inverted U-shaped time trend (the estimated coefficients for Q_i and Q_i^2 were 0.07 and $-4.76E-04$ respectively, both significant at $p < 0.001$; $R^2 = 0.035$). We obtain standardized residuals from the model, denoted by $CITERESID_i$, which can be regarded as a time-corrected citation measure of academic impact. We retained the top 200 articles ranked on this academic impact measure.

Third, we examined the *MGS* articles in this top 200 and excluded the 71 articles that did not consider a marketing subject, because they could not possibly be "marketing" science. Next, we calculated the extent to which each of the 129 remaining marketing articles is a marketing "science" article. We found the task of defining marketing "science" difficult. After many discussions with experts, we came to the following working definition: "Marketing science is the development and use of quantifiable concepts and quantitative tools to understand marketplace behavior and the effect of marketing activity upon it."[2]

To determine whether a specific article satisfied this definition, we asked five pairs of two marketing science experts – members of the *Marketing Science* and *IJRM* Editorial Boards, and leading marketing intermediaries – to individually code 100 articles published in the four journals in a hold out sample published in 2004–2005,[3] as marketing science articles, or not. The proportion of agreement between the raters was 0.77, which translated into a proportional reduction of loss (PRL) inter-rater reliability measure of 0.72 (Rust & Cooil, 1994), satisfactory for the exploratory nature of our research. We created a variable that took the value 1 if both raters agreed it was a marketing science article, 0 otherwise.

Next, we inventoried the number of equations to measure an article's mathematical sophistication (also used by Stremersch & Verhoef, 2005), the methodologies an article uses, going from qualitative techniques to time series and analytical models, and the number of referenced articles in econometrics, statistics and mathematics. Stepwise logistic regression revealed two significant predictors: the number of equations and whether the methodology used factor and/or cluster analysis or not. The more equations an article contains, the higher the likelihood of it being considered a marketing science article. Articles that use factor or cluster analyses are generally less perceived as a

---

[2] This definition aligns closely to the definition of marketing analytics of Germann et al.'s (2013).

[3] We selected 25 articles from each of the four journals. Article selection was random for JM, JMR, and *Marketing Science*. For *Management Science*, we inventoried 25 articles from 2004 to 2005 that were marketing-related. The list of 100 articles is provided in Web Appendix 1.1.

130   J.H. Roberts et al. / Intern. J. of Research in Marketing 31 (2014) 127–140

Table 1
The 100 academically most impactful papers in marketing science (ordered by practice impact, and then by academic impact; complete bibliography is available in the Web Appendix 3).

Rank	Authors, publication year	Cites total	*CITERESID*	*PROBMKS*	Academic impact: *MKSIMPACT*	Practice impact: *INTIMPACT*
1	Green and Srinivasan (1990)	292	4.34	0.47	2.04	4.22
2	Louviere and Woodworth (1983)	195	2.99	0.78	2.35	3.56
3	Aaker and Keller (1990)	170	2.21	0.45	1.00	3.50
4	Cattin and Wittink (1982)	152	2.48	0.45	1.12	3.25
5	Guadagni and Little (1983)	431	7.44	0.80	5.94	3.22
6	Mahajan et al. (1990)	268	3.82	0.87	3.31	3.11
7	Rust et al. (1995)	146	2.88	0.77	2.22	3.00
8	Hauser and Shugan (1983)	152	2.21	0.93	2.04	3.00
9	Fornell, Johnson, Anderson, Cha, and Bryant (1996)	136	3.29	0.45	1.48	3.00
10	Griffin and Hauser (1993)	166	2.62	0.47	1.23	2.89
11	Day (1994)	321	6.63	0.45	2.98	2.67
12	Punj and Stewart (1983)	263	4.40	0.47	2.07	2.67
13	Fornell (1992)	159	2.55	0.80	2.04	2.67
14	Vanheerde et al. (2003)	25	2.01	0.72	1.45	2.63
15	Hunt and Morgan (1995)	149	2.95	0.45	1.33	2.63
16	Anderson, Fornell, and Lehmann (1994)	217	4.18	0.65	2.73	2.44
17	Simonson and Tversky (1992)	213	3.37	0.53	1.80	2.38
18	Boulding et al. (1993)	250	4.23	0.42	1.79	2.38
19	Parasuraman, Zeithaml, and Berry (1985)	765	12.08	0.45	5.44	2.25
20	Keller (1993)	250	4.23	0.45	1.90	2.25
21	Yu & Cooper (1983)	192	3.13	0.47	1.47	2.25
22	Urban, Carter, Gaskin & Mucha (1986)	162	2.07	0.57	1.19	2.25
23	Carpenter & Nakamoto (1989)	157	1.97	0.55	1.09	2.22
24	Zeithaml, Berry & Parasuraman (1996)	191	2.65	0.45	1.19	2.13
25	Dickson & Sawyer (1990)	160	2.09	0.45	0.94	2.13
26	Zeithaml, Parasuraman & Berry (1985)	225	5.41	0.14	0.76	2.13
27	Joreskog & Sorbom (1982)	133	2.04	0.84	1.71	2.11
28	Day & Wensley (1988)	233	3.14	0.45	1.41	2.11
29	Thaler (1985)	532	8.31	0.53	4.43	2.00
30	Kamakura & Russell (1989)	242	3.37	0.84	2.81	2.00
31	Zeithaml (1988)	390	5.64	0.45	2.54	2.00
32	Bolton (1998)	85	2.31	0.69	1.59	2.00
33	Tversky & Simonson (1993)	121	1.90	0.78	1.49	2.00
34	Churchill & Surprenant (1982)	262	4.58	0.13	0.60	2.00
35	Fornell & Bookstein (1982)	210	3.20	0.49	1.57	1.89
36	Mittal & Kamakura (2001)	56	2.62	0.59	1.56	1.89
37	Srivastava, Shervani & Fahey (1998)	92	2.55	0.45	1.15	1.88
38	Churchill, Ford, Hartley & Walker (1985)	161	2.14	0.45	0.96	1.88
39	Gupta (1988)	206	2.72	0.74	2.01	1.75
40	Teas (1993)	135	2.18	0.65	1.42	1.75
41	Anderson & Sullivan (1993)	200	3.34	0.65	2.18	1.67
42	Gutman (1982)	157	2.65	0.45	1.19	1.67
43	Jaworski and Kohli (1993)	411	7.64	0.53	4.07	1.63
44	Slater & Narver (1994)	238	5.22	0.45	2.35	1.63
45	Mcguire, TW & Staelin (1983)	140	2.08	0.95	1.98	1.63
46	Parasuraman, Zeithaml & Berry (1994)	178	3.14	0.57	1.80	1.63
47	Mackenzie & Lutz (1989)	208	2.82	0.47	1.33	1.63
48	Robinson & Fornell (1985)	174	2.33	0.55	1.29	1.63
49	Bitner, Booms & Tetreault (1990)	183	2.76	0.45	1.24	1.63
50	Bolton & Lemon (1999)	62	2.00	0.61	1.23	1.63
51	Henard & Szymanski (2001)	42	2.08	0.49	1.02	1.63
52	Bitner (1990)	294	4.28	0.45	1.93	1.50
53	Perreault & Leigh (1989)	168	2.13	0.65	1.39	1.50
54	Ruekert & Walker (1987)	185	2.39	0.45	1.08	1.50
55	Mackenzie, Lutz & Belch (1986)	167	2.11	0.45	0.95	1.50
56	Alba, Lynch, Weitz, Janiszewski, Lutz, Sawyer & Wood (1997)	182	5.15	0.45	2.32	1.38
57	Webster (1992)	273	4.57	0.45	2.06	1.38
58	Haubl & Trifts (2000)	60	2.26	0.49	1.11	1.38
59	Bearden, Sharma & Teel (1982)	125	1.89	0.45	0.85	1.38
60	Han, Kim & Srivastava (1998)	97	3.12	0.16	0.51	1.33
61	Dwyer & Schurr & Oh (1987)	632	9.53	0.45	4.29	1.25
62	Lynch & Ariely (2000)	83	3.35	0.47	1.58	1.25
63	Pollay (1986)	157	1.99	0.45	0.89	1.25
64	Bitner (1992)	281	4.03	0.45	1.82	1.22
65	Cronin & Taylor (1992)	399	6.82	0.21	1.45	1.22
66	Oliver (1999)	81	2.64	0.45	1.19	1.22
67	Garbarino & Johnson (1999)	114	4.15	0.13	0.54	1.22
68	Crosby, Evans & Cowles (1990)	259	3.74	0.13	0.49	1.22
69	Cronin & Taylor (1994)	153	2.62	0.45	1.18	1.13
70	Rindfleisch & Heide (1997)	92	2.43	0.45	1.09	1.13
71	Kalwani & Narayandas (1995)	117	2.12	0.45	0.96	1.13
72	Ganesan (1994)	311	6.07	0.13	0.80	1.13
73	Doney & Cannon (1997)	218	6.05	0.13	0.79	1.13
74	Morgan and Hunt (1994)	690	14.52	0.45	6.54	1.00
75	Bakos (1997)	156	4.52	0.89	4.04	1.00

(Continued overleaf)

Table 1 (*continued*)

Rank	Authors, publication year	Cites total	CITERESID	PROBMKS	Academic impact: MKSIMPACT	Practice impact: INTIMPACT
76	Narver & Slater (1990)	440	6.83	0.45	3.08	1.00
77	Anderson, Hakansson & Johanson (1994)	139	2.55	0.45	1.15	1.00
78	Deshpande, Farley & Webster (1993)	119	1.92	0.45	0.87	1.00
79	Kohli & Jaworski (1990)	442	6.73	0.45	3.03	0.89
80	Jeuland & Shugan (1983)	185	2.87	0.96	2.76	0.89
81	Gorn (1982)	170	2.99	0.45	1.35	0.89
82	Anderson & Coughlan (1987)	213	2.89	0.45	1.30	0.89
83	Phillips, Chang & Buzzell (1983)	166	2.57	0.45	1.16	0.89
84	Gaski (1984)	164	2.30	0.45	1.03	0.89
85	Novak, Hoffman & Yung (2000)	92	3.77	0.13	0.50	0.89
86	Lovelock (1983)	191	2.98	0.45	1.34	0.78
87	Solomon, Surprenant, Czepiel & Gutman (1985)	158	2.12	0.45	0.96	0.75
88	Anderson & Narus (1990)	442	6.67	0.13	0.88	0.75
89	Zirger & Maidique (1990)	150	1.93	0.45	0.87	0.67
90	Deshpande & Zaltman (1982)	248	4.19	0.13	0.55	0.67
91	Sinkula (1994)	152	2.60	0.45	1.17	0.63
92	Anderson & Weitz (1989)	185	2.39	0.45	1.08	0.63
93	Hirschman & Holbrook (1982)	234	4.12	0.45	1.86	0.56
94	Huber & McCann (1982)	133	2.10	0.67	1.41	0.56
95	Tse & Wilton (1988)	175	2.21	0.47	1.04	0.56
96	Anderson & Weitz (1992)	265	4.18	0.17	0.73	0.56
97	Hoffman & Novak (1996)	287	7.31	0.45	3.29	0.50
98	Slater & Narver (1995)	197	3.54	0.45	1.59	0.44
99	Ferrell & Gresham (1985)	290	4.27	0.45	1.92	0.33
100	Gerbing and Anderson (1988)	453	6.64	0.21	1.41	0.33

Notes:
1. In the case of ties in practice impact, we reverted to academic impact to determine which articles got into the top 20.
2. *CITERESID* is age-adjusted citation impact, measured by the residual from the negative binomial model with citations as the dependent variable and quarters since publication and its square as the independent variables.
3. *PROBMKS* is the probability that the article is a marketing science article, see Section 2.2.3 for details.
4. *MKSIMPACT = CITERESID × PROBMKS*.
5. *INTIMPACT* is awareness-adjusted impact, which is the average impact across all respondents assuming that the impact is 0 for articles of which the respondent is not aware.

marketing science article, probably because these are exploratory techniques. The fit of this model is reasonable; the hit rate was 75%, which compares favorably to chance (50.5%). We applied these model coefficients, calibrated on the out-of-sample 2004–2005 articles, to the 129 marketing articles identified earlier and retrieve an estimated probability that an article is marketing science, denoted as $PROBMKS_i$.

We then weighted the age-adjusted citation impact ($CITERESID_i$) by the likelihood of the article being marketing science ($PROBMKS_i$) to obtain our final measure of marketing science academic impact for each article ($MKSIMPACT_i$). We rank-ordered the 129 articles on this latter measure and selected the top 100. We provide the full list of 100 articles and all metrics in Table 1. Complete references are included in Web appendix 1.3. Table 1 shows that our methodology leads to credible results, with substantial face validity. For instance, Guadagni and Little (1983) and Mahajan, Muller, and Bass (1990) are more likely to be regarded as being marketing science articles than Morgan and Hunt (1994) and Jaworski and Kohli (1993).

Because one of our goals is to survey academics and intermediaries on the impact on practice of individual marketing science articles, we needed to reduce the list of 100 articles to 20, to make the task manageable for our respondents. In the final reduction from 100 articles to 20, we wanted to account for practice impact and asked 34 marketing intermediaries to rate the practical impact of four randomized blocks of 25 articles. The respondents were from a larger pool of 54 intermediaries (63% response rate) who worked in marketing science intermediary roles in firms such as AC Nielsen, Mercer, GfK, and McKinsey. These intermediaries were specifically selected because (i) they had previously published papers in or were on the Editorial Board of *Marketing Science*, and/or (ii) were past or current members of the Practice Committee of *INFORMS ISMS*. We asked these 34 respondents if they were aware of each article and, if so, the impact on practice that they believed that it had had, using a 5-point verbally anchored scale (1 = no influence; 5 = extremely influential). We gave a score of 0 to those articles of

which the respondents were not aware, assuming that there could not be a direct impact if the respondent was not even aware of the article when prompted. We then calculated an average impact across all respondents for each article, calling it an awareness-adjusted practice impact score (denoted as *INTIMPACT*). Rank-ordering all 100 articles on *INTIMPACT* allowed us to select the 20 highest ranked articles, which we used in our large-scale survey of academics and intermediaries. We found no significant differences in the average awareness-adjusted practice impact score across the four groups of intermediaries.

We acknowledge that starting with a citation screen (as well as a screen in terms of journal outlet) may preclude consideration of some papers with high impact on practice, but low impact on scholarship. Our intention though was not to measure which were the marketing articles with the highest practice impact per se. Rather our intention was to identify marketing papers with high dual impact, including both academic and practice impact.

2.3. The participants: Managers, intermediaries and academics

We use samples from each participant population (managers, intermediaries, and academics) to inventory the impact of marketing science on marketing practice, along the marketing science value chain, described in Fig. 1. We do not expect marketing managers to be aware of many, if any, academic articles, even where those articles have been incorporated into the marketing science tools that they routinely use. Thus, marketing managers can inform us only on knowledge conversion (tools) and knowledge application (decisions). However, we also calibrate managers' perceived importance of different areas of marketing decision making.

2.3.1. Sample of managers

Our sample of senior marketing managers consisted of Marketing Science Institute and Institute for the Study of Business Markets

J.H. Roberts et al. / Intern. J. of Research in Marketing 31 (2014) 127–140

(ISBM) members and company contacts. Both institutes graciously emailed a request from us to their members. In total, we solicited survey participation from 477 managers, of whom 94 (20%)[4] provided usable responses. While this group comes from a well-defined population, it almost certainly has a bias towards greater sophistication. This sophistication is likely to introduce an upward bias in the perceived impact of tools and their influence in different areas (the absolute impact of marketing science). However, there is no reason to believe that this bias will be very different for different tools and decision areas, meaning any bias in the relative effects will likely be considerably less.

2.3.2. Sample of intermediaries

We used four sources to create the sample of intermediaries. First, we examined all articles published by practitioner analysts in *Marketing Science* and included those authors in our sample. Second, we examined the editorial boards of our target journals and included any intermediaries on these boards. Third, the Marketing Science Institute contacted the marketing intermediaries among their members on our behalf. Finally, we surveyed marketing intermediaries attending the 2007 ISMS Marketing Science Practice Conference, held at the Wharton School. In total, we solicited participation from 93 intermediaries, of whom 34 (37%) participated in the main survey. 21 of these respondents worked at marketing and/or management consulting firms such as McKinsey, AC Nielsen, and Millward Brown, while 13 respondents worked in firms such as General Motors, IBM, and Campbell Soup.

2.3.3. Sample of academics

We defined the sampling frame of marketing academics to be academic marketing science members of the editorial boards of the target journals. We excluded the authors of the current paper from this sampling frame. To identify the "marketing science" members of those editorial boards, we used a peer review process, in which we asked ten marketing science experts to indicate whether they would classify members of these editorial boards (223 in total) as marketing scientists or not.[5] Of the 223 editorial board members in total, 126 were classified as marketing scientists, of whom 84 (67%) ultimately responded to our survey.

2.4. The instruments: Surveys among participants

Our instruments are as follows (see Web Appendix 1.2 for details). The survey to managers measured: (1) the overall influence of each of the 12 tools on marketing practice; (2) the overall influence of marketing science on each of the 12 marketing decision areas; and (3) the importance of the 12 marketing decision areas to their company. The survey to intermediaries and academics measured: (1) the overall influence of the 20 marketing science articles on marketing practice; (2) the overall influence of the 12 tools on marketing practice; and (3) the overall influence of marketing science on the 12 marketing decision areas. We also collected respondent background data for each sample.

Additionally, we surveyed the authors of the top 20 dual impact articles to probe: (1) other scholars who influenced the development and execution of the article; (2) academic ideas underlying the article, including the important papers on which the article was built; (3) practitioner influence on the development and execution of the article; (4) the practical ideas underlying the article; (5) whether there was cooperation with practitioners when developing the article; (6) any diffusion efforts the authors undertook to diffuse their work to academics

---

[4] The response rate for the MSI sample was 53% and for the ISBM sample (where the participant request was less personalized), it was 16%. Note that our email solicitation included a URL, which increases the likelihood of the email being classified by spam filters as spam and thus not reaching many members of our sample. As a result, the response rate we report is a lower bound. This comment applies to all three samples (managers, intermediaries, and academics).

[5] The inter-rater reliability using a separate sub-sample was 0.90, sufficiently high to indicate that our classification procedure is reliable.

and practitioners; (7) the stage of their career in which they wrote the article; and (8) the reasons that may have made the article impactful. We summarize our data collection approach in Fig. 2.

3. Results

Moving up the value chain illustrated in Fig. 1, we present the results of our research in four stages: the relative impact of marketing science on different decision making areas (Section 3.1), the impact that different marketing science tools and approaches have had on marketing practice (Section 3.2), the impact of the twenty articles on marketing decisions and tools (Section 3.3), and the antecedents of "dual" (academic and practice) impact from a survey of the authors of 20 top articles (Section 3.4). In Section 3.5, we identify trends since 2004 in the application and use of marketing science.

3.1. Impact of marketing science on marketing decisions

To inventory the impact of marketing science on marketing decision areas, we first present the self-stated importance of each decision area by manager respondents. Next, we present the extent to which our respondents felt that marketing science had impacted each marketing decision area. We end with graphically presenting the alignment between impact of marketing science on and the importance of the decision areas.

3.1.1. Importance of decision areas

In Table 2, we present the self-stated importance of each of the decision areas to the company, classified by type of firm (B2B, B2C, both B2B and B2C, and total). Overall, pricing management is rated the most important (aggregated across types of firms). New product management is rated the least important. However, there are notable differences across B2B and B2C firms. Managers of B2B firms consider pricing management to be the most important decision area, followed by customer/market selection and product portfolio management. Managers of B2C firms consider brand management and new product management to be the most important decision areas.

3.1.2. Impact of marketing science on decision areas

In Table 3, we present the perceived impact of marketing science on specific marketing decision areas, as perceived by academics (A), intermediaries (I), and managers (M). According to managers, marketing science has had the biggest impact on brand management decisions and pricing decisions (mean = 3.77 for both), and new product/service management and customer/market selection (mean = 3.66 for both). Academics feel that marketing science has made the biggest impact on brand management, new product/service management and promotion management. Intermediaries sense that marketing science has made the biggest impact on pricing management, promotion management, and new product/service management.

Interestingly, academics believe that marketing science had the biggest impact on promotion management among all decision areas (mean = 3.76), while managers consider that it had the smallest influence among all areas (mean = 3.14). For other areas, such as new product/service management, both seem to agree much more as to the relatively large extent to which marketing science has impacted such decisions (means = 3.70 and 3.66 respectively for academics and managers). Overall, Table 3 shows that while there is consensus between the academic and intermediary groups ($\rho_{AI} = 0.62$) and some moderate level of consensus between the intermediary and manager groups ($\rho_{IM} = 0.39$), there is much disagreement between academics and managers ($\rho_{AM} = 0.17$), pointing to the bridging role of marketing intermediaries.

In Table 3, we also present how managers perceived the impact of marketing science on different decision areas, split by type of firm. As expected, the results indicate some differences by type of firm. While

J.H. Roberts et al. / Intern. J. of Research in Marketing 31 (2014) 127–140   133

Stimuli

Article selection	Tool and Decision selection
What is marketing science? ⎤ *Marketing Science* Who is a marketing scientist? ⎦ Editorial Board Screening of 100 most cited ⎤ 34 Marketing marketing science articles to 20 ⎦ Intermediaries	What are the key areas ⎤ of marketing decisions? ⎥ MSI ⎥ Executive What are the key tools ⎥ Committee and approaches used? ⎦

Main Questionnaire

Manager Survey (N = 94)	Intermediary Survey (N = 34)	Academic Survey (N = 84)
Importance of decision areas Impact of marketing science on marketing decision areas Impact of marketing science tools	Impact of marketing science on marketing decision areas Impact of marketing science tools Impact of articles	Impact of marketing science on marketing decision areas Impact of marketing science tools Impact of articles

Transition Matrices

Manager Survey (N = 4)	Intermediary Survey (N = 5)	Academic Survey (N = 4)
Impact of 12 marketing science tools on 12 marketing decision areas	Impact of 12 marketing science tools on 12 marketing decision areas Impact of 20 Articles on 12 marketing science tools Impact of 20 Articles on 12 marketing decision areas	Impact of 12 marketing science tools on 12 marketing decision areas Impact of 20 Articles on 12 marketing science tools Impact of 20 Articles on 12 marketing decision areas

Antecedents of impactful papers

Survey of authors of 20 marketing science articles with high academic and practice impact
• Influence (academic, industry, literature, problem   • Industry co-operation • Effort to diffuse findings   • Author background (experience)

Fig. 2. Overview of the primary data collection approach.

B2B managers perceive the biggest impact on pricing management, B2C managers perceive the impact to be largest on customer insight management. However, there is moderate consistency ($\rho_{B2B, B2C} = 0.45$).

3.1.3. Alignment between importance of decision areas and impact of marketing science

To examine whether the impact of marketing science on decision areas is aligned with the importance of the decision area to managers, we plot the importance against (managerial perceptions of) impact in Fig. 3. Considering the differences in importance as well as perceived impact across managers from different types of firms, we present the B2B and B2C plots separately. (We have not included the plots for firms that do both since these largely lie between the two).

Table 2
Average importance of decision areas according to managers in different types of firms (ordered per Table 3).

Decision areas	B2B (N = 59)	B2C (N = 10)	B2B & B2C (N = 25)	Total (N = 94)
Brand management	3.51	4.60	4.04	3.77
Pricing management	4.03	4.30	4.12	4.09
New product/service management	3.78	4.60	3.80	3.87
Customer/market selection	3.79	4.20	3.84	3.85
Product portfolio management	3.79	4.20	3.76	3.83
Customer insight management	3.16	4.20	3.80	3.45
Service/product quality management	3.57	3.80	3.52	3.58
Channel management	3.24	4.10	3.72	3.46
Relationship management	3.62	3.60	3.56	3.60
Salesforce management	3.62	4.30	3.60	3.69
Advertising management	2.69	3.90	3.24	2.97
Promotion management	2.68	4.00	3.12	2.95

Scale: 1: Of no importance. 5: Extremely important.

Both plots indicate that, by and large, the impact of marketing science is aligned with the perceived importance of the decision area. The most notable examples of under-performance are sales force management and service/product quality for both groups, relationship management for B2B, and advertising and channel management for B2C.

Table 3
Average impact of marketing science on decision areas (ordered by managers' perceptions; numbers represent average impact given awareness).

Decision areas	Academics	Intermediaries	Managers			
			All	B2B	B2C	B2B & B2C
Brand management	3.75	3.56	3.77	3.80	4.10	3.54
Pricing management	3.53	3.85	3.77	3.82	3.80	3.63
New product/service management	3.70	3.68	3.66	3.68	3.90	3.50
Customer/market selection[b]	3.24	3.58	3.66	3.70	3.60	3.58
Product portfolio management[b]	2.94	3.26	3.55	3.55	3.60	3.54
Customer insight management[b]	2.95	3.31	3.42	3.29	4.20	3.38
Service/product quality management	3.37	3.13	3.41	3.36	3.30	3.58
Channel management[b,c]	2.72	2.71	3.40	3.40	3.44	3.38
Relationship management	3.29	3.25	3.37	3.40	3.56	3.21
Sales force management[a,c]	3.43	2.80	3.26	3.29	3.44	3.13
Advertising management	3.22	3.47	3.15	2.93	3.40	3.54
Promotion management[b,c]	3.76	3.71	3.14	3.04	3.60	3.17
Average perceived impact	3.32	3.36	3.46	3.44	3.66	3.43

Scale: 1: No influence at all 5: Extremely influential.
[a] Academics–intermediaries significantly different at $p < 0.05$.
[b] Academics–managers significantly different at $p < 0.05$.
[c] Intermediaries–managers significantly different at $p < 0.05$. Significance assessed with the Welch–Satterthwaite t-test.

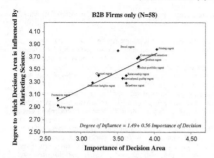

B2B Firms only (N=58)

Degree of Influence = 1.49 + 0.56 Importance of Decision

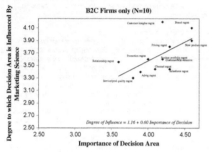

B2C Firms only (N=10)

Degree of Influence = 1.16 + 0.60 Importance of Decision

Fig. 3. Impact of marketing science versus importance of decision area (both according to managers).

3.2. Impact of marketing tools on marketing practice

Having gauged the decisions that are important to the firm and the extent to which marketing science has influenced them, we examine the tools that provide one route by which that influence is felt. In Table 4, we present the average impact of marketing science tools on marketing practice, as perceived by academics, intermediaries and managers. We also provide a split of manager perceptions, according to whether they are in a B2B, B2C, or both B2B and B2C firm.

According to managers, the top three marketing science tools and approaches are: (1) marketing segmentation tools (mean = 4.02), (2) marketing metrics (mean = 3.73), and (3) customer satisfaction models (mean = 3.59). While segmentation tools are also the number 1 pick of academics and intermediaries, opinions diverge on the other ones. Survey-based choice models (number 2 among intermediaries, mean = 4.15) and perceptual mapping techniques (number 2 among academics, mean = 3.99) had less of an impact on marketing practice, according to the marketing managers (means = 3.25 and 3.19 respectively for survey-based choice models and perceptual mapping techniques). Other tools that were consistently found to significantly impact practice are pre-test market models (number 3 or 4 in the three groups) and new product models (number 5 or 6 in the three groups). The different samples also consistently agree on the lack of practical impact of game theory models. The agreement between groups as to the impact of different tools is a lot stronger than the agreement we found on the impact of marketing science on the different decision areas: $\rho_{AI} = 0.80$, $\rho_{IM} = 0.70$, and $\rho_{AM} = 0.73$. Managers' average awareness of marketing science tools was close to 90%, which is

Table 4

Average impact of marketing science tools on marketing practice, according to academics, intermediaries, and managers (ordered by intermediaries' perceptions, numbers represent average impact given awareness).

Tools/approaches	Academics	Intermediaries	Managers			
			All	B2B	B2C	B2B & B2C
Segmentation tools[c]	4.29	4.44	4.02	4.00	4.30	3.96
Survey-based choice models[a,b,c]	3.71	4.15	3.25	3.06	3.50	3.58
Aggregate marketing mix models[a,b,c]	3.36	4.06	2.99	2.88	3.40	3.00
Pre-test market models[b,c]	3.93	3.94	3.38	2.98	4.30	3.71
Marketing metrics	3.54	3.77	3.73	3.72	3.67	3.76
New product models[b]	3.78	3.74	3.37	3.27	3.67	3.48
Customer life time value models[b,c]	3.84	3.63	3.07	3.18	2.70	3.00
Panel-based choice models[b,c]	3.76	3.58	2.82	2.73	3.11	2.87
Perceptual mapping[a,b]	3.99	3.53	3.19	3.14	3.80	3.04
Customer satisfaction model[a]	3.83	3.39	3.59	3.66	3.33	3.52
Sales force allocation models[b]	3.62	3.23	3.07	3.02	3.25	3.13
Game theory models	2.18	2.12	2.41	2.51	2.44	2.19
Average Perceived Impact	3.65	3.63	3.24	3.18	3.46	3.27

Scale: 1: No influence at all 5: Extremely influential.
[a] Academics-intermediaries significantly different at $p < 0.05$.
[b] Academics-managers significantly different at $p < 0.05$.
[c] Intermediaries-managers significantly different at $p < 0.05$. Significance assessed with the Welch-Satterthwaite t-test.

encouraging. But again, we note that our sample is likely biased toward high levels of sophistication.

3.3. Impact of articles on marketing tools and directly on marketing practice

We continue to calibrate practice impact up the value chain in Fig. 1 by examining select marketing science articles and the effect that they have had both on marketing science tools and directly on marketing decision making. We first report results from our precalibration of the top 100 marketing science papers according to academic impact among marketing intermediaries, after which we report on the results from the complete survey of the authors of the top 20 marketing science papers with "dual" impact.

In Fig. 4, we plot the academic impact of the top 100 marketing science articles in Table 1 (*MKSIMPACT*) against the awareness-adjusted impact on practice as perceived by the 34 marketing intermediaries from the precalibration (*INTIMPACT*). Individual points may be identified by reference to Table 1. While there is a significant relationship between academic and practice impact, it is weak ($\rho = 0.19$). We find it more insightful to divide the graph into four quadrants, through a median split on both dimensions. Articles in the bottom left quadrant of Fig. 4 have not had a major impact on practice (e.g., Gerbing & Anderson, 1988), and are also below the median for these 100 articles on academic impact. (Note that all 100 candidates for inclusion fall in the top 5% of age-adjusted citation in the profession's top four quantitative journals.) The articles on the bottom right are primarily knowledge drivers — that is, articles that have had above-median academic impact (relative to the 100 papers in this pool), but have had below-median practice impact (e.g., Morgan & Hunt, 1994). The articles on the top left are practice drivers — articles that have had below-median academic impact among the top 100 pool, but have had above-median practice impact (e.g., Aaker & Keller, 1990). The top right quadrant consists of articles that have had dual impact, exceptional academic as well as practice impact (e.g., Guadagni & Little, 1983). The selection from top 100 on academic impact to top 20 on dual impact represent articles from both the top-left and the top-right quadrants in Fig. 4 (see Web Appendix 2.2 for articles by quadrant).

J.H. Roberts et al. / Intern. J. of Research in Marketing 31 (2014) 127–140   135

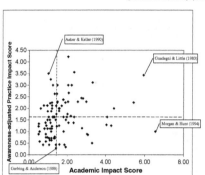

Notes:
1. Awareness adjusted practice impact score is *INTIMPACT* from Table 1. It is the average impact of the article assuming that the impact=0 for articles of which respondents are not aware.
2. Academic Impact Score is *MKSIMPACT* from Table 1, which is the age-adjusted citation score, further adjusted by the probability of the paper being marketing science.

Fig. 4. Contrast of academic and practice impact of 100 selected articles. Notes: Awareness adjusted practice impact score is *INTIMPACT* from Table 1. It is the average impact of the article assuming that the impact = 0 for articles of which respondents are not aware. Academic Impact Score is *MKSIMPACT* from Table 1, which is the age-adjusted citation score, further adjusted by the probability of the paper being marketing science.

In Table 5, we present the results of asking our sample of intermediaries (N = 34) and academics (N = 84) to evaluate the practice impact of each of the 20 dual-impact articles we identified earlier. In this table, we present the impact score given awareness for each article[6] as well as awareness-adjusted practice impact. Although we need to be careful in drawing very strong conclusions (given quite large standard deviations), Guadagni and Little (1983) and Green and Srinivasan (1990) show the highest impact on practice, both as perceived by academics (mean = 4.28 and 4.17 respectively) and intermediaries (mean = 4.17 and 3.97 respectively). Overall, the ranking across the two samples is quite consistent (ρ_{AI} = 0.63). Notable exceptions include Louviere and Woodworth (1983), Vanheerde, Gupta, and Wittink (2003), and Simonson and Tversky (1992), all of which intermediaries accredit a significantly higher impact on practice than academics, while only Fornell (1992) shows the opposite. Finally, there is a correlation of 0.65 between the practice impact of these 20 articles gauged from the pre-calibration sample of intermediaries and the calibration sample of intermediaries. (Respondents in the precalibration and calibration samples responded to different tasks, precluding any aggregation of data across samples).

Table 3 describes the impact that marketing science has had on different marketing decisions, and Tables 4 and 5 show the influence of different tools and articles, respectively. We also solicited the more detailed transition matrices of individual articles' impact on individual tools and decisions, and individual tools on individual decisions, from a sub-sample of our respondents. We include and discuss these transition matrices in the marketing science value chain in Web Appendix 2.1. Additionally, many respondents provided open ended comments (included as Web Appendix 2.2). Perhaps the most interesting aspect of those is the variety of "mental maps" with which managers, intermediaries and academics think about marketing science applications.

[6] As before, although we also report conditional impact (impact given awareness), our awareness adjusted impact assumes that for an article to have impact a respondent must have awareness of it when prompted.

3.4. Antecedents of practice impact among dual impact marketing science articles

As described earlier in our methodology section, we surveyed the authors of the twenty dual-impact articles, shown in Table 5, to learn from their experiences that go beyond the obvious, or possibly deviate from some norms in our field. Participation in our survey of these author teams was 100% (by article). 17 out of the 20 papers had multiple authors. Of those 17, multiple authors in 9 cases responded to our survey. Unsurprisingly, many expected themes emerged from these responses; themes that have been previously identified in the academic and practitioner literature. They include advice from authors to look for gaps in the literature, to ensure a strong grounding in prior theory, to find interesting, unsolved problems that are important to managers, and to fuel the diffusion process, not relying on good ideas to automatically be adopted. Below we focus on the three most interesting new themes that emerged. In addition, Guadagni and Little (2008) share their recollection in a *Marketing Science* commentary, which they based on our survey to them.

3.4.1. Symbiosis with consulting

Many of the authors referred to the symbiosis of their research with consulting as a fertile ground for dual impact papers. Rick Staelin describing Boulding, Kalra, Staelin, and Zeithaml (1993) stated "This paper started with a "consulting" project for the School [Fuqua School of Business, Duke University] trying to improve the service quality of our teaching/delivery system." Jordan Louviere speaking of Louviere and Woodworth (1983) said "[The problem] came from a consulting project in Australia. I was asked by the Bureau of Transport Economics to help them forecast demand for Qantas flights on transpacific routes."

Many of the authors also (co-)founded professional services companies to commercialize their work. For example, Roland Rust mentioned forming a company to commercialize the approach of Rust, Zahorik, and Keiningham (1995). John Little attributes his logit model's practical success largely to the commercialized products based on it. Louviere worked with DRC to commercialize the method he had developed. MDS started selling Hauser and Shugan's (1983) Defender model. Hauser joined Bob Klein in founding Applied Marketing Science, Inc. to commercialize the "voice of the customer" methodology (Griffin & Hauser, 1993).

3.4.2. Going against the grain at the right time

A common topic in many responses was that they went against the grain at the right point in time. Times were either ripe for the radical innovation the authors introduced or the authors rode on a new technology wave that came to transform industry. About the former, Roland Rust nicely phrases it as follows: "We went against the grain, which meant that acceptance of our ideas ensured minds were changed." Peter Guadagni and John Little attribute part of the success of Guadagni and Little (1983) more to the latter, an impeccable sense of timing: "Much of the impact was due to its early use of data from UPC scanners."

This does not mean that dual impact author teams were not also firmly grounded in basic theory, despite going against the grain. For example, Peter Guadagni and John Little say: "Consumers make choices to maximize utility. This came from basic economic theory." In the same vein, John Hauser on Hauser and Shugan (1983) mentions: "There was the Brandaid model by John Little in which he used a multiplicative form for the effects of advertising and distribution. Coupled with Lancaster's model, this gave us an empirically-relevant, but analytically tractable model with which to study the problem." Indeed, it is of interest that the 20 top papers by practice impact in Table 1 contained an average of 12 equations and 54 references (compared to 5 and 37 respectively for articles ranked 21–100, $p < 0.05$).

3.4.3. Working with experience

A long track record of some of the authors and influencers seems to be an essential component of dual impact teams. All author teams have

136 *J.H. Roberts et al. / Intern. J. of Research in Marketing 31 (2014) 127–140*

Table 5
Average impact of marketing science articles on marketing practice (ranked by intermediaries' perceptions of impact).

Article	Intermediaries (I) (N = 34).					Academics (A) (N = 84).					Difference test in A–I impact
	Awareness (%)	Impact (Avg|Aware)	Std. Error	Rank (impact)	Awareness-adjusted impact	Awareness (%)	Impact (Avg|Aware)	Std. Error	Rank (impact)	Awareness-adjusted impact	
Guadagni and Little (1983)	85	4.17	0.19	1	3.56	98	4.28	0.11	1	4.18	0.50
Green and Srinivasan (1990)	85	3.97	0.18	2	3.38	96	4.17	0.10	2	4.02	1.02
Louviere and Woodworth (1983)	76	3.92	0.21	3	3.00	81	2.76	0.14	15	2.24	−4.60[a]
Griffin and Hauser (1993)	74	3.64	0.22	4	2.68	94	3.32	0.12	6	3.12	−1.32
Keller (1993)	85	3.48	0.20	5	2.97	94	3.78	0.11	4	3.56	1.35
Cattin and Wittink (1982)	85	3.41	0.20	6	2.91	92	3.23	0.13	9	2.96	−0.75
Parasuraman et al. (1985)	65	3.41	0.25	7	2.21	94	3.87	0.11	3	3.64	1.69
Mahajan et al. (1990)	91	3.35	0.20	8	3.06	98	3.13	0.13	11	3.06	−0.93
Fornell et al. (1996)	76	3.27	0.20	9	2.5	90	3.63	0.12	5	3.29	1.59
Aaker and Keller (1990)	79	2.96	0.20	10	2.35	92	3.30	0.12	7	3.02	1.43
Vanheerde et al. (2003)	74	2.96	0.19	11	2.18	89	2.43	0.11	18	2.17	−2.46[b]
Hauser and Shugan (1983)	74	2.92	0.24	12	2.15	93	3.03	0.12	14	2.81	0.40
Simonson and Tversky (1992)	71	2.88	0.22	13	2.03	87	2.27	0.13	19	1.98	−2.38[b]
Rust et al. (1995)	71	2.83	0.19	14	2.00	92	3.12	0.12	12	2.86	1.28
Anderson et al. (1994)	59	2.75	0.22	15	1.62	92	3.10	0.11	13	2.85	1.46
Boulding et al. (1993)	68	2.74	0.16	16	1.85	82	2.74	0.14	16	2.25	0.00
Punj and Stewart (1983)	65	2.73	0.24	17	1.76	79	2.73	0.14	17	2.14	0.00
Day (1994)	65	2.68	0.27	18	1.74	86	3.19	0.12	10	2.74	1.71
Fornell (1992)	62	2.48	0.21	19	1.53	90	3.29	0.12	8	2.98	3.30[a]
Hunt and Morgan (1995)	47	2.44	0.27	20	1.15	73	2.02	0.13	20	1.46	−1.39
Average across articles	73	3.15				90	3.17				

Notes:
1. Scale: 1: No influence at all to 5: Extremely influential.
2. [a]$p < 0.01$, [b]$p < 0.05$, using the Welch–Satterthwaite t-test to test for differences in impact given awareness across academic and intermediary samples.
3. Awareness-adjusted impact is equal to *awareness proportion* multiplied by *impact given awareness*. Awareness-adjusted impact assumes that the impact of an article is 0 if the respondent is not aware of the article. Correlation between the two measures is 0.94 for intermediaries and 0.99 for academics.

at least one scholar with an academic career of over 15 years before co-authoring the paper (with the exception of Keller, 1993 article). The most senior author in 14 of the top 20 papers by practice impact in Table 1 held a named chair, in contrast to 23 out of the remaining 80 high academic impact articles ($p < 0.01$). It appears that significant academic experience is close to a prerequisite to writing an article that has large dual impact. In addition, industry experience may help. Authors who responded to our survey also had an average 6.75 years of experience in industry.

Authors frequently mentioned close liaison with industry. Eight out of 20 teams worked with practitioners on developing at least part of their ideas. Many other sources are mentioned on the practitioner side, both at intermediaries and marketing companies. Top sources are the Marketing Science Institute (mentioned by 5 author teams out of 20) as a source of inspiration. As individual practitioners, these authors mention people such as Bob Klein, Steve Gaskin, Richard M. Johnson, and Steve Cohen (3 or more mentions).

Academic colleagues with an influence are mainly scholars' co-authors, colleagues from the same department, or scholars on whose work authors built. Within the marketing profession, Glen Urban and Al Silk received three or more mentions. John Hauser notes on Hauser and Shugan (1983): "There were many influences. Chief was the Assessor model by Silk and Urban, which was a pre-test market model to predict the shares of new products. However, for every innovator, there were many defenders. We wanted to know what was the best defensive strategy." Authors also cite inspiration from well-known scholars outside their own field. Scholars mentioned in that category are Doug Carroll, Dan McFadden, Albert Hirschman, Herman Wold, and Frank Andrews (2 or more mentions).

3.5. Trends since 2004

It is useful to examine changes in the environment in the past nine years and to use our findings to consider likely trends in the impact of marketing science. To do that, we return to the marketing science value chain and examine separately changes to the decisions managers make, the tools that they use, and the articles that have driven the development of those tools.

3.5.1. Trends in management decisions

Clearly, a number of environmental changes have affected the way in which managers need to relate to their marketplaces. These include a greater availability of addressable data (i.e. big data) and the rise of digital and mobile communications, both in terms of access to markets and communications between consumers (such as social networks). To formalize our examination of these trends, we assessed the changing content of marketing management textbooks. We examined marketing management texts rather than cutting edge methodology books because, at this stage of the marketing science value chain, it is the overall managerial decision making environment we wish to study. An examination of sales lists at amazon.com shows that Kotler/Kotler and Keller's Marketing Management (in its various guises) dominates this market. For example, on February 23, 2013 "A Framework for Marketing Management" (5th edition) was 6632 on the best seller list with the closest non-Kotler competitor coming in at 56,620. Therefore, we looked at the evolution of this text over time: before the beginning of our study (1980), four years into our study (1988), at the end of our study (2003), and most recently (2012). The results are included as Web Appendix 3.1. We note the rising importance of branding, customer management and integrated marketing over this time.

Because textbooks may be backward looking, we also examined trends in the Marketing Science Institute's Research Priorities which are, themselves, derived from surveys among academics and their members, who are all senior managers (Web Appendix 3.2). As expected, we see more recent topics in this list such as understanding mobile marketing opportunities, the role of social networks, and the harnessing of "big data." The survey of our authors would suggest that these environmental shifts in possibility and priority bring with them the opportunity to go against the grain at the right time. An obvious analogy is John Little's view that his adoption of logit modeling was a direct result of the availability of vast quantities of panel scanner data which enabled a new, less aggregate way of modeling response to changes in the marketing mix.

J.H. Roberts et al. / Intern. J. of Research in Marketing 31 (2014) 127–140   137

3.5.2. Trends in tools available

Clearly, many changes have occurred in the statistical tools available to the industry marketing analyst (and marketing intermediary) since 2004. Kluwer's Series in Quantitative Marketing, edited by Josh Eliashberg, provides an excellent resource describing advances in many of the tools available. Many of these are driven by the availability of vast amounts of customer data and with them, the rise of data mining (see Humby, Hunt, & Phillips, 2008 for an example). Much of this work is being conducted by information systems groups rather than marketers. As well as models that account for observed heterogeneity, models that account for unobserved heterogeneity are also gaining traction. Lilien (2011) speaks to the relative success of models that may be implemented by automatic algorithm, rather than as a managerial decision aid, which is an interesting distinction.

To gain a more systematic view of trends in the tools being used in industry, we examined the programs of the American Marketing Association's Advanced Research Techniques (ART) Forum from 2002 to 2013. The ART Forum is an annual meeting of academics, intermediaries, and practicing managers which discusses new and emerging marketing science techniques, as well as conducting tutorials in newly-established ones. A summary of these programs is included as Web Appendix 3.3. We observe that a number of 12 types of tool we identified continue to be important over the following nine years (including discrete choice conjoint analysis, customer lifetime value models, and segmentation techniques). Second, we notice the introduction of new sets of tools, of which the most important are social media and network analysis methods from 2010 to 2013, including viral models, recommendation systems, and user generated content. Also of growing importance are text mining methods (2012) and agent-based modeling (2008 and 2012). Finally, many of the tools that we have described have undergone substantial development and enhancement. Primary among those are the areas of survey based and panel based choice models. The Bayesian treatment of heterogeneity (from 2002 onwards), introduction of new measurement bases such as MaxDiff, and data augmentation techniques stand out. In a rare study of the prevalence of marketing science tool usage, Orme (2013) notes fourteen major trends over the past ten years in the use of Sawtooth software (probably the leader in conjoint/choice analysis software). Primary among those are the mainstreaming of Hierarchical Bayes, the decline of ratings based conjoint, the emergence of MaxDiff scaling, and new applications/methods such as menu based choice, optimization, and adaptive designs.

3.5.3. Trends in marketing science articles

We undertook an examination of the papers published in *IJRM*, *JM*, *JMR*, *MGS*, and *MKS* for the period 2004 to 2010. We included *IJRM* given the more recent time period of study and its recognized importance as a top academic journal (Pieters, Baumgartner, Vermunt, & Bijmolt, 1999). We obtain a *CITERESID* (see Section 2.2.3) on each of the journals separately (given that we search for recent trends, they may pop up in one journal specifically). In this model, we used the number of quarters to December, 2010 as a measure of age of the article. Next, we have ranked *CITERESID* per journal and provide the top 10 per journal in Table 6. Note that we validated that the inclusion of *IJRM* was appropriate by estimating CITERESID also on the full sample of all articles jointly and found *IJRM* had 2 representatives in the top 50 (3 in top 100), marking the gradual maturation of *IJRM* as the youngest member of top journals in marketing.

A content-analysis of the 50 papers in Table 6 indicates that the topics of research that have been cited the most are word of mouth and social networks and relationship marketing/management.

In the absence of a formal survey of the impact of marketing science articles since 2004, one way to gain some feel for those that have affected the tools that intermediaries (academics and managers) use to address marketing decisions is to look at those articles that have been mentioned in patents. Because such citations are likely to indicate an article providing the foundation of new tools, we undertook a search using

Google Patents for mentions of articles in our target journals in patents issued by the US Patents and Trade Office (USPTO). To allow comparability with our sample period of 1983 to 2003, we also looked historically at that period as well. The results are included as Web Appendix 3.4. Marketing papers from the five target journals received a total of 1317 citations from patents issued by the USPTO. The first paper to receive a patent citation was published in the *Journal of Marketing* in 1940. The data indicate a significantly increasing trend of marketing papers being cited in patents. Almost half of the citations (625) to historical marketing papers published in the five target journals have come from patents issued since 2004. Marketing papers published since 2004 have attracted 39 of those 625 citations. The 39 patent citations were obtained by a total of 27 papers published since 2004 in *IJRM* (2 papers), *JM* (2), *JMR* (5), *MGS* (5), and *MKS* (13). Papers on the following topics received more than one citation: pricing and promotions (10), movies (4), online behavior models (4), retail assortment models (3), customer lifetime value models (2), conjoint (2), forecasting (2), innovation (2), and social networks (2).

One interesting trend is the level of engagement of marketing intermediaries and managers in the knowledge generation process. In 1983 (the beginning of our sample period), approximately half of the participants at the ISMS Marketing Science Conference held at the University of Southern California came from industry. By 2012, only 37 out of 930 attendees (4%) were from industry. However, general conferences have been replaced by specialized conferences such the biennial ISMS Practice Conference. Similarly, the Gary Lilien ISMS-MSI Practice Prize has maintained industry connections with our top journals in terms of authors. The proportion of industry authors of *Marketing Science* articles fell from 7% in the period 1983 to 2003 to 5% between 2004 and 2012. However, 35 of these 68 industry authors from 2004 to 2012 were a part of Practice Prize Finalist papers, showing the important role special events can have in stemming the disconnect between academic researchers in marketing and those who have to use their research.

3.5.4. Other marketing science trends

A number of other trends emerged in the development and application of marketing science over the past nine years. First, it has become more international at all levels of the value chain. In terms of managerial decision making, globalization has become a major driver of change. In terms of tools, at the American Marketing Association Advanced Research Techniques Forum, the ratio of North American academic presenters to those from other continents went from 15/1 in 2003 to 22/6 in 2008 and 19/6 in 2013. At the other end of the value chain, the number of authors publishing from outside North America in the top marketing journals is increasing. Looking at the authorship profile of the top 100 articles (by age-adjusted citation impact) published in the five top journals from 2004 to 2010, we find that 22% of the authors of papers from 2004 to 2007 were from non-US locations, while this number increased from 11% in 2004 to 33% in 2010. (See Stremersch & Verhoef, 2005 for evidence of globalization of authorship on the same sample of journals, but including all articles between 1964 and 2002, not merely the top cited articles). Also special fora that aim to bridge the gap between academics and practitioners can enable globalization. 11 of the 25 finalists of the Lilien ISMS-MSI Practice Prize Competition since its inception have come from outside North America (seven from Europe, three from Australia, and one from the Asia Pacific region). Entries from Europe have won the prize four out of the seven times.

4. Discussion

4.1. Summary

We have calibrated the relative impact of marketing science research on practice, using our marketing science value chain as a central framework. It is reassuring to see that the impact of marketing science on marketing decisions has been largely felt in areas that are of the greatest importance to the firm (see Fig. 3). Moreover, the managers

138   *J.H. Roberts et al. / Intern. J. of Research in Marketing 31 (2014) 127–140*

Table 6
Top 10 Articles from 2004 to 2012, listed by journal in order of age-adjusted citations.

Articles by journal	Total citations	Age-adjusted impact	Topic
International Journal of Research in Marketing			
Reinartz, Haenlein & Henseler (2009)	40	7.31	Research methodology/SEM
Peres, Muller & Mahajan (2010)	26	5.70	Diffusion/innovation
Dholakia, Bagozzi & Pearo (2004)	169	5.53	Social networks
Burgess, Steenkamp (2006)	71	3.91	Emerging markets
Bagozzi & Dholakia (2006)	83	3.61	Social networks
Street & Burgess & Louviere (2005)	83	3.31	Research methodology/choice
Goldenberg, Libai & Muller (2010)	18	3.19	Network externalities
Du, Bhattacharya & Sen (2007)	47	3.15	Corporate Social Responsibility (CSR)
Verhoef, Neslin & Vroomen (2007)	51	3.14	Multichannel shoppers
De Bruyn & Lilien (2008)	30	2.80	Word of Mouth (WOM)
Journal of Marketing			
Vargo & Lusch (2004)	1029	10.47	Marketing theory
Schau, Muniz & Arnould (2009)	82	5.37	Customer communities
Palmatier, Dant, Grewal & Evans (2006)	215	4.61	Relationship Mktg & Mgmt
Trusov, Bucklin & Pauwels (2009)	72	4.59	WOM/networks
Kozinets, de Valck, Wojnicki & Wilner (2010)	40	2.82	WOM/networks
Luo & Bhattacharya (2006)	146	2.78	CSR
Tuli, Kohli & Bharadwaj (2007)	110	2.73	Mass customization
Brakus, Schmitt & Zarantonello (2009)	55	2.70	Brand
Palmatier, Dant & Grewal (2007)	94	2.49	Relationship Mktg & Mgmt
Rust, Lemon & Zeithaml (2004)	310	2.39	Customer equity
Journal of Marketing Research			
Chevalier & Mayzlin (2006)	284	10.05	WOM
Bergkvist & Rossiter (2007)	200	8.14	Research methodology/survey research
Gupta, Lehmann & Stuart (2004)	187	6.03	Customer equity
Mazar, Amir & Ariely (2008)	91	6.02	Behavioral theory
Reinartz, Krafft & Hoyer (2004)	190	5.78	Relationship Mktg & Mgmt
Srinivasan & Hanssens (2009)	64	5.24	Metrics and firm value
Rindfleisch, Malter, Ganesan & Moorman (2008)	81	4.13	Research methodology/survey research
Trusov, Bodapati & Bucklin (2010)	21	2.95	Social networks
Nair, Manchanda & Bhatia (2010)	18	2.77	Social networks
Petrin & Train (2010)	25	2.52	Research methodology/choice
Marketing Science			
Fiebig, Keane, Louviere & Wasi (2010)	46	8.13	Research methodology/choice
Godes & Mayzlin (2009)	54	7.36	WOM
Keller & Lehmann (2006)	128	7.18	Brand
Hauser, Tellis & Griffin (2006)	122	6.80	Diffusion/innovation
Godes & Mayzlin (2004)	224	5.81	WOM/networks
Gupta & Zeithaml (2006)	90	4.76	Metrics and firm value
Rust & Chung (2006)	79	4.06	Relationship Mktg & Mgmt
Zhang (2010)	23	3.39	Learning
Van den Bulte & Joshi (2007)	52	2.97	Social networks/innovation
Eliashberg, Elberse & Leenders (2006)	61	2.91	Movies
Management Science			
Ghose & Yang (2009)	41	6.55	Search
Cachon & Swinney (2009)	37	3.92	Pricing
Chen & Xie (2008)	54	3.36	WOM/social networks
Su (2007)	75	3.26	Pricing
Franke, Schreier & Kaiser (2010)	19	3.04	Mass customization
Rahmandad & Sterman (2008)	44	2.83	Diffusion/innovation
Atasu, Sarvary & Van Wassenhove (2008)	32	2.41	Remanufacturing
Fleder & Hosanagar (2009)	23	2.33	Recommender systems
Forman, Ghose & Goldfarb (2009)	27	2.27	Online marketing
Grewal, Lilien & Mallapragada (2006)	72	2.04	Social networks

Note: Age-adjusted impact is estimated as the residual from a journal-specific negative binomial model relating number of citations to the age of the article (as measured by the number of quarters to December, 2012). The model includes linear and squared age terms to capture the non-linear time trend of citations.

in our sample are aware of the marketing science tools available to them, and there is a correlation between managers, academics, and intermediaries on the perception of the impact of those tools. Marketing science articles that have influenced practice come in a wide range of flavors. Some articles do not include empirical work (e.g., Hauser and Shugan's Defender model), while others use only laboratory data (e.g., Aaker and Keller's brand extension work). The survey among authors of top dual impact articles provides excellent pointers as to what it takes to write a top-journal article that achieves high academic and practice impact: symbiosis with consulting, going against the grain at the right time, and working with experience. Examining

more recent developments in our field since 2004, we were able to document the rise of digitization, mobile communications, and social networking, as well as further globalization of academia and the important role of special fora. We now discuss implications of our research for academia and practice, limitations of our research, and ideas for future research in this area.

4.2. Implications for academia

Many marketing science academics may not see impacting practice as their primary goal, letting the practice impact occur as a by-product

J.H. Roberts et al. / Intern. J. of Research in Marketing 31 (2014) 127–140   139

at best. A goal of practical impact might even be seen as counterproductive from the perspective of academic impact, distracting researchers from their primary mission and potentially compromising the rigor and integrity with which a problem is studied. Our study points to several counterarguments as to why the two goals may not necessarily be in conflict. First, practical problems may provide inspiration for new breakthroughs as old tools are found inappropriate to solve them (e.g., Louviere & Woodworth, 1983). Second, practical problems lure academics away from the ivory tower, in which they may be held captive by dominant paradigms.

Scholars who seek high practical impact may want to focus their research on decisions that are of greater importance to firms. In Table 2, we identified such areas to be pricing management, new product management, customer and market selection, and product portfolio management. While scholars may very well choose their research area using other inputs as well, we are able to offer scholars general advice on the challenging road to practical impact, from surveying top 20 dual impact authors. Research in symbiosis with consulting may prove to be a fertile ground for dual impact papers. The right timing in tackling the problem and the willingness to go against the grain seem crucial as well. Too early and radical a new idea may not find acceptance yet, too late and a colleague may beat the researcher to the punch. That dual impact papers require a strong grounding both in marketing science and practice, may explain why we find a disproportionate number of highly experienced scholars in our 20 top dual impact papers.

4.3. Implications for practice

Research in marketing science has relevance to many marketing decisions. At least that is what we find from the practitioners we surveyed. Even though our samples may be biased towards the sophisticated end of practice, our results are encouraging. Intermediaries consider segmentation tools and survey-based choice models to be most influential relative to other tools. Intermediaries find individual articles, such as Guadagni and Little (1983), Green and Srinivasan (1990), and Louviere and Woodworth (1983) to be very influential on practice.

Our paper provides a good primer on marketing science for marketing practitioners. It reviews an impressive body of top marketing science articles with dual impact. Therefore, it provides a guide to marketing science research for (i) marketing practitioners with an interest in discovering new areas or (ii) young market research professionals. This paper can help them discover for which decisions or tools it is useful to turn to marketing science research, as well as which specific articles provide potentially useful insights and tools to which they should be exposed.

4.4. Limitations and future research

In undertaking any research with as many dimensions as in our study, researchers must make a number of choices and assumptions. Our primary motivation in designing our research was to have a methodology that was objective and verifiable. To do so, we set up criteria upon which to design our study, carefully evaluating those criteria and obtaining input from a variety of knowledgeable sources at each stage of the research. Yet, we understand that other scholars may have approached the study differently and/or identified other study design criteria. Some significant limitations of our research include the following:

- *Citations as a screening mechanism.* We are acutely aware of the irony of starting to measure impact on practice with a list ranked by academic impact (i.e., citations). We tried to minimize this effect by including a pre-calibration stage. At worst, however, we can claim to have gauged the practice impact of the population of highly cited marketing science articles (what we call dual impact).
- *Biased sample.* The use of MSI and ISBM led to practitioner samples that were likely skewed towards greater sophistication. While this likely skew might improve the reliability of responses (and the

response rate), we believe that it could introduce considerable bias. We have attempted to address this by focusing largely on *relative* rather than absolute effects.

- *Alternative knowledge diffusion routes.* Textbooks, magazines and newspapers represent important, alternate ways by which new marketing knowledge diffuses. Similarly, organizations such as ACNielsen, Sawtooth, and Advanis are responsible for knowledge generation that may not always begin in journal articles. Because we are not claiming a complete catalog of the sources and transition nodes of marketing science knowledge diffusion, this is less of a problem.
- We focus on success and that brings with it a number of benefits, as well as being easier to observe. However, the lack of a control sample of "failures" means that we cannot discriminate between that which works and that which does not (though we can, to some extent, examine correlates of drivers of the degree of success).

Having taken the first step in an effort to calibrate the effect of marketing science on marketing practice, we find ourselves faced with a number of interesting but unanswered questions. These include the possibility of a more comprehensive mapping and measures built up from marketing practice, rather than down from journal articles. In terms of a more comprehensive mapping, it would be useful to consider other knowledge vehicles (e.g., textbooks, magazines and newspapers), routes (e.g., user knowledge generation and seminars), and participants (e.g., specialist training educators). More representative samples would allow inferences to be drawn about absolute impact rather than just relative impact. Finally, the unit of analysis we used is that of articles published in the period 1982–2003. Had it been scholars or over a longer timeframe, other researchers may have been more strongly represented.

The measure of relative rather than absolute impact raises another issue; that of market penetration of marketing science knowledge and tools (e.g., Roberts, 2000). Marketing science tools and the articles on which they are based may be used in a wide variety of marketing decision making situations (i.e., the opportunity set is large). A more appropriate benchmark might perhaps be, "Of all the situations to which these tools could have provided insight, in what per cent are the tools actually being applied?" Our sense is that the number is low. If this is indeed the case, it is presumably hard for us to argue that the marketing science tools currently in the market are in any way "standard" approaches to marketing and the measurement of its effect. We could contrast this penetration to that of approaches taught in other management disciplines, such as accounting and finance, for example.

Overall, we hope that we have identified the basis for a continued and richer study of the marketing science value chain.

Acknowledgments

We were inspired and supported by the Practice Prize Committee of the INFORMS Society for Marketing Science, the Marketing Science Institute (MSI) and the Institute for the Study of Business Markets (ISBM) in the execution of this work. Many individuals have also contributed to the ideas contained in the paper, particularly Gary Lilien and Bruce Hardie. We would like to thank the Guest Editor, Area Editor and two anonymous reviewers who provided constructive and insightful feedback to us. John Roberts acknowledges support from the London Business School Centre for Marketing and Stefan Stremersch from the Erasmus Center for Marketing and Innovation.

We have conducted many secondary analyses in the context of this project, which we do not report in the interest of brevity. Please contact the first author should you have an interest in obtaining supplementary materials.

Appendix A. Supplementary data

Supplementary data to this article can be found online at http://dx. doi.org/10.1016/j.ijresmar.2013.07.006.

References

Aaker, D. A., & Keller, K. L. (1990). Consumer evaluations of brand extensions. *Journal of Marketing*, 54(1), 27–41.

Anderson, E. W., Fornell, C., & Lehmann, D. R. (1994). Customer satisfaction, market share, and profitability: Findings from Sweden. *Journal of Marketing*, 58(3), 53–66.

Boulding, W., Kalra, A., Staelin, R., & Zeithaml, V. A. (1993). A dynamic process model of service quality — From expectations to behavioral intentions. *Journal of Marketing Research*, 30(1), 7–27.

Bucklin, R. E., & Gupta, S. (1999). Commercial use of UPC scanner data: Industry and academic perspectives. *Marketing Science*, 18(3), 247–273.

Cattin, P., & Wittink, D. R. (1982). Commercial use of conjoint-analysis — A survey. *Journal of Marketing*, 46(3), 44–53.

Day, G. S. (1994). The capabilities of market-driven organizations. *Journal of Marketing*, 58(4), 37–52.

Fornell, C. (1992). A national customer satisfaction barometer — The Swedish experience. *Journal of Marketing*, 56(1), 6–21.

Fornell, C., Johnson, M.D., Anderson, E. W., Cha, J. S., & Bryant, B. E. (1996). The American customer satisfaction index: Nature, purpose, and findings. *Journal of Marketing*, 60(4), 7–18.

Gerbing, D. W., & Anderson, J. C. (1988). An updated paradigm for scale development incorporating unidimensionality and its assessment. *Journal of Marketing Research*, 25(2), 186–192.

Germann, F., Lilien, G. L., & Rangaswamy, A. (2013). Performance implications of deploying marketing analytics. *International Journal of Research in Marketing*, 2, 114–128.

Geyskens, I., Steenkamp, J. E. B.M., & Kumar, N. (1998). Generalizations about trust in marketing channel relationships using meta-analysis. *International Journal of Research in Marketing*, 15(3), 223–248.

Green, P. E., & Srinivasan, V. (1990). Conjoint-analysis in marketing — New developments with implications for research. *Journal of Marketing*, 54(4), 3–19.

Griffin, A., & Hauser, J. R. (1993). The voice of the customer. *Marketing Science*, 12(1), 1–27.

Guadagni, P., & Little, J.D. C. (1983). A logit model of brand choice calibrated on scanner data. *Marketing Science*, 2(3), 203–238.

Guadagni, P., & Little, J.D. C. (2008). A logit model of brand choice calibrated on scanner data: A 25th anniversary perspective. *Marketing Science*, 27(1), 26–28.

Hauser, J. R., & Shugan, S. (1983). Defensive marketing strategies. *Marketing Science*, 2(4), 319–360.

Humby, C., Hunt, T., & Phillips, T. (2008). *Scoring points: How Tesco continues to win customer loyalty.* London, UK: Kogan Page.

Hunt, S. D., & Morgan, R. M. (1995). The comparative advantage theory of competition. *Journal of Marketing*, 59(2), 1–15.

Jaworski, B. J., & Kohli, A. K. (1993). Market orientation — Antecedents and consequences. *Journal of Marketing*, 57(3), 53–70.

Keller, K. L. (1993). Conceptualizing, measuring, and managing customer-based brand equity. *Journal of Marketing*, 57(1), 1–22.

Kotler, P., & Keller, K. L. (2012). *Marketing management 14th edition.* Upper Saddle River, NJ: Prentice Hall.

Leeflang, P.S. H., & Wittink, D. R. (2000). Building models for marketing decisions: Past, present, future. *International Journal of Research in Marketing*, 17(2–3), 105–126.

Lehmann, D. R., McAlister, L., & Staelin, R. (2011). Sophistication in research in marketing. *Journal of Marketing*, 75(July), 155–165.

Lilien, G. L. (2011). Bridging the academic-practitioner divide in marketing decision models. *Journal of Marketing*, 75(2), 196–210.

Lilien, G. L., Kotler, P., & Moorthy, K. S. (1992). *Marketing models.* Englewood Cliffs: Prentice Hall.

Lilien, Gary L., Rangaswamy, Arvind, & De Bruyn, Arnaud (2007). *Principles of marketing engineering.* : Trafford.

Lilien, G. L., Roberts, J. H., & Shankar, V. (2013). Effective marketing science applications: Insights from the ISMS practice prize finalist papers and projects. *Marketing Science*, 32(2), 229–245.

Louviere, J. J., & Woodworth, G. (1983). Design and analysis of simulated consumer choice or allocation experiments — An approach based on aggregate data. *Journal of Marketing Research*, 20(4), 350–367.

Mahajan, V., Muller, F. M., & Bass, (1990). New product diffusion-models in marketing — A review and directions for research. *Journal of Marketing*, 54(1), 1–26.

Morgan, R. M., & Hunt, S. D. (1994). The commitment–trust theory of relationship marketing. *Journal of Marketing*, 58(3), 20–38.

Orme, B. (2013). *Advances and trends in marketing science from the Sawtooth Software perspective.* Orem, UT: Sawtooth Software, Inc.

Parasuraman, A., Zeithaml, V. A., & Berry, L. L. (1985). A conceptual-model of service quality and its implications for future-research. *Journal of Marketing*, 49(4), 41–50.

Pieters, R., Baumgartner, H., Vermunt, J., & Bijmolt, T. H. A. (1999). Importance and similarity in the evolving citation network of the International Journal of Research in Marketing. *International Journal of Research in Marketing*, 16(2), 113–127.

Punj, G., & Stewart, D. W. (1983). Cluster-analysis in marketing-research — Review and suggestions for application. *Journal of Marketing Research*, 20(2), 134–148.

Reibstein, D. J., Day, G., & Wind, J. (2009). Guest editorial: Is marketing academia losing its way? *Journal of Marketing*, 73(June), 1–3.

Roberts, J. H. (2000). The intersection of modelling potential and practice. *International Journal of Research in Marketing*, 13(3), 127–134.

Rust, R. T., & Cooil, B. (1994). Reliability measures for qualitative data: Theory and implications. *Journal of Marketing Research*, 31(1), 1–14.

Rust, R. T., Zahorik, A. J., & Keiningham, T. L. (1995). Return on quality (ROQ) — Making service quality financially accountable. *Journal of Marketing*, 59(2), 58–70.

Simonson, I., & Tversky, A. (1992). Choice in context — Trade-off contrast and extremeness aversion. *Journal of Marketing Research*, 29(3), 281–295.

Stremersch, S., & Verhoef, P. C. (2005). Globalization of authorship in the marketing discipline: Does it help or hinder the field? *Marketing Science*, 24(4), 585–594.

Stremersch, S., Verniers, I., & Verhoef, P. C. (2007). The quest for citations: Drivers of article impact. *Journal of Marketing*, 71(3), 171–193.

Vanheerde, H. J., Gupta, S., & Wittink, D. R. (2003). Is 75% of the sales promotion bump due to brand switching? No, only 33% is. *Journal of Marketing Research*, 40(4), 481–491.

Wierenga, B., & van Bruggen, G. H. (2000). *Marketing management support systems: Principles, tools and implementation.* Boston: Kluwer Academic Publishers.

Wittink, D. R., & Cattin, P. (1989). Commercial use of conjoint analysis: An update. *Journal of Marketing*, 53(3), 91–96.

Wittink, D. R., Vriens, M., & Burhenne, W. (1994). Commercial use of conjoint analysis in Europe: Results and critical reflections. *International Journal of Research in Marketing*, 11(1), 41–52.

[7]

Deborah J. MacInnis

A Framework for Conceptual Contributions in Marketing

Conceptual advances are critical to the vitality of the marketing discipline, yet recent writings suggest that conceptual advancement in the field is slowing. The author addresses this issue by developing a framework for thinking about conceptualization in marketing. A definition of conceptualization is followed by a typology of types of conceptual contributions. The types of conceptual contributions, their similarities and differences, and their importance to the field are described. Thinking skills linked to various types of conceptual contributions are also described, as are the use of tools that can facilitate these skills. The article concludes with a set of recommendations for advancing conceptualization in our field in the years to come.

Keywords: conceptual thinking, conceptual articles, theory, novel ideas

The 75th anniversary of Journal of Marketing (*JM*) is a fitting time for reflection on the vitality of our field, and, in particular, on its conceptual advances. More than 25 years ago, Zaltman (1983, p. 1) noted that although "the quality of our research primarily follows the quality of our ideas, the quality of our ideas needs improvement." These observations are in accord with those of the 1988 AMA Task Force on the Development of Marketing Thought, which advocated increased research on conceptualizations that enhance marketing thought. Yet in the intervening years, scholars have suggested that methodological and empirical advances have outpaced the field's conceptual advances (e.g., Kerin 1996; Stewart and Zinkhan 2006; Webster 2005; Zaltman, LeMasters, and Heffring 1985). Perhaps emblematic of this issue is the status of purely conceptual articles (e.g., integrative perspectives, reviews, propositional inventories) in our top journals. MacInnis (2004) observes a precipitous yet relatively recent decline in the number of such papers. Yadav (2010), who replicates these observations, proposes that this decline is detrimental to the field's advancement because conceptual articles not only provide new ideas but also are disproportionately more influential (e.g., in terms of citations and awards) than empirical papers. Moreover, Yadav notes that conceptual articles play an important role along the discovery–justification continuum that characterizes the knowledge development process (Hanson 1958). For example, whereas propositional inventories lay out areas in which empirical research is needed, and thus contribute to the process of discovery, integrative reviews contribute to the process of justification by validating what is known.

These concerns over conceptualization motivate this essay. In the pages that follow, I propose that our potential for making conceptual advances may be fostered by gaining clarity on (1) what conceptualization means, (2) the entities to which conceptualization applies, (3) what types of conceptual contributions academic scholarship can make, (4) what criteria should be used to evaluate the quality of conceptual ideas, and (4) how we and our future students can hone our conceptual thinking skills. The essay proceeds in four parts.

First, I define "conceptualization" and develop a novel typology of conceptual contributions that can guide academic research in marketing. The typology shown in Table 1 suggests that conceptualization can pertain to various entities, emphasizing smaller units (e.g., constructs) to very large units (e.g., science itself) (see the rows in Table 1).

Second, I argue that for each entity, conceptualization can contribute to knowledge in one or more ways, as noted in the column headings of Table 1. These types of contributions include envisioning new ideas, relating ideas, explicating ideas, or debating ideas. Within each of these four broad types of conceptual contributions, there are two subtypes that reflect contributions either to the process of discovery or to the process of justification. For example, envisioning encompasses contributions that add to the process of discovery by identifying something new. Envisioning also encompasses contributions that add to the process of justification by using new information, facts, or observations to revise an existing idea. Table 2 expands on the meaning of these more specific types of conceptual contributions.

I also discuss criteria along which different types of conceptual contributions can be judged (see also Table 2). One criterion noted in Table 2 is that of "interestingness." Murray Davis (1971) suggests that "interesting" ideas challenge strongly held assumptions about the state of the world. Interesting ideas add insight. They are not just new; they provide different perspectives that alter others' thinking. For example, if we were to believe that consumers tend to hold strong attitudes only when they think deeply about

Deborah J. MacInnis is Vice Dean for Research and Strategy, Charles L. and Ramona I. Hilliard Professor of Business Administration, and Professor of Marketing, Marshall School of Business, University of Southern California (e-mail: macinnis@usc.edu). The author thanks Allen Weiss, Valerie Folkes, Rich Lutz, Bill Wilkie, Manjit Yadav, and Ajay Kohli for their helpful comments on a previous draft of this manuscript.

© 2011, American Marketing Association
ISSN: 0022-2429 (print), 1547-7185 (electronic)

Journal of Marketing
Vol. 75 (July 2011), 136–154

TABLE 1
Types of Conceptualization and Entities Around Which Conceptualization Can Occur

General Conceptual Goal	Envisioning		Explicating		Relating		Debating	
Specific Conceptual Goal	Identifying	Revising	Delineating	Summarizing	Differentiating	Integrating	Advocating	Refuting
Entities around which conceptualization occurs								
Constructs (measurable theoretical concepts)								
Relationships/theories (linkages among constructs)								
Procedures (ways of conducting research)								
Domains (areas of study that include constructs, theories, and procedures)								
Disciplines (collections of domains that specify what a discipline studies)								
Science (the activity disciplines perform in the pursuit of knowledge)								

TABLE 2
Detailed Description of Types of Conceptual Contributions

General Conceptual Goal	Envisioning		Explicating		Relating		Debating	
Specific Conceptual Goal	Identifying	Revising	Delineating	Summarizing	Differentiating	Integrating	Advocating	Refuting
Meaning	To see that something exists; to apprehend, notice, or behold	To see something that has been identified in a new way; to reconfigure, shift perspectives, or change	To detail, chart, describe, or depict an entity and its relationship to other entities	To see the forest for the trees; to encapsulate, digest, reduce, or consolidate	To see types of things and how they are different; to discriminate, parse, or see pieces or dimensions that comprise a whole	To see previously distinct pieces as similar, often in terms of a unified whole whose meaning is different from its constituent parts; to synthesize, amalgamate, or harmonize	To endorse a way of seeing; to support, justify or suggest an appropriate path	To rebut a way of seeing; to challenge, counterargue, contest, dispute, or question
Metaphorical role of the researcher	The astronomer	The artist	The cartographer	The astronaut	The naturalist	The architect	The guide	The prosecutor
Metaphorical tool	The telescope	The paintbrush	The map	The space ship	The magnifying glass	Architectural plans	The compass	The evidence
Common name applied to contribution	Novel framework; new perspective	Revised perspective; alternative view	Conceptual framework; structural framework; propositional inventory	Review paper	Typological/ taxonomic framework; classification scheme	Integrative framework	Position paper	Critique/rejoinder/commentary
Evaluative criteria based on execution	Make us aware of what we have been missing and why it is important; reveal what new questions can be addressed from identifying the entity	Identify why revision is necessary; reveal the advantages of the revised view and what novel insights it generates; maintain parsimony	Describe what the entity is, why it should be studied, and how it works (e.g., its antecedents, processes, moderating factors); provide a roadmap for future research	Circumscribe what falls within and outside the scope of the summary; develop an organizing framework; comprehensive in article inclusion; provide clear, accurate, and relevant conclusions; simplify through reduction; develop research priorities	Indicate how entities are different and why differentiation matters; indicate what novel insights can be gleaned or what findings can be reconciled from differentiation	Accommodate extant knowledge; explain puzzling or inconsistent findings; reveal novel insights; create parsimony	Clearly state the issue and one's perspective on that issue; state premises and assumptions; provide credible and unambiguous evidence; draw conclusions that support the advocated view; avoid fallacious reasoning errors	Clearly state the issue and one's perspective on that issue; state premises and assumptions; provide credible and unambiguous evidence; draw conclusions that are consistent the refuted view; avoid fallacious reasoning errors

TABLE 2
Continued

General Conceptual Goal	Envisioning		Explicating		Relating		Debating	
Specific Conceptual Goal	Identifying	Revising	Delineating	Summarizing	Differentiating	Integrating	Advocating	Refuting
Evaluative criteria based on interestingness, suggest that....	What is unseen is seen; what is unobservable is observable; what is unknown is known; what does not matter, matters a great deal	What is seen, known, observable, or known can be seen differently	What is simple is complex; what is micro is macro; what is unrelated is related; what is holistic is particularistic	What is complex is simple; what is macro is micro; what is related is unrelated; what is particularistic is holistic	What is similar is different; what is inseparable is separable; what is organized is disorganized; what is one-dimensional is multidimensional; what is homogeneous is heterogeneous	What is different is similar; what is separable is inseparable; what is disorganized is organized; what is multidimensional is one-dimensional; what is heterogeneous is homogeneous	What is false is true; what is unacceptable is acceptable; what is wrong is right; what is inappropriate is appropriate	What is true is false; what is acceptable is unacceptable; what is right is wrong; what is appropriate is inappropriate
Similarities in thinking skills and facilitating tools	Divergent thinking: facilitated by search for metaphors; questioning assumptions, look for hidden events and outliers, engage in introspection		Logical reasoning: facilitated by mapping		Comparative reasoning: facilitated by Venn diagrams and comparison matrices		Syllogistic reasoning: facilitated by argument diagrams, argument schemes, and awareness of persuasion tactics	
Differences in thinking skills and facilitating tools	Beginner's mind: facilitated through "taking a hike," immersion in other people's views	Expert's mind and a beginner's mind: facilitated by finding anomalies, questioning assumptions, heuristic references	Deductive reasoning: facilitated by theories in use	Inductive reasoning: facilitated by outlines	Analytical reasoning: facilitated by analogies and metaphors	Analogical resoning facilitated by analogies and metaphors		

an attitude object, an interesting idea would be one that affirms the opposite—namely, that consumers tend to hold strong attitudes only when they do not think deeply about an attitude object. Davis identifies 12 ways that ideas can be interesting (see also Zaltman, LeMasters, and Heffring 1985). Notably, and as Table 2 shows, the current typology accommodates these ways (and more) but expands on Davis's work by linking the interestingness criteria to the various conceptualization types.

If the types of conceptual contributions noted in Table 1 are critical to the development of the field, it becomes important to understand what types of thinking skills and facilitating tools underlie each contribution type. By understanding these thinking skills and how they may be developed, we may be in a better position to enhance conceptualization. Table 2 and Figure 1, which constitute the third part of this article, describe these issues. In the fourth and final section, I conclude with recommendations pertinent to the next 75 years of marketing thought.

Conceptualization

Conceptualization is a process of abstract thinking involving the mental representation of an idea. Conceptualization derives from the Medieval Latin *conceptuālis* and from Late Latin *conceptus*, which refer to "a thought; existing only in the mind; separated from embodiment" (*American Heritage Dictionary* 2003). Thus, conceptualization involves "seeing" or "understanding" something abstract, in one's mind.

Conceptual thinking, then, is the process of understanding a situation or problem abstractly by identifying patterns or connections and key underlying properties. Such thinking can include a range of information-processing activities, among which are inductive and deductive reasoning, logical reasoning, and divergent thinking skills. Conceptual thinking may involve the visual representations of ideas in the form of typologies, process models, figures, flow charts, or other visual depictions. However, such representations are

FIGURE 1
Critical Skills Necessary for Conceptual Thinking

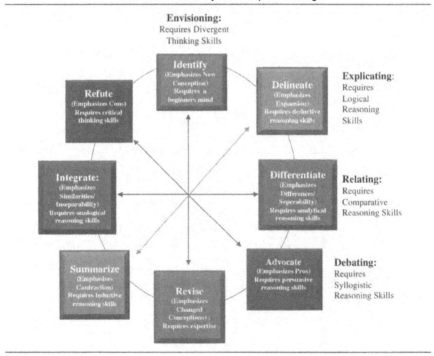

better regarded as outputs than as defining characteristics of conceptual thinking. Most academic articles (including those that take conceptual ideas and test them empirically) involve conceptualization. Identifying interesting problems, developing hypotheses, interpreting data, and deriving implications all involve thinking conceptually. Thus, conceptual thinking is at the heart of the scientific enterprise; it is critical to the development of both an individual scientist and the field of endeavor.

Conceptual articles are academic articles devoted purely to thought-based conceptions that are devoid of data (see MacInnis 2004; Yadav 2010). A differentiation is often made between conceptual and empirical articles (Elder and Paul 2009; MacInnis 2004), such that the latter include data. For example, purely conceptual articles include "conceptual frameworks," "integrative models," and "state-of-the art" reviews. Purely analytical (mathematical) articles are also examples of conceptual articles; here, ideas are represented mathematically as opposed to verbally. Purely empirical papers emphasize data mining. Other papers blend the conceptual with the empirical. For example, hypothesis-driven papers begin with conceptual ideas and test them empirically. Ethnographic papers often begin with data and use those data to build conceptual ideas. Meta-analyses also begin with data (individual papers) and use those data to understand generalizable relationships and their moderating factors.

Types of conceptual contributions, which are at the heart of this article, reflect ways in which contributions are realized. I describe such contribution types, which are represented in the columns of Table 1, in greater detail subsequently. Suffice it to say for now that (1) all contribution types reflect "seeing" or "understanding" something new in an abstract way, (2) they can pertain to the different entities shown in the rows of Table 1, (3) they reflect the nature of the research contribution and thus the criteria on which it is judged (as shown in Table 2), and (4) they differ in the conceptual skills they entail and the facilitating tools that enable them (see Table 2 and Figure 1).

Entities Around Which Conceptual Advances Can Occur

Conceptual advances can be made with respect to the entities labeled in Table 1 as constructs, relationships/theories, procedures, domains, disciplines, and science. I describe these entities in greater detail in the following subsections.

Constructs. Constructs are abstract, hypothetical concepts that are defined in a sufficiently precise manner (often along some dimension) to be operationalized or measured. For example, attitude strength, attitude valence, and attitude persistence are each unique constructs. Although all are reference "attitudes," they vary in whether the attitude is being conceptualized in terms of the confidence with which it is held (its strength), the degree to which it is favorable or unfavorable (its valence), or the degree to which is held consistently over time (its persistence).

Conceptual development pertaining to constructs is significant to academic and practitioner audiences for several reasons. First, "we see and understand things according to the concepts we have ... and [we] filter our observations through concepts" (Niehoff 1998, pp. 1–2; see also Zaltman, LeMasters, and Heffring 1985, p. 18). Thus, constructs play a critical role in knowledge representation, perspective taking, and knowledge sharing. Second, constructs "enable us to identify, compare, and distinguish dimensions of our thinking and experience.... We can never achieve command of our thoughts unless we achieve command over (properly conceptualize) the concepts and ideas in which our thought is expressed" (Elder and Paul 2009, p. 10). Third, constructs have action significance because construct labels help academics and practitioners categorize situations and decide what to do. The better marketers can understand what something is, the more effectively they can deal with it. Fourth, constructs are critical because they reflect basic units of knowledge advancement. Without conceptualizing new constructs, we would study the same constructs over and over again, limiting our perspectives on the world. Finally, the conceptualization of constructs is critical because constructs form the basis on which measures are derived and from which theories are tested. Given their centrality to knowledge advancement, several papers have articulated processes for developing "good" constructs (e.g., MacKenzie 2003; Teas and Palan 1997).

Relationships/theories. Knowledge advancement occurs not only by studying and developing constructs but also by conceptualizing their relationship to other concepts, often in a nomological network. Relationships that specify why one (or more) construct affects other constructs are called theories. Theories can also specify when (the conditions under which) and how (the process by which) given outcomes are affected. Thus, theories often include moderators and mediators as part of their specification.

Conceptual advances related to theories are also critical to both academics and managers. First, conceptualizing relationships in terms of a theory helps clarify the workings of the world around us. Second, understanding *why* fosters better prediction of the outcomes that managers care about. Thus, by conceptualizing relationships in terms of a theory, marketers can better understand how to manipulate or arrange environments so that desired outcomes can be realized. Such understanding also enables the development of process measures that have value in diagnosing whether a person is on course and what must be done to correct off-course deviations. Third, conceptual advances pertaining to theories help refine our understanding of the world by understanding the conditions under which actions will or will not produce desired outcomes. Finally, conceptual advances in theories are critical to knowledge development; theory revision avoids "saturation" (Zaltman, LeMasters, and Heffring 1985), or an emphasis on incremental tests of theories rather than the development of new ideas. Given the importance of conceptual advances pertaining to theories, researchers have given considerable thought to what constitutes a "good" theory (e.g., Darden 1991; Dennis and Kintsch 2007; Zaltman, Pinson, and Angelmar 1973).

Procedures. Some conceptual advances contribute to knowledge by articulating procedures or "best practices" for executing strategies or tactics, often with the goal of solving problems. Such procedures may be kinds of theories in that they are based on implicit or explicit theories about what will work. However, conceptual advances regarding procedures foster knowledge development by specifying how an activity should be done, often through a normative lens. Conceptual contributions at the procedure level can be of particular value to marketing practitioners who seek input on best practices. Conceptual advances related to procedures may involve identifying a new procedure; describing its implementation and/or the nature and range of the problems it solves; indicating how it solves the problems inherent in other procedures; and revealing the novel insights it can generate, the assumptions it makes, and the conditions under which it is most or least likely to be functional.

Domains. A domain is an area of study. In anthropology, domains include culture, customs, ethnocentrism, and kinship (Niehoff 1998). In psychology, domains such as attitudes, emotions, and memory assume centrality. Marketing studies domains such as relationships, services, competition, choice, strategic planning, price, and advertising. Domains are not constructs. Rather, they are broad categories of study within which specific constructs, theories, and/or procedures can be articulated. Different domains often have "different purposes, questions, information, concepts, theories, assumptions, and implications" (Elder and Paul 2009, p. 21). Domains are socially constructed, meaning that the academic or practitioner communities decide what a domain entails. Domains can encompass macrolevel phenomena (competition in the marketplace) or microlevel phenomena (e.g., preattentive processing). Moreover, domains can be hierarchically linked to other domains. For example, the domain of "consumer emotions" is part of a larger domain called "affect." Within the emotion domain, subdomains, such as "anticipated emotions," "experienced emotions," and "retrospective emotions," can be identified.

Conceptual advances at the domain level are also critical to marketing academics and practitioners. They contribute to a field's vitality by opening new and unexplored areas of study. Conceptual advances within a domain foster spheres of competence and expertise. Practitioners often rely on academics for making conceptual advances in a domain. Evidence of such advances can form the basis for practitioners' desires to connect with academic audiences. Thus, conceptual advances within a domain connect members of knowledge communities, which in turn fosters knowledge diffusion and sharing.

Disciplines. The domains and the procedures utilized in field of research constitute a discipline. Thus, the academic discipline of marketing represents the amalgamation of domains pertinent to exchange (Bagozzi 1975). Within this discipline are subdisciplines, including "consumer behavior," "marketing strategy," and "marketing models." Disciplines are the units of analysis for universities, and hiring strategies are typically organized around disciplines. Disciplines are critical for managers because disciplines have degree-granting bodies (departments and schools) that certify the breadth and depth of potential employees' knowl-

edge and thus validate their potential to enter the workforce (MacInnis and Folkes 2010).Conceptual advances within disciplines help identify research priorities and indicate ways that research in the field needs to shift to adapt to changing environments.

Science. Finally, conceptual advances can be made at the level of science. In marketing, discussions about science and the philosophy of science became salient in the 1980s and early 1990s, driven in part by alternative perspectives on the philosophy and sociology of science (e.g., Kuhn 1962). Conceptual contributions at the level of science clarify what constitutes science, what differentiates science from nonscience, and what processes are involved in scientific research (i.e., what makes for "rigorous" research and whether theories can be proved). Whereas procedures may be specific to an academic discipline or domain, contributions at the level of science are independent of discipline. Although practitioner audiences may be less concerned with conceptual contributions at the level of science, such contributions are important for academic researchers and doctoral students whose membership in the scientific academic community specifies rules of conduct to be followed in executing scientific research.

Types of Conceptual Contributions

For each of the aforementioned entities, researchers can make conceptual contributions in any number of ways (Table 1). The columns of Table 2 present four types of conceptual contributions (envisioning, relating, explicating, and debating). Within each type, I identify two subtypes, which I describe subsequently and summarize in the rows of Table 2. Various cells of Table 1 are illustrated using examples of frequently cited conceptual articles.[1] I begin by describing the more specific conceptual contributions (e.g., identification and revision) so that their linkage to the broader contributions (e.g., envisioning) can be more clearly understood. My discussion of these contributions includes a description of the criteria by which "good" papers of this type can be judged. These criteria serve as guidelines for authors who write and readers who review papers. Although the contributions are different, all move the field forward by setting an agenda for further research.[2]

---

[1]My expertise in consumer behavior inclines me to report on conceptual articles based on verbal arguments versus those based on mathematical arguments (analytical models). However, the value of analytical models cannot be disputed. Their lack of representation here merely reflects the limitations of my knowledge.

[2]Some conceptual papers (including those described here) make several types of conceptual contributions. For example, Srivastava, Shervani, and Fahey (1998) propose a revised view of the marketing discipline, suggesting that marketing's role is to create and manage market-based assets that deliver shareholder value. They also differentiate two types of market-based assets—relational and intellectual—as well as the attributes of balance sheet and off-balance sheet assets. Reflective of delineation, they propose that market-based assets (e.g., customer relationships, partner relationships) affect various aspects of market performance, which in turn affect shareholder value.

Identifying Versus Revising: Contributions That Involve Envisioning

Identifying: seeing that something exists. Researchers who make contributions through identifying establish or make known something that has yet to be established. The goal is to introduce a construct, theory, procedure, domain, discipline, or aspect of science that has yet to be apprehended or given serious study. As Table 2 shows, a metaphor for a researcher whose contribution involves identification is one of an astronomer who uses a powerful telescope to identify stars, planets, or galaxies that had previously been unseen. Purely conceptual papers that contribute in this manner are often titled with words that connote originality, for example, a novel framework or a new perspective.

Identification can occur for any of the entities in the rows of Table 1.[3] To illustrate, Glazer (1991) identifies a novel *construct* called "information intensity." He proposes that at one end of the information intensiveness continuum are products that are completely information independent. At the opposite end are information-based products. The latter may have been used initially to market a product but have since become marketable products themselves. The continuum is important because it characterizes the degree to which information is a wealth-generating asset in its own right. Hunt and Morgan (1995) present a novel "comparative advantage" *theory* of competition. The proposed theory suggests that competition is based on comparative advantage, defined as the relative resource-produced value by the firm in relation to the relative resource costs it incurs. Holbrook and Hirschman (1982) articulate a novel *domain* of consumer research, arguing that an overreliance on rational decision making and consumer information processing has blinded researchers to the role of feelings, fantasies, and fun in consumers' decision making. Day and Montgomery (1999) identify three novel *"discipline-based issues"* that the academic marketing discipline would face upon entering the new millennium: (1) providing meaningful measures, inferences, and calibration; (2) crossing boundaries and understanding functional interfaces; and (3) rethinking the role of theory.

As Table 2 shows, articles that contribute to identification make us aware of what we have been missing. This can be accomplished by providing evidence that the identified entity is real and moreover that its study is important. Reality and significance are often illustrated by reference to real-world problems, issues, or observations (see Day and Montgomery 1990; Glazer 1991). In some cases, these real-world examples reveal what is missing by comparison to prevailing views (Holbrook and Hirschman 1995; Hunt and Morgan 1995). In still other cases, they identify a novel entity by pointing to aligned research areas that have failed to intersect. For example, Ward (1974) argues that whereas marketing academics have studied consumers and develop-

mental psychologists have studied children, the field of consumer behavior had yet to examine children's learning as it pertains to the marketplace—a domain he labels "consumer socialization." Good papers also reveal what new insights can be gained from the entity's study. Good papers provide clear and unambiguous definitions of the identified entity. They are also generative; they guide future research by indicating novel research questions fostered from identification. These latter two characteristics are true of all papers that contribute conceptually, including those described subsequently.

Revising: seeing what has been identified in a different way. Revision involves reconfiguring or taking a novel perspective on something that has already been identified. Thus, whereas identifying is consistent with the logic of discovery, revision takes empirical evidence on the identified entity into account and modifies it. Contributions based on revising gain insight from alternative frames of reference. The visual metaphor might be that of an artist who uses a paintbrush to depict a landscape as a series of colored dots (as in pointillism) or a series of shapes (as in cubism). A different visual metaphor is that of a person who turns a dial on a kaleidoscope to reveal a new image. Common labels for purely conceptual papers with this goal are revised perspectives or alternative views.

To illustrate, Shugan (1980) presents a revised perspective on the *construct* of information costs. Whereas traditional economic models assumed that information was provided at no cost to consumers, Shugan views information as costly. His reconceptualization has made it possible to assess the costs of various decision-making strategies or rules. It also helps us understand when consumers are likely to make suboptimal choices from limited decision making. Anderson's (1982) "theory of the firm" provides a different *theoretical* perspective from which to understand organizational issues in marketing. MacInnis, Moorman, and Jaworski (1991) reconceptualize the *domain* of advertising executional cues. Rather than categorizing cues as "central" or "peripheral," the authors conceptualize cues in terms of their potential to enhance consumers' motivation, ability, and opportunity to process information. Webster (1992) suggests reconceptualizing the marketing *discipline*. His reconceptualization moves away from a focus on profit maximization and transactions and toward a view of marketing that emphasizes long-term relationships with customers, strategic alliances, and partnerships. Also from the standpoint of the marketing *discipline*, Van Waterschoot and Van den Bulte (1992) offer a revised perspective on the marketing mix—one that overcomes the limitations of the prevailing four P scheme. Finally, at the level of *science*, Thompson, Locander, and Pollio (1989) provide a revised (existential phenomenology) paradigm for understanding the consumer experience. In contrast with the extant Cartesian view (rooted in logical positivism), the revised view regards consumer experiences in context, understanding experiences as they are lived.

As Table 2 shows, good papers that contribute through revision can be evaluated according to the following criteria: They should describe the need for a revised perspective.

---

[3]To prevent tedium in reading, I do not attempt to provide illustrations of each individual cell in Table 1. The goal is to provide illustrative examples that clarify the meaning of the type of conceptual contribution.

In some cases, this is accomplished by revealing and questioning the validity of hidden or explicit assumptions, foundational premises, or tenets in the extant view and indicating their limiting features. In other cases, they reveal the prevailing metaphor used to guide thinking and illustrate its limitations in understanding the entity (see Thompson, Locander and Pollio 1989). Relaxing or altering these assumptions or using a different metaphor reveals what novel insights can be gained from the revised perspective (Shugun 1980). In still other cases, the need for a revised perspective is reinforced by reference to dynamic changes in firms or the marketplace that make the prevailing view outdated (see Hoffman and Novak 1996; Webster 1992). Good papers also indicate what new issues the revised view provides that the extant view cannot accommodate. They may also show how the new perspective provides a different way of understanding the meaning of various findings (MacInnis, Moorman, and Jaworski 1991) or activities (Peter and Olson 1983). Good papers that make contributions to a domain may also reveal aspects of identification, in that the new perspective may identify novel constructs, theories, and procedures that have yet to be studied.

Similarities and differences between identifying and revising. Conceptual contributions based on identifying and revising are similar yet distinct, in the ways noted in Table 2. Identifying something new and providing a revised perspective are similar in that both involve "envisioning"—that is, conceiving a new reality. Yet identifying is more closely related to the context of discovery because it involves observing that reality for the first time. In contrast, revision is more strongly related to the context of justification because it takes what is known or presumed to be and sees it differently. Identifying and revising also reflect opposing criteria of interestingness, as shown in Table 2. Articles that contribute through identification are interesting by suggesting that what is unseen is seen, what is unobservable is observable, what is unknown is known, or what does not matter actually matters a great deal. Articles that contribute through revision are interesting by suggesting that what is seen, known, observable, or of importance can be seen differently or by suggesting that what matters a great deal matters for a different reason than what was previously believed.

Delineating Versus Summarizing: Contributions that Involve Explicating

Delineation: detailing an entity. Delineation entails the goal of detailing, articulating, charting, describing, or depicting an entity. Often, this charting helps researchers consider how the entity they study (e.g., their "hometown") relates to the broader conceptual world around it. Papers aimed at delineation put the researcher in the metaphorical role of a cartographer, whose goal is to gain better grounding on a focal entity by mapping it out. Papers with a goal of delineation are often called conceptual frameworks, structural frameworks, or propositional inventories that describe an entity and identify things that should be considered in its study.

To illustrate, MacInnis and De Mello (2005) delineate the *construct* of hope, describing its implications for evaluation judgments, satisfaction processes, and risk taking. At the level of *relationships and theory*, Parasuraman, Zeithaml, and Berry (1985) delineate factors that drive consumers' perceptions of service quality (e.g., gaps between customers' perceptions and marketers' actions). Churchill's (1979) classic article on the development of marketing measures details a *procedure* for developing marketing measures. Frazier (1983) delineates the *domain* of interorganizational exchange behavior in marketing channels, articulating factors that affect the initiation of interorganizational exchanges, the processes involved in reviewing whether such exchanges should be enacted, the processes involved in implementing the exchange, and the outcomes of each of these processes. Alba and Hutchinson (1987) delineate the domain of consumer expertise. They examine the impact of expertise on a set of cognitive processes that include cognitive effort and automaticity, cognitive structure, analysis, elaboration, and memory. They develop logically derived hypotheses about the antecedents and consequences of expertise and factors that characterize experts as opposed to novices. Sherry (1983) delineates the domain of gift giving. He articulates the social, personal, and economic underpinnings of gift giving and develops a model of the gift giving process.

As Table 2 shows, "good" papers that contribute through delineation detail what the entity under study is (MacInnis and De Mello 2005), why its study is important, and how it changes or the processes by which it operates or is executed (Churchill 1979; Frazier 1983; Parasuraman, Zeithaml, and Berry 1985; Sherry 1983). Such papers may also consider what factors circumscribe the entity's study or moderating conditions that may affect it (Alba and Hutchinson 1987). They provide a roadmap for understanding the entity, sometimes in the form of boxes and arrows that demonstrate cause and effect relationships (Frazier 1983), pictorial models that depict processes (Sherry 1983), or propositional inventories or novel hypotheses (Alba and Hutchinson 1987).

Summarization: seeing the forest for the trees. The goal of summarization is to take stock of, digesting, recapping, and reducing what is known to a manageable set of key takeaways. Whereas delineation often specifies what relationships might exist (consistent with the context of discovery), summarization typically takes empirical evidence into account to derive conclusions about what is known (consistent with the context of justification). As Table 2 suggests, the visual metaphor of the researcher is one of an astronaut whose view from the spaceship allows him or her step back from the mountains, deserts, cities, and seas to see Earth in its entirety. Purely conceptual papers with the goal of summarization are commonly labeled review papers or critical syntheses (empirical papers with this goal are called meta-analyses).

For example, Gardner (1985) summarizes what is known about the *construct* of mood in consumer behavior. She reviews various mood induction methods and discusses the direct and indirect effects of positive mood on consumer behavior, memory, and product evaluation. She also reviews what is known about service encounters, point-of-purchase stimuli, and communications as factors that may affect consumers' moods in the marketplace. Rindfleisch and Heide (1997) summarize research that draws on transaction cost analysis *theory*. Wright (1980) reviews research on the use of thought verbalization *procedures* (support arguments, counterarguments, source derogations) in persuasion research. Kerin, Varadarajan, and Peterson (1992) review empirical studies on the *domains* of order of entry and first-mover advantages. Folkes (1988) reviews what is known about attributions in consumer behavior. Wilkie and Moore (2003; see also Kerin 1996) summarize how the *marketing discipline* has changed across time; they summarize prior work by clustering it into four broad "eras" of marketing thought. Reviews such as the *Annual Review of Psychology*'s consumer behavior reviews (e.g., Loken 2005) summarize what is known about a *discipline* or subdiscipline.

As Table 2 shows, papers that contribute through summarization indicate why summarization is needed or is particularly timely. They circumscribe what falls within and outside the entity encompassed in the review, from the standpoint both of a substantive focus and of sources and time frames along which their summary relies (Rindfleisch and Heide 1997; Wilkie and Moore 2003). They often develop a useful organizing framework within which the summarized material can be couched and logically linked. For example, as mentioned previously, Wilkie and Moore (2003) organize the field of marketing in terms of eras. Gardner (1985) organizes mood research in terms of what is known about effects in different contexts (e.g., service encounters, marketing communications). Folkes (1988) organizes her review on attributions in terms of antecedents and consequences. Good papers are comprehensive in reviewing the papers that meet inclusion criteria, and their conclusions are clear, accurate, and consistent with the data at hand. They identify knowledge gaps and lay out research priorities (Folkes 1988; Rindfleisch and Heide 1997). They may also develop managerial implications that pertain to the summarized findings (Gardner 1985).

Similarities and differences in delineating and summarizing. Both delineating and summarizing involve explication—that is, articulating, explaining, or drawing out ideas and relationships (see Table 2). Both also emphasize generalities and abstractions as opposed to particulars. Thus, whereas studying exceptions are appropriate for contributions based on envisioning (identifying or revising), such study is not the goal of delineation or summarization. Delineation and summarization emphasize the rule, not the exception. Both can involve statements of relationships—though with delineation, such statements may be in the form of hypotheses, while summarization statements are in the form of generalizations.

Delineation and summarization are different, however. Delineation involves mapping or charting what might be (e.g., what a construct might entail, what a domain might encompass, what relationships might exist), as would be true with the context of discovery. In contrast, summarization involves taking stock of what is empirically known from many disparate instances, as would be true with the

context of justification. They also differ in that delineation involves expansion, by mapping out the components of a construct, theory, or domain. In contrast, summarization emphasizes contraction, or the distilling of many empirical instances to a set of manageable conclusions.

As Table 2 suggests, delineation and summarization have parallel bases for interestingness. Interesting ideas aimed at delineation suggest that what is simple is complex, what is micro is macro, what is small is big, and what seems to be unrelated is actually related. In contrast, when it comes to summarization, interesting ideas are those that suggest that what is complex is simple, what is big is small, and what is idiosyncratic is general.

Differentiating Versus Integrating: Contributions that Involve Relating

Differentiation: seeing differences. Differentiation involves conceptual advances that add insight by distinguishing, parsing, dimensionalizing, classifying, or categorizing an entity (e.g., construct, theory, domain) under study. The goal of differentiation evokes a visual metaphor of a naturalist who uses a magnifying glass to classify and categorize flora and fauna into various taxonomic and hierarchical categories. Purely conceptual papers with the goal of differentiation are sometimes labeled typological, taxonomic, or classificational frameworks (Bailey 1994; Doty and Glick 1994). Several illustrations follow.

Houston and Rothschild's (1978) unpublished but often-cited paper brought great clarity to the involvement *construct* by suggesting the need to differentiate among the entities with which one could be involved: a brand, product, response, or situation. This differentiation was viewed as critical because involvement in one entity (e.g., a brand) did not necessarily imply involvement in a different entity (e.g., a product category). Moreover, theories about one construct (brand involvement) may be inappropriately applied to theories of a different construct (e.g., ad involvement). At the level of *procedure*, Jarvis, MacKenzie, and Podsakoff (2003) argue that there is a critical distinction between using formative versus reflective indicators of constructs. They differentiate the two and develop a set of procedures to help researchers identify when each should be used. They suggest that failure to specify construct indicators correctly as either formative or reflective has resulted in model misspecification in prior marketing research. Lovelock (1983) suggests that the *domain* of services can be differentiated in terms of the nature of the service act (whether it deals with tangible or intangible actions), who receives the service (people or things), the nature of the service delivery (discrete or continuous), and the presence or absence of a relationship between the firm and customers (membership relationship or no formal relationship). Likewise, the domain of "affect" can be decomposed into subcategories of emotions, mood, and attitudes (Cohen and Areni 1991). At the level of *science*, Calder, Phillips, and Tybout (1981) argue for the need to differentiate research goals in terms of whether they are designed to apply effects (to determine whether effects generalize to a different setting) or to determine whether theory can be generalized to different settings. They argue that this distinction is important because the two goals represent different philosophical and scientific approaches to the conduct of research.

Papers that contribute through differentiation demonstrate how entities are different. They may do so by revealing the underlying dimensions along which entities can be compared or by recognizing their differing antecedents, manifestations, or effects. For example, Calder, Phillips, and Tybout (1981) compare effects-oriented and theory-oriented research in terms of differences in selecting respondents, operationalizing independent and dependent variables, choosing a research setting, and selecting a research design. Good papers also articulate why differentiation matters. Differentiation may matter because seeing the differences adds clarity, reduces confusion, or makes sense of out of what were previously regarded as inconsistent effects (Houston and Rothschild 1978) or viewpoints (Calder, Phillips, and Tybout 1981). Differentiation may matter because it adds precision to thinking, making it easier to compare findings across papers, or it may matter because lack of differentiation creates errors in reasoning about entities or developing findings that pertain to them. In other cases, differentiation matters because the articulation of differences helps identify novel contingencies. For example, classifying services in terms of the extent to which they involve a discrete or continuous set off transactions (Lovelock 1983) adds new insight into the conditions under which being market driven matters.

Integration: seeing the simplicity from the complex. Like revision, integration involves seeing something in a new way, and like summarization, it involves a holistic perspective. However, true integration does more than lay out what has been found. It takes what is known and has been theorized and transforms it into something entirely new. Integration draws connections between previously differentiated phenomena, finding a novel, simplified, and higher-order perspective on how these entities are related. Integration involves synthesis—that is, the creation of a whole from diverse parts. Integration leads to overarching ideas that can accommodate previous findings, resolve contradictions or puzzles, and produce novel perspectives. Thus, integration provides a simple and parsimonious perspective that accommodates complexity. The metaphorical role of the researcher is that of an architect who creates a new building from a set of pipes, cement, steel, wiring, and windows. The metaphorical tool is the architectural plan that both depicts the building in its entirety and notes how the building's specific elements fit together to make this novel structure. Common words for papers that make such contributions are integrative frameworks—though that term is sometimes (perhaps inappropriately) applied to papers that actually emphasize delineation or summarization.

Belk (1988) provides an integrated perspective on the *construct* of possessions, suggesting that they are part of our extended selves. This perspective is developed by leveraging research on possessions in self-perception, research on the loss of possessions, and research that demonstrates investment of the self into possessions. Drawing on literature from multiple disciplines, he describes the functions of having an extended self, and he describes processes by which possessions become incorporated into the self. Dickson (1992) develops a *theory* of competitive rationality that integrates other paradigms (e.g., Adam Smith's "invisible hand," Schumpeter's entrepreneurial "creative destruction," Simon's bounded rationality). Petty and Cacioppo's (1986) "elaboration likelihood model" provides an overarching and simplified perspective that accommodates myriad theories of attitude formation. Bettman, Luce, and Payne (1998) develop an integrated theory of consumer choice that blends two perspectives on contingent choice—the effort/ accuracy perspective and the perceptual approach. Stern and Reve (1980) propose the "political economy framework" for understanding the *domain* of distribution channels. This framework, which integrates the economic and behavioral approaches to understanding distribution channels, considers the economic and sociopolitical factors that affect distribution channel behavior and performance.

Papers that contribute through integration accommodate extant knowledge. Thus, they account for well-accepted findings while explaining puzzling findings. In this way, they provide clarity by resolving apparent inconsistencies across studies. For example, Petty and Cacioppo's (1986) elaboration likelihood model shows that many of the prevailing theories of attitude formation have validity; yet their value in explaining consumers' attitude formation processes depends on whether consumers' motivation, ability, or opportunity to process information is high or low. Good papers also contribute by noting the parsimony achieved through the integrated perspective. The elaboration likelihood model achieves parsimony by taking the myriad theories of attitude formation processes and suggesting that they fall into two general buckets—those based on thoughtful processing (which occurs when motivation, ability, and opportunity to process information are high) and those based on less thoughtful processing (which occurs when motivation, ability, and/or opportunity to process information are low).

Similarities and differences between differentiating and integrating. The goals of differentiating and integrating are similar insofar as both involve comparing—that is, seeing how wholes and parts are related. Yet differentiation involves comparisons that decompose an entity by breaking it down into its constituent parts and noting contrasts or dimensions along which the entities differ and can be compared. In contrast, integration involves finding links or similarities that connect previously disparate entities; it involves seeing a new whole (e.g., a cake) instead of its constituent elements (flour, sugar, eggs, baking soda, and chocolate). Consistent with the notion that differentiation and integration are different but related forms of reasoning, Gardner (2008), uses the terms "lumpers" and "splitters" to describe people whose thinking style reflects integration and differentiation, respectively. Lumpers are people whose thinking style emphasizes putting things together and finding similarities among them. Splitters are people whose thinking style emphasizes distinctions and contrasts.

As Table 2 shows, these two contribution types have parallel interestingness criteria. In differentiation, ideas are interesting because they suggest that what has been previously regarded as similar is different, what is inseparable is separable, what is unidimensional is multidimensional, what is homogeneous is heterogeneous, what is organized is disorganized, and what is holistic is particularistic. Integration involves the opposite set of interestingness criteria.

Advocacy Versus Refutation: Contributions that Involve Debate

Advocating: endorsing a way of seeing. Advocacy involves argumentation to justify or support a given conclusion. With advocacy, the researcher recommends or pushes for something, or speaks in support of a particular view. The metaphorical role of the researcher is that of a guide who relies on a compass to direct the path forward. The common label for purely conceptual papers that emphasize advocacy is a position paper, an editorial, or a perspective.

Zajonc (1980; see also Zajonc and Markus 1982) advocates a *theory* that in the relationship between affect and cognition, affect is primary — it causes cognitions. Preferences (affect) need not rely on cognition, because preferences can be acquired incidentally and nonconsciously through exposure; as exposure increases, so does affect. To illustrate, Szymanski (1988) argues for the importance of studying declarative knowledge as a critical *domain* that affects sales performance effectiveness. Hunt (1992) advocates a deontological philosophical approach to the academic marketing *discipline*, arguing that the field should be viewed in terms of its responsibilities and obligations. As a discipline within a university, our field's ultimate obligation is to serve society, but its other responsibilities are to serve students, marketing practitioners, and the academy. Also at the level of the *discipline*, Leone and Schultz (1980) suggest that a science of marketing should emphasize marketing generalizations. By identifying such generalizations, we can better understand what we do and do not know. Moreover, a general goal in the science of marketing is to use generalizations to build and modify extant theories.

Refuting: rebutting a way of seeing. In contrast to advocating, refuting involves argumentation aimed at rebutting, challenging, disputing, or contesting a given perspective. The metaphorical role of the researcher is that of a prosecuting attorney whose exhibits to the jury cast doubt on the defendant's innocence. Papers that refute a given perspective are commonly labeled "critiques," "rejoinders," or "commentaries."

To illustrate, Moore (1982) suggests that we abandon further research on the *construct* of subliminal perception in light of evidence suggesting that its impact on consumer behavior is limited. Lazarus (1981) issues one of a series of critiques against Zajonc's *theory*, suggesting that Zajonc's theory of affect primacy underestimates the role of cognition in affect generation. Olshavsky and Granbois (1979) critique the *domain* of "consumer decision making," arguing that in many consumer contexts (budgeting, purchase allocation decisions, store patronage, and brand purchase), decision making does not resemble the classic mode; indeed, decision making appears absent. Sheth (1992) criticizes the *subdiscipline* of consumer behavior for its "unim-

pressive impact" on understanding consumers, particularly for practitioner and policy audiences.

Similarities and differences between advocacy and refutation. Contributions based on advocacy and refutation are similar because both involve the process of debate — that is, putting forward reasons designed to convince others about the validity of an idea. Debate differs from explication because it is not designed to *explain ideas* but rather to *change beliefs* or alter the confidence with which beliefs are held (Walton 2006). In contrast to explication, both advocacy and refutation involve an assumption that there is an issue or something to be debated, and both involve a stance on that issue. Both also involve an action orientation designed to convert belief systems to be in line with one's own. Both involve a normative orientation reflecting one's perspective on what others should (or should not) believe. Thus, in contrast to the previously discussed contribution types, these types of contributions emphasize change of social opinions.

The criteria that make advocacy and debate papers good are also similar. Good papers state the premises and assumptions on which their argument is based. They put forth evidence that is credible, unambiguous, consistent with the stated conclusion, and not subject to fallacious reasoning. Providing multiple sources of evidence that point to the same conclusion adds validity. Conclusions are stated clearly and align with the argument, premise, and evidence.

Advocacy and refutation differ: Whereas advocacy is designed to enhance confidence in an idea, refutation is designed to undermine such confidence. As such, advocacy and refutation can be conceptualized as opposite sides of a persuasive debate, with advocacy involving a proponent who puts forward a set of ideas and refutation involving a respondent who rebuts the argument or points out logical weaknesses that undermine the validity of an idea.

Because advocacy and refutation are designed to persuade by taking a stance on an issue about which there may be varying opinions, interesting propositions suggest that prevailing beliefs about an issue or its normative appropriateness are, in fact, in error. Thus, with advocacy, interesting propositions argue that what is considered false is actually true, what is considered unacceptable is actually acceptable, what is considered wrong is right, and what is considered inappropriate is actually appropriate. Interesting propositions pertaining to refutation suggest the opposite.

Skill Building and Facilitating Tools

The conceptual contributions described in the previous section can form the basis for purely conceptual contributions. However, as noted, the conceptualization is pertinent to any paper that has a conceptual element, even if it is an empirical paper. For example, positioning a paper may involve identifying a new construct, relationship, or domain; providing a revised perspective on that entity; and/or articulating its significance and differentiating it from previously studied entities. Delineating constructs, domains, and/or relationships is critical to many papers that publish hypotheses or propositions. Advocacy is used to convince readers of the importance of a topic and why its study matters. Refutation is used when rival hypotheses that may otherwise explain results are developed and then ruled out (see Platt 1964). Literature reviews and discussion sections entail summarization of what is known, while the development of hypotheses and the interpretation of data can involve integration of ideas into novel ones as well as the ability to advocate a particular position and refute others. Thus, the skills involved in conceptual thinking should apply to most published papers, whether they are purely conceptual or conceptual–empirical blends.

Given the central role of conceptualization in knowledge development, it is important to understand what skills these types of conceptual advances entail and how these skills may be fostered. I turn to this issue next. Figure 1 and the bottom two rows of Table 2 play an organizing role in the discussion that follows. As this figure and table show, the eight thinking skills are not only similar and different in the ways previously mentioned, they also require similar and different thinking skills and facilitating tools.[4]

Identifying and Revising

Skills. Both identifying and revising involve divergent thinking skills, both of which are critical to creativity (see Figure 1). Creative thinking results from "originality of thought, having the ability or power to create or produce, having or showing imagination and artistic or intellectual inventiveness, stimulating the imagination and inventive powers" (Elder and Paul 2009, p. 13). Both identifying and revising entail the ability to break free from an attachment to a familiar, comforting, prevailing frame of reference or worldview to see things that are not obvious (Zaltman, LeMasters, and Heffring 1985).

Yet they differ in other skills identified in Figure 1. Identification involves seeing something that has not yet been seen. Thus, it requires a beginner's mind. A beginner's mind can look at something as if seeing it for the first time and without inference or judgment. However, revision involves understanding the prevailing view, which requires expertise in the entity under study. Yet this expertise must be coupled with the creative capacity to see things anew and reconfigure the prevailing view in a different manner. Thus, such a perspective requires both a beginner's mind and an expert's mind and the ability to articulate why the revised view offers improved understanding over the prevailing view (Li 1996).

Facilitating tools. If identification and revision involve divergent thinking, how are divergent thinking skills fostered? An often-heralded method is the use of metaphors (see Thompson, Locander, and Pollio 1989). For example, Li (1996) describes how John von Neumann developed a new theory of mathematics and economic behavior (game theory) by thinking of decision making between two parties in terms of a game. Morgan's (2006) classic book on organizations shows how the use of different metaphors for organizations (as machines, organisms, brains, cultures,

political systems, psychic prisons, or instruments of domination) has yielded novel constructs and theories about organizations. Thompson, Locander, and Pollio (1989) use metaphors in developing and articulating a revised perspective on science. They compare the machine and container metaphors characteristic of logical positivism with a pattern and figure-ground metaphor that characterizes existential phenomenology.

Identification and revision can also be fostered by questioning strongly held assumptions that may be at variance with the way the world actually operates. Such is the case with Shugun's (1980) work on the cost of thinking and Holbrook and Hirschman's (1982) paper on experiential consumption. Identification and revision can also be fostered by a search for anomalies, hidden events (Zaltman 1983), differences, and things that go against the trend as opposed to nonoutliers, things that are expected, similarities, and supportive findings.

Additional devices may foster the open-mindedness necessary for identification. Facilitating tools include "taking a hike" to adjacent disciplines, seeing new vantage points from which disciplines view related phenomena, and considering how their respective vantage points can fill blind spots in our field's understanding (Zaltman 2000). Thus, understanding a construct such as "brand relationships" can be facilitated by examining the study of human relationships in sociology and psychology, mechanical relationships (as in the study of magnets in physics), or principal–agent relationships in economics. Introspection can facilitate identification because it allows a person to think about a new idea in terms of whether it "feels right." Immersion in an area of study can also provide insight, particularly if the researcher adopts a beginner's mind and observes without predetermined perspective, which, by definition, blocks the ability to see something new.

Additional devices to foster revision include the use of heuristic devices, or previously identified bases for thinking about things. For example, whereas early research on attitude formation processes considers consumers' motivation, ability, and opportunity to process ad information, the motivation, ability, and opportunity framework may also be a useful heuristic for thinking about other things, such as a salesperson's performance, consumers' abilities to delay gratification, factors that affect involvement in brand communities, and advertising executional cues. (The latter is true of MacInnis, Moorman, and Jaworski's (1991) work. Abbott (2004) identifies a set of different heuristics (beyond motivation, ability, and opportunity) that he used to provide revised perspectives on known phenomena.

Delineating and Summarizing

Skills. From a skills perspective, delineation and summarization require logical reasoning skills, defined as the ability to relate what is known in a linear, rational, internally consistent, and compelling manner (Elder and Paul 2009). Thus, they require the capacity to draw coherent conclusions on the basis of established findings. Such reasoning may be expressed in the form of verbal arguments or mathematical arguments that lay out predictions based on

---

[4]The discussion emphasizes the dominant (not the only) set of skills aligned with each type of conceptual contribution.

mathematical criteria. Halpern (1989) proposes that such reasoning uses knowledge about one or more related statements to determine whether another statement is logically true.

Notably, however, the two conceptualization types differ in other reasoning skills (see Figure 1 and Table 2). Delineation involves a process of deductive reasoning. Such reasoning occurs when a person begins with a statement known or believed to be true and then uses this statement to make conclusions about something else. A conclusion is valid if it necessarily follows from some statements called premises. To illustrate, if it is known that A affects B and that B affects C, it can logically be deduced that A should also affect C through the mediational effect of B. Deductive reasoning skills are useful in developing logical arguments on which hypotheses and propositions are based. In contrast, summarization involves inductive reasoning. Such reasoning begins with individual observations and then collates these observations into a higher-order set of conclusions. Thus, if it is observed that consumers tend to make decision-making errors when they are in crowded stores, when there is music playing, or when their children are around, it might be induced that decision-making errors are caused by distraction, which interferes with information processing. Because all three situations have distraction as a common feature, it becomes an overarching explanation that ties the individual observations together.

Facilitating tools. Because delineation involves charting, researchers have often benefited from a facilitating tool known as mapping (Novak 1998). A map is a visual representation of an area and its boundaries. It is constructed in a manner that enables someone who has never traveled the route to understand how to get from point A to B. Maps delineate where things are in relation to one another. With mapping, entities are typically labeled with words and lines (or arrows) that are used to denote the relationship between one entity and other. Frazier (1983, see Figure 1) provides an example of mapping a domain. So, too, does Parasuraman et al.'s (1985) theoretical model of the determinants of perceived service quality (see also Sherry 1983). With mapping, a person states what is known (I can get from point A to point B in 30 minutes; I usually travel at 60 miles an hour) and uses this knowledge to draw conclusions (A and B must be 30 miles apart).

When delineating theories, researchers might benefit from a "theories-in-use" approach (e.g., Argyris and Schon 1974). Such an approach fosters theory development by understanding a phenomenon from the perspective of the self or someone who is experiencing it. This tool also involves immersion in a phenomenon and uses immersion to understand relationships. Zaltman, LeMasters, and Heffring (1985) illustrate this approach through the example of a salesperson who views his or her role as that of a consultant (as opposed to being an advocate) for a good being sold. This consultant perspective allows the theorist to develop novel propositions by listening to or thinking through if/then logic. "If I appear to be concerned with understanding the consumer's problem, and if I offer general advice about solving that problem, then the consumer

will perceive me to be on his or her side and thus relatively more objective, and hence is more likely to accept suggestions I make." From there, logical propositions can be deduced (e.g., "The more oriented a salesperson is to understanding consumers' problems, the more likely it is that the consumer will accept his or her advice.... The more the salesperson displays a consulting role [as opposed to an advocacy role], the more likely it is that the consumer will accept his or her advice" (Zaltman, LeMasters and Heffring 1985, p. 115). Zaltman, LeMasters, and Heffring recommend that a theories-in-use approach should also include unsuccessful practices. Such unsuccessful practices are useful for charting boundary conditions under which the theory may or may not hold.

Mapping is also useful for summarization, though maps can show the underlying features or properties that connect specific instances to a higher-order entity. For example, an "organizational chart"–type map might be used to suggest that "distraction" is the higher-order construct that connects crowds, music, and children with reduced information processing. Summarization is also facilitated by outlines, which use devices such as headings and subheadings to organize materials into categories that relate studies to one another (see Folkes 1988; for examples of useful headings, Gardner 1985). Boxes in maps represent major headings in an outline, which in turn organize prior research in a way that allows for synthesis. Subheadings further organize what is known, with research organized into headings that support a given linkage, others that do not support it, and still others that identify contingent factors.

Differentiating and Integrating

Skills. Various skills related to differentiating and integrating can also be identified. Contributions based on differentiation and integration are similar: Both involve comparative reasoning skills, which involve the act of examining resemblances based on similarities and differences. However, differentiation requires analytical reasoning skills, defined as the capacity to see the details of something and to characterize them in terms of its elements or constituent parts (Elder and Paul 2009). For example, the construct of hope can be decomposed into its constituent appraisals. That is, a person feels hope when an outcome is appraised as desirable, as consistent with that person's goals, and as uncertain but possible. Differentiation makes it possible to see how hope differs from potentially related constructs. Wishing is similar to hope, but whereas hope is related to future outcomes believed to be possible, wishing is often related to outcomes that are desirable but impossible. By distinguishing the essential elements or properties underlying hope, it is possible to understand how it is similar to and different from other constructs. In contrast, integration involves analogical thinking, which is defined as the ability to think of something in terms of something else. Integration also requires the expertise characteristic of revision because understanding similarities and differences requires prior knowledge. It also requires imagination—a characteristic linked to identification.

Facilitating tools. Several tactics foster the comparative reasoning skills associated with differentiating and integrating (see Marzano, Pickering, and Pollock 2004). Assessing similarities and differences is fostered by exercises that ask for comparisons of similarities and differences. Such exercises may be accompanied by graphic devices, such as Venn diagrams, in which similarities are represented by the intersections of circles and differences are represented in nonoverlapping areas. Comparison matrices are other graphic devices in which people develop a grid with items to be compared along the matrix columns and characteristics linked to the items in the matrix rows. The goal is to identify features, characteristics, or dimensions along which the items can be compared and then to indicate whether these comparisons reflect similarities or differences (see, e.g., Calder, Phillips, and Tybout 1981).

The development of integrative thinking skills is particularly challenging; research indicates that people who are skilled at integrative thinking cannot articulate how they developed their integrated ideas (Dixon 2005). However, it is possible that the ability to think analogically can be fostered by training in solving analogies (e.g., book is to human as _____ is to bear) or thinking metaphorically. For example, at least three theories have been proposed to explain consumer satisfaction: expectancy disconfirmation, equity theory, and attribution theory. In developing an integrative theory, perhaps analogies can be drawn between the theories (e.g., expectation is to product as fairness is to person). By examining what aspects of one theory do and do not map onto aspects of other theories, a novel metaphor might be uncovered that accommodates both the elements on which the theories are comparable and those on which the theories are not comparable.

Advocacy and Refutation

Skills. Both advocacy and refutation involve syllogistic reasoning, which involves deciding whether a conclusion can be inferred from one or more premises (Halpern 1989, p. 128). With advocacy, the researcher attempts to provide undisputed premises from which a conclusion logically follows. With refutation, the researcher disputes the premises and/or shows that the conclusion does not follow logically from them. Notably, a single researcher can engage in advocacy and refutation with respect to his or her own ideas, first advocating an idea and then being critical of the persuasive logic. Elder and Paul (2009) call this process "dialectical reasoning."

Refutation and advocacy differ, however, in the necessity of critical reasoning skills, defined as skills of careful judgment, reflection, or observation aimed at questioning, finding fault with, and determining the merit or accuracy of a conclusion and/or its premises (Elder and Paul 2009). Such critical reasoning skills are an essential component of refutation.

Facilitating tools. The facilitating tools linked to advocacy and refutation are similar, as Table 2 shows. However, their application differs as researchers use these tools in an advocacy form to argue for what is true or should be believed or followed. With refutation, these tools are used

to dispute or argue against a view or suggest what should not be believed. Walton (2006; see also Walton, Reed, and Macagno 2008) suggests that evaluating the plausibility of persuasive arguments can be fostered by argument diagrams. With argument diagrams, verbal arguments are translated into a set of diagrams that visually depict the premises and the conclusions derived from them. This diagramming makes the premises and conclusions explicit, making it easier for the evaluator to determine whether they are defensible.

Researchers can also be trained to identify argumentation schemes, which are various types of plausible arguments whose validity can be assessed by a set of questions. A common argument scheme is to appeal to an expert. For example, "Jones is an expert in marketing relationships. Jones claims that power imbalances between two parties will undermine the relationship's tenure. Therefore, power imbalances do indeed undermine a relationship's tenure." When the scheme is identified, a set of questions can be asked that help validate the plausibility of this conclusion. With such appeals to expert schemes, a researcher can ask (1) Is Jones indeed a credible expert? (2) Is Jones an expert in the area of marketing relationships? (3) Is Jones's assertion based on solid evidence? and (4) Is the conclusion consistent with what other experts would say? Walton (2006) identifies a set of other argument schemes and associated questions. Such schemes include arguments based on popular opinions, arguments based on analogy, arguments that use correlation to assume causation, and arguments based on purported consequences, among others. In each case, the goal is to articulate a set of questions designed to help assess whether the premise and the conclusions drawn from it are valid.

Advocacy and refutation can also be based on known persuasion tactics, the awareness of which can facilitate refutation. For example, researchers can be trained to check for fallacies, such as the use of false dichotomies, circular reasoning, the provision of irrelevant reasons, the use of weak or inappropriate analogies, the use of emotional (suggestive or propaganda-like) language, the use of appeals, tradition, oversimplification, and incomplete or erroneous comparisons, among others. Gula (2007) provides excellent examples of these reasoning fallacies.

Moving Forward

I conclude with a set of recommendations for moving our field forward in making future conceptual advances. These recommendations are clustered into four categories: (1) valuing conceptualization, (2) addressing shortages, (3) developing/sustaining a beginner's mind, and (4) fostering training in conceptual skill development.

Valuing Conceptualization

Conceptualization is critical to vitality of academic fields—whether it is manifest in purely conceptual papers or in conceptual–empirical blends. Yet our field seems to have swung in the direction of valuing the empirical over the conceptual (e.g., Kerin 1996; Stewart and Zinkhan 2006; Webster 2005; Zaltman, LeMasters, and Heffring 1985).

This movement is evident not only in the decline in purely conceptual papers in our field's top journals but also in the fact that empirical advances (in methods, statistics) and empirically focused PhD coursework have outpaced conceptual advances and courses. Empirical methods are essential, but unless they are accompanied by good and interesting ideas, their value diminishes.

Moreover, whereas all articles (empirical and conceptual) are essential to the advancement of the field, conceptual articles play a special role by addressing big issues for which an accompanying empirical component may be impossible, particularly in the space of an academic journal article. Such papers are more likely to have an impact in both their influence on other's work and the external recognition they receive (Yadav 2010). The precipitous decline of such articles suggests that the field may be missing important ideas.

It might be argued that our field *is* open to conceptual papers, but their exposition is best suited to books (versus journal articles). Indeed, some of the most highly cited works in marketing and consumer behavior have appeared in books (e.g., Bettman 1979; Howard and Sheth 1969). Yet books are no longer valued in promotion and tenure decisions, giving authors little incentive to write them. Moreover, many of the most provocative conceptual pieces that appear in books today come from the practitioner community. This outcome undermines the credibility of the academic community, which in turn can taint our reputation as thought leaders.

It might also be suggested that the field *is* open to conceptual papers by pointing to articles (AMA Task Force 1988; Yadav 2010) and editorials (e.g., Kohli 2009; Monroe 1993) that acknowledge their importance. Indeed, some of the field's most respected and influential thought leaders express this view. Yet these calls remain largely unheeded. Why? Maybe we lack of a framework for thinking about conceptualization. The articulation of such a framework has been the goal of this paper. However, perhaps our field has an empirical bias that disinclines reviewers to accept such papers (which in turn disinclines authors to write them). This state of affairs would be unfortunate. An astounding number of fundamental and interesting constructs, theories, domains, and procedures were introduced to the marketing field from 1952 to 1977 (see Wilkie and Moore 2003, Table 5) because openness to thinking conceptually was deemed important.

This openness needs to be recaptured. Editors play a central role in directing this openness. They should be explicit (as is Kohli 2009) in communicating their receptivity to conceptual papers. Editorials, meet-the-editor sessions, and editorial review board meetings should be opportunities to discuss their stance on such papers. Yet editors alone do not bear the responsibility of driving the direction of the field. Reviewers should be sufficiently open-minded to accept articles based *not* on the nature of their execution (i.e., whether they are empirical or conceptual) but rather on the rigor and quality of their ideas. Finally, authors should be emboldened to write conceptual papers. In addition to writing papers that emphasize incremental findings (e.g., understanding moderators and mediators of a known rela-

tionship), authors should assume responsibility for addressing interesting and novel domains, theories, constructs, and procedures that will augment the field's vitality.

Attending to and Addressing Shortages

My "armchair review" of the conceptual articles published in the field's top journals over the past 25 years reveals a preponderance of articles that emphasize differentiation and delineation. Summarization papers are increasingly rare and are often relegated to specialized journals or book chapters. Furthermore, current standards seem to demand that summarization-type articles be complemented by empirical validation, as is true with meta-analysis. Meta-analysis is an extremely valuable procedure. Yet not all entities have a sufficient level of development or comparability to make for a useful meta-analysis. Meta-analysis may be most relevant to well-entrenched research domains in which researchers have examined similar phenomena that vary in context and procedures. They may be less useful for understanding an entity for which research is emergent, yet not yet entrenched.

Relatedly, although we do have articles that are called "integrative reviews," many (including my own) are summarization (not integration) papers. True integration papers are rare. Perhaps this is because they require a full set of conceptual thinking skills. In addition to expertise and a beginner's mind, they require the ability to see differences, the ability to think inductively about how various perspectives are related, the ability to take a creative stance on the entity, the ability to use deductive reasoning to put forth new arguments, and the ability to do so persuasively. Perhaps some forms of integration may be most successful when accompanied by structural models that test an integrative perspective (e.g., MacKenzie, Lutz, and Belch 1986). Nonetheless, the value of integration cannot be underestimated. Consider, for example, the incredible productivity engendered by the elaboration likelihood model of persuasion, which is a truly integrative perspective on attitude formation processes.

Debate exists, but with the exception of the recent "Dialogues" sections in *Journal of Consumer Psychology*, it is rare. Indeed, some journals discourage debate by having a policy that excludes rejoinders. Perhaps debate is discouraged because it is perceived as instilling ill will among researchers and fragmenting a research community. Furthermore, authors may consider debate risky. Those who attempt to refute the ideas of other authors may find their own work rejected by these same individuals. Perhaps debate is less prevalent in marketing than in other disciplines because debate in other disciplines often centers on theories; in marketing, we have been less adept at developing, proposing, and debating theories than in borrowing theories developed elsewhere. To the extent that we borrow a theory, we do not spend time debating its validity.

Relatively few purely conceptual papers emphasize new constructs or theories. Perhaps new constructs and theories are more likely to appear in empirical than in purely conceptual papers. However, I fear that our discipline lacks a sufficient emphasis on developing new constructs and theories (see also Stewart and Zinkhan 2006). Empirical papers that emphasize new relationships seem to study "effects" (e.g., relationships between variables). Even if they include moderators that identify contingencies for the effects or mediators that specify the process by which effects are observed, they often stop short of using these observations to build novel theory.

Identifying shortages is important because all types of conceptualizations add value. To the extent that our field emphasizes one type of thinking over another, knowledge in the field may be stunted. Indeed, the eight types of contributions noted in Figure 1 might be characterized as reflecting the process by which knowledge of an entity evolves. Knowledge begins when something new is first identified. Research advances by efforts to delineate it. Through delineation, complexities are realized that, in turn, require differentiation, which ensues from deeper thinking. Clarity from differentiation gives way to agreed-on views that are advocated and seem true. Subsequent thought may give way to a revised perspective, with summarized views on the revised view giving way to integrated perspectives. Refutations of the integrated view give rise to the identification of novel ideas. In this view, the eight conceptual contributions reflect the evolution of conceptual ideas about the entities in Table 1 from their early identification to more complete perspectives on them. Thus, the eight types of conceptual skills capture the development of knowledge and ultimately reflect the engine of scientific progress. As such, attentiveness to the underrepresentation of certain types of conceptualizations and their bases is important.

Developing and Sustaining a Beginner's Mind

Big areas of research begin with the process of identification. Indeed, it might be argued that identification is the most important of the conceptualization types. Yet our field does little to support the beginner's mind that is conducive to identification. In fact, it seems to dampen it. The people who are perhaps most adept at identification are first-year PhD students. Yet, they are immediately "indoctrinated" to learn a prevailing paradigm. Thus, they are trained as "game theorists," "information processing researchers," or "transaction cost analysis researchers" according to their advisor's interests and expertise. Such training may suggest that prevailing views are "right," silencing new ways of thinking. Among more experienced academics, indoctrination creates levels of comfort, which may minimize identification by disinclining the researcher to movement outside

his or her comfort zone. Moreover, instead of developing a beginner's mind, researchers often immerse themselves in the academic literature for sources of inspiration. Turning to the literature is useful, but it can stymie identification by inclining us to understand something in terms of established ideas.

A critical avenue for cultivating a beginner's mind stems from immersion in the phenomenon of interest. Interesting new insights can come from observing managers, consumers, and retailers and from understanding their day-to-day realities. For example, a student doing a dissertation on social media may uncover new ideas from reading blogs, following people on Twitter, and reading posts of reviewed products. Immersion in the phenomenon encourages those with strong conceptual thinking skills to identify what others have not yet discovered. Yet immersion is rarely encouraged, except among scholars who adhere to the consumer culture theory paradigm. We need to support a beginner's mind. Supporting a beginner's mind through immersion can further enhance the impact of marketing scholars on the managerially, socially, and politically significant issues that face consumers and marketers alike. To the extent that we deeply understand the phenomena we study, we may have more credibility with external constituents (e.g., the press, managers, policy makers, students).

Training in Conceptual Thinking Skills

Finally, it strikes me that conceptualization and its attendant thinking skills are not emphasized in doctoral training. Instead, the importance of conceptualization and knowledge of conceptual thinking skills is often tacit, making it possible and even likely that gaps in conceptual thinking skills arise. This is unfortunate because conceptual thinking skills are critical to all scholarly works—even those that blend conceptual ideas and empirical data. It is also unfortunate because literature pertaining to these thinking skills is both extensive and eminently teachable. For example, outside marketing, it is relatively easy to find work that describes skill development related to persuasion and logical thinking skills (e.g., Walton, Reed, and Macagno 2008), induction (Holland et al. 1987), and deduction (Bonevac 2003), among others. We should offer students a language for these conceptual thinking skills and provide guidelines for how such skills might be developed. It is my hope that this article, and the typology it describes, provides a starting point for making these ideas explicit, in turn making contributions a priority for the next generation of marketing scholars.

REFERENCES

Abbott, Andrew (2004), *Methods of Discovery: Heuristics for the Social Sciences*. New York: W.W. Norton.

Alba, Joseph W. and J. Wesley Hutchinson (1987), "Dimensions of Consumer Expertise," *Journal of Consumer Research*, 13 (4), 411–54.

AMA Task Force (1988), "AMA Task Force on the Development of Marketing Thought," *Journal of Marketing*, 52 (October), 1–25.

American Heritage Dictionary of the English Language, 4th ed. (2003), Boston: Houghton Mifflin.

Anderson, Paul F. (1982), "Marketing, Strategic Planning and the Theory of the Firm," *Journal of Marketing*, 46 (Spring), 15–26.

Argyris, Chris and Donald Schon (1974), *Theory in Practice*. San Francisco: Jossey-Bass.

Bagozzi, Richard P. (1975), "Marketing as Exchange," *Journal of Marketing*, 39 (October), 32–39.

Bailey, Kenneth D. (1994), *Typologies and Taxonomies: An Introduction to Classification Techniques*. Thousand Oaks, CA: Sage Publications.

Belk, Russell W. (1988), "Possessions and the Extended Self," *Journal of Consumer Research*, 15 (September), 139–69.

Bettman, James R. (1979), *An Information Processing Theory of Consumer Behavior*. Reading, MA: Addison-Wesley.

——, Mary Frances Luce, and John Payne (1998), "Constructive Consumer Choice Processes," *Journal of Consumer Research*, 25 (December), 187–217.

Bonevac, Daniel (2003), *Deduction: Introductory Symbolic Logic*. Malden, MA: Blackwell.

Calder, Bobby J., Lynn W. Phillips, and Alice M. Tybout (1981), "Designing Research for Application," *Journal of Consumer Research*, 8 (2), 197–207.

Churchill, Gilbert A., Jr. (1979), "A Paradigm for Developing Better Measures of Marketing Constructs," *Journal of Marketing Research*, 16 (February), 64–73.

Cohen, Joel and Charles S. Areni (1991), "Affect and Consumer Behavior," in *Handbook of Consumer Behavior*, Thomas S. Robertson and Harold H. Kassarjian, eds. Englewood Cliffs, NJ: Prentice Hall, 188–240.

Darden, Lindley (1991), *Theory Change in Science: Strategies from Mendelian Genetics*. New York: Oxford University Press.

Davis, Murray S. (1971), "That's Interesting! Towards a Phenomenology of Sociology and a Sociology of Phenomenology" *Philosophy of the Social Sciences*, 1 (2), 309–344.

Day, George S. and David B. Montgomery (1999), "Charting New Directions for Marketing," *Journal of Marketing*, 63 (Special Issue), 3–13.

Dennis, Simon and Walter Kintsch (2007), "Evaluating Theories," in *Critical Thinking in Psychology*, Robert J. Sternberg, Henry L. Roediger III, and Diane F. Halpern, eds. New York: Cambridge University Press, 143–60.

Dickson, Peter Reid (1992), "Toward a General Theory of Competitive Rationality," *Journal of Marketing*, 56 (January), 69–83.

Dixon, Roz (2005), "Integrative Thinking: Building Personal, Working Models of Psychology That Support Problem Solving," *Psychology Learning and Teaching*, 5 (1), 15–22.

Doty, D. Harold and William H. Glick (1994), "Typologies: A Unique Form of Theory Building: Toward Improved Understanding and Modeling," *Academy of Management Review*, 19 (April), 230–51.

Elder, Linda and Richard Paul (2009), *A Glossary of Critical Thinking Terms of Concepts: The Critical Analytic Vocabulary of the English Language*. Dillon Beach, CA: Foundation for Critical Thinking.

Folkes, Valerie S. (1988), "Recent Attribution Research in Consumer Behavior: A Review and New Directions," *Journal of Consumer Research*, 14 (March), 548–65.

Frazier, Gary L. (1983), "Interorganizational Exchange Behavior in Marketing Channels: A Broadened Perspective," *Journal of Marketing*, 47(Winter), 68–78.

Gardner, Howard (2008), *5 Minds for the Future*. Boston: Harvard Business School Press.

Gardner, Meryl Paula (1985), "Mood States and Consumer Behavior: A Critical Review," *Journal of Consumer Research*, 12 (3), 281–300.

Glazer, Rashi (1991), "Marketing in an Information-Intensive Environment: Strategic Implications of Knowledge as an Asset," *Journal of Marketing*, 55 (October), 1–19.

Gula, Robert J. (2007), *Nonsense: Red Herrings, Straw Men and Sacred Cows: How We Abuse Logic in Our Everyday Language*. Mount Jackson, VA: Axios Press.

Halpern, Diane F. (1989), *Thought and Knowledge: An Introduction to Critical Thinking*. Mahwah, NJ: Lawrence Erlbaum Associates.

Hanson, Norwood Russell (1958), *Patterns of Discovery*. Cambridge, UK: Cambridge University Press.

Hoffman, Donna L. and Thomas P. Novak (1996), "Marketing in Hypermedia Computer-Mediated Environments: Conceptual Foundations," *Journal of Marketing*, 60 (July), 50–68.

Holbrook, Morris B. and Elizabeth C. Hirschman (1982), "The Experiential Aspects of Consumption: Consumer Fantasies, Feelings, and Fun," *Journal of Consumer Research*, 9 (2), 132–40.

Holland, John H., Keith J. Holyoak, Richard E. Nisbett, and Paul R. Thagard (1987), *Induction*. Cambridge, MA: MIT Press.

Houston, Michael J. and Michael L. Rothschild (1978), "A Paradigm for Research on Consumer Involvement," working paper, University of Wisconsin–Madison.

Howard, John and Jagdish Sheth (1969), *The Theory of Buyer Behavior*. New York: John Wiley & Sons.

Hunt, Shelby (1992), "Marketing Is…," *Journal of the Academy of Marketing Science*, 20 (4), 301–311.

—— and Robert M. Morgan (1995), "The Comparative Advantage Theory of Competition," *Journal of Marketing*, 59 (April), 1–15.

Jarvis, Cheryl Burke, Scott B. MacKenzie, and Philip M. Podsakoff (2003), "A Critical Review of Construct Indicators and Measurement Model Misspecification in Marketing and Consumer Research," *Journal of Consumer Research*, 30 (2), 199–218.

Kerin, Roger A. (1996), "In Pursuit of an Ideal: The Editorial and Literary History of the Journal of Marketing," *Journal of Marketing*, 60 (January), 1–13.

——, P. Rajan Varadarajan, and Robert A. Peterson (1992), "First-Mover Advantage: A Synthesis, Conceptual Framework, and Research Propositions," *Journal of Marketing*, 56 (October), 33–52.

Kohli, Ajay (2009), "From the Editor," *Journal of Marketing*, 73 (January), 1–2.

Lazarus, Richard B. (1981), "A Cognitivist's Reply to Zajonc on Emotion and Cognition," *American Psychologist*, 36 (February), 222–23.

Leone, Robert P. and Randall L. Schultz (1980), "A Study of Marketing Generalizations," *Journal of Marketing*, 44 (Winter), 10–18.

Li, Rex (1996), *A Theory of Conceptual Intelligence*. Westport, CT: Praeger.

Loken, Barbara (2005), "Consumer Psychology: Categorization, Inferences, Affect and Persuasion," *Annual Review of Psychology*, 57, 453–85.

Lovelock, Christopher H. (1983), "Classifying Services to Gain Strategic Marketing Insights," *Journal of Marketing*, 47 (Summer), 9–20.

MacInnis, Debbie (2004), "Where Have All the Papers Gone?" Association for Consumer Research Newsletter, (Spring), 1–3.

—— and Gustavo E. de Mello (2005), "The Concept of Hope and Its Relevance to Product Evaluation and Choice," *Journal of Marketing*, 69 (January), 1–14.

—— and Valerie S. Folkes (2010), "The Disciplinary Status of Consumer Behavior: A Sociology of Science Perspective on Key Controversies," *Journal of Consumer Research*, 36 (April), 899–914.

——, Christine Moorman, and Bernard J. Jaworski (1991), "Enhancing and Measuring Consumers' Motivation, Opportunity, and Ability to Process Brand Information from Ads," *Journal of Marketing*, 55 (October), 32–53.

MacKenzie, Scott B. (2003), "The Dangers of Poor Construct Conceptualization," *Journal of the Academy of Marketing Science*, 31 (3), 323–26.

——, Richard J. Lutz, and George E. Belch (1986), "The Role of Attitude Toward the Ad as a Mediator of Advertising Effectiveness: A Test of Competing Explanations," *Journal of Marketing Research*, 23 (May), 130–43.

Marzano, Robert J., Debra Pickering, and Jane E. Pollock (2004), *Classroom Instruction That Works: Research-Based Strategies for Increasing Student Achievement*. Alexandria, VA: Association for Supervision and Curriculum Development.

Monroe, Kent (1993), "Editorial," *Journal of Consumer Research*, 20 (December), i–iii.

Moore, Timothy E. (1982) "Subliminal Advertising: What You See Is What You Get," *Journal of Marketing*, 46 (Spring), 38–47.

Morgan, Gareth (2006), *Images of Organizations*. Thousand Oaks, CA: Sage Publications.

Niehoff, Arthur (1998), *On Being a Conceptual Animal*. Bonsall, CA: The Hominid Press.

Novak, Joseph. D. (1998), *Learning, Creating, and Using Knowledge: Concept Maps as Facilitative Tools in Schools and Corporations*. Mahwah, NJ: Lawrence Erlbaum Associates,

Olshavsky, Richard W. and Donald H. Granbois (1979), "Consumer Decision Making-Fact or Fiction?" *Journal of Consumer Research*, 6 (2), 93–100.

Parasuraman, A., Valarie A. Zeithaml, and Leonard L. Berry (1985), "A Conceptual Model of Service Quality and Its Implications for Future Research," *Journal of Marketing*, 49 (Fall), 41–50.

Peter, J. Paul and Jerry C. Olson (1983). "Is Science Marketing?" *Journal of Marketing*, 47 (Fall), 111–25.

Petty, Richard E. and John T. Cacioppo (1986), *Communication and Persuasion: Central and Peripheral Routes to Attitude Change*. New York: Springer-Verlag.

Platt, John R. (1964), "Strong Inference—Certain Systematic Methods of Scientific Thinking May Produce Much More Rapid Progress Than Others," *Science*, (October 16), 347–53.

Rindfleisch, Aric and Jan B. Heide (1997), "Transaction Cost Analysis: Past, Present, and Future Applications," *Journal of Marketing*, 61 (October), 30–54.

Sherry, John (1983), "Gift Giving in Anthropological Perspective," *Journal of Consumer Research*, 10 (September), 157–68.

Sheth, Jagdish N. (1992), "Acrimony in the Ivory Tower: A Retrospective on Consumer Research," *Journal of the Academy of Marketing Science*, 20 (4), 345–53.

Shugan, Steven M. (1980), "The Cost of Thinking," *Journal of Consumer Research*, 7 (2), 99–111.

Srivastava, Rajendra K., Tasadduq A. Shervani, and Liam Fahey (1998), "Market-Based Assets and Shareholder Value: A Framework for Analysis," *Journal of Marketing*, 62 (January), 2–18.

Stern, Louis W. and Torger Reve (1980), "Distribution Channels as Political Economies: A Framework for Comparative Analysis," *Journal of Marketing*, 44 (Summer) 52–64.

Stewart, David W. and George M. Zinkhan (2006), "Enhancing Marketing Theory in Academic Research," *Journal of the Academy of Marketing Science*, 34 (Fall), 477–80.

Szymanski, David M. (1988), "Determinants of Selling Effectiveness: The Importance of Declarative Knowledge to the Personal Selling Concept," *Journal of Marketing*, 52 (January), 64–77.

Teas, R. Kenneth and Kay M. Palan (1997), "The Realms of Scientific Meaning Framework for Constructing Theoretically Meaningful Nominal Definitions of Marketing Concepts," *Journal of Marketing*, 61 (April), 52–67.

Thompson, Craig, William Locander, and Howard R. Pollio (1989), "Putting Consumer Experience Back into Consumer Research: The Philosophy and Method of Existential-Phenomenology," *Journal of Consumer Research*, 16 (2), 133–46.

Van Waterschoot, Walter and Cristophe Van den Bulte (1992), "The 4P Classification of the Marketing Mix Revisited," *Journal of Marketing*, 56 (October), 83–93.

Walton, Douglas (2006), *Fundamentals of Critical Argumentation*. New York: Cambridge University Press.

——, Christopher Reed, and Fabrizio Macagno (2008), *Argumentation Schemes*. New York: Cambridge University Press.

Ward, Scott (1974), "Consumer Socialization," *Journal of Consumer Research*, 1 (September), 1–14.

Webster, Frederick E., Jr. (1992), "The Changing Role of Marketing in the Corporation," *Journal of Marketing*, 56 (October), 1–17.

—— (2005), "A Perspective on the Evolution of Marketing Management," *Journal of Public Policy & Marketing*, 24 (Spring), 121–26.

Wells, William D. (1993), "Discovery Oriented Consumer Research," *Journal of Consumer Research*, 19 (March), 489–504.

Wilkie, William L. and Elizabeth Moore (2003), "Scholarly Research in Marketing: Exploring the Four Eras of Thought Development," *Journal of Public Policy & Marketing*, 22 (Fall), 116–46.

Wright, Peter (1980), "Message-Evoked Thoughts: Persuasion Research Using Thought Verbalizations," *Journal of Consumer Research*, 7 (2), 151–75.

Yadav, Manjit (2010), "The Decline of Conceptual Articles and Implications for Knowledge Development," *Journal of Marketing*, 74 (January), 1–19.

Zajonc, Robert B. (1980), "Feeling and Thinking: Preferences Need No Inferences," *American Psychologist*, 35 (2), 151–75.

—— and Hazel Markus (1982), "Affective and Cognitive Factors in Preferences," *Journal of Consumer Research*, 9 (2), 123–31.

Zaltman, Gerald (1983), "Presidential Address," in *Advances in Consumer Research*, Vol. 10, Richard P. Bagozzi and Alice M. Tybout, eds. Ann Arbor: Association for Consumer Research, 1–5.

—— (2000), "Consumer Researchers: Take a Hike!" *Journal of Consumer Research*, 26 (March), 423–28.

——, Karen LeMasters, and Michael Heffring (1985), *Theory Construction in Marketing: Some Thoughts on Thinking*. New York: John Wiley & Sons.

——, Christian Pinson, and R. Angelmar (1973), *Metatheory in Consumer Research*. New York: Holt, Rinehart & Winston.

8

Publishing marketing strategy papers in scholarly journals

V. Kumar

Introduction

Research forms a core precept of higher learning. In an academic setting, this endeavor is formally recognized as scholarship. Boyer et al. (2015) view scholarship to extend beyond simply engaging in original research to also include bridging theory and practice, integrating ideas from across disciplines, and effective communication of research findings to the knowledge community. In essence, scholarship can infuse vigor and vitality to the academic institution and can help create a proclivity towards knowledge creation. The aura behind the scholarly research is aptly captured by William Bowen, the former president of Princeton University. He offers that scholarly research "reflects our pressing, irrepressible need as human beings to confront the unknown and to seek understanding for its own sake. It is tied inextricably to the freedom to think freshly, to see propositions of every kind in ever-changing light. And it celebrates the special exhilaration that comes from a new idea" (Bowen 1987, p. 269). Such exalted viewpoints of scholarly research propelling the academic community to a higher plane of learning lead us to the natural question. How then, should scholarly research be conducted? Even more so, how should rigorous and relevant scholarly research that has actionable implications be conducted?

I believe the path towards impactful scholarly research (that is, rigorous and relevant research), especially in the area of marketing strategy, firmly rests in well-thought-out ideation – the process of identifying, developing, and nurturing impactful research ideas. As a result, high-quality scholarly research is bound to emerge out of strong and robust ideas that are precisely structured, articulated, and argued. In this regard, I expand on the ideation process, and structure this chapter into two sections. In section 1, I explore the process of ideation that typically involves identifying and developing research ideas, conceptualizing the research, and executing the research. In section 2, I provide examples of studies that can serve as case studies to illustrate the ideation process discussed in section 1. In addition, these case studies showcase the significance of rigor and relevance in marketing research and highlight the critical role of generating actionable insights for practitioners. Throughout the chapter, I also provide relevant examples of marketing strategy studies published in scholarly marketing journals, to aid readers in better understanding the process of ideation.

A brief note on the purpose of this chapter. This chapter is primarily intended for doctoral students and early-career researchers, who are looking for ways to establish a strong research regimen and avoid the common mistakes made when conceptualizing and executing the study. The goal of this chapter is not to present a comprehensive list of steps/actions to publish scholarly research. Rather, more modestly, this chapter aims to highlight some critical aspects related to the development of research ideas and carrying them through to potential publication outlets. The aspects covered here can be considered as "guideposts" and "warning signs" that will be of help to researchers. In this regard, this chapter is designed to provide a balanced approach to developing insightful research ideas. While all attempts have been made to make this chapter as broad-based as possible to inform readers about publishing scholarly research in the area of marketing strategy, areas where further reading and understanding will be helpful have been identified for the benefit of interested readers.

Ideation

The ideation component of scholarly research is comprised of four critical steps – (a) generating ideas, (b) understanding scientific philosophies, (c) conceptualizing the research, and (d) executing the research. The ideation process forms the foundation of scholarly research and enables researchers to demonstrate and home in on their original research contributions. Not surprisingly, this step is also where researchers ought to be spending most of their time. To understand this better, a deeper look into the three steps of ideation is warranted.

Idea generation

Any branch of knowledge relies on the generation of ideas to thrive. Moreover, imagination fuels the process of generating ideas that encourage researchers to explore the unknown (Zaltman 2016). In this regard, creative marketing thought has been conceptualized as imaginative, new-to-the-world, marketing ideas (Levitt 1986). Specifically, imagination is seen as an effective tool for researchers to explore the realm of "aboutness" – or the ability to explain how and/or why a particular effect occurs; and can serve as an effective conduit for developing richer theories that are also broadly applicable (Calder and Tybout 2016). Examples of studies that have adopted an "aboutness" viewpoint include, among others, investigating how customer relationship management (CRM) implementation influences a firm's efficiency and profitability (Krasnikov, Jayachandran, and Kumar 2009); examining how customer data is being captured and analysed by firms, and, how it can be improved upon (Wedel and Kannan 2016); understanding the antecedents of chief marketing officer (CMO) turnover (Nath and Mahajan 2017); and developing a theory to value customer contributions to firms (Kumar 2018).

In addition to "aboutness," I believe imagination can also be effectively used along the lines of "why not-ness." In a why-not approach, an observed occurrence in the marketplace is flipped on its head, to explore the existence or viability of alternate viewpoints. This could also imply questioning the conventional wisdom, and seeking newer insights. Examples of studies that have successfully toed such an approach include whether managing customer loyalty is the same as managing customer profitability (Reinartz and Kumar 2002); can firms make money from product returns (Petersen and Kumar 2010); and whether cross-selling is always good for the firm (Shah and Kumar 2012), among others. By questioning the prevailing wisdom, these studies were able to generate new and novel insights that provided a better understanding of the focal topic. In adopting such an approach, however, researchers must take precautions to stay relevant to the research question(s), as it is easy to lose focus on the research topic.

Researchers have also identified creativity to be a more practical tool compared to the imagination, since creative ideas tend to connote originality and appropriateness, while imagination can, at times, end up being not relevant (Kilgour, Sasser, and Koslow 2013). The importance of generating unique and novel ideas is best understood from the following concern expressed by Reibstein, Day, and Wind (2009, pp. 1–2):

> The prevailing research paradigm in most parts of marketing academia is to begin with a new methodology, dataset, or a behavioral hypothesis and only then occasionally ask where it might be applied. This reduces the odds of addressing a pressing marketing issue. The resultant conclusions are of some relevance to other researchers, but they offer little guidance for marketing decision making.

So then, where does one look for research ideas?

While ideas exist all around us, three critical sources of ideas that can serve as credible starting points are (a) existing research literature, (b) business community, and (c) other disciplines. Table 8.1 provides the major sources of ideas, the ways to incorporate them into research, and some exemplar marketing studies that have adopted such an approach.

Existing research literature forms an important component of our combined knowledge pool. As members of academia (students and faculty), we are constantly exposed to research literature that has offered original findings. Such studies continuously inform us of learnings and insights and spur us to expand the knowledge. The popular phrase by Sir Isaac Newton aptly captures this thought – "If I have seen a little further, it is by standing on the shoulders of Giants." Specifically, existing literature contributes to idea generation by helping us understand the topic (to extend the findings), and close any research gaps.

The call to address real-world challenges through research has been voiced over the years (Reibstein, Day, and Wind 2009; Jaworski 2011). This line of research constitutes providing solutions for observed market needs, or actively collaborating with a firm to solve specific challenges (Kumar et al. 2011; Kumar, Sunder, and Leone 2014). As a result, researchers can develop research ideas that involve observing issues faced by firms and pursuing them to solve the issues.

By integrating and utilizing knowledge from other disciplines – such as psychology, epidemiology, management, statistics, finance, and international business – researchers can uncover potential research ideas that can be developed further. Consider the field of epidemiology, and how it can aid research in marketing. The diffusion of products has been observed to be different across countries and has been explained by the lead-lag effect (Kumar and Krishnan 2002). A typical problem with the introduction of any new brand is to develop a suitable marketing strategy. If a brand is priced lower, then it can be perceived as a cheap brand but may diffuse faster. On the contrary, if the brand is priced higher, then diffusion may be slower, but perception could be a high-quality brand. So, a potential question is "is it a balance between speed of diffusion and positioning" or "Can speed and the desired positioning be obtained through a better understanding of the theories/influence from

Table 8.1   Generating research ideas

Sources of information	Recommendations for generating ideas	Exemplar marketing studies and their study focus
Existing research literature	*Identify* and *close* research gaps by exploring knowledge areas	• Lewis (2006) – examines the relationship between the depth of acquisition discounts and the value of customer assets • Mizik and Jacobson (2009) – develop a new valuation approach that incorporates brand characteristics in valuing branded businesses • Shah, Kumar, and Kim (2014) – examine the role of consumer habits in understanding customer behavior beyond repeat purchases
Business community	*Observe* and *pursue* to solve real-world business challenges	• Kumar et al. (2013) – measure the success of social media efforts at Hokey Pokey • Kumar, Bhagwat, and Zhang (2015) – show that the stronger the first-lifetime relationship with the firm, the more likely a customer is to accept the win-back offer • Kumar and Shah (2011) – develop an Emotion Quotient (EQ) Tool for Prudential to redefine its marketing and sales approach along a proactive (as opposed to responsive) market orientation paradigm
Other disciplines	*Integrate* and *utilize* cross-disciplinary findings	• Fornell, Morgeson, and Hult (2016) – examine the impact of customer satisfaction efforts on stock returns of a firm • Kumar et al. (2018) – develop a "mixture cure–competing risks" model to understand how a reacquired customer relationship evolves and possibly ends again • Morgan, Feng, and Whitler (2018) – understand whether and how international marketing capabilities differ from domestic marketing capabilities

other disciplines?" (Krishnan, Bass, and Kumar 2000). Understanding this process can help businesses to better-predict diffusion rates and better match pricing and distribution strategies with business goals. In this regard, epidemiology can offer insights and potential research ideas. Similarly, insights from other disciplines can serve as valuable starting points in identifying research ideas. However, one must be careful to ensure that the research thrives based on the original idea(s) of the researcher, and does not depend solely on the insights from other disciplines.

Understanding the scientific philosophies
As marketing researchers, our thought cycles are naturally tuned towards identifying interesting research questions, formalizing conceptual/empirical/analytical investigations into the issues, and advancing insights based on the study. In this cycle of thought, we may, at times, fail to recognize that any impactful research output is always hoisted upon a scientific philosophy that informs about the ontological (relating to the nature of a phenomenon) and epistemological (relating to the methods, validity, and scope of a particular branch of knowledge) issues. An understanding of these scientific philosophies is essential to understanding a phenomenon better, and in a manner that can best contribute to the existing knowledge base.

It should be noted that many of us, even unbeknownst to us, adopt the scientific philosophies practiced by our teachers and mentors. In such a case, it is imperative that we create an opportunity to review the alternate scientific philosophies that may lead us towards more insightful findings. In effect, it is important to recognize that the scientific philosophy we use is a matter of choice and not inheritance. To highlight the importance of scientific philosophies, Table 8.2 provides a classification of popular scientific philosophies adopted in research.

The objective of this section and Table 8.2 is to provide a flavor of the various scientific philosophies, and therefore not an attempt at providing a comprehensive review of the philosophies. For a comprehensive review, the following marketing studies can serve as excellent starting points – Deshpande (1983), Anderson (1983), Peter and Olson (1983), Arndt (1985), and Hunt (2003). By recognizing such diverse approaches, researchers can create more avenues for the interchange of ideas, models, and critical thinking.

Further, it is worth noting that while the current practice of many marketing doctoral programs not focusing on the various philosophies of science needs to be revisited, the practice itself should not be seen as diminishing the importance of scientific philosophies. On the contrary, scientific philosophies provide us with the necessary tools and frameworks to study various phenomena and enables us to evaluate alternative ways of understanding the issues surrounding us. More importantly, they help us in conceptualizing the research in a better manner.

Conceptualizing research in marketing strategy
Equipped with the information on the scientific philosophies, in this step, the researcher looks to switch from a phase of idea generation/imaginative thoughts to conceptual thinking. MacInnis (2011) defines conceptual thinking as the process of understanding a situation or problem abstractly by identifying patterns or connections and key underlying properties. As a result, the idea seed is shaped to consist of a

Table 8.2   Classification of scientific philosophies

Philosophy	Characterization	Implications	Major Criticisms
Logical Positivism	• Claims that are based on empirical observations alone are considered important and meaningful.	• No room for logical justifications.	• Never possible to arrive at a single theory.
Logical Empiricism	• Science begins with real-world observations, following which an a priori model is hypothesized and subjected to empirical tests, which then provides tentative support for the model.	• The existence of multiple confirming instances is critical in establishing the science.	• Suffers from the problem of induction. • Relies heavily on observations, and therefore subject to measurement errors and observation bias.
Relativism	• Truth is a subjective evaluation that is context-dependent and theory-informed.	• No single method or approach to science. • Recognizes the possibility of an external world that is independent of the researcher.	• The lack of distinction between truth and belief is untenable.
Humanism	• Advocates participation of the researcher in the research investigation.	• Aims to develop idiographic knowledge. • Researcher and phenomenon are mutually interactive.	• Participatory nature of the researcher gives rise to legal and moral research issues.
Realism	• The real world exists independently of our attempts to know it, and the knowledge about that world is determined by how the world is.	• Accepts existence of unobservables. • Theories capture such unobservables as they exist in the real world.	• The notion of mind-independent existence is considered to be obscure and/or incoherent.
Critical Realism	• Rejects the existence of a priori principles that explain reality.	• Advances in empirical investigations without generalizing the outcomes, because the reality is made of several overlying structures.	• Assumes that there is a reality, but it is usually difficult to grasp. Therefore, the reality is always surmised.

definite form, relationships, and linkages that can explain the core idea. This step allows the researcher to think, in abstract terms, about how the initial idea(s) can be elucidated. Apart from giving a structure to the research idea, this step can also help generate a road-map to execute the research. It is important to note that this step is important for all types of studies – conceptual, analytical, or empirical. In other words, this step forms the core of the research and has the potential to help further knowledge creation significantly. Several marketing studies provide an exposition on conceptualizing studies and carrying it forward towards publishing impactful manuscripts that can be applied to all areas of marketing (MacInnis 2011; Yadav 2010; Summers 2001; Stewart and Zinkhan 2006). Further, with specific reference to marketing strategy, several studies serve as exemplars in how to conceptualize and execute research studies (Gupta, Pansari, and Kumar 2018; Kumar 2014; Kumar 2010; Wind and Robertson 1983; Kumar, Pozza, and Ganesh 2013). The section to follow presents a few vital aspects in conceptualizing an impactful research study, with specific reference to marketing strategy.

Choice of research topic in marketing strategy   While the idea generation step discussed earlier would greatly determine the topic of research, the choice of the topic concerning timeliness and relevance is critical to the study's ultimate impact. The selection of a timely topic aids the researcher in at least three distinct ways. First, it establishes an instant connection to the topic of study. Such a ready connect primes the knowledge seekers for the study insights, thereby creating a receptive audience for the study. This especially plays out well after the study has been published. Second, a timely topic can also place the study front-and-center of the academic discourse, thereby generating a healthy exchange of ideas. Such an exchange would also add immensely to the knowledge base of the topic of study.

Finally, a timely and relevant topic readily lends itself for immediate investigation and/or implementation, as it would likely draw the attention of the relevant audience. The periodic hosting of thought leadership conferences relates towards this aspect. For instance, consider the topic of customer engagement (CE). In 2009, a Thought Leadership Conference on "Managing the Interface between Firms and Customers" was held in Germany where CE was the theme of the conference, owing to the prevailing popularity of the topic at that time. This turned out to be a significant event in the academic discussion on CE, which also led to the subsequent special issue on CE in the *Journal of Service Research* in August 2010 (Verhoef, Reinartz, and Krafft 2010). Following this event, several studies on CE continue to be published that has immensely enriched this field of inquisition (Brodie et al. 2011; Pansari and Kumar 2017; Kumar et al. 2019; Hollebeek, Srivastava, and Chen 2019; Kumar and Pansari 2016), including another special issue on CE titled "Understanding and Managing Customer Engagement Using Customer Relationship Management" in the *Journal of the Academy of Marketing Science* in May 2017 (Venkatesan 2017).

Definitions and explananda   In conceptualizing any research, clarity on the meaning and usage of the terms used in the study is of vital importance. Specifically, researchers have to be clear on the following four levels of abstraction, at the very least – concepts, constructs, variables, and measures.

A concept is defined as a linguistic operation that establishes a relationship between a focal term and one or more terms (Bagozzi 1984). Examples of concepts formalized in the marketing literature include customer, relationship, and engagement that have been defined from various perspectives. Bagozzi (1984) also offers that constructs can be defined based on (a) their attributes, characteristics, or properties, (b) the relationships among the various elements, and (c) the intrinsic nature of the concept. For instance, Varadarajan (2010) proposes the foundational premises of marketing strategy that serves as an example of conceptualization in this area.

A construct is defined as a conceptual term used to describe a phenomenon of theoretical interest (Edwards and Bagozzi 2000). However, constructs are subject to interpretation based on the study context, not always objective, and not always observed directly. As a result, the precise understanding of a construct is best understood through the variable(s) that impact/explain the phenomenon. For instance, in the area of marketing strategy, employee engagement (the construct) has been understood in light of the attitudes and behaviors of employees towards the firm (the variables). Although each of the attitudes and behaviors of the employees can, in turn, be considered as separate constructs, at a more abstract level, employee engagement can be thought of as a multidimensional construct (Kumar and Pansari 2014).

A variable, as the name suggests, is something that changes in value over time. It is this variance that is of importance to researchers, often in diagnosing a research phenomenon. Continuing with the earlier example of employee engagement, while the variables capture the values reflected by the constructs (for example, the employee commitment variable captures part of the value in the employee engagement construct), the scales capture the variance in the variables that is informative in understanding the constructs. That is, to measure employee's commitment, Kumar and Pansari (2014) use scales that include employees' level of knowledge of the brand, their commitment in delivering the brand promise to the customers, and how much the firm means to them.

A measure is an observed score of a construct (Edwards and Bagozzi 2000). In most cases, it is a numerical representation of what is being studied. Since the numbers convey meaning about the construct being measured, researchers must have a rule for assigning the numbers that accurately describes the observation. Examples of measures include satisfaction scores (for example, numbered scores) and performance ratings (for example, letter grades). It is important to note that measures are not the same as the instrument(s) used to collect the measures.

Whereas multiple classifications of terms in varying levels of abstraction have been proposed (Bacharach 1989; Kaplan 1964), researchers are advised to adopt the classification type that can distinctly and clearly lay out the subject matter in the best possible manner. This is because such a clear understanding has important potential implications for further problem identification and subsequent theory development.

Defining the research problem   As the adage goes, "Well begun, is half done," a study enjoys a favorable disposition when the problem statement is clearly defined. Van de Ven (2007) defines the research problem as any problematic situation, phenomenon, issue, or topic that is chosen as the subject of an investigation (p. 73).

Further, he identifies that the challenges involved in stating the research problem revolve around (a) identifying which audience group(s) are going to benefit from the study, (b) avoiding complexities in problem-wording, (c) motivating the study that accurately reflects the reality, and (d) leading to the development of a theory that extends beyond simply understanding/answering the immediate problems.

Kumar (2018) serves as a precise example to illustrate the importance of problem definition. Specifically, the study explored the concept of customer value that is rooted in the distinctions between valuing investor assets and valuing customer assets (through an evaluation of economic and financial theories). Further, this study proposed a customer valuation theory that conceptualized the generation of value from customers to firms. In addition to proposing a theory, this study also advanced strategies that firms can implement to measure, manage, and maximize customer contributions. In doing so, this study effectively handled the challenges highlighted by Van de Ven (2007), as mentioned in the earlier paragraph. That is, this study (a) clearly identified the firms as the key beneficiaries of the study, (b) was simply worded to frame the research question firmly around customer value measurement and management, (c) was motivated with inter-disciplinary theories that dealt with similar valuation approaches, and (d) advanced a theory that went beyond just a valuation approach to also include implementable strategies that were demonstrated to yield multi-million dollar gains for implementing firms.

Establishing the study context   The precision in identifying the study context is of critical importance. The critical nature of the study context is best understood by the link it serves between abstract ideas and the investigation-driven outcomes. In this regard, Alford (1998) provides that "Abstract concepts never perfectly fit the complexity of reality. Evidence never contains its own explanation" (p. 29). Further, contexts provide researchers the right environment to develop and test theories. Arnould, Price, and Moisio (2006) offer that contexts lend veracity and texture to theories, because contexts have the potential to engage audiences, foster discovery, and facilitate discussion.

However, if one were not cautious, contexts can work against researchers. For instance, in a qualitative research setting, McCracken (1988) offers that an inability of researchers to distance themselves from respondents' lives can hinder the results of the study. In such a case, the researcher is said to be engulfed within the context. Alternatively, readers too may get engulfed by the study context. This occurs when the readers are not able to distinguish the substantive context from the theoretical context, and thereby dismiss a study for its lack of generalizability. In this regard, Mook (1983) contends that external validity need not always be the goal of the researcher. If the goal of the researcher is to understand the boundary conditions of theories, then it is imperative that the researcher carefully elucidate the context in a manner that sets up the right context for the readers.

Scope for theory development in marketing strategy   Marketing strategy research studies often traverse the familiar route of advancing research propositions, testing them, and advancing empirical generalizations. However, the increasing intensity of such manner of research has been observed to lead to possible narrow empirical generalizations (Bass and Wind 1995), and less useful insights to managers (Day and Montgomery 1999). In this regard, MacInnis (2011) observes that conceptualizing with theory development in mind helps in (a) explaining better how the world works, (b) eliciting better predictions about outcomes, (c) clarifying conditions that will not produce desired outcomes, and (d) creating new knowledge.

So, what constitutes a good theory? The process of theory construction has been covered in detail in the organizational studies literature (Kaplan 1964; Dubin 1978; Weick 1989; Weick 1995). Whetten (1989) contends that a good theory not only describes the who, what, and where of a phenomenon being studied, but also explains the how, when, and why it occurs. Alternatively, Sutton and Staw (1995) identify elements such as (a) references to theory, (b) data used in the study, (c) lists of variables or constructs, (d) visual representations such as figures and charts, and (e) hypotheses contained in a study alone do not represent/contribute towards theoretical development; and (f) contend that theory relates to the "underlying processes so as to understand the systematic reasons for a particular occurrence or nonoccurrence" (p. 378). In this regard, Bacharach (1989) offers that a theory is a "system of constructs and variables in which the constructs are related to each other by propositions and the variables are related to each other by hypotheses" (p. 498).

In marketing, there is significant debate on the definition of theory (Burton 2005), and on the role and relevance of theory to practitioners (Cornelissen 2002). Hunt (1983) observed that to develop general theories, marketing literature has largely adopted two structural forms – a hierarchical form that is based on basic principles or axioms (for example, Bagozzi 1975), and a collection of sub-theories form that is a systematic integration of several smaller theories (for example, Bartels 1968). Despite these differences, Shaw (2014) concludes that there is significant agreement in the literature regarding the elements (for example, components, axioms, sub-theories) required to build a general theory of marketing, and calls for renewed efforts towards the construction of such a general theory. As mentioned earlier, Kumar (2018) clearly demonstrates that theory development is possible in the marketing strategy domain. Therefore, any attempts by marketing researchers towards theory construction would further the ongoing scientific progress made in this discipline.

Executing the research

As the research progresses from the conceptualization stage to the execution stage, the distinction regarding the specificity of research actions between the two stages somewhat blurs. The reason for this being, the researcher is also in a position to actively consider some facets of the research execution alongside the conceptualization. This is, of course, *not to* say that researchers must or ought to think of research execution in tandem with the research development stage. This implies that some aspects, as described in this section, lend themselves naturally also to be thought of during the conceptualization stage. However, there are a few distinguishing elements in executing research that warrants attention.

Data needs   Data (that is, an aggregation of observations) relating to the phenomenon under inquiry is a critical component in solving a particular research problem. The sources, types, and uses of data, along with other data-related issues, in marketing research have been widely covered in scholarly articles (Leeflang and Wittink 2000; Lilien and Rangaswamy 2000; Wedel, Kamakura, and Böckenholt 2000) and marketing textbooks (Kumar et al. 2019; Zikmund et al. 2013). However, two aspects are specifically noteworthy.

First, data and problem statement are interrelated. In this regard, Hanson (1965) notes that conducting research inquiry and collecting data about it are not independent, but are interactive and interwoven. As a result, the act of having a precise problem statement may not always lead to clarity and success in data collection. For instance, managers often identify problems in their firms based on deviations from the normal trend. In such cases, an accurate understanding and measurement of the "normal" are critical. Additionally, in the current environment of open marketing (Day 2011) and network organizations (Achrol and Kotler 1999), "normal" is likely to depend on many other things happening in the firm. In such cases, the identification of the problem, and therefore the collection of data, may constitute an iterative process, along with the presence of certain assumptions. In the context of marketing strategy, this corresponds to not just collecting data about the focal variables, but to also adopting data capture technologies that are aligned with the incentive structure of the firm (Petersen et al. 2009).

Second, ascertaining the unit of analysis is critical. Examples of a unit of analysis in marketing include at the individual-level (for example, customers, employees), segment-level (for example, customers, employees), firm-level, brand-level, and market-level. While the topic of study can provide a ready indicator for the unit of analysis (for example, individual- or segment-level for customer profitability studies, firm-level for firm value and stock returns studies and brand-level for brand awareness studies), the networked nature of firms may not always permit this. That is, in some cases (for example, studies on country culture, product quality) researchers may not be able to observe the focal variables directly, and therefore may have to rely on accepted policies or indicators (for example, Hofstede's index for country cultures, and six-sigma ratings for product quality) as data indicators. Additionally, the unit of observation may be different from the unit of analysis. As a result, researchers will have to exercise caution in making conclusions in such situations. For instance, the finding that, on average, a customer buying four products from a firm cannot be inferred to apply to all customers of the firm. Similarly, a low rating on industry-wide satisfaction scores (for example, based on the American Customer Satisfaction Index) cannot be inferred to apply to all firms within the industry.

Methodological skills   The extent of a researcher's toolkit significantly determines the ability to successfully execute a research study. Scholars have identified several desired skillsets for researchers in the literature. For instance, guidance on case studies (Bonoma 1985), observational methods (Grove and Fisk 1992), qualitative methods (Belk 2007), survey research methods and how to incorporate them (Kumar et al. 2019), causal models (Hulland, Chow, and Lam 1996), and experimental designs (Kuhfeld, Tobias, and Garrett 1994), among others have been presented to assist marketing researchers in conducting impactful studies. A balanced and well-rounded development of the methodological skills would thus bode well for the long-term progression of early career researchers.

In updating the methodological skills, researchers do not have to do it alone but instead can seek the help and assistance of the research community. In this regard, conducting research workshops and/or presenting the initial research at various conferences and symposia would secure valuable feedback for refining various aspects of the study, and particularly the data analysis section. This is because, by presenting the early findings to a diverse audience, the feedback will highlight the potential applications and implications of the study, along with any missed opportunities that the researcher might have overlooked. When the researcher compiles all the feedback, the study prospects widen. However, in inviting feedback, researchers must also look out for potential viewpoints that may be a distraction or a digression from the original line of inquiry.

Hypothesis development   A critical component of study execution is the development of research hypotheses. A hypothesis is a formal statement that explains a possible outcome regarding a particular relationship/phenomenon. Alternatively, it can be seen as a likely conclusion in light of a specific line of argument. The hypothesis also represents the claim or answer that is being proposed to the topic of inquiry. In this regard, statements that form the premises of the argument are first presented, and from therein, a hypothesis is formulated. Finally, the hypothesis is justified when it is demonstrated that it is the logical conclusion of a valid argument.

Typically, effective hypotheses have two distinct features – specificity, and discrimination (Van de Ven 2007). For example, consider the following claim: Market development leads to superior financial performance. This claim is too general and is not very informative. A more specific claim would be: In markets consisting of unbranded competition for products and services, market development leads to superior financial performance. While the new claim is specific, it is not discriminating against the alternatives and other key conditions. Now, consider this: In markets consisting of unbranded competition for products and services, market development delivers better financial performance than market orientation (Sheth 2011). By recognizing the alternatives (that is, market orientation), and its subsequent negation, the final version of the claim becomes a discriminating proposition that firmly establishes the conclusion by way of related arguments. In fact, more than the affirmatory outcome, it is the negation of alternatives that lends a hypothesis precision and nuance. For a detailed exposition on hypotheses development, readers are encouraged to refer to Freeley and Steinberg (2014), Giere, Bickle, and Mauldin (2006), and Ramage, Bean, and Johnson (2015).

Ensuring rigor and relevance   A common theme in academic discussions, the choice between rigor and relevance is of scholastic importance. Over the past decades, several scholars have weighed in on the issue of whether to focus on rigor or relevance in research studies, and whether there is a tradeoff between the two (Varadarajan 2003; Shrivastava 1987). There is also a belief among scholars that the leaning towards rigor by the marketing journals is a cause for this situation (Lehmann, McAlister, and Staelin 2011; Ellison 2002). Overall, the consensus indicates a rigor *and* relevance approach, as opposed to a rigor *vs.* relevance approach (Hunt 2002); with some studies also identifying ways to ensure rigor and relevance in marketing research (Wind 2008; Mentzer 2008). I too, subscribe to this consensus and propose a few steps through which we can achieve rigor and relevance in research.

To ensure rigor in research, identifying the sources of rigor is essential. Rigor in research is not confined to empirical rigor, but also includes conceptual and analytical rigor (Varadarajan 2003; Houston 2016; Kumar 2017). Rigor in studies can be ensured by (a) reviewing the literature in scholarly journals (for example, *Journal of Marketing*, *Journal of Marketing Research*, *Journal of Consumer Research*, and *Marketing Science*); (b) integrating techniques from other disciplines (for example, Economics, Statistics, and Psychology); and (c) interacting with peers in academia. On this note, I make the following appeal to the reviewer community. Often, studies are rejected during the review process citing insufficient rigor (a blanket observation). Instead, when reviewers (a) evaluate whether the article is rigorous in all applicable areas of contribution, and (b) indicate how the authors "can be rigorous," researchers will benefit immensely in improving the study of interest and the findings (Kumar 2016).

One way of ensuring relevance is to make the research more accessible to the practitioner community. In this regard, Kumar (2017) identified that managerially relevant studies typically includes (but is not limited to) (a) solving unique and relevant managerial problems that have received little or no research attention, (b) advancing the theoretical and/or conceptual principles that are also accessible to the practitioner community, and (c) questioning the conventional wisdom and creating new research stream(s). Essentially, when studies comprehensively answer the "What's in it for me?" question (as viewed from the practitioners' perspective), they would have addressed the relevance issue and secured the attention of the practitioner audience. In addition to managerial relevance, Varadarajan (2003) identifies various aspects of relevance that studies can ensure, such as latent relevance, the breadth of relevance, and duration of relevance, among others. In this regard, when preparing the manuscript, researchers would face favorable odds of manuscript acceptance when they establish relevance by pre-emptively answering the "Yeah … So what?" question. Such a line of discussion would ensure that the managerially relevant issues come to the forefront and get sufficient coverage.

Ideation in marketing strategy studies – a case illustration
Until now we reviewed how the four critical steps in the ideation process of a scholarly output – (a) generating ideas, (b) understanding scientific philosophies, (c) conceptualizing the research, and (d) executing the research – can guide researchers in their pursuit of publishing impactful studies. While the above discussion of the ideation process benefitted from perspectives from various disciplines, in this section I will review a comprehensive illustration of how research ideas were generated and executed in a series of recently conducted marketing studies that I was a part of. In doing so, I aim to highlight the critical aspects of the ideation process discussed in the previous section, and how they all come together in the final research output. To present this illustration, I choose the issue of customer reacquisition and customer churn to competition.

Study 1 – regaining lost customers

In 2014, my colleagues and I looked into understanding the issue of customer reacquisition (Kumar, Bhagwat, and Zhang 2015). This was an issue that was high on managerial relevance and warranted critical attention. Every marketing firm, no matter how successful, is inevitably faced with customer churn. Dissatisfied customers will terminate their relationships with a given firm for a variety of reasons. As one marketing executive described the problem:

> In any subscriber industry, businesses are focused on providing the best products and service experiences to retain customers. Despite all efforts, there are always customers who decide to leave. While we always strive to improve retention and customer satisfaction, the reality is that there will always be customers who choose to leave for various reasons....
> (Kumar, Bhagwat, and Zhang 2015, p. 34)

However, there is no reason to assume that some of these customers cannot be reacquired – indeed, strategic win-back initiatives can be undertaken to target those lost customers who defect to competitors. The question, then, is how to devise optimal win-back strategies and successfully implement them?

To identify the best customer win-back strategies, we first hypothesized that companies can leverage the customer data already collected for lost customers, and use this information to make a series of determinations on two critical areas: (a) which lost customers are the most profitable to seek to win back, and (b) how should these customers be targeted for reacquisition? Based on the conceptual framework of hypothesized relationships, data gleaned from the customer's first lifetime (FLT) – such as referrals, complaints, and service recovery – can be assessed in tandem with the reason for defection, and all of this information can be analysed as key predictors of future behaviors. Not only can the probability of reacquisition be gauged according to this information, but the duration of the customer's second lifetime (SLT) can be determined as well.

Following this, a series of studies were conducted with both individual level transaction data and survey data from a U.S.-based telecommunications products and services firm, which tracked the activities of each of the firm's customers for seven years. Using a large-scale randomized field experiment, whereby randomly selected "lost customers" were sent win-back offers, we were able to model the probability of reacquisition, SLT duration, and profitability per month. Support for the hypothesized relationships was generated by the results of this methodology. Further, a simulation study was undertaken to help determine how best to match customers with the right win-back offer.

In empirically demonstrating the relationship between the FLT experiences and reacquisition, this research generated practical implications and, in effect, proposed a baseline foundation for reacquisition strategies. Specifically, the following findings were of vital significance:

- The quality of the first-lifetime experience is closely connected to reacquisition. That is, positive first-lifetime experiences influence the likelihood of lapsed customers returning to the firm. Further, we found that customers that refer the firm to others in their first lifetime are more likely to accept the win-back offer.

- The reason for defection is positively associated with the likelihood of reacquisition. We found that customers that leave due to price-related reasons can be attractive as they are the most willing to accept win-back offers. Although they are not as profitable as customers who left for service-related reasons, they stay longer in their second lifetime and thus are worth pursuing win-back initiatives.
- Customers who defect due to service reasons are the least likely to return to the firm. Specifically, we found that customers who likely left due to dissatisfaction with the service quality were riskier options for win-back since such customers cannot trust that the firm will deliver better service quality the second time around.
- A win-back offer including a price discount and service upgrade is most effective when reacquiring lapsed customers. However, firms should use caution when offering bundled price and service win-back offers. Customers will be inclined to accept such offers but also may defect again and quickly.
- Depending on the type of firm, it can be advantageous to initially focus on reacquisition rather than maximizing customer duration and profitability. In a saturated market where competition is intense, growing the customer base and market share should be most important.

Moreover, the insight that FLT experiences can predict not only the effectiveness and profitability of reacquisition efforts but also the duration of the SLT, yields even more managerial possibilities. For example, the conventional wisdom that customers who defect for price-related reasons are likely to quickly defect a second time was determined to be false – such customers are desirable to court with win-back offers and can prove valuable during their second lifetimes.

Study 2 – investigating customers' repeat churn behavior
While winning back customers may seem rewarding for firms, it is not without concerns. A question that looms large in this aspect among managers is, how to know if the reacquired customers will remain, or leave again. In 2018, my colleagues and I addressed some of the challenges that arise in light of successful customer win-back initiatives (Kumar, Leszkiewicz, and Herbst 2018). For if a firm can reacquire customers and initiate an SLT, it can always lose the same customers a second time. Having made considerable headway on investigating customer reacquisition, SLT, and profitability, the marketing field now requires a serious investigation of repeat customer churn and how SLT churn and FLT churn differ. Such research should seek to address the problem of developing retention strategies unique to the SLT context. In other words, this study sought to expand on the knowledge pool regarding churn behavior, and contribute towards the formation of a holistic SLT management approach so that managers can continually seek insights.

To do so, we began our investigation by conceptualizing two types of SLT customers – cured and uncured. Cured customers may potentially defect, but not for the same reason that they defected from their FLT. In reacquiring these customers, the firm has thoroughly addressed the initial grievance of circumstance that led to the initial breakaway. Uncured customers, however, may still defect for any reason.

With these two "types" of reacquired customers in mind, we sought to address, via an elaborate modeling framework, the when and the why of repeat customer churn, to bolster real-time SLT retention strategies.

From this conceptual standpoint, we used data from a U.S.-based telecommunications provider, consisting of individual-level data on a random sample of 10,000 reacquired customers, who were then tracked throughout four years of their SLT. Working with this dataset, we developed a model of repeat churn behavior which accounts for both cured and uncured customers. Based on a survival analysis framework, our proposed joint model combined a competing risks model – which predicts when and under what circumstances SLT churn will happen – and a mixture cure model. Within the parameters of this modeling approach, the reasons for SLT churn serve as competing risks, while win-back offers act as cures. Specifically, some of the interesting findings from this study include, among others: (a) customers ending their SLT early are more likely to do so again for the same reason, (b) customers bringing more monthly SLT revenue exhibit longer SLT tenures, (c) customers who engage in traditionally-desirable behaviors, like cross-buying and referring, also exhibit longer SLT tenures, (d) customers who file more complaints have shorter SLTs, and (e) increased service recovery efforts have a positive association with the duration of customers' SLT. This framework, by drawing upon literature and managerial inputs, aptly accounts for many of the unique complexities of SLT churn, which differs from FLT churn regarding reason and time dependence.

Managers can use these findings to design proactive retention strategies for the SLT, based on the relationship between customer-specific behaviors and marketing activities with the SLT duration and repeat churn behavior. Using current data allows firms to intervene at the right time during the SLT when customers are most at risk of churning again. Based on these findings, managers should send marketing communications through various media outlets to extend customers' SLT. Initially, such SLT communications should emphasize improvements made (with regard to FLT churn reasons); and later expand to a holistic retention strategy. Managers should incorporate the cure predictors enabling the firm to leverage its knowledge about customers' FLT and identify which reacquired customers have a high potential of becoming long-term customers. The joint model developed for this study serves as a managerially useful tool that tracks which reacquired customers are at risk of churning again, when, and why. By segmenting the reacquired customer base according to a cured versus uncured framework, and using this segmentation to identify potential long-term customers, managers can better target marketing communications to extend these customers' SLT.

Study 3 – competitive intelligence in combating customer churn
Assuming that a firm can reasonably predict which customers will defect, which customers it should seek to win back, and which of those reacquired customers are prone to repeat churn, there is still the ineluctable fact that there are some customers who, despite the firm's best efforts, will defect a second time. A new question then emerges: which customers are defecting to which competitor? The answer to this question can bolster a firm's SLT retention strategies even further, and yet it requires a substantial quotient of competitive intelligence to solve. While competitive

intelligence (CI) has been routinely identified in the marketing literature as a key prerequisite of enhanced organizational outcomes, there has been no systematic approach for generating such intelligence. Additionally, competitive information obtained from external databases or industry reports is often inaccurate, outdated, and inadequate for strategic decision making as firms are typically very secretive about their operations (Gelb et al. 1991; Xu and Kaye 2007).

In our ongoing research, we invoke the goal programming literature to outline a methodological approach to the real-time generation of competitive intelligence (Kumar et al. forthcoming). This requires the development of a market-sensing matrix, which includes products, firms, geographic markets, and time as its four dimensions. This matrix-balancing approach enables firms to (a) synthesize information from multiple (and often conflicting) sources on products, competitors, and markets by prioritizing information based on the level of uncertainty, and (b) generate intelligence and real-time insights by continuously incorporating up-to-date information about the marketplace.

To do so, we situate the problem in the context of a multiproduct offering at a Fortune 500 company. After identifying the two competitors of the focal firm, and the three sources of information on which CI is founded – internal firm data, survey data, and market data – we proceed to transpose relevant product, firm, and market values to the market-sensing cube. Now, while the filling in of gaps and discrepancies in the cube resembles a traditional matrix-balancing problem, important differences emerge as well, regarding data from different sources of varying importance. This results in the need for a weighted integer goal programming (GP) method.

This study holds significant substantive and methodological contributions. First, this study extends the competitive intelligence literature by developing an approach that enables firms to generate complete market intelligence on a real-time basis. Despite the academic and managerial importance of generating competitive intelligence to inform strategic actions, scholars have provided little practical guidance on how to generate the competitive intelligence in a real-world scenario using a simple and robust tool. Second, this study offers a methodological contribution to the matrix balancing literature in which the cell values of a matrix are adjusted to satisfy the given set of linear restrictions. Firms often face such a discrepancy in real-world scenarios because they seek information from multiple sources and these sources gather or estimate competitive information independently following their approaches. The proposed tool based on goal programming (TBGP) in this study can overcome this limitation of the mathematical programming method. Using this approach, managers can (a) develop optimal product mix offerings, (b) efficiently allocate the marketing budget, and (c) better assess the impact of marketing decisions.

The theoretical implications of this study are five-fold. First, this study establishes that firms need real-time CI at the individual product-market level for efficient resource allocation. Second, this study establishes that firms can gather CI at the product-firm-market level with acceptable accuracy promptly using the firm's internal and various external sources of information. Third, this study highlights the importance of incorporating multiple sources of information to leverage managerial insights and historical information on generating effective strategies. Fourth, this study offers the TBGP which is capable of accommodating primary and secondary data gathered from disparate and independent sources and provides a reliable solution despite having conflicting information. Finally, the proposed methodology also allows for the periodic refreshing of the cell-level information in the matrix by incorporating lagged effects and generating real-time CI.

In reviewing the three studies discussed above, it becomes clear that well-conceived ideas that are evolved in conjunction with theoretical and practical underpinnings do have the potential to develop into viable research studies. When the ideas are put through the conceptualization stage, clear enunciations of concepts, refinements to the topic of inquiry, precise identification of study scope, and potential for theory development have to be convincingly delineated. As the study moves to the execution stage, data, methodology, and data analysis needs have to be addressed to elicit meaningful results. The studies mentioned above went through this process judiciously. As a result, these studies were able to generate relevant insights through a rigorous approach that were not only meaningful but also actionable.

Concluding thoughts

In this chapter, I have attempted to highlight the vital role of ideation in marketing strategy research through the lens of the major stages of a research study – idea generation, understanding the scientific philosophies, conceptualizing the research, and executing the research. Such a viewpoint, in my opinion, provides not only a good vantage point to understand the role and power of ideas, but also to see it in comparison with the final knowledge outcome it aspires to. While these stages are essential to the maturation of an idea to its ultimate fruition, in conclusion, I would like to highlight two forces that serve as credible undercurrents – the research community, and research collaborations – that should always be acknowledged.

The research community is a vital source of inspiration, guidance, and validation that is available to all scholars. As mentioned earlier, research workshops, symposiums, and conferences are great avenues for researchers to reach out to the academic community. At every stage of the study, researchers would benefit by presenting their ideas and research approach and receiving critical feedback. Further, seeking input and guidance from all members of the research community (senior faculty, junior faculty, mentors, and doctoral students) provides researchers with a wide range of suggestions that can help further refine the study.

Research collaborations with academic colleagues and practitioners are an important part of generating scholarly output. A meeting of similar, or even diverse, minds can spur creativity and imagination that can further lead to novel studies. When identifying potential research collaborators, it is important to recognize that not all collaborations are alike. For instance, when working with academic colleagues, the interests of the researchers are likely to be aimed towards understanding the problem domain and explaining a phenomenon. However, research collaborators may differ on the various elements of the study (for example, focus of the inquiry, research approach, research methodology), and negotiating the study approach up front is critical in avoiding an unpleasant working relationship.

When working with practitioners, the interests of the academic researcher and the practitioner may not align from an early stage. For instance, the practitioner may be more interested in identifying a specific answer to the problem, while the academic researcher may be more interested in the general class of phenomena of which the particular problem is a part of. In such cases, an open and upfront conversation about the progression of the study is essential to iron out any possible discontent among the research team. One way of resolving the opposing focus of the collaborators is when the academic researcher agrees to serve as a consultant to solve the practitioner's problem in exchange for data and information needed to pursue their independent research agenda. Regardless of how the negotiation materializes, it is important in such relationships for parties to realize that their differences are complementary in reaching a goal; and that goal is to understand a particular occurrence that is too big or complex for any one party to investigate alone (Van de Ven 2007). Such a realization early on would lead to an inclusive relationship where the focus would be on the said problem, and not on resolving intellectual disagreements along the way.

Despite being informative and rewarding, idea generation and subsequent study development do have an important side effect – the generation of knowledge waste. Not all early ideas are interesting, viable, executable, or insightful. This becomes evident not only in the idea generation stage but also throughout the life of the study process. Further, differences in research focus/approach among collaborators may also cause some ideas to be shelved. Essentially, learning involves waste, and it is unavoidable. However, the waste is not permanent, but only temporary. When all the ideas are systematically cataloged, it becomes a ready-reference and knowledge pool for the researcher when they work on their future projects. Also important to catalog are the false starts and the dead ends, as they too can be instructive in avoiding such mistakes in the future. In essence, learning and knowledge accumulation is the fuel source for generating ideas and impactful studies, and the renewable nature of this fuel makes it a valuable asset in any researcher's toolkit.

Throughout this chapter, I have discussed the idea generation process to develop impactful research studies in the domain of marketing strategy that balances scholarship in general, and in particular with reference to marketing. I hope this chapter directs marketing scholars' attention towards the importance and role of idea generation in producing important insights. It is also my hope that this chapter provides a starting point for the generation of a treasure chest of marketing strategy ideas that can continue to power the next generation of marketing strategy scholars.

References

Achrol, Ravi S. and Philip Kotler (1999), "Marketing in the Network Economy," *Journal of Marketing*, 63, 146–63.

Alford, Robert R. (1998), *The Craft Of Inquiry: Theories, Methods, Evidence*. New York: Oxford University Press.

Anderson, Paul F. (1983), "Marketing, scientific progress, and scientific method," *Journal of Marketing*, 47 (4), 18–31.

Arndt, Johan (1985), "On making marketing science more scientific: role of orientations, paradigms, metaphors, and puzzle solving," *Journal of Marketing*, 49 (3), 11–23.

Arnould, Eric J., Linda Price, and Risto Moisio (2006), "Making contexts matter: Selecting research contexts for theoretical insights," in *Handbook of Qualitative Research Methods in Marketing*, Russell W. Belk, ed. Cheltenham, UK and Northampton, MA, USA: Edward Elgar Publishing, pp. 106–25.

Bacharach, Samuel B. (1989), "Organizational theories: Some criteria for evaluation," *Academy of Management Review*, 14 (4), 496–515.

Bagozzi, Richard P. (1975), "Marketing as exchange," *Journal of Marketing*, 39 (4), 32–9.

Bagozzi, Richard P. (1984), "A prospectus for theory construction in marketing," *Journal of Marketing*, 48 (1), 11–29.

Bartels, Robert (1968), "The general theory of marketing," *Journal of Marketing*, 32 (1), 29–33.

Bass, Frank M. and Jerry Wind (1995), "Introduction to the special issue: empirical generalizations in marketing," *Marketing Science*, 14 (3, Supplement), G1–G5.

Belk, Russell W. (2007), *Handbook of Qualitative Research Methods in Marketing*. Cheltenham, UK and Northampton, MA, USA: Edward Elgar Publishing.

Bonoma, Thomas V. (1985), "Case research in marketing: opportunities, problems, and a process," *Journal of Marketing Research*, 22 (2), 199–208.

Bowen, William G. (1987), *Ever the Teacher: William G. Bowen's Writings as President of Princeton*. Princeton, NJ: Princeton University Press.

Boyer, Ernest L., Drew Moser, Todd C. Ream, and John M. Braxton (2015), *Scholarship Reconsidered: Priorities of the Professoriate* (2nd edn). New York: John Wiley & Sons.

Brodie, Roderick J., Linda D. Hollebeek, Biljana Juric, and Ana Ilic (2011), "Customer engagement: Conceptual domain, fundamental propositions, and implications for research," *Journal of Service Research*, 14 (3), 252–71.

Burton, Dawn (2005), "Marketing theory matters," *British Journal of Management*, 16 (1), 5–18.

Calder, Bobby J. and Alice M. Tybout (2016), "What makes a good theory practical?," *AMS Review*, 6 (3), 116–24.

Cornelissen, Joep (2002), "Academic and practitioner theories of marketing," *Marketing Theory*, 2 (1), 133–43.

Day, George S. (2011), "Closing the marketing capabilities gap," *Journal of Marketing*, 75 (4), 183–95.

Day, George S. and David B. Montgomery (1999), "Charting new directions for marketing," *Journal of Marketing*, 63 (4), 3–13.

Deshpande, Rohit (1983), "'Paradigms lost': on theory and method in research in marketing," *Journal of Marketing*, 47 (4), 101–10.

Dubin, Robert (1978), *Theory Building* (2nd edn). New York: Free Press.

Edwards, Jeffrey R. and Richard P. Bagozzi (2000), "On the nature and direction of relationships between constructs and measures," *Psychological Methods*, 5 (2), 155–74.

Ellison, Glenn (2002), "Evolving standards for academic publishing: A q-r theory," *Journal of Political Economy*, 110 (5), 994–1034.

Fornell, Claes, Forrest V. Morgeson III, and G. Tomas M. Hult (2016), "Stock returns on customer satisfaction do beat the market: Gauging the Effect of a marketing intangible," *Journal of Marketing*, 80 (5), 92–107.

Freeley, Austin J. and David L. Steinberg (2014), *Argumentation and Debate* (13th edn). Belmont, CA: Cengage Learning.

Gelb, Betsy D., Mary Jane Saxton, George M. Zinkhan, and Nancy D. Albers (1991), "Competitive intelligence: Insights from executives," *Business Horizons*, 34 (1), 43–8.

Giere, Ronald N., John Bickle, and Robert F. Mauldin (2006), *Understanding Scientific Reasoning* (5th edn). Belmont, CA: Cengage Learning.

Grove, Stephen J. and Raymond P. Fisk (1992), "Observational data collection methods for services marketing: an overview," *Journal of the Academy of Marketing Science*, 20 (3), 217–24.

Gupta, Shaphali, Anita Pansari, and V. Kumar (2018), "Global customer engagement," *Journal of International Marketing*, 26 (1), 4–29.

Hanson, Norwood Russell (1965), *Patterns of Discovery: An Inquiry into the Conceptual Foundations of Science*. Cambridge, UK: Cambridge University Press.

Hollebeek, Linda D., Rajendra K Srivastava, and Tom Chen (2019), "S-D logic-informed customer engagement: Integrative framework, revised fundamental propositions, and application to CRM," *Journal of the Academy of Marketing Science*, 47 (1), 161–85.

Houston, Mark B. (2016), "Is 'strategy' a dirty word?," *Journal of the Academy of Marketing Science*, 44 (5), 557–61.

Hulland, John, Yiu Ho Chow, and Shunyin Lam (1996), "Use of causal models in marketing research: A review," *International Journal of Research in Marketing*, 13 (2), 181–97.

Hunt, Shelby D. (1983), "General theories and the fundamental explananda of marketing," *The Journal of Marketing*, 47 (4), 9–17.

Hunt, Shelby D. (2002), *Foundations of Marketing Theory: Toward a General Theory of Marketing*. Armonk, NY: M.E. Sharpe.

Hunt, Shelby D. (2003), *Controversy in Marketing Theory: For Reason, Realism, Truth and Objectivity*. Armonk, NY: M.E. Sharpe.

Jaworski, Bernard J. (2011), "On managerial relevance," *Journal of Marketing*, 75 (4), 211–24.

Kaplan, Abraham (1964), *The Conduct of Inquiry: Methodology for Behavioural Science*. New York: Routledge.

Kilgour, Mark, Sheila Sasser, and Scott Koslow (2013), "Creativity awards: Great expectations?,"

Creativity Research Journal, 25 (2), 163–71.

Krasnikov, Alexander, Satish Jayachandran, and V. Kumar (2009), "The impact of customer relationship management implementation on cost and profit efficiencies: evidence from the US commercial banking industry," *Journal of Marketing*, 73 (6), 61–76.

Krishnan, Trichy V., Frank M. Bass, and V. Kumar (2000), "Impact of a late entrant on the diffusion of a new product/service," *Journal of Marketing Research*, 37 (2), 269–78.

Kuhfeld, Warren F., Randall D. Tobias, and Mark Garratt (1994), "Efficient experimental design with marketing research applications," *Journal of Marketing Research*, 31 (4), 545–57.

Kumar, V. (2010), "A customer lifetime value-based approach to marketing in the multichannel, multimedia retailing environment," *Journal of Interactive Marketing*, 24 (2), 71–85.

Kumar, V. (2014), "Understanding cultural differences in innovation: A conceptual framework and future research directions," *Journal of International Marketing*, 22 (3), 1–29.

Kumar, V. (2016), "My reflections on publishing in *Journal of Marketing*," *Journal of Marketing*, 80 (1), 1–6.

Kumar, V. (2017), "The role of university research centers in promoting research," *Journal of the Academy of Marketing Science*, 45 (4), 453–8.

Kumar, V. (2018), "A theory of customer valuation: Concepts, metrics, strategy, and implementation," *Journal of Marketing*, 82 (1), 1–19.

Kumar, V. and Trichy V. Krishnan (2002), "Research note. Multinational diffusion models: An alternative framework," *Marketing Science*, 21 (3), 318–30.

Kumar, V. and Anita Pansari (2014), "The construct, measurement, and impact of employee engagement: A marketing perspective," *Customer Needs and Solutions*, 1 (1), 52–67.

Kumar, V. and Anita Pansari (2016), "Competitive advantage through engagement," *Journal of Marketing Research*, 53 (4), 497–514.

Kumar, V. and Denish Shah (2011), "Uncovering implicit consumer needs for determining explicit product positioning: Growing prudential annuities' variable annuity sales," *Marketing Science*, 30 (4), 595–603.

Kumar, V., Yashoda Bhagwat, and Xi Zhang (2015), "Regaining 'lost' customers: The predictive power of first-lifetime behavior, the reason for defection, and the nature of the win-back offer," *Journal of Marketing*, 79 (4), 34–55.

Kumar, V., Agata Leszkiewicz, and Angeliki Herbst (2018), "Are you back for good or still shopping around? Investigating customers' repeat churn behavior," *Journal of Marketing Research*, 55 (2), 208–25.

Kumar, V., Ilaria Dalla Pozza, and Jaishankar Ganesh (2013), "Revisiting the satisfaction–loyalty relationship: empirical generalizations and directions for future research," *Journal of Retailing*, 89 (3), 246–62.

Kumar, V., Sarang Sunder, and Robert P. Leone (2014), "Measuring and managing a salesperson's future value to the firm," *Journal of Marketing Research*, 51 (5), 591–608.

Kumar, V., Vikram Bhaskaran, Rohan Mirchandani, and Milap Shah (2013), "Creating a measurable social media marketing strategy: Increasing the value and ROI of intangibles and tangibles for hokey pokey," *Marketing Science*, 32 (2), 194–212.

Kumar, V., Eli Jones, Rajkumar Venkatesan, and Robert P. Leone (2011), "Is market orientation a source of sustainable competitive advantage or simply the cost of competing?," *Journal of Marketing*, 75 (1), 16–30.

Kumar, V., Robert P. Leone, David A. Aaker, and George S. Day (2019), *Marketing Research* (13th edn). Hoboken, NJ: John Wiley & Sons.

Kumar, V., Bharath Rajan, Shaphali Gupta, and Ilaria Dalla Pozza (2019), "Customer engagement in service," *Journal of the Academy of Marketing Science*, 47 (1), 138–60.

Kumar, V., Alok R. Saboo, Amit Agarwal, and Binay Kumar, "Generating competitive intelligence with limited information: A case of multimedia industry." *Production and Operations Management*, forthcoming.

Leeflang, Peter S.H. and Dick R. Wittink (2000), "Building models for marketing decisions: Past, present and future," *International Journal of Research in Marketing*, 17 (2), 105–26.

Lehmann, Donald R., Leigh McAlister, and Richard Staelin (2011), "Sophistication in research in marketing," *Journal of Marketing*, 75 (4), 155–65.

Levitt, Theodore (1986), *The Marketing Imagination*. New York: The Free Press.

Lewis, Michael (2006), "Customer acquisition promotions and customer asset value," *Journal of Marketing Research*, 43 (2), 195–203.

Lilien, Gary L. and Arvind Rangaswamy (2000), "Modeled to bits: Decision models for the digital, networked economy," *International Journal of Research in Marketing*, 17 (2), 227–35.

MacInnis, Deborah J. (2011), "A framework for conceptual contributions in marketing," *Journal of Marketing*, 75 (4), 136–54.

McCracken, Grant (1988), *The Long Interview*. Newbury Park, CA: Sage Publications.

Mentzer, John T. (2008), "Rigor versus relevance: why would we choose only one?," *Journal of Supply Chain Management*, 44 (2), 72–7.

Mizik, Natalie and Robert Jacobson (2009), "Valuing branded businesses," *Journal of Marketing*, 73 (6), 137–53.

Mook, Douglas G. (1983), "In defense of external invalidity," *American Psychologist*, 38 (4), 379–87.

Morgan, Neil A., Hui Feng, and Kimberly A. Whitler (2018), "Marketing capabilities in international marketing," *Journal of International Marketing*, 26 (1), 61–95.

Nath, Pravin and Vijay Mahajan (2017), "Shedding light on the CMO revolving door: A study of the antecedents of Chief Marketing Officer turnover," *Journal of the Academy of Marketing Science*, 45 (1), 93–118.

Pansari, Anita and V. Kumar (2017), "Customer engagement: The construct, antecedents, and consequences," *Journal of the Academy of Marketing Science*, 45 (3), 294–311.

Peter, J. Paul and Jerry C. Olson (1983), "Is science marketing?," *Journal of Marketing*, 47 (4), 111–25.

Petersen, J. Andrew and V. Kumar (2010), "Can product returns make you money?," *MIT Sloan Management Review*, 51 (3), 85–9.

Petersen, J. Andrew, Leigh McAlister, David J. Reibstein, Russell S. Winer, V. Kumar, and Geoff Atkinson (2009), "Choosing the right metrics to maximize profitability and shareholder value," *Journal of Retailing*, 85 (1), 95–111.

Ramage, John D., John C. Bean, and June Johnson (2015), *Writing Arguments: A Rhetoric with Readings* (10th edn). New York: Pearson.

Reibstein, David J., George Day, and Jerry Wind (2009), "Is marketing academia losing its way?," *Journal of Marketing*, 73 (4), 1–3.

Reinartz, Werner J. and V. Kumar (2002), "The mismanagement of customer loyalty," *Harvard Business Review*, 80 (7), 86–94.

Shah, Denish and V. Kumar (2012), "The dark side cross-selling," *Harvard Business Review* (December), 21–3.

Shah, Denish, V. Kumar, and Kihyun Hannah Kim (2014), "Managing customer profits: The Power of habits," *Journal of Marketing Research*, 51 (6), 726–41.

Shaw, Eric (2014), "The quest for a general theory of the marketing system," *Journal of Historical Research in Marketing*, 6 (4), 523–37.

Sheth, Jagdish N. (2011), "Impact of emerging markets on marketing: Rethinking existing perspectives and practices," *Journal of Marketing*, 75 (4), 166–82.

Shrivastava, Paul (1987), "Rigor and practical usefulness of research in strategic management," *Strategic Management Journal*, 8 (1), 77–92.

Stewart, David W. and George M. Zinkhan (2006), "From the editors: Enhancing marketing theory in academic research," *Journal of the Academy of Marketing Science*, 34 (4), 477–80.

Summers, John O. (2001), "Guidelines for conducting research and publishing in marketing: From conceptualization through the review process," *Journal of the Academy of Marketing Science*, 29 (4), 405–15.

Sutton, Robert I. and Barry M. Staw (1995), "What theory is not," *Administrative Science Quarterly*, 40 (3), 371–84.

Van de Ven, Andrew H. (2007), *Engaged Scholarship: A Guide for Organizational and Social Research*. New York: Oxford University Press.

Varadarajan, P. Rajan (2003), "Musings on relevance and rigor of scholarly research in marketing," *Journal of the Academy of Marketing Science*, 31 (4), 368–76.

Varadarajan, Rajan (2010), "Strategic marketing and marketing strategy: Domain, definition, fundamental issues and foundational premises," *Journal of the Academy of Marketing Science*, 38 (2), 119–40.

Venkatesan, Rajkumar (2017), "Executing on a customer engagement strategy," *Journal of the Academy of Marketing Science*, 45 (3), 289–93.

Verhoef, Peter C., Werner J Reinartz, and Manfred Krafft (2010), "Customer engagement as a new perspective in customer management," *Journal of Service Research*, 13 (3), 247–52.

Wedel, Michel and P.K. Kannan (2016), "Marketing analytics for data-rich environments," *Journal of Marketing*, 80 (6), 97–21.

Wedel, Michel, Wagner Kamakura, and Ulf Böckenholt (2000), "Marketing data, models and decisions," *International Journal of Research in Marketing*, 17 (2), 203–8.

Weick, Karl E. (1989), "Theory construction as disciplined imagination," *Academy of Management Review*, 14 (4), 516–31.

Weick, Karl E. (1995), "What theory is not, theorizing is," *Administrative Science Quarterly*, 40 (3), 385–90.

Whetten, David A. (1989), "What constitutes a theoretical contribution?," *Academy of Management*

Review, 14 (4), 490–95.

Wind, Yoram Jerry (2008), "A plan to invent the marketing we need today," *MIT Sloan Management Review*, 49 (4), 21–8.

Wind, Yoram and Thomas S. Robertson (1983), "Marketing strategy: New directions for theory and research," *The Journal of Marketing*, 47 (2), 12–25.

Xu, Mark and Roland Kaye (2007), "The nature of strategic intelligence, current practice and solutions," in *Managing Strategic Intelligence: Techniques and Technologies*, Mark Xu, ed. Hershey, PA: IGI Global, pp. 36–54.

Yadav, Manjit S. (2010), "The decline of conceptual articles and implications for knowledge development," *Journal of Marketing*, 74 (1), 1–19.

Zaltman, Gerald (2016), "Marketing's forthcoming age of imagination," *AMS Review*, 6 (3–4), 99–115.

Zikmund, William G., Barry J. Babin, Jon C. Carr, and Mitch Griffin (2013), *Business Research Methods* (9th edn). Mason, OH: Cengage Learning.

9

So, you want to write policy-relevant articles?

Ronald Paul Hill

Orienting remarks

So, you want to write policy-oriented articles ... in marketing journals? Well, the competition is tough and getting tougher. At one time in the history of the larger field, top journals such as *Journal of Marketing* (*JM*) not only welcomed such topics but encouraged them and often would give updates on governmental activities for organizations like the Federal Trade Commission (FTC). Additionally, at the start of the *Journal of Consumer Research* (*JCR*), some of the most important topics included issues of deception that were germane to consumer researchers as well as public policymakers. While both outlets yield space to an occasional article with a policy bent, much of this work now is contained in the *Journal of Public Policy & Marketing* (*JPP&M*) or the *Journal of Consumer Affairs* (*JCA*). One bit of good news is that both outlets continue to advance in prestige, allowing for the rise of several scholarly communities that include the *Transformative Consumer Research* (*TCR*) conference and movement, the public policy and marketing conference attendees, and the subsistence marketplace conference attendees (for example, Mick 2006).

Yet what is appropriate for submission and the accompanying review process has and will continue to change over time. Both of these outlets, along with associated organizations and affiliations, are moving targets in terms of acceptable content. For example, *JCA* has increasingly viewed its domain as consumer well-being, moving away from *public* policy toward *social* policy as its primary focus. *JPP&M* editors have expressed similar sentiments and topics such as social marketing, social entrepreneurship, poverty, and even meditation fill its pages alongside more traditional fare. This dynamic environment is likely welcome in circles such as *TCR*, which has had a number of special issues over the past decade. However, it means the momentum has shifted significantly in a new direction that requires potential authors' consideration.

I have had the pleasure of editing both policy-oriented journals and have served on a number of editorial boards as well as an ad hoc reviewer for all major journals in the marketing field. My belief is that we are in for a major shift in how research is reviewed and disseminated regardless of subfield. However, I'll couch my remarks in the context of public policy and marketing research for the benefit of authors seeking publication at these outlets. I begin by discussing what comes to mind from my time as an editor, and then move to where I see the subfield advancing over time. The next section includes discussion of the future of academic publishing in general that considers subsequent decades. I close with recommendations on how to manage this evolving terrain. Let me note here that I could be wrong ... but you are getting my reflections from the cat-bird seat! Yet, I am convinced, as sung by Sam Cooke, "Change's gonna come!"

Editorial musings

I was able to act as the *Policy Watch* section editor of *JPP&M* for several years, followed by two three-year terms as the editor (2006–2012). My next editorship is with *JCA*, and it is ongoing as of the writing of this chapter (2018–present). They are very different outlets in many ways, for reasons that I will make clear. First, *JPP&M* is housed by the American Marketing Association (AMA) and has firm roots in the larger field of marketing. This association has historically had an academic and practitioner focus on public policy issues, but the inclusion of *JPP&M* in its portfolio of journals relegated such discussion away from generalist journals to this one outlet. Some scholars in this space bemoan the shift, especially if they are in institutions that only give credence to a handful of elitist journals. However, a positive side effect is that *JPP&M* is now in a small subset of AMA offerings that are widely considered the top of the larger field across universities. Thus, while a handful of places distinguish between *Journal of Marketing Research* (*JMR*), *Journal of International Marketing* (*JIM*), *JM*, and *JPP&M*, most among us see the portfolio as moving in the same positive reputational direction.

JCA, on the other hand, was created by scholars in the consumer economics field, and it is widely recognized as a top journal for their purposes of tenure and promotion. Given its origin, you will often find a variety of scholars from the original human ecology domain submitting articles on topics like vulnerability and financial planning (Anderson, Strand, and Collins 2018), to marketing faculty seeking to publish research on warning labels (Gallopel-Morvan, Hoek, and Rieunier 2018). Their supervising organization is the American Council on Consumer Interests (ACCI), and it is considerably smaller and more intimate that the AMA. As a result, their meetings and communications, as well as their oversight of the Journal, suggest that they value both originating fields but with an emphasis that is removed from marketing strategy or tactical discussions that often dominate marketing outlets.

One change over time is that *JPP&M*, and to a lesser extent *JCA*, now have standards and acceptance rates that rival the most exclusive journals in marketing. It is no surprise to receive reviews from the editor, associate editor, and three reviewers that go on for 5 to 10 pages of single-spaced notes. This review team does not consider its charge as different from, say, *JM*, and the expectation is that *JPP&M* is the author's preferred outlet and s/he is willing to go through a grueling review process to gain acceptance. In fact, many of these reviewers are associate editors and editorial review board members at other elite journals, and they use the same rigorous yardstick to evaluate manuscript drafts. My experience is that they are less likely to reject *everything* that comes their way than with other journals, but ultimate acceptance requires meeting or exceeding the same standards.

There is also an openness to different ways of discovering truth that is beyond most of the other journals that seem to care about consumer well-being. *JCR* and *Journal of Consumer Psychology* (*JCP*), for example, promote experimentation over different forms of discovery (see Rapp and Hill 2015 for a review of *JCR*), and other offerings, such as *JMR* and *Marketing Science* (*MS*) tend to focus on methods that reflect complex modeling. Interestingly, the multiple or endless parade of experiments or sophisticated mathematical models are welcome but not dominating by any means, and the use of qualitative techniques, including ethnography, have healthy representation (see Arnould 2001 as an example). In fact, it seems that the policy subfield is one of the few places in marketing that is agnostic as to method, although multiple approaches to truth in the same submission may increase the odds of eventually gaining acceptance. What seems to be the metric is what have you uncovered that is new or novel and can be of use to scholars and policymakers, and the latter is often broadly defined and beyond simply individuals in the legislative branch of government or agencies.

Most interestingly, topical areas of prominence show how the past still informs the present, with new ideas infusing the mix. Consider that we still publish research on tobacco and alcohol, two industries that have received much attention but require still more in terms of novel solutions (James and Cude 2009). Part of the reason for continued look at these areas is the rapidly changing landscape. For instance, tobacco products are moving away from traditional methods of smoking toward vaping, and younger generations are getting hooked on nicotine under the mistaken belief that there is no subsequent harm. As consumers move from one nicotine delivery system to the next, how do scholars and policymakers ensure that the impacted publics remain safe? Also, small quantities of some alcoholic beverages may actually be healthful, but many consumer segments such as college students often engage in binge drinking. This subpopulation has been told not to drink and drive, which seems to have impacted their behavior, but are we failing to recognize the long-term potential costs of binging?

New industries and issues are at the forefront of the subfield's discussions that offer a different take on public policy research. One industry that defies previous research paradigms is the burgeoning market for cannabis in the U.S. This market represents the first and only example of a previously illegal good that has become legal, at least at the state level. True, alcohol was prohibited during parts of the 1920s and 1930s, but it already had a long history of legal purchase. What makes this market particularly interesting is the geographic divide between who has access and who does not, and whether intoxication in one place bars intoxication in another. Further, the federal government maintains its status as a prohibited substance, leaving the possibility of a federal crackdown at some point. Scholars who embrace this topic will have opportunities to inform policymakers for many years to come, especially if they chronicle and inform the dynamic nature of legislation and consumer behavior.

A look at new issues requires nothing more than a survey of the topics covered by the transformative consumer research movement (Davis, Ozanne, and Hill 2016). Over time, these scholars have tackled the most difficult societal issues associated with poverty, social status and stigma, too much food and too little, gender roles and empowerment as well as abuse, and a host of others. Consider the way food plays out across societies. It is clear that nearly half the world's population lives in real poverty, and many in this group are undernourished and underfed. Juxtapose this situation with the spread of obesity in developed nations, where 40% of adults in countries like the U.S. are considered overweight or obese and subject to health-related ailments. In these same countries, their poor find dense but often unhealthy food options from places like fast food outlets to be inexpensive in the short-term but the cause of other long-term problems. Clearly, such topics offer considerable space for more research.

Despite so many options for new and advancing scholars to find a place in the subfield, many still struggle to get their work accepted. There are several possible reasons but we will discuss only a few. First, the opening section and the theoretical setup often leave reviewers wanting. These offerings tend to organize previous literature to meet their needs, cherry-picking articles that help them justify their hypotheses without a deeper look at what has been done in the past. Some of this problem is caused by the way we now read papers. Instead of regularly getting journals delivered to our doors and giving the entire issue attention, we now use search engines that take a handful of keywords and use whatever pops up (along with our own research) to determine what is relevant. To an expert in the field, the result comes across as noncritical and superficial at best, souring his or her mood for the remainder of the paper. While some reviewers may have the ability to see value in a well-run study that is poorly positioned, my experience suggests that they are few-and-far-between.

Another issue has to deal with data sources. There is likely a place for use of students for certain kinds of investigations, but they often are inappropriate for many policy studies. (One exception that comes to mind could be their perceptions of vaping nicotine mentioned earlier because they are the center of this target market.) For instance, if you are looking at how low literacy impacts navigation of the marketplace, you will need people with poor reading skills. Some students might qualify, but artificially creating a system by which they are forced into illiteracy is not appropriate. This discussion brings to mind a review team I faced once that appreciated our use of a dataset of tens-of-thousands of consumers at the base-of-the-pyramid, but they asked us to run an experiment to show the *truth* of our findings. I noted that it would only work if we took all hope for a better future away from subjects, something that IRBs are loath to support! We make compromises all the time between internal and external validity, but public policy research must have the latter to be an effective tool for change.

As you might expect, the final area of concern is the close. The policy subfield has been a dumping ground for experimental research that was rejected from top-ranked consumer behavior journals, which may offer interesting and novel insights about consumption. Unfortunately, these scholars may have been literally through hell to get their work published, only to find after two or three rounds that they are rejected. While the best policy journals typically do not play this editorial game and make decisions earlier in the review process, it does not mean that all work in consumer behavior will have a place with us. Further, many of these types of submissions are relatively unchanged except for a reference or two and a paragraph at the end of the paper that simply says policymakers should care about this issue. Frankly, our reviewers are typically angered by such offerings, especially if they remain in a different style guide format that suggests the authors did not even bother to make necessary changes. If you want to get rejected fast, make sure the review team views your paper as a sophisticated research project that had no consideration of public policy in any form, but it was rejected so they are lucky to receive it!

Public policy and marketing research comes of age

So, where are we going as a subfield? Well, you can intuit some of my reactions from the previous material but let me be as explicit as possible. One direction is a movement away from the traditional center of the subfield and its focus on regulatory agencies at the federal level to other issues and stakeholders. A possibility that has yet to come full circle is an emphasis on governmental organizations outside of the U.S. federal level. Much legislation and its subsequent enforcement happens at state and local levels that are often ignored by scholars. Consider, again, the marijuana marketplace. Legal decisions at the state level ignore federal mandates and are overturned at the city/community level. What is a consumer to do? Can you be consistent with one in your purchasing and usage behaviors but simultaneously in violation of others? How about global dictates that come through nongovernmental organizations such as the United Nations or the World Health Organization? Does U.S. exceptionalism make sense in light of the gender/racial inequities that exist in our marketplaces? Much is left to be discovered!

This begs the question as to whether a U.S.-centric focus for these journals is appropriate. Both *JPP&M* and *JCA* have published research on base-of-the-pyramid consumers with special issues that are wide-ranging in their coverage (for example, Venugopal, Viswanathan, and Jung 2015). At the time of this writing, *JCA* has a novel issue seeking manuscripts that considers how well-being manifests differently in Asian nations relative to the developed west, and it portends a rethinking of what we mean by consumption and quality of life. As scholars from around the world face higher standards of publication for tenure and/or advancement, they will continue to flood our journals with their work. At one time, these papers were often off-base and lacked the theoretical and methodological sophistication of their peers at western universities, but that inferiority is quickly evaporating. Further, this work is moving away from research that repeats what was done previously in U.S. contexts to issues that are particularly germane to other cultures. This new globalism will likely continue.

This dynamic context moves forward our previous discussion of what it means to be a policymaker in this new environment. While our research would indict what happens at agencies like the FTC, most scholars failed to discuss exactly who and where in the organization actors are charged with the ability to make changes, or if legislative action is necessary, who would be a likely candidate to initiate changes. Is more specificity needed in the future or will our desire for greater acceptability in the larger marketing academic community continue to lead us toward theoretical emphasis over practicality? This question is also germane as the moniker is expanded to include other actors outside formal government including nonprofit executives, NGO officials, social marketers and entrepreneurs, religious leaders, and additional managers in leadership roles. It seems appropriate to look closely at who is responsible so that we can influence the organizational design and makeup of the institutions involved.

It also seems that the newest generation of scholars is beginning to show its intellectual might and they have started to fill the pages of our journals with innovative and expansive research. *JPP&M* was initially started by a small group of scholars that understood the importance of the government–business intersection; of course, with a strong marketing orientation. They often adopted some of the same ideas that they used to organize *JCR*, and issues associated with how consumers processed information and were subject to deception and its remedies was front-and-center. However, Generation Y scholars are much broader thinkers and less likely to concentrate on federal agencies in lieu of pressing societal ills (see Davis, Ozanne, and Hill 2016). As noted earlier, topics like obesity, global poverty, racial discrimination, sexual harassment and violence have links to governmental acts but include other forms of response from nonprofit organizations, community advocates, and individual consumers. As their work takes center stage, it is possible that our research portfolio will discuss responsibilities of a variety of stakeholders rather than simply "government."

Taken together, these changes that are upon us now may require a new way of organizing our journals as well as how best to disseminate our research findings. Both outlets highlighted here have maintained the same basic formats for years and this strategy has served them well. Yet, we may wish to reorganize how we solicit and manage articles and papers for maximum impact. For instance, an author will submit a manuscript, wait three months for reactions, revise the paper accordingly with a similar timeframe, send it back for another round of reviews, and enter another loop before a final publication decision is reached. What once may have been a novel idea is now a year older, possibly making it less relevant and timely. One answer is to get it up on websites soon after acceptance, since the time lag to showing up in print might be another full year. However, this newer practice does little to get it in the hands of those who need its findings the most. More on this problem in the next section.

Looking just at the various categories of publications within these journals, we see a rather dated set of options. At best, we have full-length articles, some shorter pieces, and a place for novel contributions that might include book reviews. Is it time for new thinking? What if we began publishing an extended series of "think" pieces that chronicled cutting-edge ideas about public policy and marketing from first-paper articles of dissertations and senior scholars with the insights to inform what is going to happen rather than what has already occurred? These papers could be an extended series that continues the conversation across the same and similar authors, eventually bringing data from diverse methods and sources to help us understand, navigate, and resolve associated problems. It might mean grouping manuscripts accordingly: novel paradigms or perspectives, critical analyses of current ideas, empirical evaluations and research directions, and lessons for impacted parties and other stakeholders. While it is hard to manage input without working closely with various scholarly communities, it would be a proactive versus reactive way of directing relevant scholarship.

Future of academic publishing
The last two paragraphs of the previous section lead us into this discussion. When I completed my dissertation in 1984, scholars had to physically handle journals and proceedings to determine which articles were relevant to their research ideas, taking

weeks or even months to assemble necessary documentation for review that requires a few minutes today. Papers were handwritten and transcribed, revised and then rewritten, and likely then given or mailed to other scholars for a first-level review. After a considerable time-period, the paper came to a final first-draft form and was copied, collated, bundled, and sent off to an editor for consideration. It was subsequently mailed to reviewers, who eventually completed the attached forms and wrote their reviews for author consideration. The packet was copied, filed away, and some subset was mailed to the authors. We were urged at that time to have several papers in various stages of development so that there was always something to work on as you waited. It somehow worked but often seemed convoluted. Authors would pick up the letters and use its heft as a first sign of interest or reaction to manuscripts. Of course, this was only the first round, with (potentially) more to come.

When fortunate, papers were eventually accepted and then edited and entered into the publishing/printing system of choice. The path of least resistance was often taken, and graphs, charts, figures, and even footnotes had to meet specifications that were more about publishing ease rather than quality reproduction. Some of these dictates survive even today (for example, limits or discouragement of footnotes) that seem mostly passé. However, because of cost (not ease) of high-quality, color reproductions of exhibits such as photographs, additional expenses are often passed on to the author(s). We are typically happy to pay them given university reimbursements and the desire to publish versus perish. Yet, this pass-along seems likely to continue if we still advance scholarship in the same formats that have existed since the invention of the printing press. Once again, times are changing, and the horizon looks very different from the past.

Most of the very best journals are housed or managed within associations like AMA for *JPP&M* or American Council for Consumer Interests (ACCI) for *JCA*. These parent organizations include many of the scholars who write for such outlets, also sponsoring associated conferences, webinars, formal training, and job boards for academic appointments. It is not surprising to see some researchers attend many or most of their annual events so that they can present research ideas and meet with like-minded scholars and/or coauthors. The journals typically have meet-and-greet sessions with potential authors, giving them information on what is relevant, how to improve the odds of publishing, and other nuances about these journals. In some cases, these gatekeepers pride themselves on how few papers survive the rigors of the review process, with acceptance rates in the single digits. Prestige is presented as a function of who is excluded as well as the reputations of who has published the most over time. Rarely, if ever, do journals account for the content of what is ultimately accepted unless it is for the purposes of creating a guide to capture the volume of scholarship over a defined period. It may give the impression that who is more important than what, and tenure cases at many universities are based, in part, on numbers of articles and where.

The newest generation of scholars do not seem to be enamored with a process that makes failure the most likely outcome. Sure, researchers who self-select and are selected by the most research-oriented institutions that hold three-to-five publications as the center of the universe likely will continue to perpetuate a system that seems to hold them in higher esteem. Yet many of the Gen-Y faculty see this "game" as fixed and unworthy of their time and effort. Instead, they may eschew the dictate of their Ph.D. professors who tell them to "hold off doing research that matters or is personally interesting until they reach tenure," and begin doing more meaningful scholarship as early as possible. They flock to groups such as *TCR* that place them in like-minded communities where they explore issues deeply and publish papers that inspire action. The same can be said of the public policy and marketing annual conference, where the new faculty/Ph.D. student event prior to the full conference is often filled beyond capacity.

This generation and the next are also fully engaged in social media, and they see these connections as meaningful relationships even if their older colleagues view them as no more than a pleasant diversion. While the former feels comfortable putting their personal and professional beliefs, feelings, and ideas in cyber-forums that are often unregulated, the latter remain firm that research should not be exposed to others until it receives the sanction of peer-review. At the very same time, how our work is disseminated is rapidly changing. Most associations have turned to a relatively small number of publishing giants to compile and distribute their journals because of the large costs incurred to reach a global network of interested parties. These publishing houses often have dozens if not hundreds of journals and other publication forums, and they are on the forefront of digital communication and circulation. They are finding that individual journals may soon become obsolete in an interconnected and transdisciplinary world that has traditionally been organized in silos of researchers who talk to themselves rather than in broader dialogues across fields and subfields. At *JCA*, we are currently having articles paired with others from interrelated areas without concern for their origination. What results is a richer discussion of topics for all.

The future remains murky but it is clear that the current template is not sustainable. My best guess is that associations and their hold over the collection and dissemination of research in the academic community is waning. This remark is not to say that they are obsolete but that they will have different and possibly expanded reasons for their existences in the future. Scholarship, however, may move from the journal format that at one time was mailed to interested parties and institutions to a new format that is managed by the surviving publishers who maintain a stable of scholars, other researchers, and a host of experts who seek and examine manuscripts that fit into transdisciplinary areas and issues that are marketable commodities. They reimburse researchers or their sponsors (for example, universities) for their work, and they charge individuals, institutions, or even countries for their digital use. Prestige as a function of control over outlets moves from a handful of research universities to the individuals who can bridge the chasm across disciplinary divides. Thus, reputations for excellence will reside in the person and a portfolio of marketable scholarship, allowing him or her to move seamlessly across institutions over time.

Recommendations to scholars

Hopefully, readers remember David Letterman of late-night television fame. One of his famous skits was his top-ten lists, which were humorous takes on various people or topics of the day. Mine are likely less entertaining, but they go to the very heart of what it takes to publish marketing articles in public policy-oriented journals as well as journals in professional fields. They are provided in no particular order and cover a range of issues and ideas. Together, they present a cohesive checklist for what you write and how to get it published. If they do not work for you, it is a good idea to make your own list and follow it until you no longer need guidance. Part of getting published requires rigorous adherence to detail; something that seems to escape many scholars in academic institutions. Regardless, you must have a plan in mind, especially in the beginning of your career, and allow it to mature as you pass through its various phases.

#10 Don't focus efforts on well-worn topics in the field or subfield. While this advice may go against common wisdom, I hope you will see its value shortly. I remember a time much earlier in my career when I received a paper from *JCR* to review that was elegant, sophisticated, well-written, and well-researched. However, it concentrated on a set of issues that had been so well mined that it was over-mined! The authors were furious that it was eventually rejected, but I could not get to recommending acceptance since the nuance selected for discovery seemed inconsequential. In fact, as an editor, I often get exhausted reading manuscripts that seek to find minor extensions of known theories (for example, if older consumers are subject to some forms of marketplace deception, are their differences by product category and gender or race in France?) After a while, it is like reading the same undergraduate essay exam 50 times. You get exhausted by the lack of real differences and your enthusiasm wanes over time. What we want to publish is novel looks at new ideas that bring fresh air to the field (consider Grier and Perry 2018). Try it, you will like it as well!

#9 Learn to be satisfied with less than perfection. I had a friend who occupied an office near mine as a junior faculty member that was a real perfectionist. While the rest of us were trying to get as many things under review as possible, with the belief that it increased our odds of success, s/he worked on this one paper over months and years to make sure it was without flaws. On occasion, s/he would come out of the office and ask someone to read a paragraph or to look at a statistical result. However, the idea of letting anyone view it until it was deemed perfection was an impossibility. Needless to say, this person failed to make it past a third-year review since there was little to show for 36 months of effort. In the end, you must decide between what is good enough to remain in the review process and move to the second round so that the review team can give guidance toward publication. Of course, this is not a superficial attempt that is poorly written or executed, but it need not be flawless in your mind. Reviewers will still find flaws; you just need to be good enough for them to care to correct them!

#8 Even the best schools do not teach you everything. A good friend was on an interview at a top-ranked university that she believed was above her Ph.D. granting university's station and outside her reach. However, she took the interview since one of their faculty members was at the top of her subfield interest. One of her fellow interviewees was from an even "better" institution and he announced on her arrival that he was working on a "*JCR*" paper. This incident calmed her down because of its ignorance. As one of my mentors used to say, "you are working on a paper not an article; it doesn't become an article until the editor says so!" Interestingly, this person did ask me for directions on his paper at one point because another senior colleague

suggested he do so. I was rather naïve at the time and worked hard to give him helpful ideas for modification toward publication, but his ego got in the way of his better interests. He did not get tenure and moved downstream in university prestige. The lesson here is to seek help and take heed of the lessons offered. You never know how good a "paper" it is until someone else agrees!

#7 Make sure your papers carefully follow the style guide. As editor at *JPP&M*, we would regularly get manuscripts that had been rejected at top-ranked generalist journals and resubmitted to us. My editorial board rightly believed that we were among the very best outlets in the world since we were the top-SSCI rated public policy journal in the larger business field. So, as noted previously, someone would add a paragraph or two without major revision and send it to us, only to be desk rejected for failure to make a significant contribution to public policy *and* marketing research. About half the time, they would come back with their tails between their legs and show how they had now read the Journal, included relevant articles, followed the style guide for headings and references, and expanded the policy discussion. Many of these papers did very well since they were sophisticated looks at interesting phenomena that could inform policymakers and scholars. The lesson is clear – if you want to publish in a particular place, you need to look like that was your original intention. Otherwise, you seem like an unwanted stranger or intruder!

#6 Get to know the full range of the topic under consideration. As an editor, I personally find it disconcerting when someone suggests they know a constituency well but have never met or spoken with someone in that domain. At a recent conference, I was a discussant on a session that had scholars and policymakers discuss how impoverished consumers navigate the market. I listened carefully as they described the reactions of such persons who were part of a panel of respondents in one of the largest pools of research subjects. My reaction was that these folks may have been the socioeconomic bottom of the subject pool, but they did not represent the bottom tier in our society. To reach that community, they would need to go outside such panels and find alternative ways of gaining access. Unfortunately, their comfort zone was sitting in an office and watching the data come in across their computers. My advice to you is to listen, learn, and report, and doing so may require you to find novel ways of access to people who provide the best intel.

#5 Actively engage the right people and attend the appropriate events. This dictate may sound presumptuous, but it is well-meaning. By "right" people I mean scholars who are doing research in the same areas as you are. Take, for instance, the focus of this chapter on public policy and marketing research. There are several events that host these scholars, including the annual public policy and marketing conference (held every other year in DC to ensure that some policy folks are in attendance) and the biannual *TCR* dialogic conference. The former follows a more traditional path of papers and discussants, while the latter places people in rooms for days as they work on intractable societal problems. The former also has a well-attended preconference that showcases cutting-edge research by some of the most notable professors and practitioners in the field, and the latter requires the inclusion of young scholars in each of its tracks. One of the most notable differences between these events and most others is the willingness of more senior faculty to engage, share ideas, and mentor new colleagues. Try it and see!

#4 Think in transdisciplinary ways about topics of interest. I was the internal dean at one institution and vividly remember a conversation with the external dean. He was interested in the development of research "pods" that would house scholars who were willing to work across disciplinary boundaries that seemed artificial barriers to more effective solutions to business and social problems. I told him that interdisciplinary was passé, and that the new direction was to be *transdisciplinary*. As you might imagine, he was unsure if I was right, so he continued to use the language that was more common at the time. However, I still think this revised approach is much better because it moves away from a melting pot of individual ideas to an open, almost agnostic view of different perspectives on the same issues. Consequently, scholars must carefully look at how a variety of disciplines and subdisciplines capture areas of research interest conceptually, theoretically, and methodologically. Rather than making judgments about viability from the vantagepoint of one's field, scholars rise above these restraints and look to find the best of the best to inform their research. This way we do not "reinvent the wheel" but build a better car!

#3 Intersectionality provides a different avenue for extending current research. Almost every research project conducted by social science scholars adds a series of questions to find possible differences beyond the stated hypotheses. For instance, information on demographic variables are regularly collected so that nuances of how other variables play out can be explored. Sometimes they work, other times nothing is significant. Maybe we are doing nothing more than "fishing" for important results. Yet, there are other directions that might yield important nuances that represent what *TCR* scholars call intersectionality. This term is often used to describe how various issues come together with other areas of concern to form a more cohesive whole. One example from my own work is poverty. In and of itself, it is worthy of our efforts because it has a major impact on the consumptive quality of life of nearly half of all human beings. But the fuller impact seems also to be related to race (being black versus white) and gender (being female versus male) (for example, Hill and Dhanda 1999). Taken together, they are better able to show the face of impoverished consumers, why it continues to persist, and what solutions can make a difference.

#2 Be more than an author – become a reviewer as well. Like most faculty members, I would spend much more time dwelling on negative teacher evaluations versus the overwhelming number of positive reviews and remarks. However, when I became a department chair and had the opportunity to see my entire department's evaluations, my viewpoint changed. I began to recognize that *everyone* has at least some detractors no matter how much effort they put into class preparation, giving me a new perspective on this process. The same thing may happen for you once you begin reviewing the work of others in areas where you have expertise. My guess is that you will find that many papers are well-meaning but superficial, incomplete, and subject to alternative interpretations to guide public policy. Thus, you may learn that your own attempts are better than you were aware, hopefully making you more confident and willing to risk rejection. It is also possible that you feel your work is subpar, but your reading of such manuscripts yields new ideas on how to advance your research. At a minimum you will have a better understanding of the topics and quality of scholarship that compete for the same journal pages as you do!

#1 Work in research areas that are meaningful to you. It sounds so simple as to become trite, but many scholars in this field were told to avoid "meaningful" topics until tenure or even beyond. I remember well the turning point in my career when I decided to write about how the poor across societies navigate the material world. A well-meaning senior colleague told me that this decision was like "putting a gun to my career and pulling the trigger." Yet, I recently had had a conversation with Terry Shimp (formerly at University of South Carolina) about why so many good scholars stop publishing after tenure. Is it because they find the process too onerous? Too demanding? Or is it that writing out of fear for one's job is not sustaining over time unless you love this form of discovery? I can honestly tell you that I look forward almost every day to the start of a novel idea or the writing of a new paper. While my preferences for what and how to contribute have shifted over many decades, my interest in solving dilemmas associated with impoverishment have never waned. Find a similar path and hang on for what surely will be a bumpy ride; nevertheless, it will be the ride of a lifetime!

References

Anderson, Drew M., Alexander Strand, and J. Michael Collins (2018), "The Impact of Electronic Payments for Vulnerable Consumers: Evidence from Social Security," *Journal of Consumer Affairs*, 52 (Spring), 35–60.

Arnould, Eric J. (2001), "Ethnography, Export Marketing Policy, and Economic Development in Niger," *Journal of Public Policy & Marketing*, 20 (Fall), 151–69.

Davis, Brennan, Julie L. Ozanne, and Ronald Paul Hill (2016), "The Transformative Consumer Research Movement," *Journal of Public Policy & Marketing*, 36 (Spring), 159–69.

Gallopel-Morvan, Karine, Janet Hoek, and Sophie Rieunier (2018), "Do Plain Packaging and Pictorial Warnings Affect Smokers' and Non-Smokers' Behavioral Intentions?," *Journal of Consumer Affairs*, 52 (Spring), 5–34.

Grier, Sonya A. and Vanessa G. Perry (2018), "Dog Parks and Coffee Shops: Faux Diversity and Consumption in Gentrifying Neighborhoods," *Journal of Public Policy & Marketing*, 37 (Spring), 23–38.

Hill, Ronald Paul and Kathy Dhanda (1999), "Gender Inequality and Quality of Life: A Macromarketing Perspective," *Journal of Macromarketing*, 19 (December), 140–152.

James, Russell N. and Brenda J. Cude (2009), "Trends in *Journal of Consumer Affairs* Featured Articles: 1967–2007," *Journal of Consumer Affairs*, 43 (Spring), 155–69.

Mick, David Glen (2006), "Meaning and Mattering Through Transformative Consumer Research," in *Advances in Consumer Research*, Vol. 33, Cornelia (Connie) Pechmann and Linda Price, eds. Provo, UT: Association for Consumer Research, 1–4.

Rapp, Justine and Ronald Paul Hill (2015), "'Lordy, Lordy Look Who's Forty!' The *Journal of Consumer Research* Reaches a Milestone," *Journal of Consumer Research*, 42 (1), 19–29.

Venugopal, Srinivas, Madhu Viswanathan, and Kiju Jung (2015), "Consumption Constraints and Entrepreneurial Intentions in Subsistence Markets," *Journal of Public Policy & Marketing*, 34 (Fall), 235–51.

10

Publishing in international marketing: challenges, opportunities, and guideposts

Constantine S. Katsikeas

Introduction

As a result of growing globalization of markets and intensifying competition worldwide, international market operations have become an integral part of the corporate life of many business organizations. Academic research in international marketing has responded accordingly to this international business phenomenon. Over the past four decades, there has been a surge of scholarly journal publications in two broad domains: (1) studies examining problems and practices of firms in their endeavors to enter and penetrate foreign markets and (2) studies investigating international consumer behavior and cross-cultural issues. Various streams of research have been followed and influential articles published that have played an important role in the advancement of knowledge in international marketing. Understandably, an abundance of literature review efforts and meta-analytic studies have been conducted in order to examine, organize, and assess the body of current knowledge within specific areas or streams of research and, in some instances, to offer an evaluation of the structure of research undertaken in the general international marketing literature (for example, Leonidou et al. 2017). International marketing is an established field with long tradition, and international market operations will continue to play a vital role for many companies' existence and long-term viability and provide significant benefits for national economies in terms of employment, productivity, and living standards improvements (Katsikeas 2018).

An important issue inherent in the particular nature of international marketing concerns the emergence of new developments and parameters in the global environment that affect customers and their behavior, competition, and the international activities and strategies of business organizations. One recent example is Brexit that currently is utterly unclear what it is and what shape it is going to take. However, this huge uncertainty associated with Brexit poses colossal challenges not only for U.K. companies with global operations, but for those from other countries with established operations within the U.K. Another significant development is the imposition of tariffs on certain imported products initiated by the U.S. and retaliatory acts by other countries, which has resulted in a kind of trade war among nations. Such developments in the international environment have significant implications for firms' overall business operations and, in particular, their international marketing strategies. In addition, a tendency has recently been witnessed among a considerable number of global companies with foreign manufacturing mainly in emerging markets (for example, China) to engage in reverse internationalization, aiming at taking gradually their overseas manufacturing operations back home, typically a developed country (for example, the U.S.). This again has important implications for firms' global business operations and marketing practices. Here, the point I would like to make is that all these developments should not be seen as pure threats to international business. Simply they constitute a change in the rules governing international business operations. From a researcher's perspective, such developments provide intriguing opportunities for future investigation of timely and important issues in international marketing.

Given the popularity of international marketing among researchers and business practitioners, along with the emergence of new attractive research opportunities on an ongoing basis, the objective of this chapter is to discuss and provide advice on how to publish in this important area in scholarly academic journals. My thinking is based essentially on my own experience and knowledge gained as academic researcher and author of a range of publications, as editorial board member of and reviewer for academic and practitioner-focused journals across marketing, strategy, and general management, and as current and past editor of several academic journals. Throughout this endeavor, I will bear in mind that advancing knowledge, focusing on addressing important international marketing problems, by publishing in scholarly academic journals is a focal issue in the intellectual development of the field. It should also be remembered that decisions in faculty promotion and appointment panels across academic institutions worldwide are primarily driven by the quality and amount of an individual's published work. Thus, I will pay attention to isolating challenges in conducting research in international marketing, considering ways of addressing practical problems, and offering tangible guidelines for helping researchers to develop and pursue interesting research projects and go through the journal publishing process.

Challenges in conducting research in international marketing

Marketing concepts, tools, and techniques are the same regardless of where firms' market operations take place (i.e., domestically, overseas, or both). However, what is different in firms' international operations concerns the multiplicity of forces, different from those in the domestic market, that shape the international environment. As a result, in international market operations, consideration should be given to a wider variety of factors influencing firms' international marketing strategies and performance. For instance, important issues in marketing (for example, customer behavior, distribution structure, salesforce management, etc.) are affected by the presence of significant differences in socio-cultural, regulatory, political, and economic systems that often exist between domestic and foreign markets. Apparently, specific marketing problems encountered by companies have their roots in the international market environment. Examples include the effects of foreign exchange fluctuations on pricing policies and strategy, the impact of political risk on foreign transactions, and the influence of language differences across countries on branding and brand management. Thus, the challenges facing firms in international expansion and foreign markets are different from those in domestic business operations.

Consequently, pursuing research in international marketing involves unique challenges for researchers in the field. First of all, rigorous conceptual models of firms' international marketing practices and performance outcomes would need to take into account the wide range of factors shaping the international market context that play an influential role. Failure to account for a good proportion of relevant and important variables would result in underspecified models. In addition, in effectively examining international marketing phenomena, there might well be a need to collect data in more than one country. This can pose major difficulties in the collection of enhanced quality primary data or the acquisition of reliable data from secondary sources particularly in developing countries.

For instance, a distinct strand of research in marketing and other business and management disciplines in both domestic and international market settings focuses on the study of behavioral aspects (for example, trust, commitment, opportunism, norms etc.) underlying interfirm collaborative exchange relationships. Often, the study of interorganizational business relationships requires the collection of dyadic data. Understandably the collection of high-quality dyadic cross-border buyer–seller relationship data is particularly challenging. Furthermore, the collection of such data or data from different countries that measure the same constructs requires the assessment of cross-cultural measure equivalence. Establishing configural, metric, and scalar invariance for the measures used in cross-cultural studies is by default a challenging task. In some cases, however, the assessment of cross-cultural measure equivalence is not possible. A typical example is the case of examining relationships of exporters with their foreign distributors who naturally are based across many different markets overseas. In such a situation, attempts to assess and establish cross-cultural measure equivalence in the measures between the exporter and importer groups would be meaningless, given that importers are scattered across different countries.

In addition, theory-based conceptualizations and empirical tests of models in international marketing often need to incorporate constructs specific to the international business or foreign market context. A typical example is the study of quanxi business associations in China that have been conceptualized as having various aspects or components, which have explicitly been incorporated in models of international exchange relationships of Chinese companies. However, what we have seen more often than not in the international marketing literature is that researchers propose conceptual frameworks within an international business setting (for example, manufacturer–foreign distributor relationships) that are essentially drawn from the work on these phenomena in the domestic market, with no account taken of any particular characteristics or influences of the study's international market context. Testing such conceptual models is likely to offer limited additions to current theoretical knowledge in international marketing.

It is vitally important that international marketing studies focusing on the examination of a relatively generic issue within the particular context of an inherently international business phenomenon consider the unique elements of the empirical setting. For instance, in the study of drivers and performance outcomes of trust in international strategic alliances, it would be prudent to conceptualize trust in the unique context of international alliance partnerships comprising different aspects, dimensions, and sub-dimensions and investigate antecedents that are pertinent to this alliance context (see Robson, Katsikeas, and Bello 2009). A similar example refers to the examination of how commitment influences performance in the context of international marketing alliances (see Bello, Katsikeas, and Robson 2010). In addition to isolating those aspects of commitment that are of particular relevance to international marketing alliances, the study introduced a new mechanism (i.e., accommodation along with monitoring) that is meaningful within the particular alliance context, enabling such alliances to cope with the problems of adaptation and evaluation and thus connect different alliance commitment aspects with performance outcomes. Importantly, such studies can contribute to the advancement of knowledge not only in international strategic alliances but also in interfirm exchange relationships.

A practical approach to conducting research in international marketing
Undertaking scholarly research that leads to journal publications can be viewed as an ongoing project that involves a process through which promising research ideas are conceptualized and modeled, studies are conducted and publications achieved, and importantly new research avenues emerge that facilitate continuing conceptual development and empirical study. It is essential for individual researchers to effectively manage this process concerning the growth and development of their studies and building their own research agenda. Subsequently, I provide a practical approach to pursuing research in international marketing and offer some guideposts for researchers working in the field. To this end, I refer to my own experiences as author, reviewer, and editor and offer examples from influential work in international marketing. Figure 10.1 provides a framework that I find helpful for organizing my thoughts and highlighting key issues in successfully conducting research in the field.

Pursuit of effective publication strategy
Getting published in academic journals in general marketing, management, and international business has increasingly become highly competitive. This is due in part to the fast growth of business schools worldwide, the increasing globalization of business education, and focused attempts among academic institutions to recruit and retain faculty capable of publishing academic research of high quality. Faculty though need to be realistic about their publication strategy and the journals they target. We live in an era of quite low acceptance rates, more often than not less than ten percent, and in the case of successful submissions there is a relatively long review process. Comparatively few academics across business and management disciplines manage to publish in a leading, top-tier journal in their academic career, and some believe that this is even more challenging for faculty based in non-U.S. institutions (see Wright 2014). However, it should be noted that the benefits of publishing in a leading journal for career progression are significant.

Broadly, one should be aware that building a curriculum vitae on the basis of a stream of publications in low level journals might not impress senior administrators in research-active business schools and may have a negative effect on career development. It would be more appropriate to pursue research and publications that count in the institution's tenure and promotion systems. Realistically not every project and manuscript has the trappings required for meeting the stringent quality

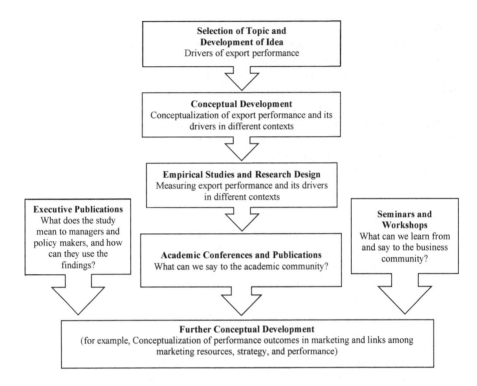

Figure 10.1   A practical approach to conducting research in international marketing

standards of a top-tier journal. It would thus be more effective to pursue a strategy aiming at publishing in journals that meet a certain quality threshold and are recognized by the school. Publishing in journals that count, while avoiding placing work in those that do not, would improve a faculty member's satisfaction and confidence with positive effects on undertaking better quality research and publishing in more prestigious journals. Concerning research in international marketing, it should not be assumed that submission of such papers is limited only to journals specializing in publishing international marketing and cross-cultural consumer behavior studies (for example, *Journal of International Marketing*) or in more broad-based international business journals (for example, *Journal of International Business Studies*). Nowadays, general marketing journals including the leading ones are open and receptive to international marketing papers, provided that these submissions meet their editorial objectives and standards and, in the case of top-tier journals, their stringent quality thresholds.

Selection of topic and development of idea

An initial issue for a researcher is to select a promising area to conduct research that exhibits potential to have impact. The topic of research should be both managerially relevant and theoretically interesting, not over-researched as it might be challenging to find important gaps in the literature that warrant consideration, but not very new and undefined as it might prove difficult to make a significant contribution within a reasonable timeframe. As noted earlier, international marketing is a dynamic field that offers many excellent opportunities for investigation that can have impact not only in terms of theory development but addressing such problems can also have important implications for business practice and public policy. A stream of my own research, resulting in dozens of publications over the past three decades, focuses on factors influencing the export performance of the firm. This is a topic that has been investigated widely but is not over-researched, and current developments in the international business landscape provide new opportunities for investigation. In addition to its theoretical significance, the study of export performance and its drivers is of particular relevance to business practitioners and public policy makers concerned with the development of effective national export promotion policies.

Broadly, within this context, identification of a major unresolved problem can be the epicenter of a promising research idea to work on. For instance, some time ago, I worked with colleagues on the particularly important but contentious issue of the performance effects of international marketing strategy standardization versus adaptation, with hundreds of articles in the field considering directly or indirectly this issue. This controversial issue was resolved in Katsikeas, Samiee, and Theodosiou (2006), and this project generated significant interest and a stream of research has been pursued and influential articles published since then. The lesson from this and other similar projects is that, despite the challenges and uncertain outcomes, addressing important unresolved problems has strong potential to result in highly impactful publications for scholarly and practical advancement, generate a large number of citations, and open new avenues of future investigation.

An important issue in the selection of a topic and its impact potential is whether the evidence provided involves a degree of novelty in resolving an important problem. The key point is whether the research conducted, and findings reported would facilitate new ways of thinking about the issue studied. Here, novelty refers to the extent to which the evidence provided by a study "would change the conversation that is already taking place in a given literature" (Colquitt and George 2011, p. 433). For instance, in Katsikeas, Samiee, and Theodosiou (2006), the study offered new evidence, suggesting that neither marketing strategy standardization across markets nor adaptation to foreign market requirements is superior, but it is the achievement of co-alignment or fit between the strategy deployed (whether standardization, adaptation, or any combination of the two) and environmental imperatives that results in enhanced performance outcomes. This evidence not only resolved a long-standing and highly contentious debate in the literature, but also provided new thinking that attracted attention and generated significant research activity in international marketing.

Conceptual development
The development of a strong theory section is a key aspect of any submission to a scholarly journal. This is a particularly relevant issue in international marketing, as a number of critical assessments of this literature have criticized early work and certain streams of research in the area as largely atheoretic with many endeavors conducted in isolation without paying attention to linking the study to prior research (for example, Katsikeas, Leonidou, and Morgan 2000; Leonidou et al. 2007). Undoubtedly,

the picture is totally different nowadays, as the field has grown and developed significantly on the basis of well-conducted theory-based research. Often, in international marketing and other areas as well, researchers pay insufficient attention to conceptual development; many submissions suffer from a lack of conceptual rigor, which limits the chances of a paper's favorable review. To enhance knowledge and advance the maturity of the international marketing field, authors should pay focal attention to the quality of conceptual development in their papers. Emphasis should be given to issues including the engagement and treatment of relevant literature, clarity and precision of conceptual definitions, use of conceptual logic to support position, and treatment of complementary and competing theoretical viewpoints (see Varadarajan 2003). Research in international marketing is prone to falling short of robustness along these lines, "as we tend to 'borrow' from underlying disciplines without always having a deep understanding of their conceptual base. In addition, we often introduce new constructs to capture novel phenomena, without fully doing the proper construct development work" (Bello and Kostova 2012, p. 540).

From a more practical standpoint, there are two fundamental aspects that mark out excellent publications in scholarly academic journals. The first concerns the development of an overarching theoretically anchored conceptualization. This entails that the various study constructs are brought together under the umbrella of a clear theory-based conceptual story. A common problem that we experience is the absence of such an overall theoretical base, along with the presence of individual research hypotheses that are often unconnected on the basis of a clear theoretical foundation and convincing rationale. Such an omission is widely considered a major weakness that would probably result in rejection, particularly in the case of a top journal. The second aspect concerns the development of individual hypotheses. Often, researchers develop hypotheses that are simply based on findings of previous studies, lack compelling conceptual logic, fall short of rational consistency, and/or fail to be part of a coherent set with a clear conceptual premise. As authors, we can certainly contribute by making greater efforts to develop more pragmatically and theoretically interesting hypotheses that exhibit a certain degree of complexity, sophistication, and clarity of conceptual logic.

Empirical studies and research design
In empirical studies, methodological rigor is a key criterion for assessing the quality of scholarly research. The main challenge facing researchers in the design of their projects is matching research designs to address their study questions. However, in an era of heightened journal demands and low manuscript acceptance rates, researchers are pushed to deploy optimal research designs but often find that external factors and particular study characteristics limit their ability to pursue such research based on ideal quality data (McGrath 1981). This is particularly the case for research in international marketing. Often, in addition to the need to establish cross-cultural measure equivalence in certain studies, addressing effectively many research problems in international marketing requires primary data scattered across different countries, the collection of which is typically an overwhelming task. Access to companies and rich data, as well as significant commitments of managers and employees in certain positions required for the participation in academic research,

pose a major problem for international marketing researchers. If such restrictions play a central role in research design decisions, the outcome will be a study that is weaker than expected or that the results are subject to a number of plausible alternative explanations, eventually leading to rejection from a scholarly academic journal or publication in a lower quality journal and the waste of substantial time, effort, and resources (Bono and McNamara 2011).

Changes of basic research design choices are not possible at an advanced stage (for example, during the crafting or revision of a paper). Research design decisions thus affect essentially the validity of the results, confidence in the study conclusions and implications, and the extent to which potential alternative explanations can be ruled out. A number of research design issues have been identified, among editors of and reviewers for scholarly journals, as particularly important to the quality of empirical research (see Bono and McNamara 2011; Varadarajan 2003). I refer to those methods-related issues that, if given insufficient attention in a study, constitute fundamental causes of rejection. First, measurement issues concerning the operationalization of the study constructs, along with the use of rigorous measure validation procedures to establish reliability and validity, require careful consideration. The measurement of a construct needs to effectively capture the construct's conceptual domain. Thus, prior to dealing with measurement issues, it is essential that researchers place emphasis on articulating clear conceptual definitions for the constructs included in the study. In the case of introducing a new construct or adapting a construct established in another field, which is commonly the case in international marketing research, attention should be given to specifying the boundaries of such a construct, explaining how it differs from existing constructs, and avoiding the blatant use of a measurement scale developed in a different context. A fatal flaw of many submissions is the inconsistency between the measures used and the definitions provided for the constructs in a study. Failure of a key construct's measure to adequately tap the conceptual domain of this construct would result in rejection.

Second, the implementation of appropriate sampling and data collection procedures is crucial for effectively addressing the research question. Nowadays, convenience samples – commonly the case in early studies in international marketing – make it difficult for researchers to successfully target academic journals. Likewise, there is a widely held negative bias among editors and reviewers toward the use of student samples in experimental research, as college students are criticized for their inability to represent, and student samples capture, actual customer attitudes and behavior. The use of excellent data is key to testing complex conceptual models, especially in the context of research in international marketing considering the challenges involved in gaining access to or collecting data in more than one country. It is important to describe the data collection and analysis procedures followed, providing clear steps of how sources of data are identified, respondent participation encouraged, experiments organized, and data are collected, cleaned, and analysed using appropriate statistical methods. It should be noted that clarity, precision, and justification of decisions and choices made in sampling and data collection is particularly important. For instance, illustrating how to develop a sampling frame for international marketing alliances using complementary sources (for example, Bello, Katsikeas, and Robson 2010) or undertaking proactive steps and post hoc checks for ensuring informant quality in the study of export ventures (for example, Spyropoulou et al. 2018) is quite painful but excellent practice, often recognized in the review process.

Third, dealing with omitted variables in model specification has become an increasingly important issue in research in international marketing. In this regard, editors and reviewers of international marketing papers, particularly when submitted to highly prestigious journals, now pay greater attention than ever before to the use of appropriate endogeneity tests as well as to the proper inclusion of control variables. Endogeneity is an important problem in much of the research in the general marketing field, indicating that an independent variable is associated with the error term of the regression equation. Lack of attention to accounting for endogeneity is likely to yield biased parameter estimates, which "undermine the validity of the results obtained from regression-type analyses of observational data ... [or from the presence of] correlation between an endogenous variable and its own effect" (Sande and Ghosh 2018, pp. 185–6). Similarly, the inclusion of appropriate control variables results in better specified models and enhances confidence in empirical findings. In practice, however, it may be impossible to include every control in the estimation of a model. It is not feasible that international marketing researchers in particular are able to have data on all possible control variables in the database being employed. Nonetheless, the careful selection of relevant control variables during the research design phase can prove rewarding later on when the manuscript is under publication consideration. In many cases, researchers do not use control variables at all or make choices based on convenience in an effort to account for relevant factors connected with the study's international marketing problem or context, often leading to the use of "unimportant" variables that unnecessarily soak up degrees of freedom and bias results. The inclusion of a variable as a control requires a clear expectation that it is related to the dependent variable(s) in the study on the basis of theoretical logic or previous findings (see for discussion Bono and McNamara 2011).

Academic conferences and publications
Once the selection of an intriguing research topic is made, the conceptual framework developed, sound data collected, and necessary analyses conducted, the focus of attention should move to publishing the work in scholarly academic journals. To this end, many established researchers recommend that participation in international academic conferences is an important means of presenting a new project to get feedback, often from established colleagues who may share similar interests, which can tangibly help the authors advance their work. Internationally recognized research meetings and academic conferences, not only those specializing in international marketing and business but also more general marketing ones, play a crucial instrumental role in advancing a project and strengthening its quality. Thus, excellent mentors always encourage young faculty and doctoral students to present their work in prestigious academic conferences and pursue opportunities to discuss their research with other researchers on the subject and leading scholars in the general field.

Next, emphasis should be placed on *crafting* the paper for submission to a scholarly academic journal. Authors need to decide explicitly on the journal they will target and make sure that they have a clear idea of the key features, author guidelines, and idiosyncrasies of this journal, the types of articles it publishes, and how these are organized and presented. Here, I refer to some issues that authors may wish to consider in crafting a manuscript, as these usually attract the attention of editors and reviewers and are raised in their reports.

Introduction and positioning   The introduction is perhaps the most important section of a manuscript, as it focuses on articulating the framing and positioning of the study in the international marketing literature and, in turn, enables authors to specify the distinct ways that their study significantly contributes to the body of existing knowledge. The opening paragraph often focuses on highlighting the nature and significance of the focal phenomenon examined. The aim is to generate strong interest and curiosity about the paper. Then, attention is given to providing an account of prior work on the issue and specifying key streams of research that have been pursued on the issue under study. Next, authors need to establish important gaps in the literature that are worthy of investigation. Identifying a lacuna of knowledge that is of little interest for international marketing theory and practice, or just isolating an issue that has not been investigated before, but which is trivial or uninteresting, does not constitute a gap that can serve as a platform for building a study. Authors should find it prudent to explain how a specific gap limits our understanding of the phenomenon investigated and justify the importance of addressing this gap. Clarity and precision here lead smoothly to setting interesting research questions or objectives that are linked to prior research and to establishing the contributions of the study to the literature that must also be outlined in the introduction.

Authors can contribute in a number of different ways. A manuscript can focus on resolving the presence of mixed findings concerning the significance of a widely researched issue, for example, the performance outcomes of trust in international strategic alliance relationships (for example, Robson, Katsikeas, and Bello 2008). Alternately, a paper can investigate an important controversial issue in the literature, for instance, the study of performance effects of international marketing strategy standardization versus adaptation (for example, Katsikeas, Samiee, and Theodosiou 2006). In such a case, the authors may find advantage in seeking to bring a new theoretical lens to an established area. They should also show the limits inherent in existing approaches or the conditions under which current approaches work and explain how the new lens enables us to consider an issue differently. Another approach would be to introduce a new variable or mechanism that explains important connections between constructs or sheds light onto discordant findings in the literature. Such an example is the introduction of accommodation and monitoring as the mechanism enabling international marketing alliances to address adaptation and evaluation problems commonly experienced by such partnerships and, in turn, link commitment aspects to performance in the alliance (see Bello, Katsikeas, and Robson 2010).

Regardless of the study and issue addressed, the ways in which the study contributes to the literature need to be explicitly stated. There is no prescription as to how you can do this. One approach is to craft a meaty well-structured paragraph to specify an overall, grand contribution to existing theoretical knowledge and one or two specific contributions to the issue or topic being studied. Another approach that is widely used is presenting the study contributions in separate paragraphs. This is more appropriate when a study makes a number of contributions to knowledge in different research strands that are of equal magnitude. Crafting the contributions can be challenging and requires the author's full attention, as failing to do so would raise doubts among editors and reviewers about the significance of the study and predispose them negatively toward the added value of the research findings.

When authors target a specialized international marketing or business journal, in crafting the introduction of their manuscript attention should be given to highlighting the need to fill the gaps that the authors identify in, along with the contributions that the study makes to, the international marketing and/or international business literature. However, a different approach is needed when an international marketing paper is targeted at a more broad-based journal. In developing a convincing positioning of an international marketing study for submission to a general marketing journal, it is essential to isolate the limitations in current debates and research in the general marketing literature and demonstrate how recourse to an international marketing context and its unique characteristics and contingencies helps shed new light and/or offers new evidence that runs contrary to traditional thinking (cf. Wright 2014). This is a subtle but important issue that many authors working on specific issues within relatively narrow areas or specialized fields tend to overlook in their journal targeting choices, which can determine the editorial decision about a paper.

Conceptual framework and hypotheses   A systematic review of the literature should focus on the issues and constructs considered in the study and avoid an extensive coverage of the whole literature in an area that fails to provide a clear foundation and rationale for the present study. As noted earlier, introducing an overarching conceptual framework helps the development of hypotheses to fit together in a coherent theory-based fashion, rather than advancing individual hypotheses in isolation (Wright 2014). Researchers need to justify the appropriateness of selecting to apply or draw from a particular theory or multiple theories. Drawing from more than one theoretical perspective is common in international marketing, due in part to the potential of such research to generate new insights in terms of theoretical and practical advancement of knowledge on the subject being investigated. However, the challenge facing researchers is to integrate the different theoretical perspectives that they draw from for the development of their conceptual framework and research hypotheses. The problem that often arises is that researchers choose to draw from multiple theories that are not compatible, which makes any attempt to develop an integrated conceptual framework and subsequent empirical analyses unsubstantiated and meaningless.

Methods and results   All empirical papers need to have a section on the methodology and another on the analysis and results that explicitly explain the suitability of the data and measures employed and the appropriateness and rigor of the data analysis methods used for addressing the research questions. Well-presented and structured methods and results sections, explaining the data collection procedures and data analysis and presenting the results, can play an instrumental role in convincing editors, reviewers, and their broader audience that proposed frameworks, conceptual arguments, and expected relationships are validated (partly or fully) or otherwise. These sections send positive signals about the quality of the empirics employed in the study and the extent to which researchers have done things 'according to the book'. Nevertheless, as methods and results sections may seem, prima facie, not very exciting and/or sometimes are viewed as not playing a critical role, many researchers tend to place less emphasis on developing them – which is wrong. In practice, many scholars begin the construction of their papers with the drafting of the methods and results sections, and then move to the development of earlier parts.

Importantly, method and results sections crafted in a way that demonstrates methodological rigor and attention to detail can make a real difference in the minds of editors and reviewers about a study and its potential and, in turn, whether to make a revision request or recommend rejection (Zhang and Shaw 2012). This is an issue of particular importance to empirical research in international marketing, given the difficulties involved in collecting high quality data in cross-cultural studies and/or across more than one country. My own experience strongly suggests that, more often than not, taking the time and feeling the pain to employ a rigorous methodology, collect excellent data, and use appropriate methods of analyses is a rewarding task and one of the key elements triggering a revision invitation. There are no recipes concerning the best way to follow in crafting the methods and results sections. Though the primary purpose and basic characteristics of the methods and results sections have considerable similarities across studies, the structure of these sections, details included, and degree of justification provided are likely to differ from one study to another. Zhang and Shaw (2012) suggest that methods and results sections should each be developed on the basis of three fundamental principles, these being completeness, clarity, and consistency, and provide valuable insights together with a set of broad guidelines for crafting each of these sections.

Discussion   Researchers tend to consider the discussion section the last mandatory obstacle they need to climb and thus accelerate their paper's move to the "under review" stage. The discussion section provides a great opportunity to researchers to strengthen and sharpen the big message conveyed by the study and fully convince editors and reviewers of its wider impact, underlying value, and contribution. This section may also offer the chance to more fully introduce and embed the study and its contribution in the body of current knowledge, thus engaging other researchers in a deep, value-enhancing discussion and even shaping the future direction in the area (Geletkanycz and Tepper 2012). The discussion section essentially contains the theoretical and pragmatic implications (for example, managerial and, if relevant, policy), commonly presented in two separate subsections. Limitations and future research directions can also be presented in a subsection of the discussion or, quite often, are organized as a separate section.

Authors agree that, often, the discussion should start with outlining the research problem or questions and how the study and evidence has tackled those. Particular attention should be given to the theoretical implications of the study findings, which should be presented in a value-enhancing way that demonstrates how they significantly add to or extend existing theoretical knowledge, and/or deepen understanding of the phenomenon or issue investigated. Unexpected or surprising findings should be highlighted, and attempts made to explain them. Researchers often undertake additional analyses in the endeavor to explain such evidence and also rule out alternative explanations and enhance confidence in their conceptualization and findings. If limited, the results of such analyses are reported in the discussion or in the limitations (sub)section. If further analyses are extensive, these are commonly reported in a separate subsection of the results or parts of these that involve considerable detail can be placed as Web appendices.

A common observation with many papers is that, while researchers concentrate on effectively addressing a big controversy or major issue of particular theoretical and managerial importance, this focus often disappears by the time they reach the discussion of their findings. However, it should be remembered that the discussion needs to convincingly resolve the research problem and fill the gaps in the literature identified initially. To stress the significance of their work, researchers sometimes make claims about the study's contributions that are not supported by the results, which attracts the attention and discomfort of reviewers. This section should instead help readers ease the tension and/or complexity involved and resolve the puzzle that underpins the need or motivation for the execution of the study. A good discussion would need to address the question of "so what?" in a very convincing and robust fashion and "articulate ... how the study changes, challenges or otherwise fundamentally refines understanding of extant theory" (Geletkanycz and Tepper 2012, p. 257). In addition, the discussion section should consider the overall picture of the evidence provided in the study and assess the findings in a unified, aggregate way that cultivates and promotes the advancement of a strong single message underpinning the conceptual framework and research hypotheses. Researchers often make the mistake of organizing their discussion around individual research hypotheses or focus on summarizing the results of individual tests, which is at the expense of attention to explaining the results and examining their added value. What we also experience is that researchers attempt to claim and examine many theoretical implications that appear unconnected to each other, which undermines coherence in the discussion and overall contribution of the study to existing theoretical knowledge.

The role of seminars and workshops

The growth and development of the international marketing literature is largely based on scholarly investigation focusing on research, models and hypotheses, or dependent and independent variables of particular interest to companies, managers, and sometimes public policy makers (cf. Varadarajan 2003). The pragmatic relevance of the bulk of research in international marketing is reflected in the emphasis placed on examining factors that practitioners, and less often policy makers, can control or influence. It is thus vital for researchers to develop and maintain a deep understanding of the key challenges facing companies in establishing and sustaining international market operations. Highly influential research in international marketing is driven by the interests and priorities of business practitioners concerning their firms' international marketing strategies.

Engagement in practitioner-based seminars and workshops plays a critical role in establishing a healthy connection to business practitioners with the view to understanding how they think, act, and make decisions and choices in their international market operations. Seminars and workshops are widely seen as an effective means of connecting one's research agenda to current priories in the business world. They enable researchers to communicate their findings to parts of the business community interested in the study and its practical implications. It is an obligation of academic researchers to do so, not only because companies and managers often endorse and participate in academic studies, but because they also constitute a natural recipient of the findings of academic research. Regular involvement in seminars and workshops also enables researchers to keep track with the real world, appreciate practitioners' current problems, and ultimately identify opportunities for new projects on important and timely issues. Further, through interaction with practitioners, researchers can improve their conceptual models and research designs. For instance, it was initially a series of workshops with managers that helped us appreciate that, in studying the performance effects of trust in cross-border buyer–seller relationships, we had to use a time lag in the collection of data on trust and performance outcomes as managers appeared consistent in their perceptions that good performance enhances trust, rather than vice versa (see Katsikeas, Skarmeas, and Bello 2009).

Executive publications
Given the central role that academic researchers in marketing and other business disciplines play in serving the business community, it is essential that academics disseminate research findings among practitioners in a way that makes sense to them. However, executives have questioned the managerial usefulness of academic research. They often make noises about the practical value of academic publications, which they find too complex and cannot see how research findings can help them resolve their problems (for example, Jaworski 2011; Reibstein, Day, and Wind 2009). It should be noted that, in reality, the bulk of research in international marketing and other marketing areas aims at publications in scholarly academic journals, which essentially determines tenure and promotion decisions in research-driven business schools all over the world. The vast majority of researchers thus pay little (if any) attention to writing for and communicating their results to the business world or even forget to go back to companies participating in academic research projects, with a practitioner-friendly summary of the main findings and their implications for business.

Although this situation is up to a certain extent understandable, the gap between research on marketing issues and its relevance to organizations and society (for example, Bolton 2011 seriously questions the contribution of marketing within the firm (for example, Lehman, McAlister, and Staelin 2011). Therefore, within the context of international marketing, it is vital that, in addition to publishing in scholarly academic journals, researchers need to place emphasis on communicating their findings and implications of their work to international business practitioners and other decision makers (for example, public policy makers, consumers) interested in these. One way of doing this is through publications in prestigious practitioner-journals, including *Harvard Business Review*, *Sloan Management Review*, *California Management Review*, which involve a selective screening and review process. Articles in these journals in fact count in many business schools.

Another way is pursuing publications in less demanding outlets (for example, *Business Strategy Review*, *LSE Review*) established by individual business schools to communicate with their own business network and maintain an ongoing relationship with their alumni. Editors of these outlets often look proactively for interesting academic articles and pursue the consent of the authors to develop a short managerial version for their audience. Furthermore, researchers can pursue other avenues including business magazines (for example, *Marketing Week*, *Fortune*, *Business Today*), local and national newspapers, business conferences and executive workshops, and/or websites in their business schools. In sum, to elevate the standing of the field within the firm, it is important to demonstrate to practitioners that researchers not only understand the current problems their firms experience in international market operations, but also provide readily interpretable guidelines for effectively resolving these problems.

Further conceptual development

A particularly healthy step in the research trajectory of an academic researcher is, when a project is completed with articles being published in academic and practitioner-focused journals and seminars and workshops delivered among managerial audiences, to engage in continuing conceptual development that would serve as a platform for the next project. The experiential knowledge that a researcher has gained through the process of design and execution of the research, along with the challenges in crafting, revising, and ultimately publishing manuscripts from the project, is a valuable asset that can play an instrumental role in the researcher's pursuit of other, perhaps more ambitious, projects. A typical example from the international marketing literature is a highly influential article on reviewing and evaluating, on the basis of theory-based criteria, the export performance measures identified in the pertinent empirical literature (see Katsikeas, Leonidou, and Morgan 2000). The learning from this evaluation exercise was the driving force for the authors to embark on a much larger and more ambitious project on assessing performance outcomes in marketing, which covered all the empirical studies in marketing with one or more performance outcome variable over a 33-year period. The project was published quite recently in the *Journal of Marketing*, and early signs indicate that this is a highly impactful article (see Katsikeas et al. 2016). It should be noted that, without the knowledge gained from the first project, which was more focused and narrower, it would not have been possible for the authors to conceptualize, undertake, and deliver the second project, which was much broader, more demanding in terms of effort, time, and resources, and more challenging to complete.

There are different ways that researchers can follow in capitalizing on the knowledge that they acquire from their projects. In addition to the earlier example, it would be fruitful if researchers engaged in new projects that build on the findings and/or limitations of a study that has just been completed and the paper is in print. For instance, the study of trust in international buyer–seller relationships has received considerable research attention in the international business and marketing literature. Learning from conducting research on the subject, authors worked on developing a new third-order conceptualization and operationalization of trust in international strategic alliances that was theoretically anchored, managerially meaningful, and more comprehensive than those of previous studies (see Robson, Katsikeas, and Bello 2008). Similarly, international marketing researchers should find advantage in developing measures for their study constructs based on the latest knowledge advanced in the literature. A typical case in international marketing concerns the measurement of export performance, often based on the use of global measures that tend to mask the varying effects of independent variables on diverse aspects of performance dependents. Recent developments in the general field recognize various buckets of performance measures and call for focus on specific performance aspects and the study of performance trade-offs (for example, Katsikeas et al. 2016). Such knowledge can certainly improve conceptual and methodological rigor in international market performance assessments and enable the study of theory-based performance trade-offs between different indicators in foreign market activities.

Can research in international marketing make it in leading academic journals?
A relatively small number of international marketing articles have been published in top-tier marketing journals over the past thirty years. Thus, understandably, an important question among researchers is whether international marketing is a disciplinary area that offers promising research opportunities that can lead to publications in leading academic journals, which essentially determines decisions for faculty tenure and promotion in research-led academic institutions worldwide. There is a widely held thought among academics that publishing international marketing papers in leading marketing journals is a particularly challenging task – clearly more difficult than it is in other disciplinary areas of marketing. Many marketing scholars believe that it is immensely difficult to take account of the multiple factors influencing dependent variables in international marketing studies, often resulting in underspecified models or models that have limited explanatory power.

A related issue is that researchers in international marketing have formed a view that there is some kind of bias against international marketing papers in top-tier journals in marketing. The question arising is whether there is such a negative bias among top journals in the field and, in broader terms, the extent to which it is credible to view international marketing as a particularly difficult area to publish in top-tier marketing journals. Based on my long experience as author of over a hundred articles in a wide range of journals including top-tier ones, reviewer for various journals including top ones across fields, and editor of several academic journals, I strongly suggest that this perception is unsubstantiated and that top journals are not biased at all against international marketing submissions. On the contrary, my view is that international marketing papers are very welcome not only among premier-league marketing journals, but also among such journals in other business and management fields.

The most important element of work published in leading academic journals concerns the significance of its contribution to theory, methodology, and/or practice in international marketing. For instance, a series of articles on country-specific scale construction and cross-national measurement invariance by De Jong and colleagues (2009, 2007), Baumgartner and Steenkamp (2001), and Steenkamp and Baumgartner (1998) are widely regarded as important methodological contributions that have greatly influenced thinking in and the direction of global marketing. Another example is Cavusgil and Zou's (1994) highly influential study on export product–market ventures. In response to the largely fragmented body of knowledge in the exporting literature, these authors have advanced and tested a theory-based model of internal and external factors that influence adaptation of export marketing program elements, which in turn affect export venture performance outcomes. In addition to the relevance of the topic, the timing of the study, and its substantive contribution to knowledge, this award-winning article has stimulated significant further research activity in the field. Likewise, in Morgan et al.'s (2004) impactful study, the thrust of the contribution is based on the assimilation of two distinct but competing theoretical perspectives (i.e., the industrial organization theory and the resource-based view) in an integrated model of drivers of export venture advantage and performance outcomes. In a similar vein, Bello, Katsikeas, and Robson (2010) identified discordant findings concerning the commitment–performance link in international marketing alliances. In response, the authors introduced a new theoretically anchored mechanism that addresses fundamental adaptation and evaluation problems and, thus, connects distinct commitment aspects and performance outcomes in such alliances.

A common feature in these and other international marketing articles in top-tier marketing journals is the broadness of their contribution. These studies have been designed to contribute significantly (and do so) not only to the international marketing literature, but they also pay focal attention to advancing knowledge in the broader marketing and/or management field. Many of the problems addressed and research streams developed in the context of international marketing are relevant and important issues of research interest in other fields, which makes international marketing studies eligible for targeting journals beyond marketing. For instance, Robson, Katsikeas, and Bello's (2008) study of antecedents and performance consequences of trust in international strategic alliances, a commonly researched issue in (international) marketing, was published in a leading management journal. Even more striking example is Katsikeas, Samiee, and Theodosiou's (2006) influential study on strategy fit and performance outcomes of international marketing strategy standardization, which was published in *Strategic Management Journal* – the leading strategy journal. In sum, this discussion suggests that relevant and rigorous research in international marketing, which significantly contributes to current knowledge, has the potential to make it in leading journals not only in marketing but in other business and management fields. This potential, along with the pace of change and developments in the global marketplace, makes international marketing a particularly interesting field in which to work and pursue scholarly research and publications.

Conclusion

In this chapter, I have presented challenges facing international marketing research and highlighted opportunities for undertaking scholarly research in this field. Attention has been given to considering a practical approach to conducting research in international marketing and highlighting key steps in this process and providing some guideposts for building and maintaining an effective research strategy. The message in this discussion is that international marketing is an exciting field that offers a plethora of fruitful opportunities to pursue managerially relevant and theoretically interesting research and publications in academic and practitioner journals. For some academics, publishing might seem a challenging task, especially when considering the difficulties in and commitment to conducting research in international marketing. There is no typical trajectory in international marketing research and individual researchers will be able to reflect on their own idiosyncrasies, experiences, and decision choices. Nonetheless, I very much hope that I have managed to demonstrate the benefits of continuously engaging in scholarly research, generating and disseminating new knowledge, contributing to theory and influencing decision makers (for example, managers, government officials, consumers) within the exciting domain of international marketing.

References

Baumgartner, Hans and Jan-Benedict E.M. Steenkamp (2001), "Response Styles in Marketing Research: A Cross-National Investigation," *Journal of Marketing Research*, 38 (May), 143–56.

Bello, Daniel C. and Tatiana Kostova (2012), "From the Editors: Conducting High Impact International Business Research: The Role of Theory," *Journal of International Business Studies*, 43 (6), 537–43.

Bello, Daniel C., Constantine S. Katsikeas, and Matthew J. Robson (2010), "Does Accommodating a Self-Serving Partner in an International Marketing Alliance Pay Off?," *Journal of Marketing*, 74 (November), 77–93.

Bolton, Ruth N. (2011), "The *JM* in its 75th Anniversary," *Journal of Marketing*, 75 (July), 129–31.

Bono, Joyce E. and Gerry McNamara (2011), "Publishing in *AMJ* – Part 2: Research Design," *Academy of Management Journal*, 54 (11), 657–60.

Cavusgil, S. Tamer and Shaoming Zou (1994), "Marketing Strategy–Performance Relationship: An Investigation of the Empirical Link in Export Market Ventures," *Journal of Marketing*, 58 (January), 1–21.

Colquitt, Jason A. and Gerard George (2011), "From the Editors: Publishing in *AMJ* – Part 1: Topic Choice," *Academy of Management Journal*, 54 (3), 432–5.

De Jong, Martijn G., Jan-Benedict E.M. Steenkamp, and Jean-Paul Fox (2007), "Addressing Cross-National Measurement Invariance Using a Hierarchical IRT Model," *Journal of Consumer Research*, 34 (August), 260–78.

De Jong, Martijn G., Jan-Benedict E.M. Steenkamp, and Bernard P. Veldkamp (2009), "A Model for the Construction of Country-Specific, Yet Internationally Comparable Short-Form Marketing Scales," *Marketing Science*, 28 (July–August), 674–89.

Geletkanycz, Marta and Bennett J. Tepper (2012), "Publishing in *AMJ* – Part 6: Discussing the Implications," *Academy of Management Journal*, 55 (2), 256–60.

Jaworski, Bernard J. (2011), "On Managerial Relevance," *Journal of Marketing*, 75 (July), 211–24.

Katsikeas, Constantine S. (2018), "Special Issue on the Future of International Marketing: Trends, Developments, and Directions," *Journal of International Marketing*, 26 (1), 1–3.

Katsikeas, Constantine S., Leonidas C. Leonidou, and Neil A. Morgan (2000), "Firm-Level Export Performance Assessment: Review, Evaluation, and Development", *Journal of the Academy of Marketing Science*, 28 (4), 493–511.

Katsikeas, Constantine S., Saeed Samiee, and Marios Theodosiou (2006), "Strategy Fit and Performance Consequences of International Marketing Standardization," *Strategic Management Journal*, 27, 867–90.

Katsikeas, Constantine S., Dionysis Skarmeas, and Daniel C. Bello (2009), "Developing Successful Trust-Based Exchange Relationships," *Journal of International Business Studies*, 40 (1), 132–55.

Katsikeas, Constantine S., Neil A. Morgan, Leonidas C. Leonidou, and G. Tomas M. Hult (2016), "Assessing Performance Outcomes in Marketing," *Journal of Marketing*, 80 (March), 1–20.

Lehmann, Donald R., Leigh McAlister, and Richard Staelin (2011), "Sophistication in Research in Marketing," *Journal of Marketing*, 75 (July), 155–65.

Leonidou, Leonidas C., Constantine S. Katsikeas, Dayananda Palihawadana, and Stavroula Spyropoulou (2007), "An Analytical Review of the Factors Stimulating Smaller Firms to Export: Implications for Policy-Makers," *International Marketing Review*, 24 (6), 735–70.

Leonidou, Leonidas C., Constantine S. Katsikeas, Saeed Samiee, and Bilge Aykol (2017), "International Marketing Research: A State-of-the-Art Review and the Way Forward," in *Advances in Global Marketing: A Research Anthology*, Leonidas C. Leonidou, Constantine S. Katsikeas, Saeed Samiee, and Bilge Aykol, eds. Basingstoke: Springer International, 3–33.

McGrath, Joseph E. (1981), "Dilemmatics: The Study of Research Choices and Dilemmas," *American Behavioral Scientist*, 25 (2), 179–210.

Morgan, Neal, Anna Kaleka, and Constantine S. Katsikeas (2004), "Antecedants of Export Venture Performance: A Theoretical Model and Empirical Assessment", *Journal of Marketing*, 68 (1), 90 – 108.

Reibstein, David J., George Day, and Jerry Wind (2009), "Guest Editorial: Is Marketing Academia Losing its Way?" *Journal of Marketing*, 73 (July), 1–3.

Robson, Matthew J., Constantine S. Katsikeas, and Daniel C. Bello (2008), "Drivers and Performance Outcomes of Trust in International Marketing Alliances: The Role of Organizational Complexity," *Organization Science*, 19 (4), 647–65.

Robson, Matthew J., Constantine S. Katsikeas, and Daniel C. Bello (2009), "Drivers and Performance Outcomes of Trust in International Strategic Alliances: The Role of Organizational Complexity," *Organization Science*, 19 (4), 647–65.

Sande, Jon Bingen and Mrinal Ghosh (2018), "Endogeneity in Survey Research," *International Journal of Research in Marketing*, 35 (2), 185–204.

Spyropoulou, Stavroula, Constantine S. Katsikeas, Dionysios Skarmeas, and Neil A. Morgan (2018), "Strategic Goal Accomplishment in Export Ventures: The Role of Capabilities, Knowledge, and Environment," *Journal of the Academy of Marketing Science*, 46 (1), 109–29.

Steenkamp, Jan-Benedict E.M. and Hans Baumgartner (1998), "Assessing Measurement Invariance in Cross-National Consumer Research," *Journal of Consumer Research*, 25 (June), 78–90.

Varadarajan, Rajan P. (2003), "Musings on Relevance and Rigor of Scholarly Research in Marketing," *Journal of the Academy of Marketing Science*, 31 (4), 368–76.

Wright, Mike (2014), "Getting Published in Entrepreneurship Journals," in *How to Get Published in the Best Entrepreneurship Journals*, Alain Fayolle and Mike Wright, eds. Cheltenham, UK and Northampton, MA, USA: Edward Elgar Publishing, 16–26.

Zhang, Yan (Andrea) and Jason D. Shaw (2012), "Getting Published in *AMJ* – Part 5: Crafting the Methods and Results," *Academy of Management Journal*, 55 (1), 8–12.

[11]

Sample design for research in marketing

Vikas Mittal

A major objective of publishing research in top-tier marketing journals is to make an impact on scholarly and managerial thinking. A typical journal article can achieve this goal by choosing a theoretically important topic, providing novel insights to academics and practitioners, and ensuring that the article provides results that can be trusted and applied by practitioners. The latter two goals rely on the realism and generalizability of the data used, as well as the appropriate application of research tools – statistical analysis, description and interpretation of results – to the data. Needless to say, a critical aspect of developing the data for a research paper includes the selection and implementation of an appropriate sample design process.

As defined later, the sample design process includes a systematic approach to defining a population of interest, choosing a subset of the population (that is, sample) for empirical measurement, and retaining the ability to project the results to the population of interest. In most empirical studies, the researcher will provide a brief overview of the sample design, including but not limited to source of the sample, response rate, descriptive characteristics of the sample, sample size, and criteria used to exclude specific sample units. For readers of a published article, the sample description section is a key element in deciding the extent to which the results can be projected and applied to the general population. Higher external validity – the ability to project the results from a sample to a population – helps to increase the influence of an article because managers as well as academics can use the results with a higher level of confidence in their applicability to situations beyond the original sample. As a result, researchers interested in increasing the impact of their research should carefully evaluate the pros and cons of choosing an alternative at each step of the sample design process.

This chapter provides a brief overview of sample design process, discusses issues pertaining to sample design and selection, and highlights best practices for sample design and reporting in journal articles. The goal is to help readers gain a deeper understanding of the process so that they can critically evaluate their choices at each step of the sample design process for maximizing the impact of their research.

Sample design for representing a population of interest

Sample design is a process for systematically identifying, collecting, and measuring a subset of elements from a population of interest with the goal to draw accurate, valid, and generalizable conclusions about the population. Figure 11.1 provides a general overview of the process which typically entails four specific decisions. At each stage the researcher must make several informed choices which shape the final disposition of the sample used in an empirical study.

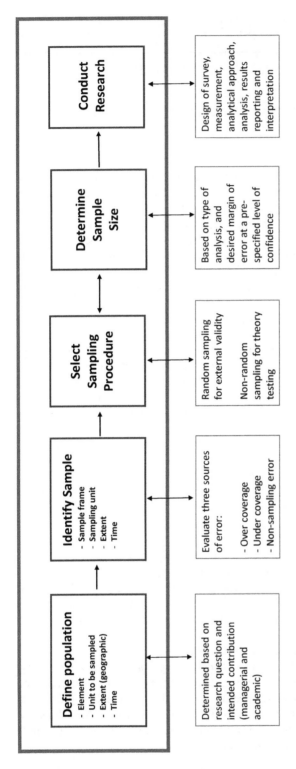

Figure 11.1   Sample design process

Implementing the sample design process entails the determination of an appropriate population, and selection of a sample. More formally, we define the population and sample as follows:

Population: Collection of all elements about which information is sought.
Sample: The subset of elements of a population that is selected to obtain information about the population.

As shown in Figure 11.1, defining the population and the sampling frame entails the research scholar to ascertain if the primary goal of the paper is to test theory or provide managerial insights. For the former, a narrowly defined population would suffice as long as the study design and analysis can ensure high internal validity. In contrast, if the goal is to provide managerially generalizable results, the sampling elements may need to be closer to the decision of interest to managers. As an example, the sample design for the American Customer Satisfaction Index (ACSI) specifically focused on seven major economic sectors in the USA, including major industry groups within each sector, and within each industry included the top two or three companies accounting for the majority of the sales. Finally, for each company, researchers interviewed 250 customers based on a national probability sample of households in the USA that had a telephone. This approach to defining the population – customers of products and services of U.S. companies – ensured that the sample was not only relevant to scholars interested in understanding customer satisfaction as a theoretical construct, but also to managers at a specific company interested in comparing their customers' satisfaction to customers of other companies – within their own industry and across industries.

Why use a sample?
A sample-based approach, widely used in marketing studies, is preferred to a census for several reasons. In a census, the goal is to measure each and every element of the population. In contrast, in a sample, a subset of elements of the population is chosen and measured. The subset can be chosen based on probability or non-probability sampling techniques.[1]

- For a given budget, obtaining a sample is much more efficient – cheaper and faster – than obtaining a census.
- In many situations, for example, pharmaceutical consumer research, a sample is preferred if contact with the population element contaminates, harms, or destroys the unit. For example, if injecting a potential patient with an experimental drug can have side effects, we would want to obtain a small sample and not a census. When conducting research on brand messaging to mitigate the effects of product harm crisis, scholars would prefer to use a sample rather than expose the entire population to the potential product harm.
- Theoretically, a sample is *more* accurate than a census when a researcher faces a budget constraint. Why? A colleague in India obtained a research grant for $4,000 to examine how narcissism affects the online behavior – posting, liking, and sharing social media posts – of consumers in India. With over 250 million

Indian consumers using social media, any attempt to survey all of them will require the majority of the budget to be spent on sending a survey to all 250 million consumers. Aside from the impracticality of this approach, it would require the researcher to cut corners in survey design and analysis, degrading the quality of the overall conclusions drawn from the data.

Given these practical constraints, virtually all of the articles appearing in marketing journals rely on some form of a sample to draw conclusions about the population of interest. Generally, it is believed that a small, representative, and unbiased sample is preferred to a much larger, biased sample.

Components of sample design

The key components of a sample include the population element, the sampling unit, the sampling frame, the time, and the extent of the sample. These are defined below:

Population element: This is the element of the population about which information is sought.

Sampling unit: This is the unit of a sample which can provide information about the population element. As described later, the sampling unit and population element can overlap but they need not be the same.

Sampling frame: This is the source from which sampling units are obtained. Examples include a mailing list of customers of a company, a list of email addresses, a group of voluntary participants for compensation in a survey, people entering a mall during a pre-specified period, product ratings on a specific website and so forth.

Sampling extent: This typically refers to the geographic reach of the sampling frame.

Sampling time: This defines the time period within which the sampling units are contacted and measured.

These concepts can be illustrated with four different hypothetical studies, summarized in Table 11.1 and described next. They are used throughout the chapter to illustrate different concepts.

Consumer research example – 1 (CB-online study)

Researchers wanted to examine how the political identity of U.S. consumers influences their brand perceptions. The study was run using Amazon Mechanical Turk (MTurk), where each participant was paid $1.00 for completing the survey. The survey was posted online from August 12 to 22, 2018, and people 21-years or older who reside in the United States were eligible to participate. A total of 310 people completed the survey, of which five were excluded because they did not pass the attention check measures.

Table 11.1   Sample design for hypothetical studies

	CB-Online Study	**CB-Field Study**	**Managerial Study**	**Quantitative Modeling Study**
Population Element	U.S. Consumers	U.S. Consumers	A company with suppliers	Customers of FurnCo
Sampling Frame	All potential MTurk workers	All consumers entering the mall during the study period	All enrollee's in the SampleCo study	FurnCo's customer database
Sampling Unit	MTurk workers who chose to participate for a $1 incentive	Consumers entering a mall in Houston, TX who choose to participate in a study for a $5 incentive	An employee at a company who is also enrolled in SampleCo's study, and who was approached for the marketing study	FurnCo customers who are also in the company's database
Time	August 12–22, 2018	December 1–7, 2017	September 10–30, 2018	May 1 2010 to May 1 2015
Extent	USA	USA	Canada, USA, Europe	Arizona, California, Nevada

Consumer research example – 2 (CB-field study)

To examine how political identity of U.S. consumers influences their brand perceptions, researchers ran a study in an upscale mall in Houston, TX. A research assistant set up a small table at one of the entrances, for the first week of December, 2017. Every fifth person entering the mall was approached with a $5 coupon that could be used at any store in the mall. Mall entrants who decided to participate in the study sat at the table, completed the study, and received their coupon. A total of 200 completed surveys were obtained.

Business-to-business research (managerial study)

Strategy researchers wanted to examine how a company's satisfaction with its supplier affects its likelihood to invite the supplier to bid on the next project that becomes available. They obtained a sample of managers from different businesses who rate one of their suppliers. The sample is provided by SampleCo, a leading business-to-business research company that provides sample lists of managers from companies in Canada, Europe, and the USA. The supplier ran the survey from September 10 to 30, 2018. A total of 2,000 managers were invited to participate. Of those, 200 managers with at least five years of work experience who have direct experience working with the supplier completed the survey. After that the study was closed to any additional participants.

Loyalty-card study (quantitative modeling study)

Researchers obtained customer data from 30,000 customers of a company, FurnCo, in California for the period May 1, 2010 to May 1, 2015. The company sells furniture in California, Arizona, and Nevada through its stores and direct-mail program. Among customers in the database, 32 percent were members of the loyalty-card program while others were not. The goal of the study was to compare loyalty-card holders and non-holders, and examine factors driving loyalty card usage among loyalty-card holders.

Table 11.1 summarizes the major aspects of the sample design process – defining the population, identifying the sample, and selecting the sampling procedure. As should be evident, research scholars can use the systematic format shown in Figure 11.1 and Table 11.1 to clearly describe the sampling process and its ramifications for their empirical study. This format can lend clarity and provide a unified approach to the research team for evaluating the sample from many different vantage points. When describing their sample for a journal article, researchers should make sure that they describe all five characteristics of the sample in the study design section, using a separate sub-heading entitled "Sample Design."

Evaluating sample quality

Assuming that the researcher has clearly and correctly identified the population of interest, the primary criterion for judging the quality of the sample used in the research study is the sample's ability to represent the population of interest. Stated differently, the quality of a sample is judged based on the representativeness of the sample, that is, the ability of a researcher to confidently project the findings from a sample to the population of interest. A typical sample will deviate from the population of interest for several reasons.

Over-coverage in the sampling frame   This occurs when the sampling frame contains units that should *not* be part of the population. Examples of this are shown in Table 11.2. This problem can be corrected by pre-screening of respondents prior to inclusion in the study.

As an example, in the CB-online study, all potential participants would be asked:

Q1.   Which category best describes your current age?
      __ Less than 21 years   __ 21 years and older
Q2.   Where do you currently reside, that is, what is your current place of residence?
      __ In the continental United States   __ Outside the continental United States

Based on the above two questions, we can retain participants who qualify for the study, and screen out participants who do not.

In the CB-field study a similar approach could be taken by asking participants their area of residence and whether they have shopped in the past three months (a surrogate for consumer status), and administering an attention check. In the quantitative study, the researcher cannot ask direct questions to study participants. Therefore, some cross-validation could be done with other company databases to ascertain if people in the database are, in fact, customers. Thus, the researcher could ask sales records for each customer to be appended to the dataset; those who do not have a sales record appended may be excluded.

In summary, over-coverage can be addressed by designing and implementing a respondent-screening process and by cross-validating participants to ensure they meet study inclusion criteria.

Under-coverage in the sampling frame   This occurs when the sampling frame systematically excludes units that should be part of the population. Typically, this occurs when the sampling frame does not include elements that are part of the population set. From a practical point of view, the inherent limitations of a sampling frame lead to issues with under-coverage. Examples of under-coverage are shown in Table 11.2.

As an example, the CB-online study suffers from a high degree of under-coverage due to its reliance on MTurk. The intended population of this study is U.S. consumers. However, the majority of U.S. consumers are not part of MTurk. This itself is not an issue, except that MTurk panelists are likely to be systematically different than non-participating consumers. Compared to the average U.S. consumer, MTurk panelists are typically younger in age, more technology friendly, more likely to be female, more likely to be more liberal, have lower income, and more motivated to do tasks in exchange for a small incentive. In other words, specific types of U.S. consumers are systematically excluded from the sample because of the composition of the MTurk panel. Due to these systematic differences, the results of the study based on MTurk participants cannot be projected back to the U.S. population of consumers. Rather,

Table 11.2   Evaluating sample quality

Source of error & remedy	CB-Online Study	CB-Field Study	Managerial Study	Quantitative Modeling Study
Over-coverage: sampling frame contains units that should *not* be part of the population.				
Issue	MTurk workers who are younger than 21 years, and/or reside outside the USA may be part of the sample.	People who are not from the USA, and who are non-consumers may come to the mall.	People who are not managers, and/or who have fewer than 5 years of work experience, and/or no direct experience with supplier may be part of the survey panel.	Non-customers may be incorrectly included in the database.
Remedy	Participant screening for age and area of residence.	Participant screening for area of residence and consumer-status.	Participant screening for 5-years work experience and direct experience working with the supplier rated in the survey.	Cross check if those in the dataset purchased anything from FurnCo during the 2010–2015 period.
Under-coverage: sampling frame excludes units that should be part of the population.				
Issue	MTurk systematically excludes most U.S. consumers such as very high income, consumers who do not use computers and so forth.	Most U.S. consumers do not shop at the mall in Houston. Further, most shoppers at the mall are from very high-income households.	People may not be managers, and/or have fewer than 5 years of work experience, and/or have no direct experience with supplier.	Customers who only pay cash may not be part of the company's database.

(Table 11.2 Continued)

Remedy	• Acknowledge the systematic exclusion and its impact on the study's conclusions. • Potentially use multiple sampling frames that include different members of the population.			Seek other sampling frames.
Non-response bias: sampling frame members who are eligible and invited to participate in the study do not do so.				
Issue	Those from the west coast may not participate due to time zone, and the sample consists mostly of east-coast participants.	Wealthy consumers entering the mall do not participate because the $5 incentive is not enough to motivate them.	Many eligible panelists did not participate because they did not find the topic of the study interesting.	Customers who are in the database may not provide complete information. Therefore, they were excluded from the final sample.
Remedy	• Compare early and late responders to identify systematic differences. • Compare responders and non-responders when possible. • Motivate participants through different incentives to increase response rate. • Carefully describe how the results and conclusions may differ with different sample characteristics.			Statistically, correct for selection bias (for example, Heckman selection correction).

they are likely to differ from results we may expect from a study of U.S. consumers. As an example, suppose the brands evaluated in the study are premium/luxury brands, and participants provide their willingness-to-pay (WTP) for each brand. The MTurk participants may not be sufficiently experienced to evaluate them and may provide WTP estimates that are downwardly biased.

The nature of under-coverage bias will be different in the CB-field study where the sampling frame consists of upscale participants from a wealthier, more upscale segment of Houston. Their views are unlikely to represent the views of a typical U.S. consumer. While the Houston mall goers may be sufficiently experienced in using luxury brands, they may lack the ability or experience to rate value brands and their WTP estimates may be upwardly biased. Similar issues can be readily identified for any other sampling frame that may be used for such a study.

Researchers should recognize there is no such thing as a perfect sampling frame. Every sampling frame will come with its own set of issues with respect to over-coverage and under-coverage. In general, researchers should use a sampling frame with over-coverage and screen out undesirable sampling units. However, issues pertaining to under-coverage which leaves out some segments of the population of interest, are difficult to rectify. Unlike over-coverage, this issue cannot be easily rectified after a particular sampling frame has been chosen for the research project. The best way forward is for the researcher to be clear-eyed about the inherent under-coverage in a specific sampling frame and discuss how the under-coverage affects the study's results and the research conclusions. These should then be clearly noted in the discussion following the results of each study, and in the research limitations of the paper.

Non-response error   This occurs when units from the sampling frame that are selected for inclusion in the sample, are not included (that is, excluded) for a variety of reasons. In a consumer study, a common reason for exclusion is the inability or unwillingness of selected customers to participate in the study. For example, if the CB-online study was opened for participation at 8:00 AM CDT, many people from California may not get the opportunity to participate while those on the east coast may be more likely to participate and fill up the study quota. Consequently, the final sample of participants may not even be representative of the MTurk panel from which it was chosen. In the CB-field study, the researcher may invite every fifth person entering the mall to participate in the study. However, people who are very wealthy may simply not be motivated by the $5 coupon to participate in the study; some of the younger participants may not like the idea of participating for money. Thus, the final sample of respondents becomes non-representative of the sampling frame (that is, shoppers at a Houston mall).

Non-response error renders the final sample systematically different from the sampling frame. In other words, the characteristics of the sampling frame are no longer applicable to the final sample since the non-response error systematically excluded some units from the final sample. If the researcher knows some basic descriptive characteristics of the members of the sampling frame units, then statistical procedures can be used to estimate and correct for the bias in the final sample due to non-response. One way to do that is to implement a Heckman selection correction that takes the characteristics of non-responders relative to responders and adjusts for the potential bias (Heckman 1979). Assuming that early responders to a survey are more representative of the sampling frame, researchers may compare early responders to late responders to glean if the sample is systematically biased due to non-response; the absence of a statistically significant difference between early and late responders may suggest that non-response bias is not an issue in the sample (Armstrong and Overton 1977). Finally, some researchers use a high response rate as evidence that their study does not suffer from non-response bias. Without comparing responders and non-responders, one cannot really be sure that a high response rate has fully addressed non-response bias.

If the sampling frame is systematically different from the population to begin with, the non-representativeness of the sample gets compounded due to non-response error. While it cannot be fully rectified, it is important for a researcher to note issues related to non-response bias in the limitations section of the paper. Therefore, in discussing the results of a study, a researcher should clearly note the potential ways in which the systematic exclusion of non-responders may have tilted the reported results, and what the results might look like with the inclusion of non-responders.

Sample design and external validity

The design of a sample can have a large influence on the external validity of a study. External validity is the extent to which inferences based on a sample can be projected or applied to the population of interest. The external validity of a sample can be compromised if:

- **The sampling frame is systematically different from the population:** Most sampling frames are not inherently designed to represent populations of interest to marketing scholars. Thus, as a sampling frame MTurk is a collection of individuals who will do a variety of tasks for compensation. One such task is filling out surveys. It is not designed to represent the "U.S. consumer." Similarly, the mailing list of customers of a manufacturing company is designed to represent its current, past, and potential customers. It is not designed to represent marketing managers. In today's day and age, obtaining sampling frames boils down to obtaining contact information for a group of people who may fit a set of pre-defined characteristics. Therefore, a mismatch between the sample list and the desired population of interest to a researcher is only to be expected, and rather pervasive in many studies reported in marketing journals.
- **From a sampling frame, participation of units is non-random:** Random sampling is at the heart of the statistical theory that allows us to generalize the conclusions from a sample to the population it represents. The key assumption enabling us to link the conclusions based on a sample to the population is that the sample is randomly selected from the population. To the extent that a sampling frame is representative of the population, randomly selecting units from a sampling frame for inclusion in a study is critical. In reality, such an assumption is routinely violated when sampling units enter into the sample at their discretion, for example, participants volunteer in a study based on their own interest. When this happens, the final sample ceases to be a randomly selected representation of the sampling frame.

In both the cases described here, the link between the final sample and the population of interest is broken so that conclusions based on the sample can no longer be applied to the population of interest. Thus, the mean estimates obtained from the sample may be systematically biased with no way of knowing whether the bias is in the upward or downward direction. This systematic bias cannot be corrected by simply obtaining a larger sample size, since the larger sample size simply helps to shrink the 95 percent confidence interval around the mean estimate without correcting the upward or downward bias in the mean estimate.

In most published studies, research scholars are sensitive to this issue, although it may not be comprehensively discussed in the text of the paper. One reason for this is that scholarly articles typically put a premium on internal validity – the soundness of the theoretical conclusion – which is based on measurement, analysis, and design of the study. That is why, in many papers, carefully designed randomized studies based on a non-representative sample may be deemed appropriate to test a theory. Moreover, as mentioned elsewhere, it is incumbent on the researcher to note the issues with sample non-representativeness and to alert the reader to the limits of the conclusions that can be drawn.

In consumer-behavior research, it is commonplace to have multiple studies in a single paper. Typically, the different studies try to achieve convergent validity by using different experimental stimuli, different measures of underlying constructs, and different product categories. To this, a sound research practice would be to add different sampling frames, that is, different sources of samples to enhance the external validity of the results. Thus, including a student sample, an online sample from MTurk, a sample obtained from a marketing research company, and potentially other sources such as a local mall or church could enhance the external validity of the results.

Reporting response rate
In most studies, especially those based on surveys, it is important and desirable for the researchers to indicate the response rate. Broadly speaking, the response rate represents the final number of units in a sampling frame from which information is obtained divided by the total number of units from which information is solicited. In published journal articles the response rates can range from a low of 1 percent to a high of 90 percent or more.

When reporting the response rate, researchers should carefully indicate the different units included at different stages of the sampling process. As an example, the following description of a brand study for consumers in the banking industry clearly describes the different units included at different stages of the sampling process:

A total of 6,000 telephone numbers were randomly generated for the survey. Of these, 1,627 were not usable because the telephone number was identified as belonging to a business listed in the Yellow Pages, non-working, disconnected, changed, and/or connected to a fax machine. The remaining 4,373 telephone numbers were dialed until 300 interviews were completed. For 1,185 telephone numbers, eligibility could not be determined for one or more of the following reasons: the telephone was never answered, there was a language barrier, the phone was not in service or a business/fax/computer tone was received. A total of 394 households were screened to be eligible. Among them, 6 were terminated because they did not belong to the 4-county area, 24 were terminated because of employment ineligibility, and 50 were terminated as they did not directly deal with a bank or were not involved in the banking decisions of the household. Thus, a total of 314 individuals qualified, among whom 14 refused to participate for a final sample size of 300 individuals.

Another study used a sample of practicing managers to test and validate the market orientation scale. The sample description of the study reads as follows (Jaworski and Kohli 1993, p. 58):

> The sampling frame for this group was the American Marketing Association membership roster, which provided the names of additional informants. From this sampling frame, 500 names were selected at random, after first eliminating those whose titles suggested that they were relatively low in their organizational hierarchy. From this set, thirteen individuals could not be reached because of incorrect addresses, resulting in an effective base of 487. The 3-wave mailing procedure described earlier was used to obtain data from this sample. A total of 230 responses were obtained, for a response rate of 47.2%.

These descriptions provide a sense of the information that readers expect to be reported in an article. In most cases, the researcher should clearly report the sample size at various stages of the sampling process. At the minimum, these include:

(a)   Size of the sampling frame and random/non-random inclusion of population elements in the sampling frame.
(b)   Number of units selected for contact, and whether the selection was done randomly.
(c)   Number of units that were discarded due to different ineligibility criteria and missing contact information.
(d)   Number of eligible units contacted.
(e)   Final number of units from which a response was received.
   From (e), some units may still be discarded if they did not meet screening criterion and/or provided incomplete information. Thus, the response rate may be calculated as:

Response rate

$$= \frac{\text{Final number of responses received–Units discarded if they fail to meet screening/provide incomplete information}}{\text{Number of eligible units contacted}}$$

In a scholarly article, it is desirable to provide information about all stages of the sampling process (see Figure 11.1), and then report the response rate. Simply reporting the response rate does not provide the reader with enough information to fully evaluate the sample. The researcher should also clearly lay out the criterion for ineligibility in stage (3), screening criteria, and the variables on which many respondents had missing information. Providing these pieces of information can help future research scholars to design better studies.

Increasing response rate

One goal of sample design is to increase the response rate from stage (4) to stage (5) of the sampling process. Doing so decreases non-response bias, ensuring the final sample mirrors the sampling frame. Thus, a sample with a 90 percent response rate will be closer to the original sampling frame than a sample with a 10 percent response rate.

Within marketing, a rich literature exists on techniques that can be used to increase the response rate of a study. A 2002 meta-analysis of 292 randomized controlled trials with 258,315 participants examined factors that affect response rates in mail surveys (Edwards et al. 2002). The authors concluded the odds of response, shown as odds ratios (in parentheses), increased when:

- The survey was designed to be of more interest to participants (2.44)
- The survey was sent using recorded delivery (2.21)
- A monetary incentive was used (2.02)
- A shorter survey was used (1.86)
- Incentives were not conditional on response (1.71)
- Participants were contacted before sending them a survey (1.54)
- There was a follow-up contact (1.44)
- Non-respondents were provided a second copy of the survey (1.41)
- Colored ink was used (1.39)
- Survey originated from a university rather than a commercial organization (1.31)
- Stamped return envelopes were used (1.26)
- Personalized surveys and letters were used (1.16)

These tactics used for increasing the response rate closely correspond to the conceptual framework of influence strategies proposed by Groves, Cialdini, and Couper (1992) and developed by Delener (1995). As Table 11.3 shows, the framework conceptually relates different influence strategies to specific tactics used to increase survey response rate. As an example, providing monetary incentives influences respondents by activating the norm of reciprocity. Researchers can and should use multiple influence strategies simultaneously to increase response rates. For most studies it is desirable to use shorter surveys, provide monetary incentives, provide pre-notification, and follow up to improve response rate. While resource-intensive, implementing these strategies can increase response rate and therefore the representativeness of the sample used in a study.

Sample size

Researchers should always report the size of the final sample utilized in the analysis of a study. If there are multiple studies reported in a single paper, the sample size of each study should be clearly reported. In the statistical analysis, the sample size is used to determine the "margin of error" or the "confidence interval" associated with the central tendency (mean or proportion) of the sample. In most marketing studies, it is customary to use the 95 percent confidence interval associated with the mean (Burns, Bush, and Sinha 2014; Lenth 2012; Mittal 2015). It can be computed once we know the sample size, the mean, and the standard deviation of the variable(s) of

Table 11.3   Increasing response rates in surveys

Influence Strategy	Conceptual Meaning	Response-Rate Strategy
Reciprocation	Comply with requests from those who have given something to you (exchange theory)	Provide monetary incentives to increase response rate
Consistency	Behave similarly in all situations	Pre-notification/pre-commitment
Social Validation	Comply if you believe similar others will comply	Cite participation by salient others
Authority	Comply with requests from those perceived as legitimately powerful	Mention survey sponsor; link survey to branded institutions like universities
Scarcity	Perceived scarcity linked to higher value	Note that only a select few people are being asked to participate in the study
Liking	People favor individuals they perceive to be similar	Try to match the characteristics of the participation requester to respondent characteristics
Low-Involvement Processing	People are not usually motivated to participate	Keep the request and the survey short and simple; use reminders and follow up

interest. Then the 95 percent confidence interval (C.I.) may be computed using the following equations:

Mean: 95% C.I. for mean $= \bar{x} \pm 2\,\dfrac{s}{\sqrt{n}}$

$\bar{x}$ = sample mean

s = sample standard deviation $= \sqrt{\dfrac{\Sigma(x-\bar{x})^2}{n-1}}$

n = sample size

$2 \approx 1.96$

Proportion: 95% C.I. for proportion $= p \pm 2\sqrt{\dfrac{p \cdot q}{n}}$

p = % saying "yes"

$q = 1 - p$

n = sample size

$2 \approx 1.96$

For the overall study and for specific sub-cells (for example, experimental sub-cells in an experiment) reporting the sample size, mean, and standard deviation enables future researchers to conduct better synthesis through meta analyses. In the long run, this can increase the impact of a study by enabling future scholars to understand the results in the context of a larger empirical literature stream.

Differences among samples and moderator analysis

Suppose we use an identical survey in the CB-online and the CB-field study but get different results. One interpretation may be that the phenomenon being tested, and the empirical methods being used were sufficiently weak so as to preclude replication. Another interpretation may be that the key result is moderated by consumers' perceived social class, status, or income (the Houston mall sample is significantly wealthier than the MTurk sample). More generally, and from a philosophy-of-science perspective, systematic differences in results obtained from two similar studies conducted with different samples should be carefully evaluated to ascertain potential reasons for the difference in results (Lynch 1982). In many cases, understanding the difference may lead to theoretically interesting discoveries that can also be applied by managers (who learn about segment-specific differences in key variables).

It is for this reason that researchers should strive to precisely disclose key descriptive features of their sample in a tabular form. These should include, but not be limited to demographics of the respondents (for example, average age, income categories, gender) and basic characteristics of the firms (for example, average sales, number of employees, the type of business). This enables future research scholars to compare their findings against published research and develop novel research hypotheses using an inductive approach to knowledge development.

Concluding comments

The design of a sampling strategy can play an important role in enhancing the external validity of the results and help improve the impact of a research article. However, doing so requires a careful consideration of many different factors rather than simply obtaining a large sample size. This chapter has attempted to highlight and discuss some of these critical issues with the hope of helping researchers improve the contribution of their scholarly work.

Note

1. Several sources provide an overview of specific sampling techniques along with a comparison of random versus non-random selection of sampling units (cf., Burns, Bush, and Sinha 2014; Deming 1990; Mittal 2015).

References

Armstrong, J. Scott and Terry S. Overton (1977), "Estimating Nonresponse Bias in Mail Surveys," *Journal of Marketing Research*, 14 (3), 396–402.
Burns, Alvin C., Ronald F. Bush, and Nilanjana Sinha (2014), *Marketing Research*. Boston, MA: Pearson.
Delener, Nejdet (1995), "An Integrative Review of Nonresponse Errors in Survey Research: Major Influences and Strategies," *Research in Marketing*, 12, 49–80.
Deming, W. Edwards (1990), *Sample Design in Business Research*. New York: Wiley.
Edwards, Phil, Ian Roberts, Mike Clarke, Carolyn DiGuiseppi, Sarah Pratap, Reinhard Wentz, and Irene Kwan (2002), "Increasing Response Rates to Postal Questionnaires: Systematic Review," *BMJ*, 324 (7347), 1183.

Groves, Robert M., Robert B. Cialdini, and Mick P. Couper (1992), "Understanding the Decision to Participate in a Survey," *Public Opinion Quarterly*, 56 (4), 475–95.

Heckman, James J. (1979), "Sample Selection Bias as a Specification Error," *Econometrica*, 47, 153–62.

Jaworski, Bernard J. and Ajay K. Kohli (1993), "Market Orientation: Antecedents and Consequences," *Journal of Marketing*, 57 (3), 53–70.

Lenth, Russell V. (2012), "Some Practical Guidelines for Effective Sample Size Determination," *The American Statistician*, 55 (3), 187–93.

Lynch Jr., John G., (1982), "On the External Validity of Experiments in Consumer Research," *Journal of Consumer Research*, 9 (3), 225–39.

Mittal, Vikas (2015), "Sample Design for Customer-Focused Research," (accessed November 26, 2018), https://papers.ssrn.com/sol3/papers.cfm?abstract_id=2638086.

SECTION III

REVIEWS AND THE REVISION PROCESS

Introduction to section III

A critical element in the publication process is the review procedure, in which individuals who have expertise in the subject matter addressed by a paper are asked to provide comments and suggestions for improvement. While some journals do ask reviewers for a recommendation about whether to publish, invite revision, or reject a paper, such a recommendation is not the primary task of the reviewer. Rather, the reviewer's objective is to make the paper better by offering constructive comments about conceptual development, methodology, logic, conclusions, implications and exposition. Whether a paper is eventually published in a particular journal or not, the insights of reviewers are a powerful tool for improving papers. Even when a paper is rejected by one journal, reviews offer a means for improving the paper before submission to another journal. Authors of rejected papers would be well advised to make revisions in response to reviewers' comments before sending a paper to another journal because there is a good chance at least one of the reviewers of the original submission will be selected by the new journal.

Reviewers are selected for different reasons. A reviewer may have expertise related to the topic addressed by the paper, but frequently at least one reviewer is selected for their methodological expertise or their familiarity with a particular theory. In some cases, especially for papers that are highly technical or that focus on a highly specialized area, a very experienced reviewer may be selected who has little direct expertise on the topic addressed by a paper but can help in making the paper better at communicating to a non-specialist reader. The multiple perspectives of the review team provide insights into the responses of the larger readership of the journal and help make the paper more accessible and more relevant to the broadest possible audience.

This section of the book focuses on reviewers and the review process. Chapter 12 is a reprint of a paper by Donald R. Lehmann and Russell S. Winer. It focuses on the role of the reviewer and the influence that reviewers can have on both individual papers and the discipline at large. Chapters 13 and 14 provide the perspectives of an editor and an author of a paper that took a long time to mature and to obtain a positive decision for publication. The paper, "Evolving to a new dominant logic for marketing," was published in the *Journal of Marketing* and has gone on to win numerous awards and become one of the most cited papers in marketing. The editor, Ruth N. Bolton, describes the editorial process as the paper moved toward acceptance for publication. One of the co-authors, Stephen L. Vargo, tells his story of the journey to publication. In the interests of full disclosure, one of the editors of this book (DS), was the editor of the *Journal of Marketing* when the paper was first submitted for publication and processed the manuscript through multiple rounds of revision and review. There are at least three lessons to be learned from this paper's journey from idea to award-winning paper. First, the paper that was eventually published was very different from the one that was initially submitted. It benefited from multiple rounds of reviews and from multiple reviewers. Second, however frustrating at times, the review process usually works. Good papers are published when the authors persist. Reviews do improve papers when authors are responsive. Third, editors want to publish good papers; it is more fun than rejection for both the editor and the author.

12

J. of the Acad. Mark. Sci. (2017) 45:587–592
DOI 10.1007/s11747-016-0501-x

EDITORIAL

The role and impact of reviewers on the marketing discipline

Donald R. Lehmann[1] · **Russell S. Winer**[2]

Published online: 16 January 2017
© Academy of Marketing Science 2017

Since John Lynch's presidential address at the 1998 annual meeting of the Association for Consumer Research (Lynch 1998), a large number of articles have appeared in the marketing literature pertaining to the review process in our field. Almost every new journal editor makes some statement about the standards and etiquette that reviewers should adopt during his or her editorial regime. For some good examples, see Shugan (2003), Desai (2011), and Kumar (2016). Other useful discussions of the review process also exist (e.g., Holbrook's 1986 paper with seven suggestions for reviewers).

The purpose of this editorial is to give our perspective on (1) how the editorial process has evolved over time, (2) the importance and benefits of the review process to the marketing field, (3) how reviewing fits into career development, and (4) the characteristics of a good review. While it is inevitable that we will cover some ground that has already been tread by previous work, we hope that from the collective 90 years we have spent involved with the review process, we can add a useful perspective to a process that is often dreaded by both authors and reviewers.

Evolution

The (good?) old days

When we entered the field, it was relatively small. For example, Russ Winer's AMA Doctoral Consortium group had 41 students. Similarly, when Don Lehmann attended the first "open" ACR annual meeting in 1969, there were 90 attendees including quantitative researchers, practitioners, and government officials. Several major marketing journals, including *JCR, Marketing Science, JCP,* and *QME,* did not exist and manuscript flow was relatively low. In 1970, when Ralph Day was the editor, *JMR* had only 21 members of the editorial board,[1] no co-editors, and no associate editors.[2] In the twentieth century, the editorial process worked as follows:

- Authors snail-mailed 5 hard copies to the editor.
- The editor chose 2–3 reviewers from the editorial board and from an ad hoc list.
- The editor mailed the hard copy papers to the reviewers.
- The reviewers mailed back their reviews.
- The editor made his/her decision and mailed it to the authors as well as copies to the reviewers.

✉ Donald R. Lehmann
drl2@columbia.edu

1 Graduate School of Business, Columbia University, New York, NY, USA

2 Stern School of Business, New York University, New York, NY, USA

---

[1] Interestingly, 9 of them were from companies.
[2] *JCR* did adopt an associate editor system in the early 1990s and was the first major marketing journal to do so.

J. of the Acad. Mark. Sci. (2017) 45:587–592

While the reject rate at the top marketing journals has always been high,[3] the manuscript flow was lower, editors needed to fill issues, and the prevailing attitude among editors was that they were looking for papers to accept. For example, as late as 2006, *JMR* and *JM* were receiving about 250 new manuscripts each year. Others, such as *Marketing Letters* (which began publishing in 1989), had closer to 100.

Currently

The pressure on editors today is intense. What has led to this?

- The size of the field has increased dramatically. The number of business schools has increased substantially with concomitant increases in marketing faculty positions and doctoral programs. For example, at the 2016 AMA-Sheth Doctoral Consortium, there were 103 students (which was fewer than in 2015), far greater than the 41 at Russ Winer's consortium.
- Many business schools that were once mainly "teaching" schools now demand some research for promotion and tenure.
- The market, which was once dominated by (and in effect limited to) the U.S. and parts of Europe, is now global with more marketing faculty in the rest of Europe and particularly in the Asia-Pacific region. Editors are seeing papers from universities in countries that were not major sources of manuscripts 10–15 years ago such as China, Turkey, and Iran.
- Business school rankings such as those of the *Financial Times* include faculty publications in international research journals as a component.
- Some schools supplement salaries with bonuses for publications in top-level international journals.
- Longer doctoral programs and pressure from promotion and tenure committees to have focused research programs have resulted in increased specialization and created more competition at the discipline-based journals.
- Electronic submission systems have reduced the costs of submission and re-submission (although not necessarily the length of the review process).

As a result, in spite of on expansion in the number of journals (Lehmann, 2005), competition for the available journal space has intensified. The number of submissions has increased dramatically to over 600 new and 800+ total submissions per year at some major journals. The journal "system" has responded in two ways. First, the former system of one editor and a review board has been replaced by a three-tier system of an Editor-in-Chief

(EIC), a team of associate/senior/area editors who synthesize the reviews and make a recommendation to the EIC/co-editor, and a review board. Several of the top journals have co-editors, who also have decision-making authority on a manuscript in addition to the EIC.

Second, the desk reject rates at all the journals have increased, in several cases to 50%, some of which is due to authors not paying sufficient attention to either journal format or the advice of editors (e.g., Palmatier 2016a, b). Without a high desk rejection rate, it would be nearly impossible to manage the manuscript flow given the number of submissions, the number of rounds of revisions (which many editors attempt to limit to two but which often extend to three or more), and the availability of reviewers with expertise in a particular area who have the capacity and willingness to do the work. Reviewing loads are heavy, and editors, appropriately, try to avoid overloading good reviewers, especially when there is little chance that their efforts will result in a publishable paper in their journal. From the author's point of view, desk rejections are discouraging and, to some, seem like a violation of "due process." On the other hand, it is generally better to know sooner rather than later if a paper will be rejected so the author can move on with alternative plans. Desk rejections are also not something new. Robert Ferber (who was the first *JMR* and second *JCR* editor) in the 1970's had three screening editors at *JCR* whose job was to (a) identify papers that stood little chance of acceptance, and (b) write a short report explaining why along with some suggestions for how to improve the paper.

The end result of all of this is that the review system is under duress. Reviewing in the field of marketing is a volunteer activity[4] and the top reviewers are already heavily committed. The larger number of papers under review means that editors are both using their current teams more intensively and seeking ad hoc (and in the case of *JCR*, "training reviewers", i.e., PhD students) reviewers at a greater rate. It is a struggle to get reviewers to agree to do reviews and an additional challenge to get them to do timely ones. Consequently, editors need to "protect" reviewers and AEs or risk losing them altogether.

This increased load has also created an attitude change among reviewers who often look for reasons to reject rather than to accept papers. Further, reviewers often focus on technical details that may or may not have little to do with the main (substantive) contribution of the paper but are frequently represented as basic requirements for publication (McAlister 2016). The additional layer of review created by the associate editor structure means more time in the system for a given manuscript and more time pressure for timely reviews. It also adds another person who can

---

[3] For example, when Russ Winer was an Associate Editor for *JCR* in the early 1990s for Editor Brian Sternthal, the acceptance rate was 5 %.

[4] Some fields such as finance pay reviewers from funds collected when manuscripts are submitted for review.

 Springer

J. of the Acad. Mark. Sci. (2017) 45:587–592

recommend rejection. Given the tendency to weight negative information more heavily, additional reviews make it harder to get a paper accepted. (Of course the additional review can also both catch errors and make useful suggestions). The use of co-editors creates a potential problem of non-uniform standards as well as increased specialization as co-editors together with AEs and reviewers are chosen to match the paper as closely as possible. This results in papers written to some degree in "code" that are mainly accessible to and read by a small fraction of the field even though they appear in general journals such as *JMR*. New papers with "out of the box" thinking have a more difficult time getting through the process partly because they don't fit into any of the narrow paradigms.

Recently, a number of well-documented cases of academic misconduct (ranging from p-hacking to outright fraud) have led journals to adopt new and more stringent rules about data and computer code disclosures when a paper is accepted. This has resulted in reviewers being asked to pay more attention to potential problems, increasing the reviewing burden. It also produces a bit of a "guilty until proven innocent" mentality in the review process. Overall, this has moved the process toward being more adversarial and legalistic (as evidence by long reviews and responses to reviewers).

When faced with two of three negative reviews and a negative reaction from an AE, most editors feel compelled to go with the majority opinion (partly to avoid antagonizing their volunteer reviewers and AEs). There is also another pernicious aspect. Typically, if one of three reviewers recommends acceptance, revisions are only sent back to the two reviewers who didn't. This in effect loads the jury against acceptance, thus disenfranchising the positive reviewer (whose position is subsequently weighted less heavily).

Importance of the review process

Despite these issues, the peer review process continues to be important and useful. A strong, effective review process helps ensure that papers that are accepted do not have fatal flaws, establishes research standards in the field, and, if operating properly, permits editors to shape the research agenda by accepting papers outside normal boundaries and in areas that might otherwise not receive sufficient attention.

Of course, one does not have to go through the review process. There are a large number of outlets today for non-peer reviewed work. Perhaps the most popular for marketing academics is the Social Science Research Network (SSRN). SSRN essentially replaces the old hard-copy working paper series that business schools used to have. This facilitates the quick dissemination of new ideas and offers authors the increased opportunity to receive comments and citations from other academics. As a result, authors often tout the number of SSRN downloads as an indication of the quality and impact of their work. However, SSRN does not peer review working

papers and therefore having a paper in the SSRN database is not a perfect substitute for having one in a peer-reviewed journal or a signal of quality. Similarly, Google Citations include a number of sources, which provides some information but not the more focused view of academic citations captured by ISI, Web of Science.

The review process as part of career development

As noted above, the marketing profession operates on a volunteer basis. Faculty expect to get good reviews when they submit manuscripts and in turn should supply good reviews to other authors. Because becoming a good reviewer is an important part of career development, younger faculty should be willing to review for a journal and many look forward to doing so. (Although as a person becomes more senior, it is "be careful what you wish for" as a good reviewer will wind up with multiple manuscripts on her or his desk.) Younger faculty can be particularly valuable for providing verification that there is nothing "wrong" technically. Importantly, reviewing is more than just "giving back" to the field; it often leads to learning. As reviewers we have been made aware of new areas of research, and research methods, and gained a general appreciation for the quality of work that is being done by our colleagues.

How does reviewing fit into the promotion and tenure process? While having published papers is clearly more important, it is generally assumed that junior faculty will do some reviewing; it would be unusual for a CV to not have a list of journals for which the tenure candidate has reviewed. A strong positive signal is membership on the editorial board of a major journal, but this is uncommon. If non-tenured faculty members are not being asked to do reviews, we recommend that they (or better a well-known senior colleague) contact the editor and/or the AEs and let them know that they are available to do reviews and have expertise in certain areas. While this may appear to be presumptuous, there is a shortage of people able and willing to do reviews, so being proactive is normally welcomed.

Ph.D. students should definitely be asked to assess published and working papers in their doctoral seminars. Whether students should become formally involved with the reviewing process in their doctoral programs is debatable. There is always something amiss even in published papers (no paper written is ever perfect), and tearing papers apart is a normal part of student training. A useful exercise is to provide students with a paper that is (or was) under review at a journal. Since journal editors and authors expect that reviews will be conducted by the faculty members themselves, we do not feel it is appropriate to let doctoral students directly insert their perspectives on a manuscript into the final review. While reviewing is a useful learning experience, in general, students do not have the experience and perspective to

590   J. of the Acad. Mark. Sci. (2017) 45:587–592

understand the extent of the incremental contribution. Students also tend to look for what is wrong with a paper as opposed to what is right/interesting. *JCR* has formalized this process by allowing for "training reviewers" to write reviews on a paper. However, an important condition is that the students are tutored on how to write a good review. Without that, many doctoral students will focus on a manuscript's perceived flaws, which is less helpful to editors, the authors of the paper, and the field.

Characteristics of a good review

Provides advice to the editor

One (the?) main purpose of a review is to provide guidance to the AE and ultimately to the editor about the disposition of the manuscript. That is, after all, the *raison d'être* of the review process. Thus, a good review helps those up the review ladder to either make an accept or reject decision or develop a coherent road map for a revision. As a result, reviewers are encouraged to divide the comments into what the reviewer feels are the most important, major points that affect the "up or down" decision, and those that are more minor, such as editorial issues. It is then up to the editor and AE to determine if the major points made are fixable (which suggests encouraging a revision) or not (i.e., requires rejection).

Where many reviews fall short is in terms of the specificity of their comments. Just to say there is an endogeneity problem is not helpful; it is much more helpful to indicate why the reviewer feels the problem exists, and even better to suggest a solution for it. Similarly, to say that the conceptual development/theory is poor/weak does not indicate where the theory falls short. Also, simply saying that other papers have covered the same ground is less helpful than if the reviewer provides specific citations.

Provides helpful comments to the author

Of course, reviewer comments are also supposed to assist authors in improving their papers whether they are revising them for resubmission to the same journal or not. The idea is that the review process should improve the next version of the paper. Essentially all senior faculty members have had their papers rejected, including, sadly, these authors (multiple times). However, the benefit of having at least three pairs of experienced eyes read a paper and provide comments is enormous.[5] (In return for this service, authors should not send in partly finished work in the hope that the reviewers will find

ways to improve it.) When Preyas Desai was the editor of *Marketing Science*, he encouraged review teams to use the "reject and resubmit" when appropriate because otherwise other journals would receive the benefits of the improvements that the journal's review team provided.

A helpful review has the same key property as one giving good advice to the editor and AE: specificity. Authors appreciate a clear roadmap for revisions and AE's and Editors want key concerns highlighted and distinguished from minor issues.

Helps determine what is a contribution

There are many ways to make a contribution, and a paper does not need to include all of them. Traditionally contributions have been categorized as theoretical, methodological, logical, or substantive. To this we would add "makes one think/ inspires future research." Because no single paper is ever completely definitive, this aspect may be the most important. A considerable amount of qualitative work falls in this category. Finally, there has been an increased focus on work that is helpful to some party, i.e., action research such as that done under the umbrella of TCR (Transformative Consumer Research) or work that impacts practice (e.g., the Lilien practice prize work in marketing science). Before reviewers conclude a paper "makes no significant contribution", they should make sure that is really true.

Components of a review

Four assessments

A review contains at least four assessments. One is for technical correctness. Here the question should be not whether the paper uses the most advanced (and often costly) approach, but whether the approach is reasonable and likely to produce a good, if not the best, result.

A second is whether the paper is conceptually coherent. This is often operationalized as "does it test a theory?" or unfortunately sometimes "does this test the theory I would test if I were doing this study?" More broadly, the field is in some cases close to strangling itself by insisting that every paper have and test a theory/theoretical basis. A better criterion is "does this paper present a result which makes one think and encourages future research, and did the author make a reasonable attempt to explain/provide a coherent story for the results?" (Interestingly and importantly, the "newer" something is, and therefore potentially more impactful, the less well it will be tied to prior theory precisely because it is new.)

The third area is an assessment of marginal contribution. Here again it is fine to provide your judgement of this as long as you recognize that others may differ in this assessment.

---

[5] This is a serious point for junior scholars to consider when revising their papers. However, how to utilize reviews is a topic for another day.

J. of the Acad. Mark. Sci. (2017) 45:587–592

The fourth area is the trickiest. It involves "taste." Taste colors judgment whether we want it to or not. It is important to identify which of your concerns are about taste, make them explicit, recognize that tastes can differ, and leave it to the editor to decide how to incorporate this into their decision.

Other considerations

Tone The tone of a review matters. While some authors are "tough" and even enjoy contesting reviews, most are not and do not. Further, most authors want to improve their work if a specific and reasonably doable path to do that is made clear to them. Thus tone matters. Even for work that you feel is well below the (your) standards, that is not justification for belittling the authors or not showing some sympathy to a fellow author who may be just starting out or at an institution without much support for research. Put differently, remember that while you are presumably an expert in some aspects of a paper, you are not "the" expert in all of them. Humility is a plus.

Rigidity There are few absolutes. Insisting on a particular way of doing things without strong evidence that (a) it is superior in this particular case and (b) doing them that way makes a material difference in the results (i.e., in the first decimal place of an estimate) is counter-productive. If an approach gives materially different results, subsequent replication attempts and meta-analyses will show that. Insisting on a single complex way of doing thing actually retards knowledge development as it perfectly confounds method with the results and precludes variation (e.g., conceptual replications).

Newness/surprise "New" is a relative term. There is essentially nothing we do that can't be related to prior work or thinking, whether by marketing scholars, scholars in other disciplines, philosophers, etc. Currently there is a tendency to dismiss a paper that doesn't have surprising findings as "not a contribution." This effectively rules out most replications (exact or conceptual) and inhibits future meta-analyses, which are critical for establishing empirical generalizations. Establishing an empirical regularity of an important phenomena is useful even if it is not exciting.

Cleverness/complexity In the behavioral area, main effect findings are often considered inferior/inadequate when in fact they can be the most meaningful (after all, $E = mc^2$ is a pretty simple formula). While it is useful and interesting to look for mediators, moderators, moderated mediation, etc., they should not be requirements for all behavioral papers. Similarly, in the empirical quantitative area, complex estimation methods are not always required or even the most appropriate (McAlister 2016).

Empathy It is always important to remember that behind every manuscript is many person-hours of hard labor. For empirical work, data collection takes time. Whether it is scraping data from the Internet, administering a survey across multiple countries with suitable translations, running 15 lab studies, or assembling secondary data, the amount of time it takes to create a suitable database can be substantial. Even without data, the author of a theory paper takes many hours to read the literature and develop and hone concepts. Many more hours are spent drafting and revising a manuscript. It is easy as a reviewer to say that more and/or different data or experiments are needed or to make flippant comments that the theory is wrong. Showing a little courtesy and empathy for authors does not hurt.

In addition, careers are at stake. For many academics, getting as few as one or two papers in the top journals can create a tenure case at their schools. While this should never be a criterion for making a recommendation on a manuscript, being careful and diligent in preparing the review as well as following the guidelines noted previously can be enormously helpful, especially to junior colleagues.

Suggestions

1. Start every review with "What I like about this paper is" and remember that as you do your review. If you think the paper is good enough to be published, go ahead and say so. A good critical review is not necessarily a negative one.

2. Remember the paper is the authors' paper, not yours, and that their name will appear on it (and not yours). Don't in effect take over and try to dictate exactly what they "must" do.

3. Remember that authors may not respond to every one of your suggestions no matter how great you think they are. They have to respond to several reviewers, an AE, and an Editor which often pull them in different directions.

4. Don't treat the review process as a legal proceeding. A paper can be acceptable even if it doesn't deal with all your concerns and suggestions. Also try not to introduce new, non-critical suggestions on subsequent rounds of the review process.

5. Be timely. It takes you no more time to review paper early than it does late.

6. Don't be upset if editors don't follow your recommendations. You are an advisor, they are the decision makers.

7. Try to complete your review in one sitting. It will save you time remembering where you were and produce a more coherent/consistent review.

8. Brevity is key. Indicate the (few) key issues succinctly. Length does not equal quality. Also, clearly separate what you think are major concerns/suggestions from minor "it would be nice to do" points.

🍁 Springer

592   J. of the Acad. Mark. Sci. (2017) 45:587–592

9. As you review, so shall you be reviewed. Nasty reviews beget more nasty reviews, thoughtful ones encourage thoughtful ones. Which would you prefer to get?

Conclusion

The demand for space in the top marketing journals has increased faster than the supply. As a result, while the so-called "A" journals in marketing have remained fairly constant for a long time, a number of journals such as *JAMS* have increased dramatically in quality (and in fact are now included in the *Financial Times* list of top journals). However, due to the growth in the number of marketing scholars around the globe, there is still intense competition for the available journal space. This has significantly increased the pressure on the peer review system since every paper submitted typically needs at least two reviewers, an AE, and an editor to make a decision.

Recruiting enough volunteers to man this system is challenge enough. To make the system work for both the journals and the authors is even harder. There are many critics of the review process; who hasn't seen criticism of reviewers on Facebook or heard it at a conference? Overall, the system is working fairly well despite its problems. Griping aside, our papers have benefited from the process and, if ultimately published, were better than the versions originally submitted. We also feel that despite the amount of information available about papers and authors on the Internet, the integrity of the review process has remained intact.

The main challenges are really at the individual reviewer level. As authors, we expect to receive fair, helpful reviews from readers who pay careful attention to our work. As reviewers, we are obligated provide nothing less than that. Our observation is that we are lucky in marketing to have a review process that is generally working. Many of us have submitted papers to journals in other fields and have suffered from long review times and cursory or unhelpful reviews. While that happens occasionally in marketing, our experience is that it is not the norm in our field.

We have provided an historical context for the review process in marketing, some observations on it, and some suggestions for how it could be better. Starting with the reviews that we are currently processing, we intend to take our own advice.

References

Desai, P. S. (2011). Editorial—marketing science: marketing and science. *Marketing Science, 30*(1), 1–3.

Holbrook, M. B. (1986). A note on sadomasochism in the review process: I hate when that happens. *Journal of Marketing, 50*(3), 104–108.

Kumar, V. (2016). My reflections on publishing in *Journal of Marketing*. *Journal of Marketing*, 90 (January), 1–6.

Lehmann, D. R. (2005). Journal evolution and the development of marketing. *Journal of Public Policy & Marketing, 24*(1), 137–142.

Lynch, J. (1998). Reviewing. *Advances in Consumer Research, 25*, 1–6.

McAlister, L. (2016). Rigor versus method imperialism. *Journal of the Academy of Marketing Science, 44*(5), 565–567.

Palmatier, R. W. (2016a). Editorial: the past, present, and future of JAMS. *Journal of the Academy of Marketing Science, 44*(1), 1–4.

Palmatier, R. W. (2016b). Improving publishing success at JAMS: contribution and positioning. *Journal of the Academy of Marketing Science*, doi: 10.1007/s11747-016-0497-2.

Shugan, S. M. (2003). Editorial: compartmentalized reviews and other initiatives: should marketing scientists review manuscripts in consumer behavior? *Marketing Science, 22*(2), 151–160.

 Springer

13

How papers get better before they get published

Ruth N. Bolton

I have been asked to contribute my recollections about the editorial review process for the article, "Evolving to a New Dominant Logic for Marketing" by Stephen L. (Steve) Vargo and Robert F. (Bob) Lusch, which was published in the *Journal of Marketing* (*JM*) in 2004. This chapter offers my recollections – with the advantage of hindsight.

Initial submission

A new editor is frequently met by a deluge of papers – some of which have met with rejection at other journals. As incoming editor at *JM*, I received a number of manuscripts that had been rejected by the previous editor, David W. (Dave) Stewart. Some of these manuscripts appeared to have been resubmitted without many changes. Perhaps the authors were hoping that a new editor would have a fresh perspective on their paper. Unfortunately, after reading the paper and the editorial correspondence, I usually reached the same conclusion that Dave Stewart had. There didn't seem to be a path forward for the manuscript.

Among these, the paper now entitled "Evolving to a New Dominant Logic for Marketing" (hereafter called the "SDL paper") stood out for several reasons. First, the cover letter from Steve Vargo and Bob Lusch candidly described the paper's history and asked me to consider their (new) version of the paper for review and potential publication. Second, *JM*'s paper files – containing previous versions of the manuscript, associated reviews and editorial correspondence – were about six inches thick![1] The authors had made substantial changes during each revision. Third, the paper was a conceptual paper with a strategic focus. These papers are often the most difficult to develop and publish – although they sometimes win awards when they are successful. They also require a committed review team who can truly add value through their comments. Last, after reading the files, I realized that the paper had evolved considerably. Clearly, many people had felt the paper had potential – but could it be realized?

Today, editors at some journals often make "reject, resubmit" decisions, so that it is not unusual to reconsider a previously rejected paper. However, in 2003, this practice was rare at marketing journals. There is a good reason for not reconsidering rejected papers. If a paper has not met the hurdle for publication after three rounds of review, it is usually better for the authors to submit the paper to a new journal. A new journal, with a new editor and reviewers, might be able to help move the paper forward in ways that the existing review team could not. Conversely, there were only a few outlets for conceptual and strategic papers in marketing other than *JM* at that time. It seemed unlikely that there was a journal better suited to finding a path to publication for this paper. The American Marketing Association gives its journal editors complete discretion over the editorial review process, so I could put the paper into the review process if I wished. I felt that I needed the fresh reviews to evaluate whether to take this paper forward, so I decided to send it out for review.

Selecting the reviewers

Steve and Bob had demonstrated that they were willing to devote considerable time and effort to improving the paper. If the paper was to continue to move forward, it was crucially important to have reviewers who could help make the paper better. For this reason, I used two reviewers who had seen the paper in the past and one new reviewer. My approach to selecting reviewers is to choose experts with complementary perspectives, to achieve both breadth and depth. For this paper, I was able to obtain three outstanding reviewers: Valarie Zeithaml, Roland T. Rust and George Day. Subsequently, all three were recipients of the AMA–Irwin–McGraw-Hill Distinguished Marketing Educator Award.

Valarie is a strong conceptual thinker, who speaks and writes extremely well. She has authored many award-winning articles. Roland is a scholar of great breadth, who has a strong focus on service topics, and has been recognized for his contributions in diverse areas. George is an expert on marketing and strategy, who has written many highly influential articles, and has extensive experience in both marketing academia and practice. Not every paper has three such notable scholars as reviewers! I knew them well and believed that they could provide the insights necessary to increase the contribution of the paper.

JM's manuscript flow was increasing, but the journal had a fixed page limit. Since conceptual articles tend to be somewhat longer than other articles, it was very important that the contribution of the article be commensurate with its length. Fortunately, during my tenure as editor, *JM* did not have an area editor structure, so I worked directly with the reviewers and authors to improve the paper. As with other papers, I sometimes spoke with the reviewers or authors on the telephone rather than writing – which helped the review process focus on critical issues and converge more quickly.

Reviewer contributions

With the passing of the years, I can't remember the details of a complex review process that incorporated multiple revisions. However, a few critical changes to the manuscript stand out in my mind. First, the authors had a deep understanding of the historical development of the field of marketing. It was important to cover this ground succinctly, so Table 1 ("Schools of Thought") and Figure 1 ("Evolving to a New Dominant Logic") were introduced into the article. These were helpful ways of summarizing the evolution of marketing thought, so that the reader encountered the new ideas offered by the manuscript earlier in the article. This change increased its focus on key conceptual arguments and its contribution to marketing science and practice.

Second, Valarie Zeithaml helped create a strong conceptual structure for the article. She suggested that the key ideas in the article be formally stated – leading to the creation of its "foundational premises." This feature crystallized the article's key ideas so that its arguments could be strengthened – and debated. Not only did it make it easier for readers to follow the authors' reasoning, it made it possible for scholars to build upon their work (for example, Ballantyne and Varey 2008). Third, a crucial insight was offered by George Day, who suggested the term "Dominant Logic." His terminology concisely encapsulated the authors' ideas about the evolution of marketing thought. It also overcame a significant impediment to publication. Specifically, previous reviewers had felt uncomfortable with language implying that the article was articulating a "new theory of marketing" or a "paradigm shift." Today, the term "Service Dominant Logic" and its acronym SDL are widely used – indicating the importance of this insight.

Last, but not least, every article benefits from a reviewer who advocates for the paper. Roland Rust was an advocate for the SDL paper – and his role was especially important due to its unique nature. Since the 1960s, an extensive literature had developed on service management and service science topics. (See Fisk, Brown, and Bitner's (1993) review article for a description of early research on this topic.) The SDL paper was simultaneously arguing for a new approach, and vindicating the conceptual work of its scholarly forerunners. Roland's in-depth knowledge of the service literature gave him an appreciation of the novelty and nuance of the SDL approach, yet he was sufficiently open-minded to embrace an evolution in marketing thought.

Collaboration and impact

Naturally, for any paper to be accepted for publication, it must be factually correct and well-reasoned. Moreover, it often makes sense to acknowledge counter-arguments within a paper. For example, in a paper that develops theory-based hypotheses, it is sometimes useful to offer one or more alternate hypotheses that (perhaps) rely on a different theory. However, Don Lehmann once told me that – to be accepted for publication – a paper doesn't have to be exactly right; it just has to be "not wrong." His view was that the issues explored in an article can always be debated and extended in subsequent articles (if they warrant it). This perspective was very important to the conclusion of the review processes for the SDL paper.

The reviewers and I recognized that the SDL paper could be controversial. We had helped the authors refine and clarify their ideas, but there were countervailing theoretical arguments, ideas and opinions. To what extent should these opposing ideas be explicitly recognized in the paper? After a few review cycles, there was a general sense that incorporating counter-arguments within the paper would have eroded the fabric of the paper, extended its length and lessened its impact.

In talking over the penultimate revision of the SDL paper, George Day suggested to me the paper could be published with a set of commentaries. I liked the idea immediately! In this way, *JM* could accommodate a variety of reactions to the paper, stimulate discussion and debate and advance the science and practice of marketing. It was important to present diverse perspectives – so I gave considerable thought to how best to achieve these goals. I decided on many short commentaries rather than inviting a single (longer) commentary. In a sense, this approach is quintessential embodiment of the SDL logic! After consulting Steve, Bob and the three reviewers,

I invited commentaries from George Day, John Deighton and Das Narayandas, Evert Gummesson, Shelby D. Hunt, C.K. Pralahad, Roland T. Rust, and Steven M. Shugan. By bundling the paper with several commentaries, synergies were created that increased the contribution of the SDL paper.

Guidance for beginning scholars

What are some of the lessons to be learnt from the evolution of the SDL paper? Naturally, authors should be persistent – but persistence is not enough. One critical success factor is that authors must accept guidance from the review team and continuously work to improve their ideas. My first letter to Steve and Bob was five pages long – excluding the reviews – and they were very responsive. In addition to responding to reviewers' comments, they sought out opportunities to present their work in different forums and acted upon the feedback they received. In my experience, authors are often reluctant to embrace change and typically make only small changes to their papers.

Second, authors must clarify and refine the presentation of their ideas. Writing clarity is essential in all published work – and especially conceptual work. Reviewers and readers will have expertise in diverse disciplinary areas. Hence, authors should use every tool at their disposal – verbal, mathematical, and pictorial – to communicate clearly. For the SDL paper, it was essential that Steve and Bob drew from multiple disciplinary perspectives and defined key terms very precisely. Moreover, the crystallization of their ideas as foundational premises helped readers grasp their key insights. Authors should consider the best way to convey each essential point.

Third, the "right" review team is important. The capabilities and resources of the editor and reviewers must match the requirements of the paper. The SDL paper was unusual in that it went through many rounds of review over a long period of time – thereby benefiting from the advice of multiple reviewers and editors. Of course, no author wants to spend ten years or more bringing a paper to publication! However, it is not uncommon for a paper to be rejected by a review team at one journal and – after major revisions – be submitted to another journal where a new review team develops it further so that it is suitable for publication. Both authors and reviewers must understand the collaborative nature of the review process.

Last, the publication process offers both risks and rewards. Beginning authors are often advised to "follow their passion" without any warnings about where their passion might lead them. However, I would add two caveats to this advice. First, authors should recognize that their work must match the positioning of the target journal. In the case of the SDL paper, there was a good match with the *Journal of Marketing* because it is committed to publishing articles that address substantive marketing questions. In contrast, a paper on a narrow, highly specialized topic might not be suitable for the *Journal of Marketing*. Second, developing a paper over a protracted period of time is a risky strategy. Scholarly developments may overtake the paper, reducing its contribution. In addition, beginning scholars usually need a body of published work to meet the requirements for promotion and tenure. Hence, a useful rule of thumb for managing these two risk factors is to "work on the paper that is closest to publication." This rule might mean putting a particular paper on the back burner to focus on moving another paper toward publication.

Closing thoughts

Don Lehmann once told me that an editor is remembered by the best papers he or she publishes – not the worst. I am happy to be remembered as the editor who published the SDL paper!

Note

1. The *Journal of Marketing* converted to an online review process in 2003. The article had been revised many times over a period of six or more years.

References

Ballantyne, David and Richard J. Varey (2008), "The service-dominant logic of marketing," *Journal of the Academy of Marketing Science*, 36 (1), 11–14.

Fisk, Raymond P., Stephen W. Brown, and Mary Jo Bitner (1993), "Tracking the evolution of the services marketing literature," *Journal of Retailing*, 69 (1), 61–103.

Vargo, Stephen L. and Robert F. Lusch (2004), "Evolving to a New Dominant Logic for Marketing," *Journal of Marketing*, 68 (1), 1–17.

14

The service-dominant logic journey: from conceptualization to publication

Stephen L. Vargo

Background

In 1992, after having sold my entrepreneurial business, I returned to school to obtain the Ph.D. that I had not finished (ABD in social psychology and human ecology) years prior, following the death of my major professor. Given that my practical expertise was in marketing and promotion and my business endeavors (most recently, in hospitality) were typically classified in terms of service, my intended focus was services marketing. Naively, without researching universities, business schools or marketing departments, I simply applied to the local university, the one I had attended previously – the University of Oklahoma (OU). I was accepted and, several years later, that naive decision proved to be fortuitous.

Fairly early in the Ph.D. program, two questions began to nag at me: First, did it really make any sense that "service economies" were "tertiary," following agricultural and industrial economies – that is, would not essentially all economic activities prior to industrialization now be classified as service? Second, did it really make any sense that there needed, effectively, to be two marketing disciplines, one for goods and the other for all else – services? This issue was exacerbated by the fact that the latter were being characterized in terms of undesirable features in comparison to the former – intangibility, inseparability of production and consumption, inability to be standardized (heterogeneity) and perishability (Zeithaml, Parasuraman, and Berry 1985, sometimes referred to as "IHIP" characteristics)?

There was also a corollary, paradoxical issue related to the combination of these questions, one that compounded them: how could it be that "advanced" economies – that is, services economies – are characterized as producing output that is considered to have inferior qualities in comparison to the previous era? In short, it seemed incoherent that the "output" of advanced "services economies" could be characterized as having qualities inferior to those of the "industrial economies" that preceded them.

Although these issues continued to haunt me, it was not until my third year in the program that a resolution began to emerge. It happened during a history of management thought seminar, conducted by Daniel Wren, a notable management historian. It was an outstanding course, showing how current thinking was a function of various bifurcations and recombination of past views and contexts. The semester project was to research and write an historical perspective on a business-related topic. The seminar was held in the Henry W. Bass Business History Collection at the Bizzell Memorial Library. It was there, in a business reference book, that I first began to appreciate the possibility that the present views about service(s) were not always agreed upon, currently or historically.

With that in mind, I spent several months essentially living in the "stacks" of the library, reading through everything having to do with service(s). The journey took me (1) back as far as the work of Aristotle and then, with pauses in the Middle Ages and the Renaissance, forward to (2) the work of Adam Smith, (3) the Industrial Revolution, and (4) contemporary economic activity, including what is often referred to as a "service economy." Of particular interest were the developments in the theoretical foundations of economic philosophy and economic science, followed by those in the business disciplines, including marketing.

There were a number of telling discoveries. First, service was considered a higher-order contribution than most other activities in some early societies. Second, Smith (1904 [1776]), in early chapters of *The Wealth of Nations*, had a primary focus on the skills and activities of people (that is, division of labor) and on what he called "real value" (value in use), the benefit received by some party, rather than on the output and for what it can be exchanged (value in exchange). Third, and most profoundly, a relatively obscure, nineteenth-century economic philosopher, Frédéric Bastiat (1964 [1848], pp. 61–2), had argued over 150 years ago that "Services are exchanged for services ... It is trivial, very commonplace; it is, nonetheless, the beginning, the middle, and the end of economic science." The story of that historical journey for Dan Wren's class became the first draft for my paper for his class and the foundation for some work I was later do with Bob Lusch (as well as a later article in the *Journal of Macromarketing* – Vargo and Morgan 2005).

I first met Bob Lusch when I started the Ph.D. program. He had just stepped down following his five-year stint as dean of the business school at OU and was teaching a seminar in marketing theory and thought. Following that, I had relatively little contact with him until I was assigned to assist him in his research, around my third year. Following Professor Wren's seminar, I showed Bob the paper I had just written, with some revisions. He found it interesting and provocative but questioned some of the insights. However, the paper, along with the fact that I had been assigned to work with him, provided us an opportunity to discuss mutual interests and discover some academic compatibilities.

About the same time, I approached Bob about a directed readings course, looking at the topic of channels of distribution as it applied to services. Sometime in the midst of reading his requisite 1,000-pages-per-credit-hour (that is, 3,000-page) assignment, coupled with the insights from my research on an historical perspective on service and conversations with Bob, a simple but potentially profound insight occurred to me: "we have all of this backward; services are not a special case of products at all; products are the distribution mechanisms for services, which is the general case." I shared it with Bob one day. His response was "damn, I think you might be right." I then developed a paper based on the historical perspective with an extension into the role of service in economic exchange, which, in addition to fulfilling the requirements of the course, formed the basis for our first collaboration.

For the next several years, in addition to writing my dissertation (on an unrelated topic) and moving to California to take a visiting position, Bob and I worked at revising the paper that I had submitted for the readings course with him, refining the central idea, streamlining or pulling out sections that did not contribute to it and developing the story line. This was not an easy task. Whereas the core idea was a fairly simple one, at least on the surface, it required considerable additional research and thought before it could be adequately extended, developed, and reconciled with traditional marketing thought and substantiated through the convergence of similar divergent thought in marketing and other business literature. Perhaps most critical was fully internalizing the perspective we were advocating.

Following that period – roughly 1996–98 – Bob indicated that he thought the paper, or at least its core idea, was *Journal of Marketing* worthy. However, also during that period, he had become the *JM* editor and thus was ineligible to submit a manuscript to that journal. He told me I had several choices: (1) submit it to another journal, (2) submit it as a sole author to *JM*, or (3) wait until his term was over and submit it to *JM* together. I opted to wait until he stepped down as editor and submit to *JM*. We submitted the manuscript in 1999 under the title "Is It All About Services?: A Paradigm Inversion."

Submission, responses, and revisions

The first reviews were mixed, as were all of the ones that followed. One reviewer, (#2), later revealed as Roland Rust, stated:

> Every once in a great while a paper comes along that is truly exciting – that has the ability to change the way people think. This is one of those papers. If this paper is published in *JM*, then it has an opportunity to be a classic in our field. I wish I had written it.

He also warned of two likely reactions: "1) it's not new, and 2) it's wrong," with "services" scholars aligning with the first reaction and "goods" scholars with the second.

At the other extreme, one reviewer took exception to his/her (incorrect) inference that we were trying to argue that "services" don't get the respect they deserve, saying "The solution is to loosely call every economic activity a service or a product of a service and to declare services thinking to have won ... but to what evident useful end or purpose." Essentially, the reviewer was arguing we were wrong. The third reviewer's assessment was somewhat more in the middle, indicating that we had made "a compelling case for the central importance of services and the transformation of companies from service firms rather than goods providers," but then contended that our view could be "better subsumed under a market orientation" – essentially arguing that there is nothing new. Dave Stewart, the *JM* editor at the time, found the manuscript "interesting" but noted, in line with the comments of several reviewers, that there was "not much new." He invited an "extensive revision."

We of course made that revision, focusing particularly on the clarity of our positioning in an attempt to state more succinctly what was new and the conceptualization of "service" we were using – the *process* of using one's resources for the benefit of another actor, rather than *units of output* (that is, "services") – and elaborating it throughout the manuscript. It was a difficult process for a number of reasons. Most difficult was getting our arms completely around the key points and how to substantiate and convey them.

Continuing to fully grasp and internalize the central idea was also problematic. I possibly had a little advantage in this regard, simply because I was still an academic novice, relatively less encumbered by traditional marketing and economic conceptualizations than was Bob. I also had been thinking about this reconceptualization longer. Bob, on the other hand, being considerably better read and experienced in academic marketing, was also perhaps a bit more encumbered by the conceptualizations he had previously internalized. I recall a particular phone conversation, several years after the beginning of our collaboration, in which it became apparent to me that we had finally embraced a common understanding, even if it was one that was still not fully developed.

Unfortunately, that common understanding, though a major breakthrough, did not fully alleviate the difficulty in getting the story across. Given the time it had taken to get on the same page on the underlying thesis, that was not entirely surprising. It was, nonetheless, quite frustrating.

Following that revision and resubmission, we received another invitation for a major, risky revision from Editor Stewart, with a particular emphasis on the following three points: (1) "a primary concern of the reviewers remains focused on the incremental contribution of the paper," (2) a feeling that "… it is probably too strong to conclude that all goods represent services in disguise," and (3) a request to "identify the boundary conditions of your premises." The boundary condition issue had become a particularly pointed one throughout the process, either explicitly or implied. It seemed that it was difficult for some to see how we could be arguing that a service-centered logic could apply to *all* economic phenomena, rather than just a subset. This was a troubling hurdle, since this was of course our central thesis. Fred Morgan had brought up the same issue in a friendly, informal review sometime before. No doubt, it was a result of the fact that the traditional classification system considered goods and services as two categories of the same class, that is, products, albeit with services somewhat inferior, as discussed above. As noted, the eventual solution of this problem was through the clarification of the intended, transcending conceptualization of "service" as a process and as a superordinate concept to "goods" and "services" (units of output). We substantiated this claim through a number of supporting citations in the literature, perhaps most notable, Gummesson's (1995, pp. 250–51) observation that "The traditional division between goods and services is long outdated. It is not a matter of redefining services and seeing them from a customer perspective; *activities render services, things render services.*"

I learned a lot about the critical role of clarity and substantiation throughout this review process. Most notably, that it is up to the writer to compellingly establish the core arguments, rather than the reviewers and editor to figure them out.

The next revision took approximately 11 months, partly because I was moving between universities in California and Bob was moving to TCU to become dean and had also taken on the job as Chairman of the American Marketing Association (in addition to being *JM* editor). Additionally, we had decided that to satisfy the diverse, sometimes contradictory, comments of the various reviewers and the editor, we needed to restructure the entire manuscript. The most notable change was the organization of the key points around eight propositions, which we called "foundational premises" – later condensed into the first two (of currently five) axioms (Vargo and Lusch 2016) – a suggestion made by a new (fifth) reviewer in the previous round. From these, we derived 13 managerial and social implications. We also reduced the manuscript by approximately 25 percent, a difficult task, given the diversity of reviewer and editorial requirements but one that was no doubt helped by the pointedness of the new organization. The story was now becoming more complete and compelling. The title was also shortened to "Is It All About Service?"

While often disagreeing in their specific views, it was clear that all of the reviewers, including reviewer #2 (Rust), who had been supportive from the beginning, as well as the editor, agreed that the manuscript in all of its forms, up to this point was controversial. In the letter to the editor, we addressed this issue directly:

> This manuscript continues to be controversial. However, we do not intend to be controversial merely for the sake of controversy. We want to challenge the profession of marketing (both educators and practitioners) to answer for themselves the central question "Is It All About Services?" In this regard we provide as much evidence, logic, and analysis possible to answer in the affirmative. Predictably, however not all may agree with our conclusion; nonetheless we feel this question needs to be debated. As Reviewer #2 stated in their initial review:
>> "The author's thesis, that service, not goods, dominate marketing and should shape marketing thought, is not new, but the extended exposition and defense of the thesis are new. I am sure that there will be two reactions: 1) it's not new, and 2) it's wrong... The paper does an excellent job of rebutting these potential criticisms."

This was submitted in August, 2001.

Bob and I felt that our reviewer responses to this revision, at a minimum, gave the editor "permission" to publish, even if they did not reflect comprehensive agreement with its position. The verdict, however, was another invitation for a risky revision and resubmission, this time with the specific instruction that it should be a "largely new effort." The decision motivated a hand-written note to me by Bob on his Dean's letterhead expressing his outrage in language I seldom heard him use – a note that I kept and have now (following his death in 2017) hung on my office wall, along with the awards the paper has received.

It was apparent to us that, while perhaps not on the verge of outright rejecting the manuscript, it was unlikely that the present editor would ever accept it. Extremely frustrated, we contemplated the alternatives. Bob wanted to withdraw the manuscript and submit it to the *Journal of the Academy of Marketing Science (JAMS)* – in fact, he drafted a transmittal letter to Rajan Varadarajan, then editor of *JAMS*, for that purpose. In spite of my very high regard for *JAMS*, I disagreed. Rather, I suggested that we hold on to this revision until the time when Ruth Bolton was to take over as *JM* editor in 2002. More specifically, I suggested that we write Ruth after she took over, outlining what we intended for the revision and asking her if that would qualify as sufficient for a "largely new effort" in her opinion and also if she could provide any guidance. My thinking was that, if she liked the overall thesis, she would signal this by offering some suggestions and, if not, we would know pursuing publication in *JM* was a dead end and could proceed with a *JAMS* submission.

Fortunately, her response was generally positive. However, she was not entirely comfortable with the thesis of a *service orientation*, as opposed to a *goods orientation*, suggesting instead a transition from an *output* to a *process* orientation. While we did not fully agree with this change, we acquiesced to her judgment. The revised manuscript was titled "Transition and Convergence: From an Output to a Process Centered View of Marketing" and then submitted in September, 2002.

Ruth Bolton's letter, along with the reviewer comments came back to us in November of the same year. Importantly, she had added a sixth reviewer, later revealed as George Day. Her summary of his input turned out to be pivotal, as well as somewhat prophetic, and probably not only contributed to its publication but, arguably, also to its impact. She noted:

> I invited a new reviewer (Reviewer 6) to prepare an evaluation – with a specific request that he/she make suggestions that could help bring closure to the review process. I felt that his/her breadth would be useful for a paper that tackles important issues related to the future of marketing, He/she found the paper "interesting and provocative" and rightly observes that it is unlikely (and perhaps undesirable) for reviewers to converge on their opinions. Reviewer 6 recommends that I ask you to create a shorter and more focused paper (that retains your key arguments.) Then, if your paper is accepted for publication, it can provide the basis for invited commentaries by distinguished scholars. I like the recommendation because it allows you to preserve the integrity of the key ideas of your manuscript (which might otherwise be diluted or distorted by the review process). At the same time, a tentative plan for invited commentaries will encourage alternative perspectives (that go beyond the scope of this paper) and foster intellectual debate about the future of marketing.

Several additional opinions expressed by the reviewers and editor were also especially significant. In reflecting on the change to output-process-transition positioning, Roland Rust (Reviewer #2, the original, strongly supportive reviewer) commented "I think the paper had it right before. It is all about service and the shift from a goods focus to a customer focus, with service broadly defined as satisfying the customer. The output vs. process characterization of this shift muddles the key concepts, in my opinion." More generally, Ruth Bolton noted that the other reviewers "are also concerned that the paper's original message has been 'diluted' due to the process/outcome distinction."

In addition to the suggestion that the paper (1) need not have reviewer consensus and (2) if published, should be done with invited commentaries, the new reviewer (Reviewer #6, George Day) made another suggestion that has created a long-term path dependency: he suggested that the transition be identified as "a shift in the dominant logic," because of "the loaded connotations of 'paradigm'." Ruth Bolton endorsed this view and, coupled with the return to the designation of a service-centered orientation, the title of the revision became "Evolving to a New Dominant Logic for Marketing." This, eventually, morphed into the name "service-dominant logic," as it became apparent that we had to move beyond the label of "new."

We also incorporated the "operand resource" (resources that must be acted on to provide benefit) and "operant resource" (resources that can act on other resources to provide benefit) distinction in this version, to capture some of the output-versus-process orientation to deepen the original, service-centered framework. Additionally, we provided evidence to support the framework through Mauss's (1966) discussion of a "total services" model of reciprocal exchange in archaic societies. The revised manuscript was submitted in February 2003, shortened to 28 pages, a 35 percent reduction from the previous version but a few more pages than the 25 requested by the editor.

Finally, in April, 2003, Ruth Bolton "conditionally accepted" the manuscript, inviting us to "polish" it and to consider a few additional suggestions from Reviewer #6, which we incorporated. The final version (the fifth) was submitted in the summer of 2003 and was accepted, over four years after the first submission and ten years since the original conceptualization and draft.

The manuscript was substantially changed from the one originally submitted at that point. Although the core ideas were intact and had actually been expanded, the organization, and substantiation were, arguably, considerably improved. These improvements were of course not just a function of Bob's and my efforts, but also the combined efforts of the various editors and reviewers, who not only pointed out where our original positioning and arguments were less than compelling but also provided specific guidance for improvement.

At the same time the manuscript was conditionally accepted, Ruth Bolton invited us to provide input into the guidance for and selection of commentators, while suggesting a list of her own. The general approach was to ask several people to take a broad approach and others to take a more focused look at specific points, roughly aligned with the foundational premises. At least two reviewers (Roland Rust and George Day) were included on the final list. Evert Gummesson was specifically selected to provide a non-U.S., "Nordic School" perspective. Other invitees were John Deighton, Das Narayandas, Shelby D. Hunt, C.K. Prahalad, and Steven M. Shugan. Publishing seven commentaries (Bolton 2004) in conjunction with a single article was a first for *JM*. Ruth Bolton also provided an introductory comment, which said in part:

> Vargo and Lusch (2004) observe that an evolution is underway toward a new dominant logic for marketing. The new dominant logic has important implications for marketing theory, practice, and pedagogy, as well as for general management and public policy. ... The ideas expressed in the article and the commentaries will undoubtedly provoke a variety of reactions from readers of the *Journal of Marketing*.

Her words were prophetic and, clearly, these commentaries were attention-provoking for the article. In approximately ten years, the article was the most cited article in *JM* since 1996, and one of the top ten most-cited articles in the history of *JM*. No doubt many of these citations have been perfunctorily motivated, as is the case with many new, novel articles and clearly some have been critical, but a very significant number have been supportive and developmental, using S-D logic foundationally to explore wide-ranging applications both within marketing and business and beyond (see Vargo and Lusch 2017).

Some lessons learned

Clearly, whether measured from the initial questioning of what would later be called the "goods-dominant (G-D) logic of marketing," the initial kernel of the idea that it is actually service that should represent the dominant logic of the market and value creation, or the submission in 1999, the road to publication was long and arduous. Just measured from the fist submission, it involved two editors, six reviewers and four major, risky revisions.

As with most submissions, to journals of all levels, the review process can be very frustrating, but it can also be very helpful. The original, strongly supportive reviewer was clearly encouraging and, arguably, might have been influential in keeping the early versions of the manuscript alive. But, in many ways, the less than enthusiastic reviewers were also instrumental in the paper's success. Of particular note were those reviewers who argued that our contentions were not sufficiently clear, cogent, or compelling. While painful to hear, all were instrumental in contributing to the eventual success of the manuscript.

Of particular note was early, general pushback that seemed to be objecting to what probably appeared to be a traditional-thought-has-it-wrong and we-are-right positioning. Given the fact that the possibility of an alternative (to G-D logic) perspective was obvious from both the historical literature as well as supported by trends in thinking and writing beyond marketing, the initial positioning was probably unreasonable. However, we realized that some of the pushback, if not outright objections, of some reviewers were probably attributable to the fact that we appeared to be stepping on their personal paradigmatic foundations.

Thus, we changed our positioning to one of capturing and accelerating a change that we saw taking place, making it less confrontational, as reflected in the shift in title from "Is it all about service" to "Evolving ...." It is a lesson I have found beneficial, repeatedly. Sounding critical of a position, especially one held by a reader (including a reviewer) that one is trying to modify is seldom effective, whereas inviting readers on an evolutionary journey that is underway, is much more palatable.

Another lesson learned is the benefit of embracing paradigmatic paradoxes. They almost always point toward opportunities for important advances. In this case, it was the notion that a service economy was characteristic of advanced societies coupled with the idea that services were seen as having qualities that were less desirable than tangible, manufactured goods that made our ideas ultimately compelling. The resolution was to (1) not define service in terms of intangible goods, but rather as a process of using one's resources for another's benefit and (2) seeing that service was the purpose of all goods. Thus, as noted, service became a transcending concept. I spend a lot of time in doctoral seminars extoling the benefits of embracing paradoxes.

There are at least two other critical lessons to learn from the review and publication process described here. The first has to do with capitalizing on the review process. Reviewers and editors are not the natural predators of authors, as is sometimes imagined. The former are themselves scholars and working, with no (direct, at least) compensation, to advance the discipline and the latter actually wants every manuscript submitted to them to be publishable. True, reviewers can be resistant to new ideas because of their own entrenched views, a particularly difficult problem. However, this can often be overcome by acknowledging and responding to their comments, using the remarks of the editor as signals of the most essential concerns. On the other hand, most negative reviews just reflect lack of clarity and substantiation of evidence on the part of the author(s) and thus, their suggestions often just indicate areas that need further development. Ultimately, given an attentive editor, the review process usually results in a considerably more impactful article than would be the case otherwise. In short, while extremely frustrating at the time, I have found the review process beneficial. The keys are listening to the editor for guidance, particularly in relation to contentious issues, being as respectful and responsive to negative reviewers as possible and building on the suggestions of positive reviewers and the editor.

The second lesson relates to the potential power and payoff of persistence. There were numerous opportunities to abandon the pursuit of the publishing of "Evolving …," at least in *JM*. Clearly, though tempting at times, that would have been a major error. Potentially impactful ideas, especially contentious ones that run counter to contemporary thought, are likely always to be difficult and frustrating to get accepted. That is, their very contentiousness provides both their strength in contribution and their weakness when seeking acceptance. The former can be best served through clarity, evidence from existing literature, and turning confrontation into a story of coalescence and convergence and the latter can be best overcome in much the same way, motivated by a deep sense of conviction.

References

Bastiat, Frédéric (1964 [1848]), *Selected Essays on Political Economy*, edited by George. B. de Huszar. Princeton, NJ: D. Van Nordstrand.

Bolton, R. (2004), "Invited Commentaries on Evolving to a New Dominant Logic for Marketing," *Journal of Marketing*, 68 (January), 18–27.

Gummesson, Evert (1995), *Relationship Marketing: Its Role in the Service Economy, Understanding Services Management*, New York: John Wiley & Sons.

Mauss, Marcel (1960), *The Gift: Forms and Functions of Exchange in Archaic Societies*, London: Cohen and West Limited.

Smith, Adam (1904 [1776]), *An Inquiry Into the Nature and Causes of the Wealth of Nations*, London: Methuen.

Vargo, S.L. and R.F. Lusch (2004), "Evolving to a New Dominant Logic in Marketing," *Journal of Marketing*, 68 (January), 1–17.

Vargo, S.L. and R.F. Lusch (2016), "Institutions and axioms: An Extension and Update of Service-Dominant Logic," *Journal of the Academy of Marketing Science*, 44 (1), 5–23.

Vargo, S.L. and R.F. Lusch (2017), "Service-Dominant Logic for 2025," *International Journal of Research in Marketing*, 34 (1), 46–67.

Vargo, S.L. and F.W. Morgan (2005), "Services in Society and Academic Thought: An Historical Analysis," *Journal of Macromarketing*, 25 (1), 42–53. doi: 10.1177/0276146705275294.

Zeithaml, V.A., A. Parasuraman, and L.L. Berry (1985), "Problems and Strategies in Services Marketing," *Journal of Marketing*, 49 (2), 33–46.

SECTION IV

FINAL THOUGHTS

Introduction to section IV

For the reader who has come this far in this book, it should be obvious that the publication process is hard work, filled with opportunities for learning and for frustration, and requiring a willingness to persist and constructively respond to criticism. It is a creative exercise that is rarely characterized by a smooth, linear route from idea to publication. The final section of this book includes two chapters designed to provide a summary of the process and advice from numerous current and former editors of leading journals in marketing. It is advice offered in the spirit of improving scholarship in the marketing discipline, developing the next generation of marketing scholars, and making the publication process more transparent and more fun.

Chapter 15 is a reprint of a paper written by one of the editors of this book (DS). It was specifically addressed to the growing number of international marketing scholars who are responsible for an increasing percent of the papers submitted to and published in the leading marketing journals. Though addressed to an international audience, the advice applies to all scholars who aspire to publish in the best marketing journals.

Chapter 16 is co-authored by a unique collection of current and former editors. The authors of the chapter have edited the *Journal of Marketing*, the *Journal of Marketing Research*, the *Journal of Consumer Research*, the *Journal of the Association for Consumer Research*, and/or *Marketing Science*, as well as numerous other publications. They are also highly accomplished scholars and authors. Their collective wisdom regarding publication in the leading journals in marketing is a fitting conclusion of this book.

[15]

Academic publishing in marketing: best and worst practices

David W. Stewart

Department of Marketing, Marshall School of Business, University of Southern California, Los Angeles, California, USA

Received August 2006
Revised August 2006,
September 2006
Accepted September 2006

Abstract

Purpose – The purpose of this paper is to offer observations regarding best and weak practices with respect to academic publishing in marketing.

Design/methodology/approach – The approach takes the form of personal reflections based on the experience of the author as an editor of the *Journal of Marketing* and *Journal of the Academy of Marketing Science*.

Findings – Interesting and novel work is most likely to be published in academic journals even when such work has methodological flaws. Research that is methodologically correct but of limited contribution is less likely to be published. Venue-driven research, replications, most extensions of prior research and data fitting exercises are unlikely to be published in the "better" marketing journals.

Practical implications – The paper offers practical advice about how to publish in the better marketing journals and how an author should manage the publication process.

Originality/value – The paper offers observations regarding best and weak practices with respect to academic publishing in marketing. It is a practical guide to the academic publication process in marketing. It will be of use to any aspiring scholar in marketing.

Keywords Publishing, Academic libraries, Research, Marketing, Best practice

Paper type Viewpoint

Introduction

I am pleased to have the opportunity to address my international colleagues who read the *European Business Review* (*EBR*). From 1999 to 2002 I served as editor of the *Journal of Marketing* (*JM*) and began a three-year term as editor of the *Journal or the Academy of Marketing Science* (*JAMS*) in June of 2006. As an editor I have managed the review process of more than 1,200 papers. I have also served as a reviewer for another 1,000 or so papers submitted to more than four-dozen journals during an academic career that has spanned more than 25 years. I have not only been involved in offering reviews of paper, I have also been on the receiving end of reviews as the author of more than 150 papers in refereed publications. This experience, as editor, reviewers and author provides a special, if not entirely unique perspective on the publication process. I am happy to share that perspective with the readers of *EBR*.

My junior colleagues, and even some of my senior colleagues, often express their concern that the publication process is stacked in favor of a few established scholars who review and recommend publication of one another's work. There is often a view that there are "right" ways to do research, or "more correct" topics, that make it more likely for a paper to successfully get through the review process. At the very least, there is a perception among many scholars that there is something mysterious about

Emerald

European Business Review
Vol. 20 No. 5, 2008
pp. 421-433
© Emerald Group Publishing Limited
0955-534X
DOI 10.1108/09555340810897943

EBR
20,5

422

the publication process. Somehow, a small number of wizards learn the secret formula of success and only rarely share it. As editor and author I can assure readers that there is no secret formula for success. Neither is success in publication the province of a few members of an in-group that controls access to the pages of major journals in marketing.

There is a formula, however and a few scholars have mastered it by virtue of their own creativity, persistence, and hard work. The formula is at once very simple in concept and very difficult in practice. Scholars are in the creativity business and creativity is difficult. There are more failures of the creative enterprise than successes. This unbalanced ratio occurs for two reasons. First, some scholars are more creative than others, just as some composers, novelists, and film directors are more creative than others. Second, even the most creative scholar, or artist, creates far more mediocre work than truly outstanding creative work. This means that the formula for success involves two things: creativity and a willingness to work very hard. The latter attribute can compensate somewhat for somewhat lower creativity but, it my experience, even remarkable creativity in the absence of a willingness to work hard is seldom a strategy for success.

There is also a misconception that methodological rigor can substitute for a lack of creativity. Methodological rigor is important and has its place, but it is not a substitute for creativity. Figure 1 provides, in graphic form, an indication of the probability of success of publication based on two dimensions, the interest value of the work (its creativity or originality) and its methodological rigor. Papers with high interest value and methodological rigor are the types of papers editors and reviewers like to see; they have a very high probability of publication. Papers on interesting topics, but that suffer some methodological problems (but are not fatally flawed) have the next highest probability of publication. This is because papers that address interesting issues in

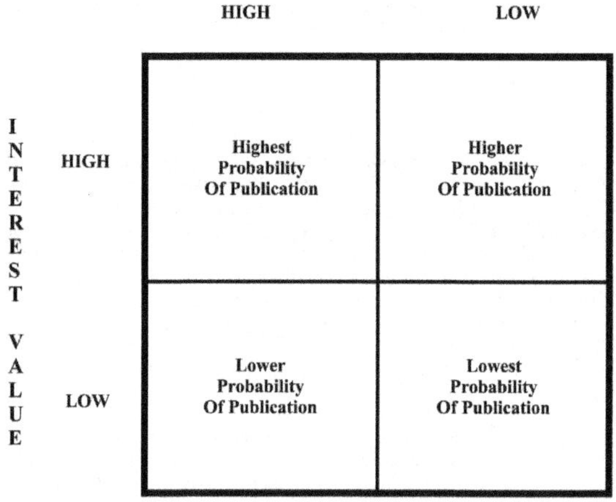

	HIGH	**LOW**
INTEREST **HIGH**	Highest Probability Of Publication	Higher Probability Of Publication
VALUE **LOW**	Lower Probability Of Publication	Lowest Probability Of Publication

Figure 1.
The probability of publishing

novel ways are often given some "slack" with respect to methodological rigor. The majority of papers ultimately published in the better journals fall into this class. One reason that some methodological slack is afforded such papers is that these papers often are both treating an important substantive issue and building a methodological road that others may follow.

Subsequent papers on the same topic are almost always, by definition, less interesting (certainly less novel) and are required to correct the methodological mistakes of the pioneer. This is why papers that have modest interest value (e.g. the 37th paper on a topic) must of necessity be methodologically rigorous. There is a point of diminishing returns with respect to interest value, which is why even the most methodologically rigorous paper has a low probability of publication if it lacks interest value. Papers that are neither rigorous nor interesting are all too common. Such papers generally reflect a need, or perceived need to publish but without either the requisite conceptual foundation for creativity or the methodological skills for rigorous research. Sometimes these papers are the result of an unwillingness to do the hard work involved in a creative enterprise and to develop the necessary skills. More often, aspiring scholars who lack the necessary theoretical and conceptual training to pursue high quality work write these papers. Sometimes, individuals early in their training write these papers; in other cases individuals trained in weak programs write them.

It is unfortunate that we do not do more to prepare scholars for their participation in the creative enterprise. Creative work requires a unique approach to management and a unique set of personal traits. Because creative work is fraught with failure it is important to develop and manage a whole portfolio of projects. The typical motion picture production company is lucky to produce one blockbuster in ten. It would be nice if than one could be identified in advance, but this is seldom the case. So, the company creates ten products in the hope that one will be the big hit. The other nine go into limited theatrical release or immediately to the video store. So it is with scholarship in marketing. A few papers out of many will have major impact. The remaining papers don't go to the video store but they do end up at journals of lesser reputation and as conference presentations. The formula for success for a marketing scholar is to always be working on a portfolio of projects and to manage that personal portfolio as a creative enterprise.

The frequency of rejection experience by a creative artist or a marketing scholar can be depressing and de-motivating. This is why so many faculty members drop out of the publication venture even when they possess substantial creative capability. This is where the hard work comes in, as well as a refusal to accept rejection of an individual paper as a rejection of the entire creative effort. It is in this area that senior scholars can be of most help to junior scholars by being unbridled cheerleaders.

Regrettably, the review process itself is too often de-motivating. I have always viewed whatever success I have had to a great deal of hard work and a more modest dose of creativity. In the hope that I might provide motivation and encouragement I will describe a formative experience in my own career. It will be all too familiar to many readers, but describing it may illustrate that the persistence can prevail. I will turn to a discussion of the factors that can increase the probability of success in publication, as well as factors that may diminish the probability of success. Finally, I wish to conclude with some observations about the differences in perspective, paradigm and focus that characterize American versus European scholarship in marketing with the hope that my observations may produce a rapprochement in the two approaches and bring about a greater complementarity in the work of scholars around the globe.

EBR
20,5

424

A formative experience

I begin with an experience as an author early in my career that shaped my own perspective as a reviewer, and ultimately as an editor. It also illustrates the influence that a reviewer can have on an author. In 1980 I submitted a paper to the *Journal of Marketing Research* (*JMR*) that provided a review of the applications and misapplications of factor analysis. The paper, which had its genesis in my applied work in an advertising agency, was subsequently published and has had some modest impact. The reviews of that paper were quite helpful and the paper was significantly improved as a result of the comments I received. However, one reviewer, after offering otherwise useful comments and suggesting the paper might have potential offered the observation that "I doubt this author has the ability to do the necessary work".

As a young scholar such a comment about my ability by an anonymous reviewer in a position of authority was a body blow. The comment was not about the paper but was about me, and my capability to improve upon my own work. I am not so easily discouraged, persisted and eventually had success. Nevertheless, there were some important lessons for me in this event and I believe there are lessons for others. This event has influenced my owe behavior as a reviewer and editor. It made clear to me how easily we might discourage creativity and innovation. It also made very salient to me the importance of reviewing papers rather than authors. Over the last 25 years I have seen similar comments by reviewers and have counseled many a scholar, including some who are not so junior, about how to handle such negative comments. The lesson for authors is to persist; the lesson for reviewers is to be constructive and focus on the paper not the author. I have admonished a number of reviewers, most who are themselves junior scholars, to be helpful and to avoid gratuitous remarks about authors. It is one thing to suggest that a paper needs to be thoroughly copy edited; it is quite another thing to suggest that the author is unable to write clearly.

The larger lesson in this personal story is that academic scholarship occurs within the context of a community. One reason that communities of creative artists arise is because they provide important support and reassurance to the artist, or scholar, in the face of rejection – rejection that all too often takes the form of a personal insult. As scholars we need to be especially cognizant of our role in the larger community of scholars and of the need to support scholarship even when our view of a single piece of work is not very positive. I devoted my first editorial statement as editor of the *JM* (Stewart, 1999) to a discussion of the role of community in academic research (see also Stewart, 2007). Reviewers and editors influence not only what is published but also the quality of what is published. Authors not only contribute to the body of scholarship, but also make the literature better by attending to and responding to constructive comments by reviewers. Readers use, apply and teach based on this literature, and this literature ultimately feeds back into the process of writing papers and the review process. All of the actors in this community, authors, reviewers, editors and readers have a strong vested interest in making the cumulative body of scholarship better. This is the goal of the community – adding to and improving the body of scholarship. Publication is not an end in itself; it is a means to an end.

Journals are just tangible artifacts of an intellectual community. Editors and reviewers certainly influence the character of these artifacts but they are really driven by authors. Most of the articles published by a new editor during her or his first year are already written and in the review process. The problems and topics on which scholars within the intellectual community are working and will work reflect the broader social and economic environment of which a discipline is a part. An editor has very modest influence on this environment, especially in the short-term. However, an editor plays an especially important role in ensuring that the best scholarship is captured and published on a timely basis. This is the common goal of the community. If we bear in mind the role that journals play, a tangible artifact, and the common goal of the intellectual community, adding to the collective body of knowledge, it is not difficult to identify practices that are more likely, and less likely to achieve the common goal. These practices also have very specific implications for authors who wish to contribute to the body of knowledge and reviewers who assist them.

Why papers are published

In an earlier paper at the close of my tenure as editor of *JM* (Stewart, 2002) I offered some practical advise about how to get published. I will repeat some of that advice here but will also try to update and broaden this advice. As I observed above, there is no mystery about why papers are published. It is also inevitable that the rejection rates of the very best journals in a field will be high. While I was editor of *JM* we rejected more than 85 percent of the papers that were submitted. We are running at a comparable rejection rate at *JAMS*. These are journals that seek to publish the best of the best papers. Many good papers are rejected; they are just not good enough. This is the nature of the creative enterprise. There are many books written, but few best sellers; there are many movies produced, but few blockbusters; there are many commercials created by only a few "big ideas".

There are things that an author can do and things an author should generally avoid doing that can increase the probability of the acceptance of a paper. They are obvious but too often unheeded. They are also the characteristics of the social fabric of scholarship that defines what is publishable work and what is not. The factors can be found in the following list:

(1) *Facilitators*:
- originality/creativity;
- interest value;
- sharing and feedback;
- listening to reviewers and editor;
- revising and resubmitting (soon);
- building on failure; and
- becoming active as a reviewer.

(2) *Inhibitors*:
- pure replications;
- venue driven research;
- simple extensions (add a variable);
- data fitting;
- lack of feedback;
- not listening to advice; and
- failure to revise on timely basis.

EBR
20,5

In journals that publish the best work in the entire field of marketing, like *JM* or *JAMS*, the articles that make broad contributions to the field will be favored. As a result, an otherwise very good paper in a narrow area may not be acceptable for publication. This does not mean that the paper is poor; rather, it means that the paper does not make enough of a general contribution to the marketing discipline to warrant its selection over other papers. The best papers on advertising compete for space against the best papers on channels of distribution. These papers, in turn, compete for space against the best papers in every other area of marketing. A significant percentage of the papers submitted to journals like *JM* and *JAMS*, are eventually published somewhere. What distinguishes the papers that are published in the premier journals from those published elsewhere is the significant of the contribution of these papers; it is what they add that is new and incremental.

Too often authors focus on what has been previously published as a guide for choosing problems on which to work. It is, of course, useful to understand what has been published in the past, but focusing on what has already appeared in the literature to identify opportunities for important incremental contributions is rather like gauging where one is in a foot race by looking backward. The work that appears in print almost certainly began at least two to three years earlier. It is old work by the time it is in print (the journal is just an archive). This is one reason it is important to be actively involved in the review process and present at conferences where thought leaders present their work. This allows one to look forward as well as backward.

Although it is a good practice to review past issues of a journal for form and content, examination of past issues is not the best guide to the incremental contribution of a paper. Past issues can indicate what is already known in an area and therefore serve as a benchmark for assessing a paper's contribution. However, just because a topic has been addressed often in prior literature is no guarantee that a paper on the same topic will be publishable. Areas of inquiry mature over time, and research on a given topic tends to become less incremental and less interesting. The 76th paper on a topic is simply not as useful or interesting as the first paper. Similarly, just because something was done in a previously published article is not, in and of itself, justification for a practice. Weak methodology or an incomplete model may be over-looked in the first article on a topic (because the topic has not been previously explored), but it is unlikely to be acceptable in subsequent work.

The most common reason by far for rejection of a paper is that it lacks a sufficient incremental contribution, i.e. it lacks sufficient interest value. I learned early in my tenure as an editor that this explanation for rejecting a paper is especially disconcerting to authors. Such a rationale is based on a subjective judgment (though informed by the opinions of reviewers). It is also difficult to tell an author exactly what must be done to improve the incremental contribution of a paper. Sometimes, the methodology in an empirical study is so flawed that the contribution could be improved only by redesigning the study. On other occasions the focus is so narrow as to be of minimal interest. More often, there is nothing wrong with the methodology and the focus is not too narrow. Rather, the issue addressed is just not very important given all of the prior work on the topic.

There are things a prospective author can do to improve the likelihood that a paper will make a significant incremental contribution. The best approach to making an important incremental contribution is to do something interesting. Whether something is interesting or not is an empirical question. It is virtually impossible to identify important questions when one is not an active participant in the larger intellectual community; it is difficult to sit alone in an office, think great thoughts and hope to publish these thoughts. Share your idea with others; ask if something to which you are considering devoting time and resources is interesting to others. Put yourself at conferences where the latest ideas are being discussed and in the presence of colleagues who can give you good feedback. You might still wish to work on the idea even if others do not find it interesting, but be aware that such ideas have a low probability of being published.

Weaker practices
There are also types of papers that are more likely to be found wanting with respect to incremental contribution. In fact, it is easier to identify the characteristics of less interesting papers than of more interesting papers. A great deal of research I have reviewed and that has been submitted to me as an editor has been justified almost exclusively by the setting in which the research is conducted. Venue is seldom a sufficient rationale for publishing a paper and immediately raises questions about incremental contribution. Just because a particular phenomenon has not been examined in a particular venue (such as a specific industry or country) is not a good reason to do a study. This is the problem with much of the research in an international or internet context. For example, it is unclear why consumer decision-making should necessarily be different in Russia versus Korea. If differences are not found, the investigation of the topic has a "so what?" quality. If it a difference is found, finding a difference alone is insufficient without an explanation for the difference. All too often the real reason for any obtained difference is trivial (consumers in one country are not as familiar with the stimulus brands as consumers in another; the required translation of the questionnaire produced differences in the meaning of the questions compared with the original instrument).

Similarly, brand, trust and reputation are important in many markets. Why would it be any different in an internet context? I was editor of *JM* during the peak of the internet bubble and received many papers related to the internet. In three years I published only one paper on the internet. Clearly, the internet was and is important; there are many interesting and unique questions related to the internet. The papers I received did not address these interesting and unique issues; rather they addressed old, worn issues in an internet context and produced such uninteresting conclusions as brand and reputation matter in an internet context. Venue-driven research bears the burden of making the case that venue should matter for some important reason and then demonstrating that the expected difference is present for the reason posited. This is a high hurdle.

Pure replications are not compelling for similar reasons. A replication that works has a "so what?" character. A replication that does not work raises questions about why. Replications may fail for many reasons, and most of these reasons are not interesting. A replication may fail because a different measure was used, a manipulation failed, or the sample was inappropriate. A failure to replicate bears the burden of explanation. Such failures can be important for the establishment of the boundary conditions of phenomena, but this too is a high hurdle. This does not mean that replications are unimportant. In fact, the stronger papers that are published often

EBR
20,5

428

include replications within them. This is one reason why some many papers often report multiple studies.

A variation of replication is the addition of a new variable. This type of research often starts with well-established research and is justified by a finding that adding a previously unexamined variable accounts for some additional variance. Such research can be interesting, especially if the new variable suggests boundaries for a phenomenon, but as with venue-driven research and replications, the burden for demonstrating the importance of a contribution is high. The questions raised are why this particular variable is examined and others are not, why the selected variable is theoretically relevant, and how important the added variance accounted for really is.

Data fitting is not usually interesting no matter how sophisticated the model or method may be. This is the problem with much of the recent work employing structural equation modeling. Merely showing that a set of data fits a model is not an especially compelling contribution. The same data may fit many different models with very different theoretical implications. Data may also fit a model for reasons as uninteresting as common method variance. The burden on the author is to make a compelling case that there is theoretical or practical significance associated with fitting a given model.

Making interesting ideas better

An interesting idea is certainly a good starting point for a strong incremental contribution, but it is usually not enough. As editor and reviewer I have written numerous comments on papers of the form: "this paper contains an interesting idea but it suffers in execution". Great thoughts need to be followed with a good deal of work and this work is not always especially interesting or glamorous. It may involve pre-testing, false starts, and the slow, deliberate process of writing in a form that communicates to the reader. Ideas get better when they are shared, feedback is sought and there is an openness to change. As an editor, I could usually identify the papers that had been read by no one other than the author before submission. Feedback helps and raises the odds of publication and often reduces the number of rounds of review. Early feedback even helps you avoid work on a project that has a low probability of success in the first instance.

The role of reviewers

Despite my earlier story, I believe most reviewers try to help, even if they are not always as constructive and nurturing as might be desirable. A common complaint from authors is that reviewers do not understand. In my experience I have found that reviewers usually do understand what they read, but authors are often not clear about what they mean. Part of the purpose of the review process is to identify and correct such in communication. Another common complaint from authors is that the reviewers do not agree. This complaint is often offered as a way of dismissing reviewers' comments. After all, if the reviewers cannot agree about how to revise the paper how can the author respond?

In fact, reviewers disagree far less often than many authors believe. Reviewers frequently agree on the problems that exist in a particular paper. Disagreements do occur, but these are more likely when reviewers offer potential solutions for these problems. For example, all the reviewers may agree that one problem with a paper is insufficient power in a statistical test. One reviewer may suggest increasing sample size to solve this problem, another reviewer may suggest using a more sensitive measure, and a third reviewer may suggest using a covariate to reduce the error variance. In such a case, it is not unusual for authors to become concerned that the reviewers disagree about the approach they should take in the revision. They lose sight of the real problem, on which all agree. It is the solution to the problem rather than the particular approach that is important.

As an editor I believe an important role that reviewers play is to suggest solutions to problems. It is far more helpful to an author to identify a problem and suggest a potential solution. The purpose of the review process is to make a paper better not simply identify its flaws. Some reviewers are very good at identifying flaws. Sometimes the flaws are so great that they cannot be readily repaired. But, the helpful review will offer constructive comments about how flaws can be corrected and how the paper can be improved.

Dealing with editors

The goal of an editor is to fill every issue of a journal in a timely manner with the best possible papers. This means that the goals of the editor and the author are very much alignment. The author wants to publish a paper and the editor wants to publish papers. The editor also wants your paper to be the best it can be. When you have a question, contact the editor. It is part of the editor's responsibility to help you through the editorial process. You should listen to what the editor asks you to do. If you are unwilling to make the changes that have been requested, you probably should withdraw the paper and submit it elsewhere. Ultimately, the editor must make a decision about your paper, however. Keep this decision in perspective; if the editor rejects your paper this is a decision about your paper; it is not about you.

If you are given the opportunity to revise a paper, do so and do so quickly. Any opportunity to revise is a victory and moves you a step closer to publication. The odds of eventually being published go up substantially when a revision is invited. During my tenure as editor of *JM* 75 percent of all papers were rejected after the initial review. Of the papers whose authors have been given the chance to revise, half were eventually published. Of the papers that have gone through a second revision, 90 percent have been eventually published, though some of these have required several more rounds of revision.

It is important to revise quickly, however. Much of the research in which we engage is time sensitive. Other scholars likely are working on similar topics, and some phenomena change over time in important ways. This means that the longer you wait to revise and resubmit a paper, the more likely its contribution will be lower by the time it is reviewed again. Authors occasionally become annoyed at the "inconsistency" of reviewers (and editors), because they were told a paper was interesting and made an important contribution in one round of reviews and subsequently were told that the paper's contribution was not great in the next round of reviews. The odds that this will happen go up the longer it takes the author to complete the revision. In such cases, the reviewers are not being inconsistent; rather, their evaluations are time dependent.

Dealing with rejection

Rejection is inevitable for active scholars; learn from rejection. Rejected papers often form the basis for new work on the same topic. The comments of the reviewers can

EBR
20,5

suggest the direction for a new paper. As I noted earlier many of the papers that are rejected by one journal are published elsewhere. The feedback from the review process can be helpful to an author in revising a paper for another journal.

Building theory

430

Much of what I have discussed, particularly with respect to weaker practices tends to apply to empirical research. In American marketing journals there is a bias toward empirical work, or at the very least, it is more difficult to publish a conceptual or theoretical paper. Nevertheless, good theoretical and conceptual papers can not only be interesting but can dramatically alter the ways in which the cumulative body of research is interpreted and directed in the future. Drawing on the work of Sutton and Staw (1995), George Zinkhan and I have offered some thoughts on what makes for a good theoretical paper (Stewart and Zinkhan, 2006). As with empirical work, it is far easier to define what is not a strong theoretical contribution than to define the characteristics of strong theoretical contributions. As Sutton and Staw (1995) observe, a theoretical paper is not a collection of references to prior work, not a lot of boxes and arrows, and not a set of definitions and constructs. Rather, a theory integrates, explains, and predicts.

It may be easier to point to good examples of conceptual work and theory building, or at least papers and books that were good examples at the time of publication. At the risk of offending some of my colleagues by omission, let me offer some exemplars of good theoretical and conceptual papers and books. I would include among these exemplars the works of Alderson (1978), Berry *et al.* (1985), Bettman (1979), Borden (1942), Hunt and Morgan (1995), and Howard and Sheth (1969). I have identified these particular works because they represent a range of conceptual and theoretical efforts over time and focused on very different phenomena. I would encourage authors who are contemplating writing a conceptual or theoretical paper to carefully study the structure and form of these works. All integrate past work in novel ways. The integration itself produces new insights and suggests new directions for research. This is what strong theoretical and conceptual papers should do.

The American bias

I would be remiss in writing to an audience that is largely outside the USA if I did not address the differences between American and European scholarship. As an editor I have often heard the complaint the American marketing journals, or at least the editors and reviewers of these journals, are biased toward American authors. While I do not doubt that there is some degree of such bias I believe there are more subtle issues at work. I believe if we understand these issues we can make scholarship in marketing stronger, whatever its source.

There is an empirical bias among American marketing scholars. This bias reflects a more general tendency among Americans to want hard data, to reduce problems to simple operational constructs that can be more easily manipulated and studied, to be skeptical of general theories and to look for solutions to immediate problems. This empirical bias, which grows out of the combined influence of American pragmatism and British empiricism, is one reason it is so difficult to publish conceptual papers in American marketing journals. It is also a reason why a growing amount of research on consumer behavior research is focused on pure effects in the absence of either theory or context. A great deal of the empirical work now being published demonstrates small and peculiar oddities in human decision making in contexts that could not remotely be described as representative of any market situation. This is unfortunate for the field.

It also represents another bias in American scholarship, at least in the social sciences generally and in marketing more specifically. American scholarship has a bias toward micro-level phenomenon, e.g. the decision making of individual consumers in very specific situations in response to well defined stimuli. There is nothing wrong with such a focus, but there are important questions that require dealing with more macro-level phenomenon that exhibit greater complexity and conceptual "messiness". Such work can be found in American scholarship but it is by far the minority of the published work.

This bias toward micro-level phenomenon often leads reviewers to ask authors of more macro-level papers to reduce the complexity and redesign systems into smaller components that are more easily studied with tools involving laboratory or statistical control. It is, of course, appropriate to ask whether such reductionism is possible. Nevertheless, it is also important to ask whether the phenomenon of interest, which is defined by complexity, disappears when reduced to a subset of its parts. The challenge for authors who treat macro-level phenomenon is to make the case that something is lost by reduction and that study of the more complex phenomenon is interesting and tractable, even if different theories and methods are required.

In contrast, Europeans have tended to be interested in the complexity, the influence of context, and systems approaches. American scholars could do with a health dose of this viewpoint. Complex, systems oriented papers do not fair so well among American reviewers because they deal with phenomena that are messier, more difficult to operationalize, and generally less prescriptive of specific solutions. At the same time the simpler empirical work that is submitted by Europeans does not fair so well with European reviewers.

This is a dilemma for the discipline because we need both strong empirical work focused on small, easily defined problems (micro-level phenomena) and work at the broad systems level (macro-level phenomena). We also need work on mid-range theories that connect narrow empirical to broader theories. Rigorous empirical research that demonstrates small idiosyncratic effects in response to experimental stage management is not helpful, but neither is grand theory that cannot be operationalized or tested. I am optimistic that the globalization of research in marketing may move the discipline in the direction of greater balance of scholarship devoted to micro- and macro-level phenomena. In the meantime, my advice to junior scholars for whom publication is a requisite for tenure is to be aware of these biases and pick the audience for your research so that it will be appreciated at the defining moment of tenure.

Some concluding thoughts

Marketing is a relatively young discipline and is still finding its way as a social science. I do believe it is a social science and not merely an engineering practice through which the theories and empirical knowledge of field such as economics and psychology find application. This means that the marketing discipline must behave like a social science. The discipline has been defined more and more narrowly in recent years. It has become increasingly tactical in practice and within the academic community has ceded enormous domains to other disciplines ranging from quality (and customer

Academic publishing in marketing

431

EBR
20,5

satisfaction) to supply chain management to product management. The discipline needs to reclaim its expertise in these areas and focus more attention on larger, more strategic questions. There is a compelling need for marketing to demonstrate its value to the customer and to the firm much as the quality movement has done over the past 50 years. This will require marketing to pay more attention to measurement of its effects on the larger entities of which it is a part, the firm, the economic system, and society at large. This requires at least two fundamental changes in marketing scholarship.

First, there must be much more attention to measuring the impact of marketing in ways that are relevant to these larger entities. For marketing within the firm this means more attention to how marketing and its associated activities influence the firm and, more importantly, how it contributes to such financial metrics as cash flow and long-term grow. I have made this case in more detail elsewhere (see Young *et al.*, 2006; Stewart, 2006) so I will not elaborate at length. It is sufficient to note that has been enormous resistance by marketers in both practice and in the academy to resist tying marketing actions to financial metrics. It is correct, as those who resist would argue, that the problem is messy and difficult. There are temporal issues and inappropriate accounting conventions to overcome. Nevertheless, I am convinced that if marketing does not take on the burden of demonstrating its effectiveness in financial terms and, as result, providing a means for continuous improvement, others will do this for us. Marketing will become ever more tactical as a discipline. In my view this is the single most important issue confronting the marketing discipline today. It is also an issue to which marketing academics could make an enormous contribution.

The firm is but one entity of which marketing is a part. Marketing has much to contribute in the domains of economic and public policy, consumer welfare, and social wellbeing. Again, in my view, too little scholarship is currently focused on the role that marketing plays and can plays within the larger economic and social systems of which it is a part. Marketing has contributed and has the potential to contribute more in terms of a unique perspective on such issues as health care (many of the problems are problems of the organization of services delivery and of consumer behavior), anti-trust (marketers define markets from a consumer perspective rather than the traditional supplier perspective offered by economists), and environmental issues (an understanding of the use of markets to change behavior of sellers and buyers), among others. If marketing is to ever take its rightful place as a social science it must be an active contributor to the social debate on these and other important global social problems.

These concluding comments bring me full circle and back to the publication process. The important areas for scholarship in marketing are also very difficult and publication of papers on these topics will be difficult (certainly more difficult that much of what is published today, even in the best journals. It will be largely new and should carry considerable interest value. We possess some tools and conceptual frameworks for addressing these issues, but they are big, complex and messy issues. We will need to develop new methods and tools to address these problems. Nevertheless, in an increasingly consumer centric world marketers are among the best equipped of the social sciences for addressing these issues.

It may be that in addressing these important issues we at last find a point for reconciliation of the American micro-level view and the European macro-level view.

Both perspectives, guided by an understanding of consumer, a belief in the power of markets, and an expertise in the design value delivery systems, have much to offer and complement one another well. The firm and society at large would certainly benefit from such work, and marketing might survive as an important business function and social science rather than be reduced to such tactical tasks as which ad copy we should run today. I hope the readers of *European Business Review* will take on the task.

Academic
publishing in
marketing

433

References

Alderson, W. (1978), *Marketing Behavior and Executive Action*, Ayer Company Publishing, Manchester, NH.

Berry, L.L., Parasuraman, A. and Zeithaml, V. (1985), "A conceptual model of service quality and its implications for future research", *Journal of Marketing*, Vol. 49 No. 4, pp. 41-50.

Bettman, J. (1979), *An Information Processing Theory of Consumer Choice*, Addison-Wesley Publishing, Boston, MA.

Borden, N.H. (1942), *The Economic Effects of Advertising*, Irwin, Chicago, IL.

Howard, J. and Sheth, J. (1969), *The Theory of Buyer Behavior*, Wiley, New York, NY.

Hunt, S.D. and Morgan, R.M. (1995), "The comparative advantage theory of competition", *Journal of Marketing*, Vol. 59 No. 2, pp. 1-15.

Stewart, D.W. (1999), "Beginning again: change and renewal in intellectual communities (editorial statement)", *Journal of Marketing*, Vol. 63 No. 4, pp. 2-5.

Stewart, D.W. (2002), "Getting published: reflections of an old editor (editorial statement)", *Journal of Marketing*, Vol. 66 No. 4, pp. 1-6.

Stewart, D.W. (2006), "Putting financial discipline in marketing: a call to action", *Corporate Finance Review*, Vol. 10, September/October, pp. 14-21.

Stewart, D.W. (2007), "New and improved! A look at the future", *Journal of the Academy of Marketing Science*, Vol. 35 No. 1 (forthcoming).

Stewart, D.W. and Zinkhan, G. (2006), "Enhancing marketing theory in academic research", *Journal of the Academy of Marketing Science*, Vol. 34 No. 4 (forthcoming).

Sutton, R.I. and Staw, B.L. (1995), "What theory is not", *Administrative Science Quarterly*, Vol. 40, September, pp. 371-84.

Young, R., Weiss, A. and Stewart, D.W. (2006), *Marketing Champions: Practical Strategies for Improving Marketing's Power, Influence and Business Impact*, Wiley Interscience, New York, NY.

About the author

David W. Stewart is the Robert E. Brooker Professor of Marketing and Chair of the Department of Marketing in the Marshall School of Business at the University of Southern California. He is a past editor of the *Journal of Marketing* and the current editor of the *Journal of the Academy of Marketing Science*. David W. Stewart can be contacted at: david.stewart@marshall.usc.edu

[16]

Responding to reviewers: lessons from 17 years of editor experience at Duke University

Christine Moorman, James R. Bettman, Joel D. Huber, Mary Frances Luce and Richard Staelin

You are reading this chapter because you have decided to try your hand at sharing your research with a journal or you have already done so and are now in the enviable position where you need to respond to reviewer advice. Good for you! We are fortunate to work in the Marketing Area of the Fuqua School of Business, Duke University, which has been home to more editors of the field's four major journals over the past fifty years (1969–2019) than any other university.[1] We thought it would be interesting to gather our perspectives as current or former editors on this topic. In the pages that follow, you will get advice from Chris Moorman (*Journal of Marketing*, 2018–2022), Jim Bettman (*Journal of Consumer Research*, 1982–1988), Joel Huber (*Journal of Marketing Research*, 2006–2009), Mary Frances Luce (*Journal of Consumer Research*, 2011–2014), and Rick Staelin (*Marketing Science*, 1995–1997). There is some convergence in our thinking, but there are also times when we disagree, which we did not edit away. We think there are a number of ways to respond effectively to reviewers, and we hope you find these tips helpful in your quest to publish your research.

Responding to reviewers: lessons from the trenches

Christine Moorman

The chance to respond to reviewers is, at one level, a gift received in return for all the hard work you have invested in your paper. Given that 30–40 percent of all papers get desk rejected (depending on the journal) and fewer than half of those that remain receive an invitation to revise, you should be thrilled with any type of revision opportunity coming from an editor. The most common type of opportunity takes the form of "major and risky" – approximately 90 percent. Therefore, do not be discouraged – you are in good company with the rest of the field. You should, however, embrace the "major" part of this decision. Usually this means a lot of work. If you want to succeed, you will have to do as much as you can to rework the positioning, predictions, data, tests, or discussion. In many cases, more than 50 percent of the paper will be new. The point is that you should not take this opportunity lightly if you want to succeed.

I share eight tips for responding to reviewers that I hope will be useful. Some of these are big picture orientations and reflect mindsets or postures that might guide you in the review process. Others are more tactical in nature and may help with implementation. In both cases, they come from my experience as an author, reviewer, associate editor, and now editor-in-chief.

First, adopt an open-minded and discerning attitude about the review process. The review process involves objective referees reading and commenting on the value of your work as well as offering ideas about how it might be improved. I think it is best to discover what you might learn from the process as opposed to adopting a defensive or combative approach to responding to reviewers. Reviewers may be wrong in some cases, but more often than not when I approached reviewer reports with an open mind, I discovered that there was something about how I had written the paper or failed to write the paper that led a reviewer to make a particular comment. Try to understand why a smart member of the profession might have written what you see in the review. Put yourself in the position of a "new" reader to your paper – this means forgetting about information coming later in the paper or your own elaborations of what you have written. Instead, consider what the words you wrote actually communicate and how you organized your paper to understand how the reviewer drew an inference or missed something. In my experience, I am at fault at least 90 percent of the time.

Second, show appreciation for the time and energy reviewers put into your work. This does not mean excessive "thank yous" in your response. Instead, it means revising your paper to reflect the actual or spirit of the recommended changes. This is the best way to please a reviewer – take actions in the paper.

Third, communicate the nature of your changes in your revision notes. However, do not repeat the text of your paper. Instead, describe the broad contours of the revision and then direct the reviewers to the page or pages of the paper where they can read the revisions in more detail. This is helpful because if you paste in the text, the reviewer has to read it once in your revision notes and again in your paper! This is costly in terms of time. In general, I think reviewer notes are too long. To reduce length without loss of information, I recommend summarizing your major revisions on a few pages at the beginning of the reviewer notes. Direct all reviewers to examine this list and note that you will refer to it. This should be the five to seven biggest issues that are resolved in the revision. I call these "Major Revisions" and number them sequentially as MR1, MR2, and so on. Exhibit 1 provides an example of how I organize these major revisions in my revision notes. Note that it can be helpful to note which members of the review team's comments prompted the revision. I do this by noting it in my response, such as writing it as "As recommended by the EIC, AE, and R1 ..." or write out your revision and then put the reviewer's initials after in parenthesis (EIC, AE, and R1).

Exhibit 1: Organization of Major Revisions

Paper Number: OVERVIEW OF MAJOR REVISIONS

We thank the associate editor and reviewers for their careful reading of our paper and for the constructive and thoughtful suggestions to improve it. We provide point-by-point responses to each question raised, but begin with this summary of the major revisions to the manuscript. We refer to these points in our responses to specific concerns raised, where appropriate. The key changes are:

1. **We did a.** Summary of actions pointing to page numbers.
2. **We did b.** Summary of actions pointing to page numbers.
3. **We did c.** Summary of actions pointing to page numbers.

Remember that you still need to respond to each reviewer's comments. However, if your response to a reviewer's comment is contained in one of your major revisions, you can thank the reviewer and point him/her to the list on the first page of your notes. If the reviewer has some idiosyncratic comments, you can say something like "Thank you for your recommendation to do a. We took the actions outlined in MR1. In addition, to resolve your additional question of b, we also took the following actions."

Fourth, when I disagree with a reviewer, I try to be polite and base my rebuttal on empirical evidence and conceptual logic. A rebuttal should not be driven by opinion or personal taste. Think about tests or analyses you can run that will challenge the reviewer's conclusion and show that your choices are legitimate. This may mean collecting additional data, taking a deeper dive into the literature, offering corroborating evidence, or talking to outside experts. My own personal motto is first, work as hard as I can to do all that I can to follow a reviewer's direction. However, if I believe the direction is not in the best interests of the paper and I have stronger evidence for my chosen path, I will try to explain my point of view as well as I can with all the evidence and logic I can muster.

Fifth, reviewers do sometimes miss things in a paper. When this happens, I gently point it out and, if I see how my writing or organization contributed to the material being missed, I take responsibility by noting that I did not make the material as clear or as central as it needed to be and describe how I changed it in the revision.

Sixth, reviewers sometimes want the paper to develop in ways that are very different from the objectives I have for the paper. There are times when the reviewers are right and the recommended direction really trumps the contribution I could make with my current approach. This happened with my 2015 *Marketing Science* paper. We had submitted the paper with a focus on how nutrition information regulation changed market structure. However, the reviewers recommended a much simpler question of whether and how the regulation affected nutrition and taste. After debating it within our team, we decided to develop the paper in this direction and ended up as a finalist for the John Little award!

Seventh, as with most aspects of our profession, it is best not to try to go solo in getting a good grasp on reviewer comments – and this is especially the case for junior authors and Ph.D. students. Ask for help from coauthors and colleagues – inside and outside your area. There is a lot of brainpower in our profession and it is always a good idea to ask others for help when you are stuck. You may not understand a particular reviewer suggestion or you may not be able to decode what seem like mixed messages. Usually, experienced authors can offer direction. However, I use my rule for when I get lost while traveling, which is to ask at least two people for directions. Doing so with reviews will help you understand whether you have some convergence of opinion or whether you have picked up on an idiosyncrasy from a colleague. Only as a last resort do you want to return to the editor for clarification. This should only be in cases where reviewers gave you different directions and neither the associate editor nor editor offered guidance about the choice.

Eighth, it is important to keep as much as possible of your paper the same across revisions. Do not change materials unless requested. There may be times when you decide a requested revision requires additional revisions on your part. However, you should be careful to not overdo it. Review teams lose confidence in a paper when tests and samples vary or if the authors flip flop too much on ideas central to the research. Importantly, if you make a change to your paper, you should share that revision with the review team. Review team members are generally not pleased to discover changes that have not been shared by the authors. Be forthright in your revision notes and communicate all changes – even those not requested by the review team. Explaining how those "extra" changes were triggered by a review team member's recommendation can also reduce concerns. As a rule of thumb, though, change as little as possible (outside of the recommended revisions).

In summary, I wish you the best of luck in the process of revising your paper. Keep an open mind, work hard, ask for help, and do not be afraid to change your paper despite years of work you may have already invested.

Four tips from Jim Bettman

James R. Bettman

Tip 1. Assume initially that the reviewer is correct: A natural reaction to a criticism from a reviewer, particularly given that many academics do not like people telling them what to do, is to start generating reasons why the reviewer is misguided or incorrect. I have found it useful to do the opposite. I assume that the reviewer is right and then try to figure out why that reviewer reacted the way s/he did and why the comment makes sense. Sometimes I have found that the wording used in the paper was misleading, causing the reviewer to interpret the writing in a different way than I intended. This is easily fixed, and saying that the writing was misleading gets a much better reaction from the reviewer than saying that the reviewer clearly misunderstood. In other cases, reviewers have different backgrounds and may bring up a different perspective of which the author(s) are not aware. This can provide an opportunity to enrich the paper.

In general, reviewers are smart people who are trying as well as they can to make sense of the article, so there is usually some grain of truth in what they are saying. Of course, sometimes an author cannot figure out why a comment is the way it is. In this case, it is best for the author to just be honest and say that s/he tried to figure out what the comment was getting at but was not able to do so.

Tip 2. Provide "resolutions" for all of the comments in reviewers' notes: This is probably "old school," but I much prefer to have authors provide detailed responses indicating how they responded to all of the comments rather than an overview of their revision plan. Not all people (including editors) prefer this, but I feel that providing such detail lets reviewers know that their hard work was given attention.

The author(s) can describe what changes they made to address the comments and, importantly, can provide a rationale for any comment(s) they did not address. Providing a reasoned argument for why something was not done can often be quite effective.

One particular case where this is useful is in providing additional data or analyses requested by a reviewer. There are times when such analyses can be quite detailed and its inclusion would detract from the flow of the paper. In such a situation, the author can say that the analyses were done, detail the results of the analyses in the reviewer notes, but say that the analyses were not put into the paper in order to maintain the flow of the manuscript. The author(s) can then say that they would be happy to put the analyses into the paper if the review team thought this would be better.

Tip 3. Make a good faith effort when asked to do something: Often reviewers or the editor or associate editor will ask for some specific change, for example to cut the length of the manuscript. From an author's perspective, the words they have painstakingly written take on great importance; however, a request to cut the length means that the author(s) should take the task of shortening and perhaps cutting some ideas very seriously. Any points that are peripheral to the main narrative/story of the paper can and should be dropped in such an effort, regardless of how attached the author is to them. A related type of specific request that involves the flow of the paper is to "redo the front end to make it less confusing." In this case, the author(s) should make a concentrated effort to lay out the main "story" of the paper in terms of a set of arguments/points that flow from one to the next and then make sure that the paper sticks to that story without distractions or detours. This can take a fair amount of effort, but the result is a paper that is more clear, focused, and coherent in making its points.

Tip 4. Write with the overall story of the paper in mind: One of the most important things for an author to accomplish, as hinted at in Tip 3, is to make sure that readers get the big picture of what the paper is about and what the paper is trying to accomplish. This is something that the author can address prior to beginning writing by doing an outline (perhaps as a set of bullet points in PowerPoint) of the flow of the paper. Having such an outline makes it easier to see if the paper is coherent and understandable and allows the author to make changes to the flow more easily. I always start with such a detailed outline and only then begin to write. Modern word processing technology offers the temptation of being able to start putting down thoughts, but my experience is that this comes with a potential cost in terms of coherence. Another tip related to writing is to always be conscious about what the reader might know at any point in the paper. One of the most common "sins" authors commit is assuming that the reader knows more than the reader actually does know, which can lead to confusion and misunderstanding by the reader (in this case, the reviewer).

Common mistakes in responding to a reviewer's points with which you disagree

Joel Huber

Many reviewer points are helpful and lead to a better paper. These are easy to handle. However, what about those points that are inaccurate and, if followed, will lead to a confusing, ill-positioned or less effective paper? Here are eight *mistakes* authors make in that common situation.

1. *Try to identify the offending reviewer.* Authors often tell editors they know the identity of a reviewer. Guessing the identity of a reviewer is almost always unproductive. Authors are surprisingly wrong about the identity of the reviewer and can hurt the paper by inappropriately adjusting the paper to the perceived biases of a person who is not the reviewer.

2. *Work to discredit a reviewer.* The points made by a reviewer may or may not be valid. Too often authors ascribe to the reviewer perverse motivations (the reviewer is protecting his own flawed work), incompetence (uses economics obsolete in 1970), or sloppiness (did not read analysis plan). Stick to the reviewer's points. Ascribing characteristics to reviewers can generate feelings of hopelessness for authors and will not be suffered gladly by editors.

3. *Treat **all** reviewer points as valid.* That also is a bad mistake, sometimes made by a young scholar who is cowed by the reviews or who is up for tenure and willing to make the paper worse just to get another publication. Authors agreeing to every point lose credibility with the associate editor and the editor. Caving everywhere implies that the authors do not have confidence in or deep knowledge of the topic. Speak truth to power, no matter how painful.

4. *Ignore a reviewer's point that offends you.* Even if the associate editor and editor do not discuss what you believe is a reviewer error, it is still unacceptable to ignore a reviewer's point. Indicate each reviewer point separately. It simply will not go away.

5. *Go behind the reviewer's back and complain to an editor.* Complaining about a reviewer directly to the editor is almost always a poor strategy. If it is the author and not the reviewers who made a mistake, then that approach is disastrous. However, it can hurt even if the author is right and the reviewer is wrong. The editor and the associate editor have to live with the reviewers, and they may themselves be unclear about who is right. Editors appropriately like to act like a judge and rule having heard both sides. Be open and honest, not sneaky and subversive.

6. *Assert the reviewer is mistaken.* That can be done, but smart authors take the blame. Indicate that the original document was not clear and that the revision takes great care to satisfy the reviewer. Perhaps even add a web appendix or a reviewer appendix that clarifies the approach taken and references others who have used that method.

7. *Tell a reviewer that adding desired references will confuse the reader or result in a less focused paper.* From an editor's perspective, it is important for authors to keep the theme focused. We are all familiar with published papers that become unreadable because the flow is interrupted by eddies that respond to multiple points made by reviewers. Here again, tact is needed. Grant that the missing references or perspectives are relevant, but their mention should be either in the introduction or general discussion.

8. *Tell a reviewer that a desired alternative analysis is either redundant or simply wrong.* Reviewers often ask for different ways to ask a question or analyse the

data. The typical appropriate response is to run a small study or reanalyse the data. If the new analysis does worse (for example, index of fit or reasonableness of the parameters), then indicate that problem in a thorough reviewer appendix, and suggest that including that analysis might weaken the overall paper and be confusing to the reader. If both methods generate the similar result, then simply mention this fact when examining the robustness of the results to different analysis or input data. If further analysis reveals that the reviewer's model or data is better, consider using that method and dropping the earlier one. Reviewers are usually pleased when they help improve an article. It is one of the main reasons they review.

Interpreting reviewer comments and decisions

Mary Frances Luce

My comments are about what happens before the reviewer response is written. Specifically, I focus on the interpretation of reviewer comments. An ideal review process is a dialogue and, as such, listening well is at least as important as communicating persuasively.

As is the case in many aspects of life, it is difficult to really listen when stakes (and emotions) run high and there is a potential for conflict. I believe it often takes reading through reviewer comments multiple times to get past your initial reactions (these reactions often run the gamut from gratitude for wise and generous comments, to embarrassment at one's own omissions, to annoyance at what seems to have been missed, and even to outrage at what seem to be too-stringent requirements). Once you experience and absorb these reactions, you are often in a better place to understand what the reviewers are saying, put reviewer comments into the context of your own research goals, and then formulate a plan for revision and ultimately the response. During this process, I find it very useful to cycle between making lists of specific requests and changes and stepping back to understand how the reviewer responded to the paper in general.

In terms of responding to the overall review packet and editorial decisions, I believe it is useful to keep in mind that there is an information asymmetry. While we all know that reviewers provide private comments to authors, it is easy to forget that the lengthy packet of reviews and editorial reports we receive as authors is not, actually, all of the relevant information. My general sense is that it is uncommon, but not exceedingly rare, for reviewers to put unique and important information into private comments to editors. These may range from simple requests (for example, "please tell the authors to cite me if you find it relevant") to serious issues (for example, "I don't think this paper is a good fit, so I gave minor comments to help the authors revise for a different journal"). Of course, it is impossible to know whether private comments contain substantive information. The best you can do is keep in mind that the editor(s) may be responding to information that is not available to you. For this and many other reasons, it is risky to challenge editorial conclusions (even weakly) on the basis of divergence from reviewer sentiments. (It is risky to challenge editors, the ultimate authorities, anyway, but doubly so if your "evidence" involves your own sense of reviewer conclusions – because the editor sees what you see and more.) In particular, you do not have full information to evaluate whether and how editors have appropriately summarized reviewer comments.

In terms of responding to reviewers, I believe it is useful to keep the dialogue as constructive as possible. This is a particular challenge when reviewers seem to have missed points or otherwise done a cursory or sloppy job. It is sometimes tempting to take a tone that illustrates for the editor(s) that the reviewer has not done as thorough a job as expected and hence perhaps that the reviewer's ideas do not merit much weight. However, I think the sure-thing principle (Savage 1954) illustrates why this is generally not the best approach. Essentially, as an author, you cannot know if a reviewer provided a good faith effort. It is often tempting, I think, to look for cues to help resolve this uncertainty and to illustrate where you have "caught" a reviewer in sloppiness or worse.

Regardless of the true state of this underlying uncertainty, I think constructive dialogue wins out. If a review reflects a good faith effort (albeit with some potential misunderstanding), then it would be very off-putting for that reviewer to receive an author response that assumes malintent that was not present. If a review does not reflect a good faith effort (and, of course, some do not), then that reviewer has already signaled he or she is not interested in putting much time into reviewing your paper and hence is particularly unlikely to do the hard work of revising his or her own position.

This does not mean that you can never challenge a reviewer. In fact, sometimes reviewers ask for things that have already been done, that are infeasible or impossible, or that would simply take the project too far from what you intended. In these cases, it is important to challenge suggestions based on statements that are incorrect or miss the point of your work. You can usually do so, however, by finding some general advice within at least the spirit, if not the details, of the reviewer request and highlighting how you leveraged the relevant insights. For instance, if something seemed to have been overlooked by the reviewer, you can make the relevant discussion clearer and more transparent. If a suggested statistical test is inappropriate, you can highlight how a more appropriate technique answers the question the suggested technique was intended to answer.

In terms of framing one's overall response, I believe it is useful to step back and think about your own goals for the research. Ideally, these can be put into conversation with the review team's comments. For instance, I typically find it very useful to provide an overview with the general strategy for the revision (whether required by the journal or not) to highlight the major impact the review team has had on the work and to subtly (and often by omission in the overview) put into context places where you could not incorporate a reviewer's comments. Once you work through the details of the review packet, it should be reasonably straightforward to create a few of the most important, general themes from the review. I think it is particularly helpful if you then are able to describe the impact of reviewer comments on your work and how these relate to the most major changes in a revision. At *Journal of Consumer Research* (*JCR*), my co-editors (Ann McGill and Laura Peracchio) and I instituted a request for "contribution statements" (detailing the authors' intended contribution) as a nudge to help keep all parties focused on the authors' major paper goals. With or without a specific contribution statement, I think it is very useful to set the context of how the review themes resonate with your goals for paper contribution.

Suggestions from an old-timer

Richard Staelin

My advice on how to respond to reviewer comments is influenced by my personal interactions with a plethora of review teams, my experience as an editor interacting with review teams and the authors while trying to shepherd papers through the review process, and my desire to continue to do research and increase the knowledge base of people interested in marketing. Let me briefly provide some more detail here so that my suggestions on how to respond have a little more context.

My experience with trying to publish my research started when I was in graduate school. After reading a journal paper on a new data analysis technique, I felt there was a statistical test that could be used in conjunction with this new approach. A faculty member suggested that I submit a note outlining the statistical test to the journal where the original paper was published. I did and almost immediately forgot that I had done so. Four months later, I received a letter from the journal saying that my note was accepted and that they would publish it as submitted. I said to myself, "That was easy." Little did I know that would be the last such letter. Every other of my initial submissions (and there have been many) was followed by requests for more work or a letter telling me that the journal no longer was interested in considering this work for publication.

My reactions to these requests or rejections has varied over the course of time. However, given my strong desire to inform others of my "contributions to knowledge," I have always tried to listen to the reviewers and learn from what they were saying. With this noted, I crafted my responses to reviewers in terms of what I felt was their role. I believe reviewers have four major responsibilities: (1) to certify that the paper is not wrong; (2) to point out aspects of the paper that are not clear and thus could be improved by a rewrite; (3) to suggest how the ideas put forward in the paper could be extended or broadened to make the paper more impactful; and (4) to inform the editor on whether or not the information conveyed in the paper merits taking up "expensive" journal pages.

With this as a backdrop, let me provide additional detail on what I believe are appropriate strategies for responding to three general scenarios associated with the opportunity to revise your paper and a fourth scenario in which your paper has been rejected. I write these suggestions in terms of the impersonal "you," but they also apply to me personally.

1. The review team is "wrong".   I put quotes around wrong because there are two types of errors that a review team can make. The first type of error is induced by you. You wrote the paper in such a manner that either misled the reviewers or did not set the stage well enough and thus the reviewers were led to counterargue whatever arguments you were presenting. In this case, the best (really the only) approach is for you to carefully read what the reviewers are saying and figure out why they are claiming that your arguments are incorrect, and then rewrite the paper to make sure that a competent reader can follow your arguments without being led astray to a different theory or method that could suggest a different conclusion. This may require you to directly address the reviewers' concerns via additional analyses or repositioning the material up front. Whatever approach you choose to pursue in revising the manuscript, you first need to carefully explain in your notes to the reviewers what changes were made and why, and then conclude with a statement thanking them and acknowledging that you were at fault for the confusion.

The second type of error is more contentious in that you believe "you are right and they are wrong." Typically, if the reviewer is saying he or she cannot certify that the paper is not wrong, the editor may not give you a chance to revise the paper. If you still get a chance to revise the manuscript, you need to provide direct proof that the reviewer is wrong. Without offending the reviewer, you need to state clearly why you are right. I personally have had to make such arguments more than once. In one instance, the editor published both my argument and the reviewers' arguments. In several other instances, I was able to convince the reviewer that he or she was wrong. The important point here is that you, as the author, need to take particular care in making sure to dot all "i's" and cross all "t's" to show why your arguments are correct. Moreover, make sure you directly address the issues raised by the review team. However, if you are misinterpreting what the reviewers are saying, then you are the one that is "wrong" (see my discussion above).

2. The review team is right, but their points are not relevant.   In my view, the review team is not there to rewrite your paper or to push it in a direction that is not where you want to go. Consequently, if you feel that the review team is making points/suggestions that are not in line with what you think are the key issues, I would suggest that you try to hold the line and point out why you do not want to pursue the suggested line of inquiry. With this noted, you need to be aware of the fact that the review team thought this was a good line of inquiry. Thus, you need to think long and hard before "fighting" their suggestions. If you choose to fight, you need to provide a compelling argument why the suggested line of inquiry is not appropriate for your paper.

3. The review team is right.   This is the easy one. Just follow their suggestions and give them appropriate acknowledgment via a footnote in the body of the paper or at the beginning in the author note section. Such suggestions are the outcome of a good review process and they make the paper better.

4. The paper is rejected.   In most cases, if my paper is rejected, my inclination is to move on and look for another review team at a new journal. In one instance, my co-authors and I decided to appeal the rejection decision because: (1) we felt the paper was too good to be rejected; (2) the reasons for rejection were too subjective; and (3) the journal was the appropriate outlet. We took some time to craft a letter asking the editor to re-evaluate the paper. He agreed and ultimately it was accepted (and later awarded a best paper award). However, I normally look carefully at the reviews that led to the rejection letter, make appropriate changes, and then send a revised paper to another journal. In most cases, the effort to improve the manuscript based on the previous reviews has helped the manuscript to be accepted at another journal. In a number of cases, the resulting publication has garnered a substantial number of cites, thereby strengthening my belief that our efforts to get a paper published are worth it, because by doing so we help others gain knowledge. The major point here, however, is that any revised published versions of the initially rejected manuscripts will reflect the comments of the reviewers who rejected it at the first journal. In other words, learn from this initial review and improve the work.

Note
1.   Our count includes Preyas Desai, Editor of *Marketing Science* (2011–2015) and Wagner Kamakura, Editor of the *Journal of Marketing Research* (2001–2003) – reflecting his editor role during his tenure at Duke.

Reference
Savage, L. (1954), *The Foundations of Statistics*, New York: John Wiley and Sons.

Index